THE AENEID OF VIRGIL

THE AENEID OF VIRGIL

VIRGIL

TRANSLATED INTO ENGLISH VERSE

THEODORE CHICKERING WILLIAMS

GYAN

Published by

GYAN

Gyan Publishing House
5, Ansari Road
Daryaganj, New Delhi-110002
Phone: 011-47034999, 9811692060
E-mail: books@gyanbooks.com

Distribution Network
gyanbooks.com
India, USA, Canada, UK, Australia

ISBN: 978-93-6208-039-4 (PB)
First Published, 1908

2nd Impression 2024

Printed at: Gyan Press, Delhi.

A LARGER GRAMMAR OF THE TAMIL LANGUAGE IN BOTH ITS DIALECTS

Author: G. U. POPE

THE
ÆNEID OF VIRGIL

THE ÆNEID OF VIRGIL

TRANSLATED INTO ENGLISH VERSE

BY

THEODORE C. WILLIAMS

χαλεπὰ τὰ καλά

BOSTON AND NEW YORK
HOUGHTON MIFFLIN COMPANY
The Riverside Press Cambridge
1908

V. C. W.

Nec Tyriae Didonis amor nec forma fefellit,
Nec fluvios Erebi monstravit diva Sibylla:
Sed profugum fato Saturnia regna secutum
Me dilecta comes ad caelos alma vocasti.

G. H. P.

I hear thy accent when I read
The change-and-time-defying creed
Of Shakespeare's youth; or when divine
Odysseus pleads in words of thine;
Through thee our England's laurelled choir
Breathed o'er my youth their generous fire:
And now these strains of Virgil's song
Not less to thee than him belong.

CONTENTS

INTRODUCTION

THE POET

VIRGIL'S has been a living name to every generation since his own. He outlived the Rome he sang; and during the long eclipse of pagan literature survived as a Christian poet. His influence upon European letters has been vast and continuous. Dante's

O degli altri poeti onore e lume!

strikes a note which all the poets of the Renaissance were to echo. They praised Homer, but imitated Virgil; and in the matchless version of Annibale Caro (1581) the Æneid became and has remained an Italian classic. All the Latin races honor Virgil as their own.

In England he has always been the poet's poet. Milton is his heir and next of kin; and formed himself not less on Virgil's masters, Homer and Euripides. Dryden gave England an Æneid, great because his own, which, after all, is less classic than rococo. Then come the eighteenth-century scholars, who (like Bernini in sculpture and the Caracci in painting) paraphrased the *bello stile* in the swollen manner of their time. The greater poets of the early nineteenth century, revolting from academic conventions, abjured latinity, and studied Nature, truth, and the Greeks.

Yet Wordsworth himself began a translation of the Æneid; and his son laid upon his bier a laurel-wreath from Virgil's tomb. Tennyson is closer to Virgil even than Milton; for the kinship is not only in style but in thought. Both were born in an age of expanding empire and dissolving beliefs; both clung as artists to a beautiful, fading past, but reached forward in prophecy to a better world. Tennyson's poem to Virgil, written for the commemoration at Mantua, is not only the homage of a great poet to an ancient master of song, but a cry of self-revelation:

Thou that seest Universal Nature moved by Universal Mind;
Thou majestic in thy sadness at the doubtful doom of human kind;
I salute thee, Mantovano, I that loved thee since my day began,
Wielder of the stateliest measure ever moulded by the lips of man.

But such discipleship from the makers of literature has not caused Virgil to be generally read. He has been the despair of translators. Lovers of Latin poetry turn oftener to Horace, Catullus, or Lucretius. Virgil remains the task-master of the schoolroom. Especially is this true in the United States, where the Æneid is relegated to beginners in Latin, and soon put away with childish things.

All great writers suffer harm if banished to schoolboy land; for there they are insulted by the ignorant and vivisected by the learned till they cease to live. Few poets have suffered more such deaths than Virgil; for his faults are those most repellent to youth; and his higher qualities such as cannot be perceived at all either by immature minds or by unimaginative erudition.

What are these faults? And how are they consistent with his claims to greatness? To answer the first of these questions is to explain why Virgil is neglected or disparaged; to answer the second is to justify his immortality.

His most conspicuous fault is nothing less than erudition. He is the scholar-poet; and therefore his poem is a mere workshop to scholars who are not poets, a mere dreamland to poets who love not study. In his greater achievement, like all the immortals, he deals directly with the world and with man, uttering an original message. But his first gesture seems, like that of a child, "As if his whole vocation were endless imitation." He has reverent memories, and has lived much with books. Behind him are Theocritus, Hesiod, Homer, Euripides, Apollonius; and also Ennius and Lucretius. His docile genius is like Raphael's. Only after loving study is it seen that such a master vitalizes what he borrows, and adds what never was on sea or land. If Virgil had translated all Homer, as he has many lines and episodes, he would still have created something incomparably Virgilian. None the less he remains the scholar-poet.

But erudition in a poet, especially to youthful readers and to distant posterity, is a form of obscurity; it obscures Milton and Dante; it darkens the counsels of Shakespearean commentators; even "Marmion" becomes hateful if used chiefly to teach the geography of Scotland. Nor does Virgil carry his erudition cheerfully, as did Shakespeare, or Sir Walter Scott. His traditional material inspires him with awe. He must picture battles between sacred kings, the conclaves of gods, haunted places, old rituals and emblems, the Sibyl's voiceful cave, the darksome country of the dead. In these solemn regions he moves with a certain priestly caution, and his march is stately but encumbered.

But after the student has forgiven Virgil's archaistic zeal, his troubles are not over. There is a fault less explicable, a defect not of form but of substance. The Æneid lacks structure; its polished fragments form an incongruous whole. In so consummate an artist, this is not due to lack of skill, but to an underlying perplexity of thought. Virgil had attempted what was rationally impossible. He tried to ennoble the childish folk-lore and fable of an unethical mythology, and fit them to his serious song. But the old bottles would not hold the new wine. His theme was the founding of Rome, by decrees of Heaven and the labors of a divine hero:

Things unattempted yet in prose or rhyme.

Nor was his heart wholly occupied with a mythical past, but with a golden future. His grander song is prophecy. Rome has been built upon the wrecks of ancient kingdoms, and Cæsar's victories have pacified the world, that justice and Saturnian peace may return to all mankind. But his Greek gods are eloquent unrealities; and Virgil knew it. His world has the double aspect it always wears to writers of "sacred history." He sees the ever-present divine agencies; he watches also the grave-browed hero, who with much pain and peril achieves what Fate intends. Such a co-operation of divine power with Man's supreme ethical struggle could not be convincingly set forth under the forms of Græco-Roman mythology. He has read Euripides, and his men and women are nobler than their gods. Turnus is braver than Mars; Venus could not love as Dido loved; Jove is pitiless, impersonal (*rex omnibus idem*), but Æneas weeps. Yet, though Virgil knew this, he keeps the Olympians in their shrines, and will bate no jot or tittle of ancient rubric. He desires, with Augustus, to re-dedicate Rome to the old gods that made her great. We feel, however, that like Hecuba and her daughters, he clings tragically to fallen powers, *victos penates*, who can no longer protect or bless:

Nos delubra deum miseri quibus ultimus esset
Ille dies, festa velamus fronde per urbem.

This paradox of pious unbelief is most bewildering when seen in the character of Æneas. He is the chosen servant of the gods, yet always trembling and perplexed. He is hero and priest; soldier unquailing, but a passive tool of higher power. He is like a weak pope; officially instructed from the skies, but timid and irresolute. Except in the Dido incident, each episode, each speech is kingly; but there is no total impression. He is not quite flesh and blood, like Dido and Turnus; nor does he personify, as they do, the commoner passions. Virgil must have seen his hero's weaknesses, for Æneas' enemies are prompt to discover them. Dido can see no "piety" in a man who has betrayed her lavish hospitality and love. Turnus laughs at a champion clothed in magic mail, and protected by the skirts of a goddess-mother. Even the gods and the ghosts are obliged to chide their favorite in severe language. In fact, to admire Æneas is a cultivated taste, and requires, as I shall try to show later, a special point of view.

These three faults, then, may be conceded as reasons why the Æneid is little read: a too visible erudition, an unconvincing epic scheme, a perplexed and perplexing hero. Why, then, in spite of all, is Virgil one of the world's four epic poets, and loved in every generation by many elect souls? May it not be that each of these faults is the defect of a quality, and that, when one has so learned to interpret it, each becomes an expression of his greatness? Let me so reconsider them.

Virgil's erudition is not that of the pedant, of the man who cares only for a vanished age and more for letters than for life. It is the erudition of a great humanist. Like Dante, Petrarch, Milton, and Goethe, his receptive genius passionately studies the past, because it explains and vitalizes the present. The scholar-poet has a philosophy of evolution. He is

The heir of all the ages in the foremost files of time.

To estimate such a writer, one must compare him, not with Homer, but with the pedantry of his contemporaries: as Shakespeare with the Euphuists; Milton with Burton; or Goethe's with the *Professoren-poesie*. In Virgil's time the fashionable pedantry was Alexandrian. Propertius boasted to be the Roman Callimachus. Of two thousand Pompeian frescoes fourteen hundred are said to have subjects from the Greek mythology. Ovid's Metamorphoses, in like manner, belittle the Olympian story to the scale of pretty pictures for a corridor. Such paintings were in the great houses of all Virgil's patrons. Alexandrian art was everywhere; nobody suspected that it was not supremely beautiful. Like all the rest, Virgil wrote his school exercises in Alexandrian Greek.

He honored his tutor Parthenius by stealing such lines as

Glauce et Panopeæ et Inoo Melicertæ,

and perhaps by translating his *Moretum*. Parthenius, though the Emperor Tiberius set up his statue, seems to have been a tenth-rate little Alexandrian erotic poet. A learned German has said, *Die Bucolica sind weniger im Stil Theokrits als der affektierten manieristen Euphorion und Gallus gehalten, und gehören daher zu den schwierigsten Gedichten in lateinischer Sprache, die uns erhalten sind.* This is severe. But the learned German knows far too much. It would be better criticism to say that an Italian provincial, the son of a lumberman, who learned from an insignificant Greekling to write in Latin such poems as the Eclogues, or even the *Moretum*, made no bad use of his schooling; and that Parthenius, if a tenth-rate poet, was a first-rate private tutor, and earned his fees. Where are Parthenius' other pupils?

It is plain enough that the Alexandrian manner was only Virgil's point of departure. The Eclogues contain, like Milton's early poems, anticipative notes of epic greatness. They show the influence not only of Theocritus, but of Lucretius. Their landscape is Italian; and they breathe that passionate love of Italy which inspires the Georgics and the later books of the Æneid. The Georgics begin, it is true, with a frigid imitation of Callimachus. But by common consent the Georgics were a new thing in literature and have never been surpassed in their kind. They were accepted at once as a national poem, for they recalled the Romans to the primitive virtues of their race. It was the life of shepherds, herdsmen, farmers, and woodmen, which Virgil had described; but it was also the life which had made the Romans masters of the world:

Hanc olim veteres victam colere Sabini
Hanc Remus et frater; sic fortis Etruria crevit;
Scilicet et rerum facta est pulcherrima Roma,
Septemque una sibi muro circumdedit arces.

Surely it was not Parthenius or Euphorion who taught Virgil to write these Roman lines.

For the imitative elements in the Æneid the excuse of youth and immaturity cannot be offered; but their importance has been exaggerated. The relation between Virgil and Apollonius of Rhodes makes an interesting academic thesis. But all critics agree that Virgil is incomparably the greater; and that the occasional resemblances are less significant than the high seriousness, the Roman strength, which separate him from that forgotten poet. The Homeric color in the Æneid is obvious. But Virgil's readers expected it, not less than Milton's audience demanded the diction of the Bible. As a scholar-poet Virgil could not ignore Homer. Yet the Æneid was hailed immediately as the supremely Roman epic. No competent student can fail to wonder at the large mass of fresh invention it contains. The whole body of its thought, its feeling, its view of life, not to speak of its passionately Italian landscapes and traditions, are utterly un-Homeric.

The truth is (respectfully be it said!) that no poet has suffered more than Virgil from pedantic criticism. Without scholarship he cannot be now understood; and from the days of Macrobius to our own the labor of commentators has been perpetual. His poetry, like his native soil, has to be constantly hoed and harrowed,

Æternum frangenda bidentibus.

All honor to the scholar's difficult and lowly toil! But there are certain diligent professors, often made in Germany, who, having no creative imagination, suppose that great poets, like themselves, are "snappers-up of unconsidered trifles"; and that immortal poems can be patched up out of old notebooks. Their own erudition being impersonal and scientific, they do not understand how a poet's reading, like all his perceptions of the world, has been selective, personal, dynamic; and how he has reshaped in his own likeness whatever his favorite books have brought him.

Critics of this unimaginative sort, the drudges of literary criticism, often miss the point, even where the borrowings and allusions really exist; and they fail to see that to the scholar-poet such allusions are not plagiaristic, but are another mode of appeal. Who can appreciate Milton without the Bible? or Keats and Shelley without a Greece behind them? or Burns without the old Scotch songs? In the *Idylls of the King* are not the archaisms of word and thought an added charm? Virgil is a master in this kind of appeal, this literature inspired by literature. He speaks to patriotism, to religion; and therefore of solemn memories and a sacred past. It is our misfortune, not his weakness, that so much of this background has vanished. Moreover, in the last half of the Æneid, as Virgil's art broadens, he uses less and less of such material as only his learned, hellenized hearers could understand. The great Roman gentlemen heard their ancestral surnames, or the names of towns, hills, rivers, of "haunted spring and dale" which all Italians knew and loved. To the modern reader some of these syllables have lost their power; for they allude to things and persons more remote from us even than the Greek tradition. We know Latona, but not Juturna; Delphi, but not Albunea; or Scamander, but not the "pale waves of Nar." This again is our misfortune. To Virgil's contemporary hearers, much of the material which to us is deadest and most foreign was what made the Roman heart beat loudest, and gave the Æneid its immediate popular success.

In short, Virgil's erudition is always the instrument of his poetic art: it makes him master of the magic phrase, the appealing name; and deepens the reader's emotion by the noble use of literary, religious, or patriotic tradition.

But what shall excuse the chief weakness of the Æneid, the inadequacy of the Greek myths and Italian folk-lore to the sublime event of building Rome? I think a sympathetic study finds even here the source of the most interesting quality of the poem. Virgil's doubting theology has made his poem more human.

He does not offer to "justify the ways of God to Man." His sense of inadequacy in this regard has kept him true to human passion and human feeling in those crises of the story where the divine agency acts unjustifiably. In this respect Dante and Milton, who believed their supernatural schemes to be true, surpass Virgil in sublimity, where they fall below him in tenderness and dramatic truth. They can view with entire serenity the myriads of the fallen

rolling vanquished in the fiery gulf,
Confounded though immortal; but their doom
Reserves them to more wrath.

Virgil, on the contrary, has tears even for the just death of Mezentius, the bloody tyrant who loved his son and his horse; and in the land of the dead, after pitying each hapless, guiltless ghost, Palinurus, Dido, and Deiphobus, he hastens by Tartarus with a *ne quaere doceri*.

It may be that Virgil's "sense of tears in mortal things" springs in no small measure from his failure to justify his gods. It therefore brings him near to such devout souls in each generation as feel the "riddle of the painful earth" even while they stand reverently at temple doors. The will of Jove is accomplished; but Troy burns, Priam dies, Æneas wanders in exile, and Hesperia is an ever-receding paradise:

per mare magnum
Italiam sequimur fugientem, et volvimur undis.

In these things Virgil spoke the deeper thought of his age, and perhaps of Cæsar himself. This fallen Troy, upon whose dying throes he spends his utmost tragic art, is but the first of a thousand cities which fell that Rome might stand; Dido's tragedy is also the doom of

Carthage, of Egypt, of the gorgeous East, and of the long train of throneless queens whose dying curses were hurled in vain against the Roman power; Pallas and Turnus are but the first princes of Italy whom a mysterious fate had disinherited for the sake of the imperial laurel. Was not the poet's own boyhood spent among the fallen cities of Etruria, and among her desecrated temples and tombs? Had not his own kin and neighbors known the bitterness of exile and expropriation?

Virgil himself was a descendant of conquered races. Therefore it is that the long story of Æneas' battles never quickened any soldier's blood. For Virgil's purpose is not, like Homer's, to describe war for the sake of the "stern joy which warriors feel," but to tell the pity of it. One hears the wail of women, as manly strength and beauty fall. Each hero dies lamented or lamenting. For six long books we expect Turnus' death: but when it comes, even Jove is sorry, and victorious Æneas is reluctant to strike. The Epic ends with a parting sigh,

Vitaque cum gemitu fugit indignata sub umbras.

This pathetic standpoint is essential if one would understand the character of Æneas. Virgil conceived him as an ideal Roman, perhaps an ideal Augustus. He saves his country's gods, founds a new nation, and performs the pious duties of a son and a father. Yet he is the instrument of divine purposes, and has no personal ambitions. Like the great Julius, he may cry *Satis vixi*, yet proceeds to fulfil his destiny. *Italiam non sponte sequor*, sums up his character. Nothing could be less Homeric than this self-conscious, unimpassioned hero. He is a Roman gentleman, whose life belongs to the state; he is priest, lawgiver, king. As a lover he is impossible, even absurd. All the loving is done by Dido, who is like a woman enamored of a statue. Rather than sacrifice Æneas' dignity as a priest and a prince, Virgil makes him merciless, inhuman, as priests and princes often are to the unhappy women who have chosen them. Æneas has been compared to Marcus Aurelius. But except for the cruelty to Dido, it might be said that Æneas is Virgil himself. He exhibits unfailing good taste, and a Hamlet-like detachment of mind. At heart he is a poet; not a man of action, but an impartial, impressionable spectator of human events.

The meagre traditions of Virgil's life confirm the conjecture that he reveals in his hero what was deepest in himself. For Virgil was neither soldier nor statesman, nor a figure in fashionable Rome, nor even a man of family. He was professionally a poet and student. There was no wife or child, nor any Lesbia, or Cinyra. His tenderest personal poem is to Syro, who taught him philosophy. His few friends speak of him with reverence. The voluptuous Neapolitans called him *Parthenios*. The audience at the theatre rose respectfully at his entrance, as if before Cæsar. Yet he was shy and slow of speech, and spent most of his life in country-seats. To accomplish his greatest work he retired to his "sweet Parthenope," where he wrote the Georgics and the Æneid, composing but a few lines a day, and, as he said, "licking them into shape as a she-bear does her cubs." His famous dying injunction to burn the Æneid, on which he meant to labor three years more, was set aside by Augustus' command. But to have made such a request reveals, as much as any poem he left, the heroic artist, who lived only that he might do his perfect work, and to whom fame was but a burden. It is said, too, that he was to give his remaining years to philosophy, as if conscious how imperfectly the practice of poetry could solve the deeper questions of his soul.

Virgil, then, like his own Æneas, was the dreamer, the idealist, the detached, contemplative mind. It is this character which gives immortality to the Æneid. No mere man of the world could hope that Augustus would restore the golden age. But in revealing to Rome her ideal self, her divine mission, Virgil began that movement of idealistic political thought, which was to be reshaped by St. Augustine and Dante. He first conceived that "Holy Roman Empire" which was to mould both Empire and Papacy throughout the Middle Age, and which still survives wherever the builders of states, democratic or monarchical, believe themselves providentially charged with a divine work.

In the Sixth Book, which is the moral climax of the poem, Virgil sets forth in terms of ethics that most genuine part of a Roman's faith, the religion of the dead. It deals with the problem of the individual, and with the life after death which redresses, both for successful crime and suffering virtue, the wavering scales of earthly justice. His conception of merit is Roman, social, humane. The family, the state, the whole unfolding of Roman story, have their causes in an unseen, diviner world. In lowest Tartarus lie traitors, adulterers, and betrayers of the poor; in brightest Elysium are all who died or labored for mankind:

Hic manus ob patriam pugnando vulnera passi.
Quique sacerdotes casti, dum vita manebat,
Quique pii vates et Phoebo digna locuti,
Inventas aut qui vitam excoluere per artes,
Quique sui memores aliquos fecere merendo.

By such thoughts was Virgil's name endeared to the Christian Rome, that was to rise on the ruins of what the Cæsars wrought. His visions are cloudy; and nothing is clear but the seriousness of his conviction that only righteousness builds nations, and only righteous souls abide in lasting joy. So great a critic as Sainte-Beuve has dared to say, *La venue même du Christ n'a rien qui étonne, quand on a lu Virgile.*

THE TRANSLATION

English translations of the Æneid are many. The first was by Caxton, the first printer. Professor Conington, in the famous preface to his prose version, gives the long list — a catalogue of forgotten dead, with Dryden sole survivor. But many others have since had the courage to be born. Of translations in verse the most notable of the recent ventures are those of Conington, Sir Charles Bowen, William Morris, James Rhoades, Harlan H. Ballard; far more poetic, and as a *tour de force* surpassing any of the above, is E. F. Taylor's Æneid in Spenserian stanza; but it is as lawlessly splendid and over-mannered as Dryden's, and marred by similar profusion of redundant lines and phrases. The best known American versions are by Cranch and

Long. All of these I have consulted freely; but, though anxious to borrow, I have almost never done so.

But why try again? My first experiments grew out of the exigencies of teaching. I thought it important that a class in Virgil should sometimes lay its Latin by, smooth out its frowning forehead, and just "hear Sordello's story told." But all the rhymed versions seemed to have a touch of the comic; and the prose ones, of course, were in that mongrel, base-bred jargon of which a man would hardly care to own the paternity unless he were a translator of the classics. Even the most scholarly and elegant versions did not admit of continuous reading aloud. It therefore became my rather desperate practice to write out selected passages, both in prose and verse, in renderings intended first of all to appeal to the ear.

From these attempts the present version has grown; for a translator once started on his thankless trade is lured along by the fascinations of difficulty.

In Italy the version of Caro is sold at railway stations, illustrated like a popular classic. But the English versions are known only to scholars, and not read even by them. Dryden's still haunts the book-stalls, but I meet no one who has read it. There is no Virgil which holds any such place as Bryant's Iliad or Palmer's Odyssey, either in the schools or outside them.

But is it possible to produce a readable Æneid, which shall be at the same time a really exact and scholarly translation? Can Virgil be commended to the increasing public of cultivated people who have forgotten Latin? The enterprise seems, I confess, a forlorn hope; for only a poet of the highest rank could entirely succeed, and no such will attempt it. It is possible that, like many others, I shall find a place among the industrious forgotten, and that I have brought to honor Virgil's shade only *inania munera.*

But certain literary aims I have had in view, which, could they be realized, would go far toward producing the ideal result.

My first aim has been lucidity. I have tried to make the narrative move swiftly and clearly; and to minimize (without loss of accuracy) the frequent artificiality and entanglement of the original phrase. Though seeking a poetic diction, bold and vivid phrases, a vocabulary rich in emotional association and words of appealing sound, I have sacrificed much to the avoidance of foreign idiom, and have not attempted the impossible task of bringing over the full magic and suggestion of every Virgilian phrase. Yet having made movement and lucidity the prime requisites (after accuracy), I have lingered long to avoid the commonplace. Only genius can attain the grand style. The translator of it must often be in the plight of the ass who tried to wear the dreadful semblance of the lion. Yet the attempt is obligatory. There must be stateliness and force. The middle way must be found between artificiality and commonness. In pursuing this, I have often avoided over-curious considerations with respect to the rendering of single words; have subordinated each word to the significance of the phrase, each phrase to its paragraph; while each page, even each entire book, is colored by its relation to the epic whole.

In the many speeches the poem contains, I have given special study to showing their dramatic and argumentative force. Virgil argues, yet remains a poet. This is a rare power. We translators are likely to lose both argument and drama — "weightier matters of the law" — in lifeless fussing about the many little things which we cannot leave undone. I have tried to let Dido and Turnus speak in character, and to give to Juno's rage, as Virgil contrives to, an Olympian dignity.

Finally, I have tried to lose nothing of the profound religious suggestiveness which Virgil's language often carries. It is a point which many translators, treating Virgil as a pagan and secular person, have largely missed. The Æneid is a book of much prayer. Supplication to the gods accompanies every great action; and Æneas first appears *duplices tendens ad sidera palmas.* It is in no irreverent spirit that I have often pressed far the use of biblical or churchly phrase. Virgil, as I have explained above, is a lover of ancient piety, of hallowed words and liturgies. In our own language all such are colored in our minds by Christian associations; yet the converse is curiously true, that the Virgilian manner has influenced not a little the religious poetry of England, and even the clerical style.

As to the vexed question, what degree of freedom a poetic translation permits, I have no dogma. I certainly have allowed myself no inventions, no licenses, such as were a translator's merry privilege in the eighteenth century, before the Germans were civilized and before the grim spirit of science invaded literature. The translation is truthful. I have added nothing, omitted nothing, nor evaded difficult and doubtful passages. But since the phrase, not the single word, is always my starting-point, this version is in no sense a "pony"; it will neither help a schoolboy to see the syntax of the Latin, nor supply him with a lexicon.

I owe thanks to many friends who have submitted to my belief that narrative poems are meant to be listened to. Mr. W. C. Collar of the Roxbury Latin School has made important comment in several books. But I owe most of all to Professor George Herbert Palmer of Harvard University, who, at his home in Boxford, has kindly read the proof-sheets of the whole work, and has from its inception offered constant encouragement and suggestion.

THEODORE C. WILLIAMS.

BOSTON, 1908.

THE ÆNEID

BOOK I

ARMS and the man I sing, who first made way,
Predestined exile, from the Trojan shore
To Italy, the blest Lavinian strand.
Smitten of storms he was on land and sea
By violence of Heaven, to satisfy
Stern Juno's sleepless wrath; and much in war
He suffered, seeking at the last to found
The city, and bring o'er his fathers' gods
To safe abode in Latium; whence arose
The Latin race, old Alba's reverend lords,
And from her hills wide-walled, imperial Rome.

O Muse, the causes tell! What sacrilege,
Or vengeful sorrow, moved the heavenly Queen
To thrust on dangers dark and endless toil
A man whose largest honor in men's eyes
Was serving Heaven? Can gods such anger feel?

In ages gone an ancient city stood —
Carthage, a Tyrian seat, which from afar
Made front on Italy and on the mouths
Of Tiber's stream; its wealth and revenues
Were vast, and ruthless was its quest of war.

'T is said that Juno, of all lands she loved,
Most cherished this, — not Samos' self so dear.
Here were her arms, her chariot; even then
A throne of power o'er nations near and far,
If Fate opposed not, 't was her darling hope
To 'stablish here; but anxiously she heard
That of the Trojan blood there was a breed
Then rising, which upon the destined day
Should utterly o'erwhelm her Tyrian towers;
A people of wide sway and conquest proud
Should compass Libya's doom;— such was the web
The Fatal Sisters spun.
                                        Such was the fear
Of Saturn's daughter, who remembered well
What long and unavailing strife she waged
For her loved Greeks at Troy. Nor did she fail
To meditate th' occasions of her rage,
And cherish deep within her bosom proud
Its griefs and wrongs: the choice by Paris made;
Her scorned and slighted beauty; a whole race
Rebellious to her godhead; and Jove's smile
That beamed on eagle-ravished Ganymede.
With all these thoughts infuriate, her power
Pursued with tempests o'er the boundless main
The Trojans, though by Grecian victor spared
And fierce Achilles; so she thrust them far
From Latium; and they drifted, Heaven-impelled,
Year after year, o'er many an unknown sea —
O labor vast, to found the Roman line!

Below th' horizon the Sicilian isle

Just sank from view, as for the open sea
With heart of hope they sailed, and every ship
Clove with its brazen beak the salt, white waves.
But Juno of her everlasting wound
Knew no surcease, but from her heart of pain
Thus darkly mused: "Must I, defeated, fail
"Of what I will, nor turn the Teucrian King
"From Italy away? Can Fate oppose?
"Had Pallas power to lay waste in flame
"The Argive fleet and sink its mariners,
"Revenging but the sacrilege obscene
"By Ajax wrought, Oïleus' desperate son?
"She, from the clouds, herself Jove's lightning threw,
"Scattered the ships, and ploughed the sea with storms.
"Her foe, from his pierced breast out-breathing fire,
"In whirlwind on a deadly rock she flung.
"But I, who move among the gods a queen,
"Jove's sister and his spouse, with one weak tribe
"Make war so long! Who now on Juno calls?
"What suppliant gifts henceforth her altars crown?"

So, in her fevered heart complaining still,
Unto the storm-cloud land the goddess came,
A region with wild whirlwinds in its womb,
Æolia named, where royal Æolus
In a high-vaulted cavern keeps control
O'er warring winds and loud concoùrse of storms.
There closely pent in chains and bastions strong,
They, scornful, make the vacant mountain roar,
Chafing against their bonds. But from a throne
Of lofty crag, their king with sceptred hand

Allays their fury and their rage confines.
Did he not so, our ocean, earth, and sky
Were whirled before them through the vast inane.
But over-ruling Jove, of this in fear,
Hid them in dungeon dark: then o'er them piled
Huge mountains, and ordained a lawful king
To hold them in firm sway, or know what time,
With Jove's consent, to loose them o'er the world.

To him proud Juno thus made lowly plea:
"Thou in whose hands the Father of all gods
"And Sovereign of mankind confides the power
"To calm the waters or with winds upturn,
"Great Æolus! a race with me at war
"Now sails the Tuscan main towards Italy,
"Bringing their Ilium and its vanquished powers.
"Uprouse thy gales! Strike that proud navy down!
"Hurl far and wide, and strew the waves with dead!
"Twice seven nymphs are mine, of rarest mould,
"Of whom Deïopea, the most fair,
"I give thee in true wedlock for thine own,
"To mate thy noble worth; she at thy side
"Shall pass long, happy years, and fruitful bring
"Her beauteous offspring unto thee their sire."
Then Æolus: "'T is thy sole task, O Queen,
"To weigh thy wish and will. My fealty
"Thy high behest obeys. This humble throne
"Is of thy gift. Thy smiles for me obtain
"Authority from Jove. Thy grace concedes
"My station at your bright Olympian board,
"And gives me lordship of the darkening storm."

Replying thus, he smote with spear reversed
The hollow mountain's wall; then rush the winds
Through that wide breach in long, embattled line,
And sweep tumultuous from land to land:
With brooding pinions o'er the waters spread
East wind and south, and boisterous Afric gale
Upturn the sea; vast billows shoreward roll;
The shout of mariners, the creak of cordage,
Follow the shock; low-hanging clouds conceal
From Trojan eyes all sight of heaven and day;
Night o'er the ocean broods; from sky to sky
The thunders roll, the ceaseless lightnings glare;
And all things mean swift death for mortal man.

Straightway Æneas, shuddering with amaze,
Groaned loud, upraised both holy hands to Heaven,
And thus did plead: "O thrice and four times blest,
"Ye whom your sires and whom the walls of Troy
"Looked on in your last hour! O bravest son
"Greece ever bore, Tydides! O that I
"Had fallen on Ilian fields, and given this life
"Struck down by thy strong hand! where by the spear
"Of great Achilles, fiery Hector fell,
"And huge Sarpedon; where the Simois
"In furious flood engulfed and whirled away
"So many helms and shields and heroes slain!"
While thus he cried to Heaven, a shrieking blast
Smote full upon the sail. Up surged the waves
To strike the very stars; in fragments flew
The shattered oars; the helpless vessel veered
And gave her broadside to the roaring flood.

Where watery mountains rose and burst and fell.
Now high in air she hangs, then yawning gulfs
Lay bare the shoals and sands o'er which she drives.
Three ships a whirling south wind snatched and flung
On hidden rocks, — altars of sacrifice
Italians call them, which lie far from shore
A vast ridge in the sea; three ships beside
An east wind, blowing landward from the deep,
Drove on the shallows, — pitiable sight, —
And girdled them in walls of drifting sand.
That ship, which, with his friend Orontes, bore
The Lycian mariners, a great, plunging wave
Struck straight astern, before Æneas' eyes.
Forward the steersman rolled and o'er the side
Fell headlong, while three times the circling flood
Spun the light bark through swift engulfing seas.
Look, how the lonely swimmers breast the wave!
And on the waste of waters wide are seen
Weapons of war, spars, planks, and treasures rare,
Once Ilium's boast, all mingled with the storm.
Now o'er Achates and Ilioneus,
Now o'er the ship of Abas or Aletes,
Bursts the tempestuous shock; their loosened seams
Yawn wide and yield the angry wave its will.

Meanwhile, how all his smitten ocean moaned,
And how the tempest's turbulent assault
Had vexed the stillness of his deepest cave,
Great Neptune knew; and with indignant mien
Uplifted o'er the sea his sovereign brow.
He saw the Teucrian navy scattered far

Along the waters; and Æneas' men
O'erwhelmed in mingling shock of wave and sky.
Saturnian Juno's vengeful stratagem
Her brother's royal glance failed not to see;
And loud to eastward and to westward calling,
He voiced this word: "What pride of birth or power
"Is yours, ye winds, that, reckless of my will,
"Audacious thus, ye ride through earth and heaven,
"And stir these mountain waves? Such rebels I—
"Nay, first I calm this tumult! But yourselves
"By heavier chastisement shall expiate
"Hereafter your bold trespass. Haste away
"And bear your king this word! Not unto him
"Dominion o'er the seas and trident dread,
"But unto me, Fate gives. Let him possess
"Wild mountain crags, thy favored haunt and home,
"O Eurus! In his barbarous mansion there,
"Let Æolus look proud, and play the king
"In yon close-bounded prison-house of storms!"

He spoke, and swiftlier than his word subdued
The swelling of the floods; dispersed afar
Th' assembled clouds, and brought back light to heaven.
Cymothoë then and Triton, with huge toil,
Thrust down the vessels from the sharp-edged reef;
While, with the trident, the great god's own hand
Assists the task; then, from the sand-strewn shore
Out-ebbing far, he calms the whole wide sea,
And glides light-wheeled along the crested foam.
As when, with not unwonted tumult, roars

In some vast city a rebellious mob,
And base-born passions in its bosom burn,
Till rocks and blazing torches fill the air
(Rage never lacks for arms) — if haply then
Some wise man comes, whose reverend looks attest
A life to duty given, swift silence falls;
All ears are turned attentive; and he sways
With clear and soothing speech the people's will.
So ceased the sea's uproar, when its grave Sire
Looked o'er th' expanse, and, riding on in light,
Flung free rein to his winged obedient car.

Æneas' wave-worn crew now landward made,
And took the nearest passage, whither lay
The coast of Libya. A haven there
Walled in by bold sides of a rocky isle,
Offers a spacious and secure retreat,
Where every billow from the distant main
Breaks, and in many a rippling curve retires.
Huge crags and two confronted promontories
Frown heaven-high, beneath whose brows outspread
The silent, sheltered waters; on the heights
The bright and glimmering foliage seems to show
A woodland amphitheatre; and yet higher
Rises a straight-stemmed grove of dense, dark shade.
Fronting on these a grotto may be seen,
O'erhung by steep cliffs; from its inmost wall
Clear springs gush out; and shelving seats it has
Of unhewn stone, a place the wood-nymphs love.
In such a port, a weary ship rides free
Of weight of firm-fluked anchor or strong chain.

Hither Æneas, of his scattered fleet
Saving but seven, into harbor sailed;
With passionate longing for the touch of land,
Forth leap the Trojans to the welcome shore,
And fling their dripping limbs along the ground.
Then good Achates smote a flinty stone,
Secured a flashing spark, heaped on light leaves,
And with dry branches nursed the mounting flame.
Then Ceres' gift from the corrupting sea
They bring away; and wearied utterly
Ply Ceres' cunning on the rescued corn,
And parch in flames, and mill 'twixt two smooth stones.

Æneas meanwhile climbed the cliffs, and searched
The wide sea-prospect; haply Antheus there,
Storm-buffeted, might sail within his ken,
With biremes, and his Phrygian mariners,
Or Capys or Caïcus armor-clad,
Upon a towering deck. No ship is seen;
But while he looks, three stags along the shore
Come straying by, and close behind them comes
The whole herd, browsing through the lowland vale
In one long line. Æneas stopped and seized
His bow and swift-winged arrows, which his friend,
Trusty Achates, close beside him bore.
His first shafts brought to earth the lordly heads
Of the high-antlered chiefs; his next assailed
The general herd, and drove them one and all
In panic through the leafy wood, nor ceased
The victory of his bow, till on the ground

Lay seven huge forms, one gift for every ship.
Then back to shore he sped, and to his friends
Distributed the spoil, with that rare wine
Which good Acestes erst in Sicily
Had stored in jars, and prince-like sent away
With his loved guest; — this too Æneas gave;
And with these words their mournful mood consoled.

"Companions mine, we have not failed to feel
"Calamity till now. O, ye have borne
"Far heavier sorrow: Jove will make an end
"Also of this. Ye sailed a course hard by
"Infuriate Scylla's howling cliffs and caves.
"Ye knew the Cyclops' crags. Lift up your hearts!
"No more complaint and fear! It well may be
"Some happier hour will find this memory fair.
"Through chance and change and hazard without end,
"Our goal is Latium; where our destinies
"Beckon to blest abodes, and have ordained
"That Troy shall rise new-born! Have patience all!
"And bide expectantly that golden day."
Such was his word, but vexed with grief and care,
Feigned hopes upon his forehead firm he wore,
And locked within his heart a hero's pain.

Now round the welcome trophies of his chase
They gather for a feast. Some flay the ribs
And bare the flesh below; some slice with knives,
And on keen prongs the quivering strips impale,

Place cauldrons on the shore, and fan the fires.
Then, stretched at ease on couch of simple green,
They rally their lost powers, and feast them well
On seasoned wine and succulent haunch of game.

But hunger banished and the banquet done,
In long discourse of their lost mates they tell,
'Twixt hopes and fears divided; for who knows
Whether the lost ones live, or strive with death,
Or heed no more whatever voice may call?
Chiefly Æneas now bewails his friends,
Orontes brave and fallen Amycus,
Or mourns with grief untold the untimely doom
Of bold young Gyas and Cloanthus bold.

After these things were past, exalted Jove,
From his ethereal sky surveying clear
The seas all winged with sails, lands widely spread,
And nations populous from shore to shore,
Paused on the peak of heaven, and fixed his gaze
On Libya. But while he anxious mused,
Near him, her radiant eyes all dim with tears,
Nor smiling any more, Venus approached,
And thus complained: "O thou who dost control
"Things human and divine by changeless laws,
"Enthroned in awful thunder! What huge wrong
"Could my Æneas and his Trojans few
"Achieve against thy power? For they have borne
"Unnumbered deaths, and, failing Italy,
"The gates of all the world against them close.
"Hast thou not given us thy covenant

"That hence the Romans when the rolling years
"Have come full cycle, shall arise to power
"From Troy's regenerate seed, and rule supreme
"The unresisted lords of land and sea?
"O Sire, what swerves thy will? How oft have I
"In Troy's most lamentable wreck and woe
"Consoled my heart with this, and balanced oft
"Our destined good against our destined ill!
"But the same stormful fortune still pursues
"My band of heroes on their perilous way.
"When shall these labors cease, O glorious King?
"Antenor, though th' Achæans pressed him sore,
"Found his way forth, and entered unassailed
"Illyria's haven, and the guarded land
"Of the Liburni. Straight up stream he sailed
"Where like a swollen sea Timavus pours
"A nine-fold flood from roaring mountain gorge,
"And whelms with voiceful wave the fields below.
"He built Patavium there, and fixed abodes
"For Troy's far-exiled sons; he gave a name
"To a new land and race; the Trojan arms
"Were hung on temple walls; and, to this day,
"Lying in perfect peace, the hero sleeps.
"But we of thine own seed, to whom thou dost
"A station in the arch of heaven assign,
"Behold our navy vilely wrecked, because
"A single god is angry; we endure
"This treachery and violence, whereby
"Wide seas divide us from th' Hesperian shore.
"Is this what piety receives? Or thus
"Doth Heaven's decree restore our fallen thrones?"

Smiling reply, the Sire of gods and men,
With such a look as clears the skies of storm,
Chastely his daughter kissed, and thus spake on:
"Let Cytherea cast her fears away!
"Irrevocably blest the fortunes be
"Of thee and thine. Nor shalt thou fail to see
"That City, and the proud predestined wall
"Encompassing Lavinium. Thyself
"Shall starward to the heights of heaven bear
"Æneas the great-hearted. Nothing swerves
"My will once uttered. Since such carking cares
"Consume thee, I this hour speak freely forth,
"And leaf by leaf the book of fate unfold.
"Thy son in Italy shall wage vast war
"And quell its nations wild; his city-wall
"And sacred laws shall be a mighty bond
"About his gathered people. Summers three
"Shall Latium call him king; and three times pass
"The winter o'er Rutulia's vanquished hills.
"His heir, Ascanius, now Iulus called
"(Ilus it was while Ilium's kingdom stood),
"Full thirty months shall reign, then move the throne
"From the Lavinian citadel, and build
"For Alba Longa its well-bastioned wall.
"Here three full centuries shall Hector's race
"Have kingly power; till a priestess queen,
"By Mars conceiving, her twin offspring bear;
"Then Romulus, wolf-nursed and proudly clad
"In tawny wolf-skin mantle, shall receive
"The sceptre of his race. He shall uprear
"The war-god's citadel and lofty wall,

"And on his Romans his own name bestow.
"To these I give no bounded times or power,
"But empire without end. Yea, even my Queen,
"Juno, who now chastiseth land and sea
"With her dread frown, will find a wiser way,
"And at my sovereign side protect and bless
"The Romans, masters of the whole round world,
"Who, clad in peaceful toga, judge mankind.
"Such my decree! In lapse of seasons due,
"The heirs of Ilium's kings shall bind in chains
"Mycenæ's glory and Achilles' towers,
"And over prostrate Argos sit supreme.
"Of Trojan stock illustriously sprung,
"Lo, Cæsar comes! whose power the ocean bounds,
"Whose fame, the skies. He shall receive the name
"Iulus nobly bore, great Julius, he.
"Him to the skies, in Orient trophies dight,
"Thou shalt with smiles receive; and he, like us,
"Shall hear at his own shrines the suppliant vow.
"Then will the world grow mild; the battle-sound
"Will be forgot; for olden Honor then,
"With spotless Vesta, and the brothers twain,
"Remus and Romulus, at strife no more,
"Will publish sacred laws. The dreadful gates
"Whence issueth war, shall with close-jointed steel
"Be barred impregnably; and prisoned there
"The heaven-offending Fury, throned on swords,
"And fettered by a hundred brazen chains,
"Shall belch vain curses from his lips of gore."

These words he gave, and summoned Maia's son,
The herald Mercury, who earthward flying,
Should bid the Tyrian realms and new-built towers
Welcome the Trojan waifs; lest Dido, blind
To Fate's decree, should thrust them from the land.
He takes his flight, with rhythmic stroke of wing,
Across th' abyss of air, and soon draws near
Unto the Libyan mainland. He fulfils
His heavenly task; the Punic hearts of stone
Grow soft beneath the effluence divine;
And, most of all, the Queen, with heart at ease,
Awaits benignantly her guests from Troy.

But good Æneas, pondering all night long
His many cares, when first the cheerful dawn
Upon him broke, resolved to take survey
Of this strange country whither wind and wave
Had driven him, — for desert land it seemed, —
To learn what tribes of man or beast possess
A place so wild, and careful tidings bring
Back to his friends. His fleet of ships the while,
Where dense, dark groves o'er-arch a hollowed crag,
He left encircled in far-branching shade.
Then with no followers save his trusty friend
Achates, he went forth upon his way,
Two broad-tipped javelins poising in his hand.
Deep to the midmost wood he went, and there
His Mother in his path uprose; she seemed
In garb and countenance a maid, and bore,
Like Spartan maids, a weapon; in such guise
Harpalyce the Thracian urges on

Her panting coursers and in wild career
Outstrips impetuous Hebrus as it flows.
Over her lovely shoulders was a bow,
Slender and light, as fits a huntress fair;
Her golden tresses without wimple moved
In every wind, and girded in a knot
Her undulant vesture bared her marble knees.
She hailed them thus: "Ho, sirs, I pray you tell
"If haply ye have noted, as ye came,
"One of my sisters in this wood astray?
"She bore a quiver, and a lynx's hide
"Her spotted mantle was; perchance she roused
"Some foaming boar, and chased with loud halloo."

So Venus spoke, and Venus' son replied:
"No voice or vision of thy sister fair
"Has crossed my path, thou maid without a name!
"Thy beauty seems not of terrestrial mould,
"Nor is thy music mortal! Tell me, goddess,
"Art thou bright Phœbus' sister? Or some nymph,
"The daughter of a god? Whate'er thou art,
"Thy favor we implore, and potent aid
"In our vast toil. Instruct us of what skies,
"Or what world's end, our storm-swept lives have found!
"Strange are these lands and people where we rove,
"Compelled by wind and wave. Lo, this right hand
"Shall many a victim on thine altars slay!"

Then Venus: "Nay, I boast not to receive
"Honors divine. We Tyrian virgins oft
"Bear bow and quiver, and our ankles white

"Lace up in purple buskin. Yonder lies
"The Punic power, where Tyrian masters hold
"Agenor's town; but on its borders dwell
"The Libyans, by battles unsubdued.
"Upon the throne is Dido, exiled there
"From Tyre, to flee th' unnatural enmity
"Of her own brother. 'T was an ancient wrong;
"Too long the dark and tangled tale would be;
"I trace the larger outline of her story:
"Sichæus was her spouse, whose acres broad
"No Tyrian lord could match, and he was blessed
"By his ill-fated lady's fondest love,
"Whose father gave him her first virgin bloom
"In youthful marriage. But the kingly power
"Among the Tyrians to her brother came,
"Pygmalion, none deeper dyed in crime
"In all that land. Betwixt these twain there rose
"A deadly hatred, and the impious wretch,
"Blinded by greed, and reckless utterly
"Of his fond sister's joy, did murder foul
"Upon defenceless and unarmed Sichæus,
"And at the very altar hewed him down.
"Long did he hide the deed, and guilefully
"Deceived with false hopes, and fair glozing words,
"Her grief and stricken love. But as she slept,
"Her husband's tombless ghost before her came,
"With face all wondrous pale, and he laid bare
"His heart with dagger pierced, disclosing so
"The blood-stained altar and the infamy
"That darkened now their house. His counsel was
"To fly, self-banished, from her ruined land,

"And for her journey's aid, he whispered where
"His buried treasure lay, a weight unknown
"Of silver and of gold. Thus onward urged,
"Dido, assembling her few trusted friends,
"Prepared her flight. There rallied to her cause
"All who did hate and scorn the tyrant king,
"Or feared his cruelty. They seized his ships,
"Which haply rode at anchor in the bay,
"And loaded them with gold; the hoarded wealth
"Of vile and covetous Pygmalion
"They took to sea. A woman wrought this deed.
"Then came they to these lands where now thine eyes
"Behold yon walls and yonder citadel
"Of newly rising Carthage. For a price
"They measured round so much of Afric soil
"As one bull's hide encircles, and the spot
"Received its name, the Byrsa. But, I pray,
"What men are ye? from what far land arrived,
"And whither going?"
When she questioned thus,
Her son, with sighs that rose from his heart's depths,
This answer gave: "Divine one, if I tell
"My woes and burdens all, and thou could'st pause
"To heed the tale, first would the vesper star
"Th' Olympian portals close, and bid the day
"In slumber lie. Of ancient Troy are we —
"If aught of Troy thou knowest! As we roved
"From sea to sea, the hazard of the storm
"Cast us up hither on this Libyan coast.
"I am Æneas, faithful evermore
"To Heaven's command; and in my ships I bear

"My gods ancestral, which I snatched away
"From peril of the foe. My fame is known
"Above the stars. I travel on in quest
"Of Italy, my true home-land, and I
"From Jove himself may trace my birth divine.
"With twice ten ships upon the Phrygian main
"I launched away. My mother from the skies
"Gave guidance, and I wrought what Fate ordained.
"Yet now scarce seven shattered ships survive
"The shock of wind and wave; and I myself
"Friendless, bereft, am wandering up and down
"This Libyan wilderness! Behold me here,
"From Europe and from Asia exiled still!"

But Venus could not let him longer plain,
And stopped his grief midway:
"Whoe'er thou art,
"I deem that not unblest of heavenly powers,
"With vital breath still thine, thou comest hither
"Unto our Tyrian town. Go steadfast on,
"And to the royal threshold make thy way!
"I bring thee tidings that thy comrades all
"Are safe at land; and all thy ships, conveyed
"By favoring breezes, safe at anchor lie;
"Or else in vain my parents gave me skill
"To read the skies. Look up at yonder swans!
"A flock of twelve, whose gayly fluttering file,
"Erst scattered by Jove's eagle swooping down
"From his ethereal haunt, now form anew
"Their long-drawn line, and make a landing-place,
"Or, hovering over, scan some chosen ground,

"Or soaring high, with whir of happy wings,
"Re-circle heaven in triumphant song:
"Likewise, I tell thee, thy lost mariners
"Are landed, or fly landward at full sail.
"Up, then! let yon plain path thy guidance be."

She ceased and turned away. A roseate beam
From her bright shoulder glowed; th' ambrosial hair
Breathed more than mortal sweetness, while her robes
Fell rippling to her feet. Each step revealed
The veritable goddess. Now he knew
That vision was his mother, and his words
Pursued the fading phantom as it fled:
"Why is thy son deluded o'er and o'er
"With mocking dreams, — another cruel god?
"Hast thou no hand-clasp true, nor interchange
"Of words unfeigned betwixt this heart and thine?"
Such word of blame he spoke, and took his way
Toward the city's rampart.

Venus then
O'erveiled them as they moved in darkened air, —
A liquid mantle of thick cloud divine, —
That viewless they might pass, nor any wight
Obstruct, delay, or question why they came.
To Paphos then she soared, her loved abode,
Where stands her temple, at whose hundred shrines
Garlands of myrtle and fresh roses breathe,
And clouds of orient sweetness waft away.

Meanwhile the wanderers swiftly journey on
Along the clear-marked road, and soon they climb

The brow of a high hill, which close in view
O'er-towers the city's crown. The vast exploit,
Where lately rose but Afric cabins rude,
Æneas wondered at: the smooth, wide ways;
The bastioned gates; the uproar of the throng.
The Tyrians toil unwearied; some up-raise
A wall or citadel, from far below
Lifting the ponderous stone; or with due care
Choose where to build, and close the space around
With sacred furrow; in their gathering-place
The people for just governors, just laws,
And for their reverend senate shout acclaim.
Some clear the harbor mouth; some deeply lay
The base of a great theatre, and carve out
Proud columns from the mountain, to adorn
Their rising stage with lofty ornament.

So busy bees above a field of flowers
In early summer amid sunbeams toil,
Leading abroad their nation's youthful brood;
Or with the flowing honey storing close
The pliant cells, until they quite run o'er
With nectared sweet; while from the entering swarm
They take their little loads; or lined for war,
Rout the dull drones, and chase them from the hive;
Brisk is the task, and all the honeyed air
Breathes odors of wild thyme.
"How blest of Heaven,
"These men that see their promised ramparts rise!"
Æneas sighed; and swift his glances moved

From tower to tower; then on his way he fared,
Veiled in the wonder-cloud, whence all unseen
Of human eyes, — O strange the tale and true! —
He threaded the thronged streets, unmarked, unknown.

Deep in the city's heart there was a grove
Of beauteous shade, where once the Tyrians,
Cast here by stormful waves, delved out of earth
That portent which Queen Juno bade them find, —
The head of a proud horse, — that ages long
Their boast might be wealth, luxury and war.
Upon this spot Sidonian Dido raised
A spacious fane to Juno, which became
Splendid with gifts, and hallowed far and wide
For potency divine. Its beams were bronze,
And on loud hinges swung the brazen doors.
A rare, new sight this sacred grove did show,
Which calmed Æneas' fears, and made him bold
To hope for safety, and with lifted heart
From his low-fallen fortunes re-aspire.
For while he waits the advent of the Queen,
He scans the mighty temple, and admires
The city's opulent pride, and all the skill
Its rival craftsmen in their work approve.
Behold! he sees old Ilium's well-fought fields
In sequent picture, and those famous wars
Now told upon men's lips the whole world round.
There Atreus' sons, there kingly Priam moved,
And fierce Pelides pitiless to both.
Æneas paused, and, weeping, thus began:

"Alas, Achates, what far region now,
"What land in all the world knows not our pain?
"See, it is Priam! Virtue's wage is given —
"O even here! Here also there be tears
"For what men bear, and mortal creatures feel
"Each other's sorrow. Therefore, have no fear!
"This story of our loss forbodes us well."

So saying, he received into his heart
That visionary scene, profoundly sighed,
And let his plenteous tears unheeded flow.
There he beheld the citadel of Troy
Girt with embattled foes; here, Greeks in flight
Some Trojan onset 'scaped; there, Phrygian bands
Before tall-plumed Achilles' chariot sped.
The snowy tents of Rhesus spread hard by
(He sees them through his tears), where Diomed
In night's first watch burst o'er them unawares
With bloody havoc and a host of deaths;
Then drove his fiery coursers o'er the plain
Before their thirst or hunger could be stayed
On Trojan corn or Xanthus' cooling stream.
Here too was princely Troilus, despoiled,
Routed and weaponless, O wretched boy!
Ill-matched against Achilles! His wild steeds
Bear him along, as from his chariot's rear
He falls far back, but clutches still the rein;
His hair and shoulders on the ground go trailing,
And his down-pointing spear-head scrawls the dust.
Elsewhere, to Pallas' ever-hostile shrine,
Daughters of Ilium, with unsnooded hair,

And lifting all in vain her hallowed pall,
Walked suppliant and sad, beating their breasts,
With outspread palms. But her unswerving eyes
The goddess fixed on earth, and would not see.
Achilles round the Trojan rampart thrice
Had dragged the fallen Hector, and for gold
Was making traffic of the lifeless clay.
Æneas groaned aloud, with bursting heart,
To see the spoils, the car, the very corpse
Of his lost friend, — while Priam for the dead
Stretched forth in piteous prayer his helpless hands.
There too his own presentment he could see
Surrounded by Greek kings; and there were shown
Hordes from the East, and black-browed Memnon's arms;
Her band of Amazons, with moon-shaped shields,
Penthesilea led; her martial eye
Flamed on from troop to troop; a belt of gold
Beneath one bare, protruded breast she bound —
A warrior-virgin braving mail-clad men.

While on such spectacle Æneas' eyes
Looked wondering, while mute and motionless
He stood at gaze, Queen Dido to the shrine
In lovely majesty drew near; a throng
Of youthful followers pressed round her way.
So by the margin of Eurotas wide
Or o'er the Cynthian steep, Diana leads
Her bright processional; hither and yon
Are visionary legions numberless
Of Oreads; the regnant goddess bears

A quiver on her shoulders, and is seen
Emerging tallest of her beauteous train;
While joy unutterable thrills the breast
Of fond Latona: Dido not less fair
Amid her subjects passed, and not less bright
Her glow of gracious joy, while she approved
Her future kingdom's pomp and vast emprise.
Then at the sacred portal and beneath
The temple's vaulted dome she took her place,
Encompassed by armed men, and lifted high
Upon a throne; her statutes and decrees
The people heard, and took what lot or toil
Her sentence, or impartial urn, assigned.
But, lo! Æneas sees among the throng
Antheus, Sergestus, and Cloanthus bold,
With other Teucrians, whom the black storm flung
Far o'er the deep and drove on alien shores.
Struck dumb was he, and good Achates too,
Half gladness and half fear. Fain would they fly
To friendship's fond embrace; but knowing not
What might befall, their hearts felt doubt and care.
Therefore they kept the secret, and remained
Forth-peering from the hollow veil of cloud,
Haply to learn what their friends' fate might be,
Or where the fleet was landed, or what aim
Had brought them hither; for a chosen few
From every ship had come to sue for grace,
And all the temple with their voices rang.
The doors swung wide; and after access given
And leave to speak, revered Ilioneus
With soul serene these lowly words essayed:

"O Queen, who hast authority of Jove
"To found this rising city, and subdue
"With righteous governance its people proud,
"We wretched Trojans, blown from sea to sea,
"Beseech thy mercy; keep the curse of fire
"From our poor ships! We pray thee, do no wrong
"Unto a guiltless race. But heed our plea!
"No Libyan hearth shall suffer by our sword,
"Nor spoil and plunder to our ships be borne;
"Such haughty violence fits not the souls
"Of vanquished men. We journey to a land
"Named, in Greek syllables, Hesperia:
"A storied realm, made mighty by great wars
"And wealth of fruitful glebe; in former days
"Œnotrians had it, and their sons, 't is said,
"Have called it Italy, a chieftain's name
"To a whole region given. Thitherward
"Our ships did fare; but with swift-rising flood
"The stormful season of Orion's star
"Drove us on viewless shoals; and angry gales
"Dispersed us, smitten by the tumbling surge,
"Among innavigable rocks. Behold,
"We few swam hither, waifs upon your shore!
"What race of mortals this? What barbarous land,
"That with inhospitable laws ye thrust
"A stranger from your coasts, and fly to arms,
"Nor grant mere foothold on your kingdom's bound?
"If man thou scornest and all mortal power,
"Forget not that the gods watch good and ill!
"A king we had, Æneas, — never man
"In all the world more loyal, just and true,

"Nor mightier in arms! If Heaven decree
"His present safety, if he now do breathe
"The air of earth and is not buried low
"Among the dreadful shades, then fear not thou!
"For thou wilt never rue that thou wert prompt
"To do us the first kindness. O'er the sea
"In the Sicilian land, are cities proud,
"With martial power, and great Acestes there
"Is of our Trojan kin. So grant us here
"To beach our shattered ships along thy shore,
"And from thy forest bring us beam and spar
"To mend our broken oars. Then, if perchance
"We find once more our comrades and our king,
"And forth to Italy once more set sail,
"To Italy, our Latin hearth and home,
"We will rejoicing go. But if our weal
"Is clean gone by, and thee, blest chief and sire,
"These Libyan waters keep, and if no more
"Iulus bids us hope, — then, at the least,
"To yon Sicilian seas, to friendly lands
"Whence hither drifting with the winds we came,
"Let us retrace the journey and rejoin
"Good King Acestes."

So Ilioneus
Ended his pleading; the Dardanidæ
Murmured assent.

Then Dido, briefly and with downcast eyes,
Her answer made: "O Teucrians, have no fear!
"Bid care begone! It was necessity,
"And my young kingdom's weakness, which compelled
"The policy of force, and made me keep

"Such vigilant sentry my wide coast along.
"Æneas and his people, that fair town
"Of Troy—who knows them not? The whole world knows
"Those valorous chiefs and huge, far-flaming wars.
"Our Punic hearts are not of substance all
"Insensible and dull: the god of day
"Drives not his fire-breathing steeds so far
"From this our Tyrian town. If ye would go
"To great Hesperia, where Saturn reigned,
"Or if voluptuous Eryx and the throne
"Of good Acestes be your journey's end,
"I send you safe; I speed you on your way.
"But if in these my realms ye will abide,
"Associates of my power, behold, I build
"This city for your own! Choose haven here
"For your good ships. Beneath my royal sway
"Trojan and Tyrian equal grace will find.
"But O, that this same storm had brought your King,
"Æneas, hither! I will bid explore
"Our Libya's utmost bound, where haply he
"In wilderness or hamlet wanders lost."

By these fair words to joy profoundly stirred,
Father Æneas and Achates brave
To cast aside the cloud that wrapped them round
Yearned greatly; and Achates to his King
Spoke thus: "O goddess-born, in thy wise heart
"What purpose rises now? Lo! All is well!
"Thy fleet and followers are safe at land.
"One only comes not, who before our eyes

"Sank in the soundless sea. All else fulfils
"Thy mother's prophecy."
Scarce had he spoke
When suddenly that overmantling cloud
Was cloven, and dissolved in lucent air;
Forth stood Æneas. A clear sunbeam smote
His god-like head and shoulders. Venus' son
Of his own heavenly mother now received
Youth's glowing rose, an eye of joyful fire,
And tresses clustering fair. 'Tis even so
The cunning craftsman unto ivory gives
New beauty, or with circlet of bright gold
Encloses silver or the Parian stone.

Thus of the Queen he sued, while wonderment
Fell on all hearts. "Behold the man ye seek,
"For I am here! Æneas, Trojan-born,
"Brought safely hither from yon Libyan seas!
"O thou who first hast looked with pitying eye
"On Troy's unutterable grief, who even to us
"(Escaped our Grecian victor, and outworn
"By all the perils land and ocean know),
"To us, bereft and ruined, dost extend
"Such welcome to thy kingdom and thy home!
"I have no power, Dido, to give thanks
"To match thine ample grace; nor is there power
"In any remnant of our Dardan blood,
"Now fled in exile o'er the whole wide world.
"May gods on high (if influence divine
"Bless faithful lives, or recompense be found
"In justice and thy self-approving mind)

"Give thee thy guerdon due. What age was blest
"By such a birth as thine? What parents proud
"Such offspring bore? O, while the rivers run
"To mingle with the sea, while shadows pass
"Along yon rounded hills from vale to vale,
"And while from heaven's unextinguished fire
"The stars be fed — so long thy glorious name,
"Thy place illustrious and thy virtue's praise,
"Abide undimmed. — Yet I myself must go
"To lands I know not where."
After this word
His right hand clasped his loved Ilioneus,
His left Serestus; then the comrades all,
Brave Gyas, brave Cloanthus, and their peers.
Sidonian Dido felt her heart stand still
When first she looked on him; and thrilled again
To hear what vast adventure had befallen
So great a hero. Thus she welcomed him:
"What chance, O goddess-born, o'er danger's path
"Impels? What power to this wild coast has borne?
"Art thou Æneas, great Anchises' son,
"Whom lovely Venus by the Phrygian stream
"Of Simois brought forth unto the day?
"Now I bethink me of when Teucer came
"To Sidon, exiled, and of Belus' power
"Desired a second throne. For Belus then,
"Our worshipped sire, despoiled the teeming land
"Of Cyprus, as its conqueror and king.
"And since that hour I oft have heard the tale
"Of fallen Troy, of thine own noble name,
"And of Achæan kings. Teucer was wont,

"Although their foe, to praise the Teucrian race,
"And boasted him of that proud lineage sprung.
"Therefore, behold, our portals are swung wide
"For all your company. I also bore
"Hard fate like thine. I too was driven of storms
"And after long toil was allowed at last
"To call this land my home. O, I am wise
"In sorrow, and I help all suffering souls!"

So saying, she bade Æneas welcome take
Beneath her royal roof, and to the gods
Made sacrifice in temples, while she sent
Unto the thankful Trojans on the shore
A score of bulls, and of huge, bristling swine,
A herd of a whole hundred, and a flock
Of goodly lambs, a hundred, who ran close
Beside the mother-ewes: and all were given
In joyful feast to please the Heavenly Powers.

Her palace showed a monarch's fair array
All glittering and proud, and feasts were spread
Within the ample court. Rich broideries
Hung deep incarnadined with Tyrian skill;
The board had massy silver, gold-embossed,
Where gleamed the mighty deeds of all her sires,
A graven chronicle of peace and war
Prolonged, since first her ancient line began,
From royal sire to son.

Æneas now
(For love in his paternal heart spoke loud
And gave no rest) bade swift Achates run

To tell Ascanius all, and from the ship
To guide him upward to the town, — for now
The father's whole heart for Ascanius yearned.
And gifts he bade them bring, which had been saved
In Ilium's fall: a richly broidered cloak
Heavy with golden emblems; and a veil
By leaves of saffron lilies bordered round,
Which Argive Helen o'er her beauty threw,
Her mother Leda's gift most wonderful,
And which to Troy she bore, when flying far
In lawless wedlock from Mycenæ's towers;
A sceptre, too, once fair Ilione's,
Eldest of Priam's daughters; and round pearls
Strung in a necklace, and a double crown
Of jewels set in gold. These gifts to find,
Achates to the tall ships sped away.

But Cytherea in her heart revolved
New wiles, new schemes: how Cupid should transform
His countenance, and, coming in the guise
Of sweet Ascanius, still more inflame
The amorous Queen with gifts, and deeply fuse
Through all her yielding frame his fatal fire.
Sooth, Venus feared the many-languaged guile
Which Tyrians use; fierce Juno's hate she feared,
And falling night renewed her sleepless care.
Therefore to Love, the light-winged god, she said:
"Sweet son, of whom my sovereignty and power
"Alone are given! O son, whose smile may scorn
"The shafts of Jove whereby the Titans fell,
"To thee I fly, and humbly here implore

"Thy help divine. Behold, from land to land
"Æneas, thine own brother, voyages on
"Storm-driven, by Juno's causeless enmity.
"Thou knowest it well, and oft hast sighed to see
"My sighs and tears. Dido the Tyrian now
"Detains him with soft speeches; and I fear
"Such courtesy from Juno means us ill;
"She is not one who, when the hour is ripe,
"Bids action pause. I therefore now intend
"The Tyrian Queen to snare, and siege her breast
"With our invading fire, before some god
"Shall change her mood. But let her bosom burn
"With love of my Æneas not less than mine.
"This thou canst bring to pass. I pray thee hear
"The plan I counsel. At his father's call
"Ascanius, heir of kings, makes haste to climb
"To yon Sidonian citadel; my grace
"Protects him, and he bears gifts which were saved
"From hazard of the sea and burning Troy.
"Him lapped in slumber on Cythera's hill,
"Or in Idalia's deep and hallowing shade,
"Myself will hide, lest haply he should learn
"Our stratagem, and burst in, foiling all.
"Wear thou his shape for one brief night thyself,
"And let thy boyhood feign another boy's
"Familiar countenance; when Dido there,
"Beside the royal feast and flowing wine,
"All smiles and joy, shall clasp thee to her breast,
"While she caresses thee, and her sweet lips
"Touch close with thine, then let thy secret fire
"Breathe o'er her heart, to poison and betray."

The love-god to his mother's dear behest
Gave prompt assent. He put his pinions by
And tripped it like Iulus, light of heart.
But Venus o'er Ascanius' body poured
A perfect sleep, and, to her heavenly breast
Enfolding him, far, far away upbore
To fair Idalia's grove, where fragrant buds
Of softly-petalled marjoram embower
In pleasurable shade. Cupid straightway
Obeyed his mother's word and bore the gifts,
Each worthy of a king, as offerings
To greet the Tyrian throne; and as he went
He clasped Achates' friendly hand, and smiled.

Father Æneas now, and all his band
Of Trojan chivalry, at social feast,
On lofty purple-pillowed couches lie;
Deft slaves fresh water on their fingers pour,
And from reed-woven basketry renew
The plenteous bread, or bring smooth napery
Of softest weave; fifty handmaidens serve,
Whose task it is to range in order fair
The varied banquet, or at altars bright
Throw balm and incense on the sacred fires.
A hundred more serve with an equal band
Of beauteous pages, whose obedient skill
Piles high the generous board and fills the bowl.
The Tyrians also to the festal hall
Come thronging, and receive their honor due,
Each on his painted couch; with wondering eyes
Æneas' gifts they view, and wondering more,

Mark young Iulus' radiant brows divine,
His guileful words, the golden pall he bears,
And broidered veil with saffron lilies bound.
The Tyrian Queen ill-starred, already doomed
To her approaching woe, scanned ardently,
With kindling cheek and never-sated eyes,
The precious gifts and wonder-gifted boy.

He round Æneas' neck his arms entwined,
Fed the deep yearning of his seeming sire,
Then sought the Queen's embrace; her eyes, her soul
Clave to him as she strained him to her breast.
For Dido knew not in that fateful hour
How great a god betrayed her. He began,
Remembering his mother (she who bore
The lovely Acidalian Graces three),
To make the dear name of Sichæus fade,
And with new life, new love, to re-possess
Her long-since slumbering bosom's lost desire.

When the main feast is over, they replace
The banquet with huge bowls, and crown the wine
With ivy-leaf and rose. Loud rings the roof
With echoing voices; from the gilded vault
Far-blazing cressets swing, or torches bright
Drive the dark night away. The Queen herself
Called for her golden chalice studded round
With jewels, and o'er-brimming it with wine
As Belus and his proud successors use,
Commanded silence, and this utterance made:
"Great Jove, of whom are hospitable laws

"For stranger-guest, may this auspicious day
"Bless both our Tyrians and the wanderers
"From Trojan shore. May our posterity
"Keep this remembrance! Let kind Juno smile,
"And Bacchus, lord of mirth, attend us here!
"And, O ye Tyrians, come one and all,
"And with well-omened words our welcome share!"
So saying, she outpoured the sacred drop
Due to the gods, and lightly from the rim
Sipped the first taste, then unto Bitias gave
With urgent cheer; he seized it, nothing loth,
Quaffed deep and long the foaming, golden bowl,
Then passed to others.
On a gilded lyre
The flowing-haired Iopas woke a song
Taught him by famous Atlas: of the moon
He sang, the wanderer, and what the sun's
Vast labors be; then would his music tell
Whence man and beast were born, and whence were bred
Clouds, lightnings, and Arcturus' stormful sign,
The Hyades, rain-stars, and nigh the Pole
The great and lesser Wain; for well he knew
Why colder suns make haste to quench their orb
In ocean-stream, and wintry nights be slow.
Loudly the Tyrians their minstrel praised,
And Troy gave prompt applause.
Dido the while
With varying talk prolonged the fateful night,
And drank both long and deep of love and wine.
Now many a tale of Priam would she crave,

Of Hector many; or what radiant arms
Aurora's son did wear; what were those steeds
Of Diomed, or what the stature seemed
Of great Achilles. "Come, illustrious guest,
"Begin the tale," she said, "begin and tell
"The perfidy of Greece, thy people's fall,
"And all thy wanderings. For now, — Ah, me!
"Seven times the summer's burning stars have seen
"Thee wandering far o'er alien lands and seas."

END OF BOOK I

BOOK II

A GENERAL silence fell; and all gave ear,
While, from his lofty station at the feast,
Father Æneas with these words began:—

A grief unspeakable thy gracious word,
O sovereign lady, bids my heart live o'er:
How Asia's glory and afflicted throne
The Greek flung down; which woeful scene I saw,
And bore great part in each event I tell.
But O! in telling, what Dolopian churl,
Or Myrmidon, or gory follower
Of grim Ulysses could the tears restrain?
'T is evening; lo! the dews of night begin
To fall from heaven, and yonder sinking stars
Invite to slumber. But if thy heart yearn
To hear in brief of all our evil days
And Troy's last throes, although the memory
Makes my soul shudder and recoil in pain,
I will essay it.

Wearied of the war,
And by ill-fortune crushed, year after year,
The kings of Greece, by Pallas' skill divine,
Build a huge horse, a thing of mountain size,
With timbered ribs of fir. They falsely say
It has been vowed to Heaven for safe return,
And spread this lie abroad. Then they conceal

Choice bands of warriors in the deep, dark side,
And fill the caverns of that monstrous womb
With arms and soldiery. In sight of Troy
Lies Tenedos, an island widely famed
And opulent, ere Priam's kingdom fell,
But a poor haven now, with anchorage
Not half secure; 't was thitherward they sailed,
And lurked unseen by that abandoned shore.
We deemed them launched away and sailing far,
Bound homeward for Mycenæ. Teucria then
Threw off her grief inveterate; all her gates
Swung wide; exultant went we forth, and saw
The Dorian camp untenanted, the siege
Abandoned, and the shore without a keel.
"Here!" cried we, "the Dolopian pitched; the host
"Of fierce Achilles here; here lay the fleet;
"And here the battling lines to conflict ran."
Others, all wonder, scan the gift of doom
By virgin Pallas given, and view with awe
That horse which loomed so large. Thymœtes then
Bade lead it through the gates, and set on high
Within our citadel, — or traitor he,
Or tool of fate in Troy's predestined fall.
But Capys, as did all of wiser heart,
Bade hurl into the sea the false Greek gift,
Or underneath it thrust a kindling flame,
Or pierce the hollow ambush of its womb
With probing spear. Yet did the multitude
Veer round from voice to voice and doubt of all.
Then from the citadel, conspicuous,
Laocoön, with all his following choir,

Hurried indignant down; and from afar
Thus hailed the people: "O unhappy men!
"What madness this? Who deems our foemen fled?
"Think ye the gifts of Greece can lack for guile?
"Have ye not known Ulysses? The Achæan
"Hides, caged in yonder beams; or this is reared
"For engin'ry on our proud battlements,
"To spy upon our roof-tops, or descend
"In ruin on the city. 'T is a snare.
"Trust not this horse, O Troy, whate'er it bode!
"I fear the Greeks, though gift on gift they bear."

So saying, he whirled with ponderous javelin
A sturdy stroke straight at the rounded side
Of the great, jointed beast. A tremor struck
Its towering form, and through the cavernous womb
Rolled loud, reverberate rumbling, deep and long.
If heaven's decree, if our own wills, that hour,
Had not been fixed on woe, his spear had brought
A bloody slaughter on our ambushed foe,
And Troy were standing on the earth this day!
O Priam's towers, ye were unfallen still!

But, lo! with hands fast bound behind, a youth
By clamorous Dardan shepherds haled along,
Was brought before our King, — to this sole end
A self-surrendered captive, that he might,
Although a nameless stranger, cunningly
Deliver to the Greek the gates of Troy.
His firm-set mind flinched not from either goal, —
Success in crime, or on swift death to fall.

The thronging Trojan youth made haste his way
From every side, all eager to see close
Their captive's face, and flout with emulous scorn.
Hear now what Greek deception is, and learn
From one dark wickedness the whole. For he,
A mark for every eye, defenceless, dazed,
Stood staring at our Phrygian hosts, and cried:
"Woe worth the day! What ocean or what shore
"Will have me now? What desperate path remains
"For miserable me? Now have I lost
"All foothold with the Greeks, and o'er my head
"Troy's furious sons call bloody vengeance down."
Such groans and anguish turned all rage away
And stayed our lifted hands. We bade him tell
His birth, his errand, and from whence might be
Such hope of mercy for a foe in chains.
Then fearing us no more, this speech he dared:
"O King! I will confess, whate'er befall,
"The whole unvarnished truth. I will not hide
"My Grecian birth. Yea, thus will I begin.
"For Fortune has brought wretched Sinon low;
"But never shall her cruelty impair
"His honor and his truth. Perchance the name
"Of Palamedes, Belus' glorious son,
"Has come by rumor to your listening ears;
"Whom by false witness and conspiracy,
"Because his counsel was not for this war,
"The Greeks condemned, though guiltless, to his death,
"And now make much lament for him they slew.
"I, his companion, of his kith and kin,
"Sent hither by my humble sire's command,

"Followed his arms and fortunes from my youth.
"Long as his throne endured, and while he throve
"In conclave with his kingly peers, we twain
"Some name and lustre bore; but afterward,
"Because that cheat Ulysses envied him
"(Ye know the deed), he from this world withdrew,
"And I in gloom and tribulation sore
"Lived miserably on, lamenting loud
"My lost friend's blameless fall. A fool was I
"That kept not these lips closed; but I had vowed
"That if a conqueror home to Greece I came,
"I would avenge. Such words moved wrath, and were
"The first shock of my ruin; from that hour,
"Ulysses whispered slander and alarm;
"Breathed doubt and malice into all men's ears,
"And darkly plotted how to strike his blow.
"Nor rest had he, till Calchas, as his tool,—
"But why unfold this useless, cruel story?
"Why make delay? Ye count all sons of Greece
"Arrayed as one; and to have heard thus far
"Suffices you. Take now your ripe revenge!
"Ulysses smiles and Atreus' royal sons
"With liberal price your deed of blood repay."

We ply him then with passionate appeal
And question all his cause: of guilt so dire
Or such Greek guile we harbored not the thought.
So on he prates, with well-feigned grief and fear,
And from his lying heart thus told his tale:
"Full oft the Greeks had fain achieved their flight,
"And raised the Trojan siege, and sailed away

"War-wearied quite. O, would it had been so!
"Full oft the wintry tumult of the seas
"Did wall them round, and many a swollen storm
"Their embarcation stayed. But chiefly when,
"All fitly built of beams of maple fair,
"This horse stood forth, — what thunders filled the skies!
"With anxious fears we sent Eurypylus
"To ask Apollo's word; and from the shrine
"He brings the sorrowful commandment home:
"'By flowing blood and by a virgin slain
"'The wild winds were appeased, when first ye came,
"'Ye sons of Greece, to Ilium's distant shore.
"'Through blood ye must return. Let some Greek life
"'Your expiation be.'
The popular ear
"The saying caught, all spirits were dimmed o'er;
"Cold doubt and horror through each bosom ran,
"Asking what fate would do, and on what wretch
"Apollo's choice would fall. Ulysses, then,
"Amid the people's tumult and acclaim,
"Thrust Calchas forth, some prophecy to tell
"To all the throng: he asked him o'er and o'er
"What Heaven desired. Already not a few
"Foretold the murderous plot, and silently
"Watched the dark doom upon my life impend.
"Twice five long days the seer his lips did seal,
"And hid himself, refusing to bring forth
"His word of guile, and name what wretch should die.
"At last, reluctant, and all loudly urged
"By false Ulysses, he fulfils their plot,

"And, lifting up his voice oracular,
"Points out myself the victim to be slain.
"Nor did one voice oppose. The mortal stroke
"Horribly hanging o'er each coward head
"Was changed to one man's ruin, and their hearts
"Endured it well. Soon rose th' accursèd morn;
"The bloody ritual was ready; salt
"Was sprinkled on the sacred loaf; my brows
"Were bound with fillets for the offering.
"But I escaped that death — yes! I deny not!
"I cast my fetters off, and darkling lay
"Concealed all night in lake-side sedge and mire,
"Awaiting their departure, if perchance
"They should in truth set sail. But nevermore
"Shall my dear, native country greet these eyes.
"No more my father or my tender babes
"Shall I behold. Nay, haply their own lives
"Are forfeit, when my foemen take revenge
"For my escape, and slay those helpless ones,
"In expiation of my guilty deed.
"O, by yon powers in heaven which witness truth,
"By aught in this dark world remaining now
"Of spotless human faith and innocence,
"I do implore thee look with pitying eye
"On these long sufferings my heart hath borne.
"O, pity! I deserve not what I bear."

Pity and pardon to his tears we gave,
And spared his life. King Priam bade unbind
The fettered hands and loose those heavy chains
That pressed him sore; then with benignant mien

Addressed him thus: "Whate'er thy place or name,
"Forget the people thou hast lost, and be
"Henceforth our countryman. But tell me true!
"What means the monstrous fabric of this horse?
"Who made it? Why? What offering to Heaven,
"Or engin'ry of conquest may it be?"
He spake; and in reply, with skilful guile,
Greek that he was! the other lifted up
His hands, now freed and chainless, to the skies:
"O ever-burning and inviolate fires,
"Witness my word! O altars and sharp steel,
"Whose curse I fled, O fillets of the gods,
"Which bound a victim's helpless forehead, hear!
"'Tis lawful now to break the oath that gave
"My troth to Greece. To execrate her kings
"Is now my solemn duty. Their whole plot
"I publish to the world. No fatherland
"And no allegiance binds me any more.
"O Troy, whom I have saved, I bid thee keep
"The pledge of safety by good Priam given,
"For my true tale shall my rich ransom be.

"The Greeks' one hope, since first they opened war,
"Was Pallas' grace and power. But from the day
"When Diomed, bold scorner of the gods,
"And false Ulysses, author of all guile,
"Rose up and violently bore away
"Palladium, her holy shrine, hewed down
"The sentinels of her acropolis,
"And with polluted, gory hands dared touch
"The goddess' virgin fillets, white and pure, —

"Thenceforth, I say, the courage of the Greeks
"Ebbed utterly away; their strength was lost,
"And favoring Pallas all her grace withdrew.
"No dubious sign she gave. Scarce had they set
"Her statue in our camp, when glittering flame
"Flashed from the staring eyes; from all its limbs
"Salt sweat ran forth; three times (O wondrous tale!)
"It gave a sudden skyward leap, and made
"Prodigious trembling of her lance and shield.
"The prophet Calchas bade us straightway take
"Swift flight across the sea; for fate had willed
"The Trojan citadel should never fall
"By Grecian arm, till once more they obtain
"New oracles at Argos, and restore
"That god the round ships hurried o'er the sea.
"Now in Mycenæ, whither they are fled,
"New help of heaven they find, and forge anew
"The means of war. Back hither o'er the waves
"They suddenly will come. So Calchas gave
"The meaning of the god. Warned thus, they reared
"In place of Pallas' desecrated shrine
"Yon image of the horse, to expiate
"The woeful sacrilege. Calchas ordained
"That they should build a thing of monstrous size
"Of jointed beams, and rear it heavenward,
"So might it never pass your gates, nor come
"Inside your walls, nor anywise restore
"Unto the Trojans their lost help divine.
"For had your hands Minerva's gift profaned,
"A ruin horrible — O, may the gods
"Bring it on Calchas rather! — would have come

"On Priam's throne and all the Phrygian power.
"But if your hands should lift the holy thing
"To your own citadel, then Asia's host
"Would hurl aggression upon Pelops' land,
"And all that curse on our own nation fall."

Thus Sinon's guile and practised perjury
Our doubt dispelled. His stratagems and tears
Wrought victory where neither Tydeus' son,
Nor mountain-bred Achilles could prevail,
Nor ten years' war, nor fleets a thousand strong.
But now a vaster spectacle of fear
Burst over us, to vex our startled souls.
Laocoön, that day by cast of lot
Priest unto Neptune, was in act to slay
A huge bull at the god's appointed fane.
Lo! o'er the tranquil deep from Tenedos
Appeared a pair (I shudder as I tell)
Of vastly coiling serpents, side by side,
Stretching along the waves, and to the shore
Taking swift course; their necks were lifted high,
Their gory dragon-crests o'ertopped the waves;
All else, half seen, trailed low along the sea;
While with loud cleavage of the foaming brine
Their monstrous backs wound forward fold on fold.
Soon they made land; the furious bright eyes
Glowed with ensanguined fire; their quivering tongues
Lapped hungrily the hissing, gruesome jaws.
All terror-pale we fled. Unswerving then
The monsters to Laocoön made way.
First round the tender limbs of his two sons

Each dragon coiled, and on the shrinking flesh
Fixed fast and fed. Then seized they on the sire,
Who flew to aid, a javelin in his hand,
Embracing close in bondage serpentine
Twice round the waist; and twice in scaly grasp
Around his neck, and o'er him grimly peered
With lifted head and crest; he, all the while,
His holy fillet fouled with venomous blood,
Tore at his fetters with a desperate hand,
And lifted up such agonizing voice,
As when a bull, death-wounded, seeks to flee
The sacrificial altar, and thrusts back
From his doomed head the ill-aimed, glancing blade.
Then swiftly writhed the dragon-pair away
Unto the templed height, and in the shrine
Of cruel Pallas sure asylum found
Beneath the goddess' feet and orbèd shield.

Such trembling horror as we ne'er had known
Seized now on every heart. "Of his vast guilt
"Laocoön," they say, "receives reward;
"For he with most abominable spear
"Did strike and violate that blessèd wood.
"Yon statue to the temple! Ask the grace
"Of glorious Pallas!" So the people cried
In general acclaim. Ourselves did make
A breach within our walls and opened wide
The ramparts of our city. One and all
Were girded for the task. Smooth-gliding wheels
Were 'neath its feet; great ropes stretched round its neck,

Till o'er our walls the fatal engine climbed,
Pregnant with men-at-arms. On every side
Fair youths and maidens made a festal song,
And hauled the ropes with merry heart and gay.
So on and up it rolled, a tower of doom,
And in proud menace through our Forum moved.
O Ilium, my country, where abode
The gods of all my sires! O glorious walls
Of Dardan's sons! before your gates it passed,
Four times it stopped and dreadful clash of arms
Four times from its vast concave loudly rang.
Yet frantic pressed we on, our hearts all blind,
And in the consecrated citadel
Set up the hateful thing. Cassandra then
From heaven-instructed heart our doom foretold;
But doomed to unbelief were Ilium's sons.
Our hapless nation on its dying day
Flung free o'er streets and shrines the votive flowers.

The skies rolled on; and o'er the ocean fell
The veil of night, till utmost earth and heaven
And all their Myrmidonian stratagems
Were mantled darkly o'er. In silent sleep
The Trojan city lay; dull slumber chained
Its weary life. But now the Greek array
Of ordered ships moved on from Tenedos,
Their only light the silent, favoring moon,
On to the well-known strand. The King displayed
A torch from his own ship, and Sinon then,
Whom wrathful Heaven defended in that hour,
Let the imprisoned band of Greeks go free

From that huge womb of wood; the open horse
Restored them to the light; and joyfully
Emerging from the darkness, one by one,
Princely Thessander, Sthenelus, and dire
Ulysses glided down the swinging cord.
Closely upon them Neoptolemus,
The son of Peleus, came, and Acamas,
King Menelaus, Thoas and Machaon,
And last, Epeüs, who the fabric wrought.
Upon the town they fell, for deep in sleep
And drowsed with wine it lay; the sentinels
They slaughtered, and through gates now opened wide
Let in their fellows, and arrayed for war
Th' auxiliar legions of the dark design.

That hour it was when heaven's first gift of sleep
On weary hearts of men most sweetly steals.
O, then my slumbering senses seemed to see
Hector, with woeful face and streaming eyes;
I seemed to see him from the chariot trailing,
Foul with dark dust and gore, his swollen feet
Pierced with a cruel thong. Ah me! what change
From glorious Hector when he homeward bore
The spoils of fierce Achilles; or hurled far
That shower of torches on the ships of Greece!
Unkempt his beard, his tresses thick with blood,
And all those wounds in sight which he did take
Defending Troy. Then, weeping as I spoke,
I seemed on that heroic shape to call
With mournful utterance: "O star of Troy!

"O surest hope and stay of all her sons!
"Why tarriest thou so long? What region sends
"The long-expected Hector home once more?
"These weary eyes that look on thee have seen
"Hosts of thy kindred die, and fateful change
"Upon thy people and thy city fall.
"O, say what dire occasion has defiled
"Thy tranquil brows? What mean those bleeding wounds?"

Silent he stood, nor anywise would stay
My vain lament; but groaned, and answered thus:
"Haste, goddess-born, and out of yonder flames
"Achieve thy flight. Our foes have scaled the wall;
"Exalted Troy is falling. Fatherland
"And Priam ask no more. If human arm
"Could profit Troy, my own had kept her free.
"Her Lares and her people to thy hands
"Troy here commends. Companions let them be
"Of all thy fortunes. Let them share thy quest
"Of that wide realm, which, after wandering far,
"Thou shalt achieve, at last, beyond the sea."
He spoke: and from our holy hearth brought forth
The solemn fillet, the ancestral shrines,
And Vesta's ever-bright, inviolate fire.

Now shrieks and loud confusion swept the town;
And though my father's dwelling stood apart
Embowered deep in trees, th' increasing din
Drew nearer, and the battle-thunder swelled.
I woke on sudden, and up-starting scaled

The roof, the tower, then stood with listening ear:
'T was like an harvest burning, when wild winds
Uprouse the flames; 't was like a mountain stream
That bursts in flood and ruinously whelms
Sweet fields and farms and all the ploughman's toil,
Whirling whole groves along; while dumb with fear,
From some far cliff the shepherd hears the sound.
Now their Greek plot was plain, the stratagem
At last laid bare. Deiphobus' great house
Sank vanquished in the fire. Ucalegon's
Hard by was blazing, while the waters wide
Around Sigeum gave an answering glow.
Shrill trumpets rang; loud shouting voices roared;
Wildly I armed me (when the battle calls,
How dimly reason shines!); I burned to join
The rally of my peers, and to the heights
Defensive gather. Frenzy and vast rage
Seized on my soul. I only sought what way
With sword in hand some noble death to die.

When Panthus met me, who had scarce escaped
The Grecian spears, — Panthus of Othrys' line,
Apollo's priest within our citadel;
His holy emblems, his defeated gods,
And his small grandson in his arms he bore,
While toward the gates with wild, swift steps he flew.
"How fares the kingdom, Panthus? What strong place
"Is still our own?" But scarcely could I ask
When thus, with many a groan, he made reply: —
"Dardania's death and doom are come to-day,

"Implacable. There is no Ilium now;
"Our Trojan name is gone, the Teucrian throne
"Quite fallen. For the wrathful power of Jove
"Has given to Argos all our boast and pride.
"The Greek is lord of all yon blazing towers.
"Yon horse uplifted on our city's heart
"Disgorges men-at-arms. False Sinon now,
"With scorn exultant, heaps up flame on flame.
"Others throw wide the gates. The whole vast horde
"That out of proud Mycenæ hither sailed
"Is at us. With confronting spears they throng
"Each narrow passage. Every steel-bright blade
"Is flashing naked, making haste for blood.
"Our sentries helpless meet the invading shock
"And give back blind and unavailing war."

By Panthus' word and by some god impelled,
I flew to battle, where the flames leaped high,
Where grim Bellona called, and all the air
Resounded high as heaven with shouts of war.
Rhipeus and Epytus of doughty arm
Were at my side, Dymas and Hypanis,
Seen by a pale moon, join our little band;
And young Corœbus, Mygdon's princely son,
Who was in Troy that hour because he loved
Cassandra madly, and had made a league
As Priam's kinsman with our Phrygian arms:
Ill-starred, to heed not what the virgin raved!
When these I saw close-gathered for the fight,
I thus addressed them: "Warriors, vainly brave,
"If ye indeed desire to follow one

"Who dares the uttermost brave men may do,
"Our evil plight ye see: the gods are fled
"From every altar and protecting fire,
"Which were the kingdom's stay. Ye offer aid
"Unto your country's ashes. Let us fight
"Unto the death! To arms, my men, to arms!
"The single hope and stay of desperate men
"Is their despair." Thus did I rouse their souls.
Then like the ravening wolves, some night of cloud,
When cruel hunger in an empty maw
Drives them forth furious, and their whelps behind
Wait famine-throated; so through foemen's steel
We flew to surest death, and kept our way
Straight through the midmost town. The wings of night
Brooded above us in vast vault of shade.
But who the bloodshed of that night can tell?
What tongue its deaths shall number, or what eyes
Find meed of tears to equal all its woe?
The ancient City fell, whose throne had stood
Age after age. Along her streets were strewn
The unresisting dead; at household shrines
And by the temples of the gods they lay.
Yet not alone was Teucrian blood required:
Oft out of vanquished hearts fresh valor flamed,
And the Greek victor fell. Anguish and woe
Were everywhere; pale terrors ranged abroad,
And multitudinous death met every eye.

Androgeos, followed by a thronging band
Of Greeks, first met us on our desperate way;
But heedless, and confounding friend with foe,

Thus, all unchallenged, hailed us as his own:
"Haste, heroes! Are ye laggards at this hour?
"Others bear off the captives and the spoil
"Of burning Troy. Just from the galleys ye?"
He spoke; but straightway, when no safe reply
Returned, he knew himself entrapped, and fallen
Into a foeman's snare; struck dumb was he
And stopped both word and motion; as one steps,
When blindly treading a thick path of thorns,
Upon a snake, and sick with fear would flee
That lifted wrath and swollen gorge of green:
So trembling did Androgeos backward fall.
At them we flew and closed them round with war;
And since they could not know the ground, and fear
Had whelmed them quite, we swiftly laid them low.
Thus Fortune on our first achievement smiled;
And, flushed with victory, Corœbus cried:
"Come, friends, and follow Fortune's finger, where
"She beckons us what path deliverance lies.
"Change we our shields, and these Greek emblems wear.
"'Twixt guile and valor who will nicely weigh
"When foes are met? These dead shall find us arms."
With this, he dons Androgeos' crested helm
And beauteous, blazoned shield; and to his side
Girds on a Grecian blade. Young Rhipeus next,
With Dymas and the other soldiery,
Repeat the deed, exulting, and array
Their valor in fresh trophies from the slain.
Now intermingled with our foes we moved,

And alien emblems wore; the long, black night
Brought many a grapple, and a host of Greeks
Down to the dark we hurled. Some fled away,
Seeking their safe ships and the friendly shore.
Some cowards foul went clambering back again
To that vast horse and hid them in its maw.
But woe is me! If gods their help withhold,
'T is impious to be brave. That very hour
The fair Cassandra passed us, bound in chains,
King Priam's virgin daughter, from the shrine
And altars of Minerva; her loose hair
Had lost its fillet; her impassioned eyes
Were lifted in vain prayer, — her eyes alone!
For chains of steel her frail, soft hands confined.
Corœbus' eyes this horror not endured,
And, sorrow-crazed, he plunged him headlong in
The midmost fray, self-offered to be slain,
While in close mass our troop behind him poured.
But, at this point, the overwhelming spears
Of our own kinsmen rained resistless down
From a high temple-tower; and carnage wild
Ensued, because of the Greek arms we bore
And our false crests. The howling Grecian band,
Crazed by Cassandra's rescue, charged at us
From every side; Ajax of savage soul,
The sons of Atreus, and that whole wild horde
Achilles from Dolopian deserts drew.
'T was like the bursting storm, when gales contend,
West wind and South, and jocund wind of morn
Upon his orient steeds — while forests roar,
And foam-flecked Nereus with fierce trident stirs

The dark deep of the sea.
All who did hide
In shadows of the night, by our assault
Surprised, and driven in tumultuous flight,
Now start to view. Full well they now can see
Our shields and borrowed arms, and clearly note
Our speech of alien sound; their multitude
O'erwhelms us utterly. Corœbus first
At mailed Minerva's altar prostrate lay,
Pierced by Peneleus' blade; then Rhipeus fell;
We deemed him of all Trojans the most just,
Most scrupulously righteous; but the gods
Gave judgment otherwise. There Dymas died,
And Hypanis, by their compatriots slain;
Nor thee, O Panthus, in that mortal hour,
Could thy clean hands or Phœbus' priesthood save.
O ashes of my country! funeral pyre
Of all my kin! bear witness that my breast
Shrank not from any sword the Grecian drew,
And that my deeds the night my country died
Deserved a warrior's death, had Fate ordained.

But soon our ranks were broken; at my side
Stayed Iphitus and Pelias; one with age
Was long since wearied, and the other bore
The burden of Ulysses' crippling wound.
Straightway the roar and tumult summoned us
To Priam's palace, where a battle raged
As if save this no conflict else were known,
And all Troy's dying brave were mustered there.
There we beheld the war-god unconfined;

The Greek besiegers to the roof-tops fled;
Or, with shields tortoise-back, the gates assailed.
Ladders were on the walls; and round by round,
Up the huge bulwark as they fight their way,
The shielded left-hand thwarts the falling spears,
The right to every vantage closely clings.
The Trojans hurl whole towers and roof-tops down
Upon the mounting foe; for well they see
That the last hour is come, and with what arms
The dying must resist. Rich gilded beams,
With many a beauteous blazon of old time,
Go crashing down. Men armed with naked swords
Defend the inner doors in close array.
Thus were our hearts inflamed to stand and strike
For the king's house, and to his body-guard
Bring succor, and renew their vanquished powers.
A certain gate I knew, a secret way,
Which gave free passage between Priam's halls,
And exit rearward; hither, in the days
Before our fall, the lone Andromache
Was wont with young Astyanax to pass
In quest of Priam and her husband's kin.
This way to climb the palace roof I flew,
Where, desperate, the Trojans with vain skill
Hurled forth repellent arms. A tower was there,
Reared skyward from the roof-top, giving view
Of Troy's wide walls and full reconnaissance
Of all Achæa's fleets and tented field;
This, with strong steel, our gathered strength assailed,
And as the loosened courses offered us

Great threatening fissures, we uprooted it
From its aerial throne and thrust it down:
It fell with instantaneous crash of thunder
Along the Danaan host in ruin wide.
But fresh ranks soon arrive; thick showers of stone
Rain down, with every missile rage can find.

Now at the threshold of the outer court
Pyrrhus triumphant stood, with glittering arms
And helm of burnished brass. He glittered like
Some swollen viper, fed on poison-leaves,
Whom chilling winter shelters underground,
Till, fresh and strong, he sheds his annual scales
And, crawling forth rejuvenate, uncoils
His slimy length; his lifted gorge insults
The sunbeam with three-forked and quivering tongue.
Huge Periphas was there; Automedon,
Who drove Achilles' steeds, and bore his arms.
Then Scyros' island-warriors assault
The palaces, and hurl reiterate fire
At wall and tower. Pyrrhus led the van;
Seizing an axe he clove the ponderous doors
And rent the hinges from their posts of bronze;
He cut the beams, and through the solid mass
Burrowed his way, till like a window huge
The breach yawned wide, and opened to his gaze
A vista of long courts and corridors,
The hearth and home of many an ancient king,
And Priam's own; upon its sacred bourne
The sentry, all in arms, kept watch and ward.

Confusion, groans, and piteous turmoil
Were in that dwelling; women shrieked and wailed
From many a dark retreat, and their loud cry
Rang to the golden stars. Through those vast halls
The panic-stricken mothers wildly roved,
And clung with frantic kisses and embrace
Unto the columns cold. Fierce as his sire,
Pyrrhus moves on; nor bar nor sentinel
May stop his way; down tumbles the great door
Beneath the battering beam, and with it fall
Hinges and framework violently torn.
Force bursts all bars; th' assailing Greeks break in,
Do butchery, and with men-at-arms possess
What place they will. Scarce with an equal rage
A foaming river, when its dykes are down,
O'erwhelms its mounded shores, and through the
 plain
Rolls mountain-high, while from the ravaged farms
Its fierce flood sweeps along both flock and fold.

My own eyes looked on Neoptolemus
Frenzied with slaughter, and both Atreus' sons
Upon the threshold frowning; I beheld
Her hundred daughters with old Hecuba;
And Priam, whose own bleeding wounds defiled
The altars where himself had blessed the fires;
There fifty nuptial beds gave promise proud
Of princely heirs; but all their brightness now,
Of broidered cunning and barbaric gold,
Lay strewn and trampled on. The Danaan foe
Stood victor, where the raging flame had failed.

But would ye haply know what stroke of doom
On Priam fell? Now when his anguish saw
His kingdom lost and fallen, his abode
Shattered, and in his very hearth and home
Th' exulting foe, the aged King did bind
His rusted armor to his trembling thews, —
All vainly, — and a useless blade of steel
He girded on; then charged, resolved to die
Encircled by the foe. Within his walls
There stood, beneath the wide and open sky,
A lofty altar; an old laurel-tree
Leaned o'er it, and enclasped in holy shade
The statues of the tutelary powers.
Here Hecuba and all the princesses
Took refuge vain within the place of prayer.
Like panic-stricken doves in some dark storm,
Close-gathering they sate, and in despair
Embraced their graven gods. But when the Queen
Saw Priam with his youthful harness on,
"What frenzy, O my wretched lord," she cried,
"Arrayed thee in such arms? O, whither now?
"Not such defences, nor such arm as thine,
"The time requires, though thy companion were
"Our Hector's self. O, yield thee, I implore!
"This altar now shall save us one and all,
"Or we must die together." With these words
She drew him to her side, and near the shrine
Made for her aged spouse a place to cling.

But, lo! just 'scaped of Pyrrhus' murderous hand,
Polites, one of Priam's sons, fled fast

Along the corridors, through thronging foes
And a thick rain of spears. Wildly he gazed
Across the desolate halls, wounded to death.
Fierce Pyrrhus followed after, pressing hard
With mortal stroke, and now his hand and spear
Were close upon: — when the lost youth leaped forth
Into his father's sight, and prostrate there
Lay dying, while his life-blood ebbed away.
Then Priam, though on all sides death was nigh,
Quit not the strife, nor from loud wrath refrained:
"Thy crime and impious outrage, may the gods
"(If Heaven to mortals render debt and due)
"Justly reward and worthy honors pay!
"My own son's murder thou hast made me see,
"Blood and pollution impiously throwing
"Upon a father's head. Not such was he,
"Not such, Achilles, thy pretended sire,
"When Priam was his foe. With flush of shame
"He nobly listened to a suppliant's plea
"In honor made. He rendered to the tomb
"My Hector's body pale, and me did send
"Back to my throne a king."
With this proud word
The aged warrior hurled with nerveless arm
His ineffectual spear, which hoarsely rang
Rebounding on the brazen shield, and hung
Piercing the midmost boss, — but all in vain.
Then Pyrrhus: "Take these tidings, and convey
"A message to my father, Peleus' son!
"Tell him my naughty deeds! Be sure and say

"How Neoptolemus hath shamed his sires.
"Now die!"
With this, he trailed before the shrines
The trembling King, whose feet slipped in the stream
Of his son's blood. Then Pyrrhus' left hand clutched
The tresses old and gray; a glittering sword
His right hand lifted high, and buried it
Far as the hilt in that defenceless heart.
So Priam's story ceased. Such final doom
Fell on him, while his dying eyes surveyed
Troy burning, and her altars overthrown,
Though once of many an orient land and tribe
The boasted lord. In huge dismemberment
His severed trunk lies tombless on the shore,
The head from shoulder torn, the corpse unknown.

Then first wild horror on my spirit fell
And dazed me utterly. A vision rose
Of my own cherished father, as I saw
The King, his aged peer, sore wounded lying
In mortal agony; a vision too
Of lost Creüsa at my ravaged hearth,
And young Iulus' peril. Then my eyes
Looked round me seeking aid. But all were fled,
War-wearied and undone; some earthward leaped
From battlement or tower; some in despair
Yielded their suffering bodies to the flame.
I stood there sole surviving; when, behold,
To Vesta's altar clinging in dumb fear,
Hiding and crouching in the hallowed shade,
Tyndarus' daughter! — 't was the burning town

Lighted full well my roving steps and eyes.
In fear was she both of some Trojan's rage
For Troy o'erthrown, and of some Greek revenge,
Or her wronged husband's long indignant ire.
So hid she at that shrine her hateful brow,
Being of Greece and Troy, full well she knew,
The common curse. Then in my bosom rose
A blaze of wrath; methought I should avenge
My dying country, and with horrid deed
Pay crime for crime. "Shall she return unscathed
"To Sparta, to Mycenæ's golden pride,
"And have a royal triumph? Shall her eyes
"Her sire and sons, her hearth and husband see,
"While Phrygian captives follow in her train?
"Is Priam murdered? Have the flames swept o'er
"My native Troy? and doth our Dardan strand
"Sweat o'er and o'er with sanguinary dew?
"O, not thus unavenged! For though there be
"No glory if I smite a woman's crime,
"Nor conqueror's fame for such a victory won,
"Yet if I blot this monster out, and wring
"Full punishment from guilt, the time to come
"Will praise me, and sweet pleasure it will be
"To glut my soul with vengeance and appease
"The ashes of my kindred."

So I raved,
And to such frenzied purpose gave my soul.
Then with clear vision (never had I seen
Her presence so unclouded) I beheld,
In golden beams that pierced the midnight gloom,
My gracious mother, visibly divine,

And with that mien of majesty she wears
When seen in heaven; she stayed me with her hand,
And from her lips of rose this counsel gave:
"O son, what sorrow stirs thy boundless rage?
"What madness this? Or whither vanisheth
"Thy love of me? Wilt thou not seek to know
"Where bides Anchises, thy abandoned sire,
"Now weak with age? or if Creüsa lives
"And young Ascanius, who are ringed about
"With ranks of Grecian foes, and long ere this —
"Save that my love can shield them and defend —
"Had fallen on flame or fed some hungry sword?
"Not Helen's hated beauty works thee woe;
"Nor Paris, oft-accused. The cruelty
"Of gods, of gods unaided, overwhelms
"Thy country's power, and from its lofty height
"Casts Ilium down. Behold, I take away
"The barrier-cloud that dims thy mortal eye,
"With murk and mist o'er-veiling. Fear not thou
"To heed thy mother's word, nor let thy heart
"Refuse obedience to her counsel given.
"'Mid yonder trembling ruins, where thou see'st
"Stone torn from stone, with dust and smoke uprolling,
"'T is Neptune strikes the wall; his trident vast
"Makes her foundation tremble, and unseats
"The city from her throne. Fierce Juno leads
"Resistless onset at the Scæan gate,
"And summons from the ships the league of powers,
"Wearing her wrathful sword. On yonder height
"Behold Tritonia in the citadel

"Clothed with the lightning and her Gorgon-shield!
"Unto the Greeks great Jove himself renews
"Their courage and their power; 't is he thrusts on
"The gods themselves against the Trojan arms.
"Fly, O my son! The war's wild work give o'er!
"I will be always nigh and set thee safe
"Upon thy father's threshold." Having said,
She fled upon the viewless night away.

Then loomed o'er Troy the apparition vast
Of her dread foes divine; I seemed to see
All Ilium sink in fire, and sacred Troy,
Of Neptune's building, utterly o'erthrown.
So some huge ash-tree on the mountain's brow
(When rival woodmen, heaving stroke on stroke
Of two-edged axes, haste to cast her down)
Sways ominously her trembling, leafy top,
And drops her smitten head; till by her wounds
Vanquished at last, she makes her dying groan,
And falls in loud wreck from the cliffs uptorn.

I left the citadel; and, led by Heaven,
Threaded the maze of deadly foes and fires,
Through spears that glanced aside and flames that fell.
Soon came I to my father's ancient seat,
Our home and heritage. But lo! my sire
(Whom first of all I sought, and first would bear
To safe asylum in the distant hills)
Vowed he could never, after fallen Troy,
Live longer on, or bear an exile's woe.

"O you," he cried, "whose blood not yet betrays
"The cruel taint of time, whose powers be still
"Unpropped and undecayed, go, take your flight.
"If heavenly wrath had willed my life to spare,
"This dwelling had been safe. It is too much
"That I have watched one wreck, and for too long
"Outlived my vanquished country. Thus, O, thus!
"Compose these limbs for death, and say farewell.
"My own hand will procure it; or my foe
"Will end me of mere pity, and for spoil
"Will strip me bare. It is an easy loss
"To have no grave. For many a year gone by,
"Accursed of Heaven, I tarry in this world
"A useless burden, since that fatal hour
"When Jove, of gods the Sire and men the King,
"His lightnings o'er me breathed and blasting fire."

Such fixed resolve he uttered o'er and o'er,
And would not yield, though with my tears did join
My spouse Creüsa, fair Ascanius,
And our whole house, imploring the gray sire
Not with himself to ruin all, nor add
Yet heavier burdens to our crushing doom.
He still cried, "No!" and clung to where he sate
And to the same dread purpose. I once more
Back to the fight would speed. For death alone
I made my wretched prayer. What space was left
For wisdom now? What chance or hope was given?
"Didst thou, dear father, dream that I could fly
"Sundered from thee? Did such an infamy

"Fall from a father's lips? If Heaven's decree
"Will of this mighty nation not let live
"A single soul, if thine own purpose be
"To cast thyself and thy posterity
"Into thy country's grave, behold, the door
"Is open to thy death! Lo, Pyrrhus comes
"Red-handed from King Priam! He has slain
"A son before a father's eyes, and spilt
"A father's blood upon his own hearthstone.
"Was it for this, O heavenly mother mine,
"That thou hast brought me safe through sword and
fire?
"That I might see these altars desecrate
"By their worst foes? that I might look upon
"My sire, my wife, and sweet Ascanius
"Dead at my feet in one another's blood?
"To arms, my men, to arms! The hour of death
"Now beckons to the vanquished. Let me go
"Whither the Greeks are gathered; let me stand
"Where oft revives the flagging stroke of war:
"Not all of us die unavenged this day!"

I clasped my sword-belt round me once again,
Fitted my left arm to my shield, and turned
To fly the house; but at the threshold clung
Creüsa to my knees, and lifted up
Iulus to his father's arms. "If thou
"Wouldst rush on death," she cried, "O, suffer us
"To share thy perils with thee to the end.
"But if this day's work bid thee trust a sword,
"Defend thy hearthstone first. Who else shall guard

"Thy babe Iulus, or thy reverend sire?
"Or me, thy wife that was — what help have I?"

So rang the roof-top with her piteous cries:
But lo! a portent wonderful to see
On sudden rose; for while his parents' grief
Held the boy close in arm and full in view,
There seemed upon Iulus' head to glow
A flickering peak of fire; the tongue of flame
Innocuous o'er his clustering tresses played,
And hovered round his brows.
We, horror-struck,
Grasped at his burning hair, and sprinkled him,
To quench that holy and auspicious fire.
Then sire Anchises with exultant eyes
Looked heavenward, and lifted to the stars
His voice and outstretched hands. "Almighty Jove,
"If aught of prayer may move thee, let thy grace
"Now visit us! O, hear this holy vow!
"And if for service at thine altars done,
"We aught can claim, O Father, lend us aid,
"And ratify the omen thou hast given!"

Scarce ceased his aged voice, when suddenly
From leftward, with a deafening thunder-peal,
Cleaving the blackness of the vaulted sky,
A meteor-star in trailing splendor ran,
Exceeding bright. We watched it glide sublime
O'er tower and town, until its radiant beam
In forest-mantled Ida died away;
But left a furrow on its track in air,

A glittering, long line, while far and wide
The sulphurous fume and exhalation flowed.

My father strove not now; but lifted him
In prayer to all the gods, in holy awe
Of that auspicious star, and thus exclaimed:
"Tarry no moment more! Behold, I come!
"Whithersoe'er ye lead, my steps obey.
"Gods of my fathers, O, preserve our name!
"Preserve my son, and his! This augury
"Is yours; and Troy on your sole strength relies.
"I yield, dear son; I journey at thy side."

He spoke; and higher o'er the blazing walls
Leaped the loud fire, while ever nearer drew
The rolling surges of tumultuous flame.
"Haste, father, on these bending shoulders climb!
"This back is ready, and the burden light;
"One peril smites us both, whate'er befall;
"One rescue both shall find. Close at my side
"Let young Iulus run, while, not too nigh,
"My wife Creüsa heeds what way we go.
"Ye servants of our house, give ear, I pray,
"To my command. Outside the city's gates
"Lies a low mound and long since ruined fane
"To Ceres vowed; a cypress' ancient shade
"O'erhangs it, which our fathers' pious care
"Protected year by year; by various paths
"Be that our meeting-place.
"But in thy hands
"Bring, sire, our household gods, and sanctities:

"For me to touch, who come this very hour
"From battle and the fresh blood of the slain,
"Were but abomination, till what time
"In living waters I shall make me clean."

So saying, I bowed my neck and shoulders broad,
O'erspread me with a lion's tawny skin,
And lifted up my load. Close at my side
Little Iulus twined his hand in mine
And followed, with unequal step, his sire.
My wife at distance came. We hastened on,
Creeping through shadows; I, who once had viewed
Undaunted every instrument of war
And all the gathered Greeks in grim array,
Now shook at every gust, and heard all sounds
With fevered trepidation, fearing both
For him I bore and him who clasped my hand.

Now near the gates I drew, and deemed our flight
Safely at end, when suddenly I heard
The sounding tread of many warriors
That seemed hard-by, while through the murky night
My father peered, and shouted, "O my son,
"Away, away! for surely all our foes
"Are here upon us, and my eyes behold
"The glance of glittering shields and flash of arms."

O, then some evil-working, nameless god
Clouded my senses quite: for while I sped
Along our pathless way, and left behind
All paths and regions known — O wretched me! —

Creüsa on some dark disaster fell;
She stopped, or wandered, or sank down undone, —
I never knew what way, — and nevermore
I looked on her alive. Yet knew I not
My loss, nor backward turned a look or thought,
Till by that hallowed hill to Ceres vowed
We gathered all, — and she alone came not,
While husband, friends, and son made search in vain.
What god, what man, did not my grief accuse
In frenzied word? In all the ruined land
What worse woe had I seen? Entrusting then
My sire, my son, and all the Teucrian gods
To the deep shadows of a slanting vale
Where my allies kept guard, I hied me back
To that doomed town, re-girt in glittering arms.
Resolved was I all hazards to renew,
All Troy to re-explore, and once again
Offer my life to perils without end.
The walls and gloomy gates whence forth I came
I first revisit, and retrace my way,
Searching the night once more. On all sides round
Horror spread wide; the very silence breathed
A terror on my soul. I hastened then
Back to my fallen home, if haply there
Her feet had strayed; but the invading Greeks
Were its possessors, though the hungry fire
Was blown along the roof-tree, and the flames
Rolled raging upward on the fitful gale.
To Priam's house I haste, and climb once more
The citadel; in Juno's temple there,
The chosen guardians of her wasted halls,

Phœnix and dread Ulysses watched the spoil.
Here, snatched away from many a burning fane,
Troy's treasures lay, — rich tables for the gods,
Thick bowls of massy gold, and vestures rare,
Confusedly heaped up, while round the pile
Fair youths and trembling virgins stood forlorn.

Yet oft my voice rang dauntless through the gloom,
From street to street I cried with anguish vain;
And on Creüsa piteously calling,
Woke the lamenting echoes o'er and o'er.
While on this quest I roamed the city through,
Of reason reft, there rose upon my sight —
O shape of sorrow! — my Creüsa's ghost,
Hers truly, though a loftier port it wore.
I quailed, my hair rose, and I gasped for fear;
But thus she spoke, and soothed my grief away:
"Why to these frenzied sorrows bend thy soul,
"O husband ever dear! The will of Heaven
"Hath brought all this to pass. Fate doth not send
"Creüsa the long journeys thou shalt take,
"Nor hath th' Olympian King so given decree.
"Long is thy banishment; thy ship must plough
"The vast, far-spreading sea. Then shalt thou come
"Unto Hesperia, whose fruitful plains
"Are watered by the Tiber, Lydian stream,
"Of smooth, benignant flow. Thou shalt obtain
"Fair fortunes, and a throne and royal bride.
"For thy beloved Creüsa weep no more!
"No Myrmidon's proud palace waits me now;
"Dolopian shall not scorn, nor Argive dames

"Command a slave of Dardan's royal stem
"And wife to Venus' son. On these loved shores
"The Mother of the Gods compels my stay.
"Farewell! farewell! O, cherish evermore
"Thy son and mine!"
Her utterance scarce had ceased,
When, as I strove through tears to make reply,
She left me, and dissolved in empty air.
Thrice would my frustrate arms her form enfold;
Thrice from the clasp of hand that vision fled,
Like wafted winds and like a fleeting dream.

The night had passed, and to my friends once more
I made my way, much wondering to find
A mighty multitude assembled there
Of friends new-come, — matrons and men-at-arms,
And youth for exile bound, — a doleful throng.
From far and near they drew, their hearts prepared
And their possessions gathered, to sail forth
To lands unknown, wherever o'er the wave
I bade them follow.
Now above the crest
Of loftiest Ida rose the morning-star,
Chief in the front of day. The Greeks held fast
The captive gates of Troy. No help or hope
Was ours any more. Then, yielding all,
And lifting once again my aged sire,
For refuge to the distant hills I fled.

END OF BOOK II

BOOK III

When Asia's power and Priam's race and throne,
Though guiltless, were cast down by Heaven's decree,
When Ilium proud had fallen, and Neptune's Troy
In smouldering ash lay level with the ground,
To wandering exile then and regions wild
The gods by many an augury and sign
Compelled us forth. We fashioned us a fleet
Within Antander's haven, in the shade
Of Phrygian Ida's peak (though knowing not
Whither our fate would drive, or where afford
A resting-place at last), and my small band
Of warriors I arrayed.
As soon as smiled
The light of summer's prime, my reverend sire
Anchises bade us on the winds of Fate
To spread all sail. Through tears I saw recede
My native shore, the haven and the plains
Where once was Troy. An exile on the seas,
With son and followers and household shrines,
And Troy's great guardian-gods, I took my way.

There is a far-off land where warriors breed,
Where Thracians till the boundless plains, and where
The cruel-eyed Lycurgus once was king.
Troy's old ally it was, its deities

Had brotherhood with ours before our fall.
Thither I fared, and on its winding shores
Set my first walls, though partial Fate opposed
Our entrance there. In memory of my name
I called its people the Æneadæ.
Unto Dione's daughter, and all gods
Who blessed our young emprise, due gifts were paid;
And unto the supreme celestial King
I slew a fair white bull beside the sea.
But haply near my place of sacrifice
A mound was seen, and on the summit grew
A copse of cornel and a myrtle tree,
With spear-like limbs outbranched on every side.
This I approached, and tried to rend away
From its deep roots that grove of gloomy green,
And dress my altars in its leafy boughs.
But, horrible to tell, a prodigy
Smote my astonished eyes: for the first tree,
Which from the earth with broken roots I drew,
Dripped black with bloody drops, and gave the ground
Dark stains of gore. Cold horror shook my frame,
And every vein within me froze for fear.
Once more I tried from yet another stock
The pliant stem to tear, and to explore
The mystery within, — but yet again
The foul bark oozed with clots of blackest gore!
From my deep-shaken soul I made a prayer
To all the woodland nymphs and to divine
Gradivus, patron of the Thracian plain,
To bless this sight, to lift its curse away.

But when at a third sheaf of myrtle spears
I fell upon my knees, and tugged amain
Against the adverse ground (I dread to tell!),
A moaning and a wail from that deep grave
Burst forth and murmured in my listening ear:
"Why wound me, great Æneas, in my woe?
"O, spare the dead, nor let thy holy hands
"Do sacrilege and sin! I, Trojan-born,
"Was kin of thine. This blood is not of trees.
"Haste from this murderous shore, this land of greed.
"O, I am Polydorus! Haste away!
"Here was I pierced; a crop of iron spears
"Has grown up o'er my breast, and multiplied
"To all these deadly javelins, keen and strong."
Then stood I, burdened with dark doubt and fear
I quailed, my hair rose and my utterance choked.
For once this Polydorus, with much gold,
Ill-fated Priam sent by stealth away
For nurture with the Thracian king, what time
Dardania's war looked hopeless, and her towers
Were ringed about by unrelenting siege.
That king, when Ilium's cause was ebbing low,
And fortune frowned, gave o'er his plighted faith
To Agamemnon's might and victory;
He scorned all honor and did murder foul
On Polydorus, seizing lawlessly
On all the gold. O, whither at thy will,
Curst greed of gold, may mortal hearts be driven?

Soon as my shuddering ceased, I told this tale
Of prodigies before the people's chiefs,

Who sat in conclave with my kingly sire,
And bade them speak their reverend counsel forth.
All found one voice; to leave that land of sin,
Where foul abomination had profaned
A stranger's right; and once more to resign
Our fleet unto the tempest and the wave.
But fit and solemn funeral rites were paid
To Polydorus. A high mound we reared
Of heaped-up earth, and to his honored shade
Built a perpetual altar, sadly drest
In cypress dark and purple pall of woe.
Our Ilian women wailed with loosened hair;
New milk was sprinkled from a foaming cup,
And from the shallow bowl fresh blood out-poured
Upon the sacred ground. So in its tomb
We laid his ghost to rest, and loudly sang,
With prayer for peace, the long, the last farewell.

After these things, when first the friendly sea
Looked safe and fair, and o'er its tranquil plain
Light-whispering breezes bade us launch away,
My men drew down our galleys to the brine,
Thronging the shore. Soon out of port we ran,
And watched the hills and cities fading far.

There is a sacred island in mid-seas,
To fruitful Doris and to Neptune dear,
Which grateful Phœbus, wielder of the bow,
The while it drifted loose from land to land,
Chained firmly where the crags of Gyaros
And Myconos uptower, and bade it rest

Immovable, in scorn of wind and wave.
Thither I sped; by this my weary ships
Found undisturbed retreat and haven fair.
To land we came and saw with reverent eyes
Apollo's citadel. King Anius,
His people's king, and priest at Phœbus' fane,
Came forth to meet us, wearing on his brow
The fillets and a holy laurel crown.
Unto Anchises he gave greeting kind,
Claimed old acquaintance, grasped us by the hand,
And bade us both his roof and welcome share.

Then, kneeling at the shrine of time-worn stone:
"Thou who at Thymbra on the Trojan shore
"Hast often blessed my prayer, O, give to me
"A hearth and home, and to this war-worn band
"Defensive towers and offspring multiplied
"In an abiding city; give to Troy
"A second citadel, that shall survive
"Achilles' wrath and all our Argive foe.
"Whom shall we follow? Whither lies our way?
"Where wilt thou grant us an abiding-place?
"Send forth, O King, thy voice oracular,
"And on our spirits move." Scarce had I spoke
When sudden trembling through the laurels ran
And smote the holy portals; far and wide
The mighty ridges of the mountain shook,
And from the opening shrine the tripod moaned.
Prostrate to earth we fall, as on our ears
This utterance breaks: "O breed of iron men,
"Ye sons of Dardanus! the self-same land

"Where bloomed at first your far-descended stem
"Shall to its bounteous bosom draw ye home.
"Seek out your ancient Mother! There at last
"Æneas' race shall reign on every shore,
"And his sons' sons, and all their house to be."

So Phœbus spoke; and mighty joy uprose
From all my thronging people, who would know
Where Phœbus' city lay, and whitherward
The god ordained the wandering tribe's return.
Then spake my father, pondering olden days
And sacred memories of heroes gone:
"Hear, chiefs and princes, what your hopes shall be!
"The Isle of Crete, abode of lofty Jove,
"Rests in the middle sea. Thence Ida soars;
"There is the cradle of our race. It boasts
"A hundred cities, seats of fruitful power.
"Thence our chief sire, if duly I recall
"The olden tale, King Teucer sprung, who first
"Touched on the Trojan shore, and chose his seat
"Of kingly power. There was no Ilium then
"Nor towered Pergama; in lowly vales
"Their dwelling; hence the ancient worship given
"To the Protectress of Mount Cybele,
"Mother of Gods, what time in Ida's grove
"The brazen Corybantic cymbals clang,
"Or sacred silence guards her mystery,
"And lions yoked her royal chariot draw.
"Up, then, and follow the behests divine!
"Pour offering to the winds, and point your keels

"Unto that realm of Minos. It is near.
"If Jove but bless, the third day's dawn should see
"Our ships at Cretan land."
So, having said,
He slew the victims for each altar's praise.
A bull to Neptune, and a bull to thee,
O beauteous Apollo! A black lamb
Unto the clouds and storms; but fleece of snow
To the mild zephyrs was our offering.

The tale was told us that Idomeneus,
From his hereditary kindgom driven,
Had left his Crete abandoned, that no foe
Now harbored there, but all its dwellings lay
Untenanted of man. So forth we sailed
Out of the port of Delos, and sped far
Along the main. The mænad-haunted hills
Of Naxos came in view; the ridges green
Of fair Donysa, with Olearos,
And Paros, gleaming white, and Cyclades
Scattered among the waves, as close we ran
Where thick-strewn islands vex the channelled seas.
With rival shout the sailors cheerly called:
"On, comrades! On, to Crete and to our sires!"
Freely behind us blew the friendly winds,
And gave smooth passage to that fabled shore,
The land of the Curetes, friends of Jove.
There eagerly I labored at the walls
Of our long-prayed-for city; and its name
Was Pergamea; to my Trojan band,
Pleased with such name, I gave command to build

Altar and hearth, and raise the lofty tower.
But scarce the ships were beached along the strand
(While o'er the isle my busy mariners
Ploughed in new fields and took them wives once more, —
I giving homes and laws) when suddenly
A pestilence from some infectious sky
Seized on man's flesh, and horribly exhaled
O'er trees and crops a fatal year of plague.
Some breathed their last, while others weak and worn
Lived on; the dog-star parched the barren fields;
Grass withered, and the sickly, mouldering corn
Refused us life. My aged father then
Bade us re-cross the waves and re-implore
Apollo's mercy at his island shrine;
If haply of our weariness and woe
He might vouchsafe the end, or bid us find
Help for our task, or guidance o'er the sea.

'Twas night, and sleep possessed all breathing things;
When, lo! the sacred effigies divine,
The Phrygian gods which through the flames I bore
From fallen Troy, seemed in a vision clear
To stand before me where I slumbering lay,
Bathed in bright beams which from the moon at full
Streamed through the latticed wall: and thus they spoke
To soothe my care away. "Apollo's word,
"Which in far Delos the god meant for thee,
"Is uttered here. Behold, he sends ourselves
"To this thy house, before thy prayer is made.

"We from Troy's ashes have companioned thee
"In every fight; and we the swollen seas,
"Guided by thee, in thine own ships have crossed;
"Our power divine shall set among the stars
"Thy seed to be, and to thy city give
"Dominion evermore. For mighty men
"Go build its mighty walls! Seek not to shun
"The hard, long labors of an exile's way.
"Change this abode! Not thine this Cretan shore,
"Nor here would Delian Phœbus have thee bide.
"There is a land the roving Greeks have named
"Hesperia. It is a storied realm
"Made mighty by great wars and fruitful glebe.
"Œnotrians had it, and their sons, 't is said,
"Have called it Italy, a chieftain's name
"To a whole region given. That land alone
"Our true abode can be; for Dardanus
"Was cradled there, and old Iasius,
"The venerated sire of all our line.
"Arise! go forth and cheer thy father gray
"With the glad tidings! Bid him doubt no more!
"Ausonia seek and Corythus; for Jove
"Denies this Cretan realm to thine and thee."

I marvelled at the heavenly presences
So vocal and so bright, for 't was not sleep;
But face to face I deemed I could discern
Each countenance august and holy brow,
Each mantled head; and from my body ran
Cold sweat of awe. From my low couch I sprang,
Lifting to heaven my suppliant hands and prayer,

And o'er my hearth poured forth libations free.
After th' auspicious offering, I told
Anchises the whole tale in order due.

He owned our stock two-branched, of our great sires
The twofold line, and that his thought had strayed,
In new confusion mingling ancient names;
Then spoke: "O son, in Ilium's doom severe
"Afflicted ever! To my ears alone
"This dark vicissitude Cassandra sang.
"I mind me now that her wild tongue foretold
"Such destiny. For oft she called aloud
"'Hesperia!' oft 'Italia's kingdom!' called.
"But who had faith that Teucer's sons should come
"To far Hesperia? What mortal ear
"Gave heed to sad Cassandra's voice divine?
"Now Phœbus speaks. Obedient let us be,
"And, warned by him, our happier lot pursue!"

He spoke: with heart of hope we all obeyed;
Again we changed abode; and, leaving there
A feeble few, again with spreading sails
We coursed in hollow ship the spacious sea.
When from the deep the shores had faded far,
And only sky and sea were round our way,
Full in the zenith hung a purple cloud,
Storm-laden, dark as night, and every wave
Grew black and angry, while perpetual gales
Came rolling o'er the main, and mountain-high
The wreckful surges rose; our ships were hurled

Wide o'er the whirling waters; thunder-clouds
And misty murk of night made end of all
The light of heaven, save where the rifted storm
Flashed with the oft-reiterate shaft of Jove.
Then went we drifting, beaten from our course,
Upon a trackless sea. Not even the eyes
Of Palinurus could tell night from noon
Or ken our way. Three days of blinding dark,
Three nights without a star, we roved the seas;
The fourth, land seemed to rise. Far distant hills
And rolling smoke we saw. Down came our sails,
Out flew the oars, and with prompt stroke the crews
Swept the dark waves and tossed the crested foam.

From such sea-peril safe, I made the shores
Of Strophades, — a name the Grecians gave
To islands in the broad Ionic main, —
The Strophades, where dread Celæno bides,
With other Harpies, who had quit the halls
Of stricken Phineus, and for very fear
Fled from the routed feast; no prodigy
More vile than these, nor plague more pitiless
Ere rose by wrath divine from Stygian wave;
Birds seem they, but with face like woman-kind;
Foul-flowing bellies, hands with crooked claws,
And ghastly lips they have, with hunger pale.
Scarce had we made the haven, when, behold!
Fair herds of cattle roaming a wide plain,
And horned goats, untended, feeding free
In pastures green, surprised our happy eyes.
With eager blades we ran to take and slay,

Asking of every god, and chiefly Jove,
To share the welcome prize: we ranged a feast,
With turf-built couches and a banquet-board
Along the curving strand. But in a trice,
Down from the high hills swooping horribly,
The Harpies loudly shrieking, flapped their wings,
Snatched at our meats, and with infectious touch
Polluted all; infernal was their cry,
The stench most vile. Once more in covert far
Beneath a caverned rock, and close concealed
With trees and branching shade, we raised aloft
Our tables, altars, and rekindled fires.
Once more from haunts unknown the clamorous flock
From every quarter flew, and seized its prey
With taloned feet and carrion lip most foul.
I called my mates to arms and opened war
On that accursed brood. My band obeyed;
And, hiding in deep grass their swords and shields,
In ambush lay. But presently the foe
Swept o'er the winding shore with loud alarm:
Then from a sentry-crag, Misenus blew
A signal on his hollow horn. My men
Flew to the combat strange, and fain would wound
With martial steel those foul birds of the sea;
But on their sides no wounding blade could fall,
Nor any plume be marred. In swiftest flight
To starry skies they soared, and left on earth
Their half-gnawed, stolen feast, and footprints foul.
Celæno only on a beetling crag
Took lofty perch, and, prophetess of ill,
Shrieked malediction from her vulture breast:

"Because of slaughtered kine and ravished herd,
"Sons of Laomedon, have ye made war?
"And will ye from their rightful kingdom drive
"The guiltless Harpies? Hear, O, hear my word
"(Long in your bosoms may it rankle sore!)
"Which Jove omnipotent to Phœbus gave,
"Phœbus to me: a word of doom, which I,
"The Furies' elder sister, here unfold:
"'To Italy ye fare. The willing winds
"'Your call have heard; and ye shall have your prayer
"'In some Italian haven safely moored.
"'But never shall ye rear the circling walls
"'Of your own city, till for this our blood
"'By you unjustly spilt, your famished jaws
"'Bite at your tables, aye, — and half devour.'"
She spoke: her pinions bore her to the grove,
And she was seen no more. But all my band
Shuddered with shock of fear in each cold vein;
Their drooping spirits trusted swords no more,
But turned to prayers and offerings, asking grace,
Scarce knowing if those creatures were divine,
Or but vast birds, ill-omened and unclean.

Father Anchises to the gods in heaven
Uplifted suppliant hands, and on that shore
Due ritual made, crying aloud; "Ye gods
"Avert this curse, this evil turn away!
"Smile, Heaven, upon your faithful votaries."
Then bade he launch away, the chain undo,
Set every cable free and spread all sail.

O'er the white waves we flew, and took our way
Where'er the helmsman or the winds could guide.
Now forest-clad Zacynthus met our gaze,
Engirdled by the waves; Dulichium,
Samè, and Neritos, a rocky steep,
Uprose. We passed the cliffs of Ithaca
That called Laertes king, and flung our curse
On fierce Ulysses' hearth and native land.
Nigh hoar Leucate's clouded crest we drew,
Where Phœbus' temple, feared by mariners,
Loomed o'er us; thitherward we steered and reached
The little port and town. Our weary fleet
Dropped anchor, and lay beached along the strand.
So, safe at land, our hopeless peril past,
We offered thanks to Jove, and kindled high
His altars with our feast and sacrifice;
Then, gathering on Actium's holy shore,
Made fair solemnities of pomp and game.
My youth, anointing their smooth, naked limbs,
Wrestled our wonted way. For glad were we,
Who past so many isles of Greece had sped
And 'scaped our circling foes. Now had the sun
Rolled through the year's full circle, and the waves
Were rough with icy winter's northern gales.
I hung for trophy on that temple door
A swelling shield of brass (which once was worn
By mighty Abas) graven with this line:
Spoil of Æneas from triumphant foes.

Then from that haven I command them forth;
My good crews take the thwarts, smiting the sea

With rival strokes, and skim the level main.
Soon sank Phæacia's wind-swept citadels
Out of our view; we skirted the bold shores
Of proud Epirus, in Chaonian land,
And made Buthrotum's port and towering town.
Here wondrous tidings met us, that the son
Of Priam, Helenus, held kingly sway
O'er many Argive cities, having wed
The Queen of Pyrrhus, great Achilles' son,
And gained his throne; and that Andromache
Once more was wife unto a kindred lord.
Amazement held me; all my bosom burned
To see the hero's face and hear this tale
Of strange vicissitude. So up I climbed,
Leaving the haven, fleet, and friendly shore.

That self-same hour outside the city walls,
Within a grove where flowed the mimic stream
Of a new Simois, Andromache,
With offerings to the dead, and gifts of woe,
Poured forth libation, and invoked the shade
Of Hector, at a tomb which her fond grief
Had consecrated to perpetual tears,
Though void; a mound of fair green turf it stood,
And near it rose twin altars to his name.
She saw me drawing near; our Trojan helms
Met her bewildered eyes, and, terror-struck
At the portentous sight, she swooning fell
And lay cold, rigid, lifeless, till at last,
Scarce finding voice, her lips addressed me thus:
"Have I true vision? Bringest thou the word

"Of truth, O goddess-born? Art still in flesh?
"Or if sweet light be fled, my Hector, where?"
With flood of tears she spoke, and all the grove
Reëchoed to her cry. Scarce could I frame
Brief answer to her passion, but replied
With broken voice and accents faltering:
"I live, 't is true. I lengthen out my days
"Through many a desperate strait. But O, believe
"That what thine eyes behold is vision true.
"Alas! what lot is thine, that wert unthroned
"From such a husband's side? What after-fate
"Could give thee honor due? Andromache,
"Once Hector's wife, is Pyrrhus still thy lord?"

With drooping brows and lowly voice she cried:
"O, happy only was that virgin blest,
"Daughter of Priam, summoned forth to die
"In sight of Ilium, on a foeman's tomb!
"No casting of the lot her doom decreed,
"Nor came she to her conqueror's couch a slave.
"Myself from burning Ilium carried far
"O'er seas and seas, endured the swollen pride
"Of that young scion of Achilles' race,
"And bore him as his slave a son. When he
"Sued for Hermione, of Leda's line,
"And nuptial-bond with Lacedæmon's lords,
"I, the slave-wife, to Helenus was given,
"And slave was wed with slave. But afterward
"Orestes, crazed by loss of her he loved,
"And ever fury-driven from crime to crime,
"Crept upon Pyrrhus in a careless hour

"And murdered him upon his own hearth-stone.
"Part of the realm of Neoptolemus
"Fell thus to Helenus, who called his lands
"Chaonian, and in Trojan Chaon's name
"His kingdom is Chaonia. Yonder height
"Is Pergamus, our Ilian citadel.
"What power divine did waft thee to our shore,
"Not knowing whither? Tell me of the boy
"Ascanius! Still breathes he earthly air?
"In Troy she bore him — is he mourning still
"That mother ravished from his childhood's eyes?
"What ancient valor stirs the manly soul
"Of thine own son, of Hector's sister's child?"

Thus poured she forth full many a doleful word
With unavailing tears. But as she ceased,
Out of the city gates appeared the son
Of Priam, Helenus, with princely train.
He welcomed us as kin, and glad at heart
Gave guidance to his house, though oft his words
Fell faltering and few, with many a tear.
Soon to a humbler Troy I lift my eyes,
And of a mightier Pergamus discern
The towering semblance; there a scanty stream
Runs on in Xanthus' name, and my glad arms
The pillars of a Scæan gate embrace.
My Teucrian mariners with welcome free
Enjoyed the friendly town; his ample halls
Our royal host threw wide; full wine-cups flowed
Within the palace; golden feast was spread,
And many a goblet quaffed. Day followed day,

While favoring breezes beckoned us to sea,
And swelled the waiting canvas as they blew.
Then to the prophet-priest I made this prayer:

"Offspring of Troy, interpreter of Heaven!
"Who knowest Phœbus' power, and readest well
"The tripod, stars, and vocal laurel leaves
"To Phœbus dear, who know'st of every bird
"The ominous swift wing or boding song,
"O, speak! For all my course good omens showed,
"And every god admonished me to sail
"In quest of Italy's far-distant shores;
"But lone Celæno, heralding strange woe,
"Foretold prodigious horror, vengeance dark,
"And vile, unnatural hunger. How elude
"Such perils? Or by what hard duty done
"May such huge host of evils vanquished be?"

Then Helenus, with sacrifice of kine
In order due, implored the grace of Heaven,
Unloosed the fillets from his sacred brow,
And led me, Phœbus, to thy temple's door,
Awed by th' o'er-brooding godhead, whose true priest,
With lips inspired, made this prophetic song:

"O goddess-born, indubitably shines
"The blessing of great gods upon thy path
"Across the sea; the heavenly King supreme
"Thy destiny ordains; 't is he unfolds
"The grand vicissitude, which now pursues

"A course immutable. I will declare
"Of thy large fate a certain bounded part;
"That fearless thou may'st view the friendly sea,
"And in Ausonia's haven at the last
"Find thee a fixed abode. Than this no more
"The Sister Fates to Helenus unveil,
"And Juno, Saturn's daughter, grants no more.
"First, that Italia (which nigh at hand
"Thou deemest, and wouldst fondly enter in
"By yonder neighboring bays) lies distant far
"O'er trackless course and long, with interval
"Of far-extended lands. Thine oars must ply
"The waves of Sicily; thy fleet must cleave
"The large expanse of that Ausonian brine;
"The waters of Avernus thou shalt see,
"And that enchanted island where abides
"Ææan Circe, ere on tranquil shore
"Thou mayest plant thy nation. Lo! a sign
"I tell thee; hide this wonder in thy heart:
"Beside a certain stream's sequestered wave,
"Thy troubled eyes, in shadowy ilex grove
"That fringes on the river, shall descry
"A milk-white, monstrous sow, with teeming brood
"Of thirty young, new littered, white like her,
"All clustering at her teats, as prone she lies.
"There is thy city's safe, predestined ground,
"And there thy labors' end. Vex not thy heart
"About those 'tables bitten,' for kind fate
"Thy path will show, and Phœbus bless thy prayer.
"But from these lands and yon Italian shore,
"Where from this sea of ours the tide sweeps in,

"Escape and flee, for all its cities hold
"Pernicious Greeks, thy foes: the Locri there
"Have builded walls; the wide Sallentine fields
"Are filled with soldiers of Idomeneus;
"There Meliboean Philoctetes' town,
"Petilia, towers above its little wall.
"Yea, even when thy fleet has crossed the main,
"And from new altars built along the shore
"Thy vows to Heaven are paid, throw o'er thy head
"A purple mantle, veiling well thy brows,
"Lest, while the sacrificial fire ascends
"In offering to the gods, thine eye behold
"Some face of foe, and every omen fail.
"Let all thy people keep this custom due,
"And thou thyself be faithful; let thy seed
"Forever thus th' immaculate rite maintain.

"After departing hence, thou shalt be blown
"Toward Sicily, and strait Pelorus' bounds
"Will open wide. Then take the leftward way:
"Those leftward waters in long circuit sweep,
"Far from that billowy coast, the opposing side.
"These regions, so they tell, in ages gone
"By huge and violent convulsion riven
"(Such mutability is wrought by time),
"Sprang wide asunder; where the doubled strand
"Sole and continuous lay, the sea's vast power
"Burst in between, and bade its waves divide
"Hesperia's bosom from fair Sicily,
"While with a straitened firth it interflowed
"Their fields and cities sundered shore from shore.

"The right side Scylla keeps; the left is given
"To pitiless Charybdis, who draws down
"To the wild whirling of her steep abyss
"The monster waves, and ever and anon
"Flings them at heaven, to lash the tranquil stars.
"But Scylla, prisoned in her eyeless cave,
"Thrusts forth her face, and pulls upon the rocks
"Ship after ship; the parts that first be seen
"Are human; a fair-breasted virgin she,
"Down to the womb; but all that lurks below
"Is a huge-membered fish, where strangely join
"The flukes of dolphins and the paunch of wolves.
"Better by far to round the distant goal
"Of the Trinacrian headlands, veering wide
"From thy true course, than ever thou shouldst see
"That shapeless Scylla in her vaulted cave,
"Where grim rocks echo her dark sea-dogs' roar.
"Yea, more, if aught of prescience be bestowed
"On Helenus, if trusted prophet he,
"And Phœbus to his heart true voice have given,
"O goddess-born, one counsel chief of all
"I tell thee oft, and urge it o'er and o'er.
"To Juno's godhead lift thy loudest prayer;
"To Juno chant a fervent votive song,
"And with obedient offering persuade
"That potent Queen. So shalt thou, triumphing,
"To Italy be sped, and leave behind
"Trinacria. When wafted to that shore,
"Repair to Cumæ's hill, and to the Lake
"Avernus with its whispering grove divine.
"There shalt thou see a frenzied prophetess,

"Who from beneath the hollow scarpèd crag
"Sings oracles, or characters on leaves
"Mysterious names. Whate'er the virgin writes,
"On leaves inscribing the portentous song,
"She sets in order, and conceals them well
"In her deep cave, where they abide unchanged
"In due array. Yet not a care has she,
"If with some swinging hinge a breeze sweeps in,
"To catch them as they whirl: if open door
"Disperse them fluttering through the hollow rock,
"She will not link their shifted sense anew,
"Nor re-invent her fragmentary song.
"Oft her unanswered votaries depart,
"Scorning the Sibyl's shrine. But deem not thou
"Thy tarrying too long, whate'er thy stay.
"Though thy companions chide, though winds of power
"Invite thy ship to sea, and well would speed
"The swelling sail, yet to that Sibyl go.
"Pray that her own lips may sing forth for thee
"The oracles, uplifting her dread voice
"In willing prophecy. Her rede shall tell
"Of Italy, its wars and tribes to be,
"And of what way each burden and each woe
"May be escaped, or borne. Her favoring aid
"Will grant swift, happy voyages to thy prayer.
"Such counsels Heaven to my lips allows.
"Arise, begone! and by thy glorious deeds
"Set Troy among the stars!"

So spake the prophet with benignant voice.
Then gifts he bade be brought of heavy gold

And graven ivory, which to our ships
He bade us bear; each bark was loaded full
With massy silver and Dodona's pride
Of brazen cauldrons; a cuirass he gave
Of linkèd gold enwrought and triple chain;
A noble helmet, too, with flaming crest
And lofty cone, th' accoutrement erewhile
Of Neoptolemus. My father too
Had fit gifts from the King; whose bounty then
Gave steeds and riders; and new gear was sent
To every sea-worn ship, while he supplied
Seafarers' kit to all my loyal crews.

Anchises bade us speedily set sail,
Nor lose a wind so fair; and answering him,
Apollo's priest made reverent adieu:
"Anchises, honored by the love sublime
"Of Venus' self and twice in safety borne
"From falling Troy, chief care of kindly Heaven,
"Th' Ausonian shore is thine. Sail thitherward!
"For thou art pre-ordained to travel far
"O'er yonder seas; far in the distance lies
"That region of Ausonia, Phœbus' voice
"To thee made promise of. Onward, I say,
"O blest in the exceeding loyal love
"Of thy dear son! Why keep thee longer now?
"Why should my words yon gathering winds detain?"
Likewise Andromache in mournful guise
Took last farewell, bringing embroidered robes
Of golden woof; a princely Phrygian cloak
She gave Ascanius, vying with the King

In gifts of honor; and threw o'er the boy
The labors of her loom, with words like these:
"Accept these gifts, sweet youth, memorials
"Of me and my poor handicraft, to prove
"Th' undying friendship of Andromache,
"Once Hector's wife. Take these last offerings
"Of those who are thy kin — O thou that art
"Of my Astyanax in all this world
"The only image! His thy lovely eyes!
"Thy hands, thy lips, are even what he bore,
"And like thy own his youthful bloom would be."

Thus I made answer, turning to depart
With rising tears: "Live on, and be ye blessed,
"Whose greatness is accomplished! As for me,
"From change to change Fate summons, and I go;
"But ye have won repose. No leagues of sea
"Await your cleaving keel. Not yours the quest
"Of fading Italy's delusive shore.
"Here a new Xanthus and a second Troy
"Your labor fashioned and your eyes may see —
"More blest, I trust, less tempting to our foes!
"If e'er on Tiber and its bordering vales
"I safely enter, and these eyes behold
"Our destined walls, then in fraternal bond
"Let our two nations live, whose mutual boast
"Is one Dardanian blood, one common story.
"Epirus with Hesperia shall be
"One Troy in heart and soul. But this remains
"For our sons' sons the happy task and care."

Forth o'er the seas we sped and kept our course
Nigh the Ceraunian headland, where begins
The short sea-passage unto Italy.
Soon sank the sun, while down the shadowed hills
Stole deeper gloom; then making shore, we flung
Our bodies on a dry, sea-bordering sand,
Couched on earth's welcome breast; the oars were ranged
In order due; the tides of slumber dark
O'erflowed our lives. But scarce the chariot
Of Night, on wings of swift, obedient Hours,
Had touched the middle sky, when wakeful sprang
Good Palinurus from his pillowed stone:
With hand at ear he caught each airy gust
And questioned of the winds; the gliding stars
He called by name, as onward they advanced
Through the still heaven; Arcturus he beheld,
The Hyades, rain-bringers, the twin Bears,
And vast Orion girt in golden arms.
He blew a trumpet from his ship; our camp
Stirred to the signal for embarking; soon
We rode the seas once more with swelling sail.

Scarce had Aurora's purple from the sky
Warned off the stars, when lying very low
Along th' horizon, the dimmed hills we saw
Of Italy; Achates first gave cry
"Italia!" with answering shouts of joy,
My comrades' voices cried, "Italia, hail!"
Anchises, then, wreathed a great bowl with flowers
And filled with wine, invoking Heaven to bless,

And thus he prayed from our ship's lofty stern:
"O lords of land and sea and every storm!
"Breathe favoring breezes for our onward way!"
Fresh blew the prayed-for winds. A haven fair
Soon widened near us; and its heights were crowned
By a Greek fane to Pallas. Yet my men
Furled sail and shoreward veered the pointing prow.

The port receding from the orient wave
Is curved into a bow; on either side
The jutting headlands toss the salt sea-foam
And hide the bay itself. Like double wall
The towered crags send down protecting arms,
While distant from the shore the temple stands.
Here on a green sward, the first omen given,
I saw four horses grazing through the field,
Each white as snow. Father Anchises cried:
"Is war thy gift, O new and alien land?
"Horses make war; of war these creatures bode.
"Yet oft before the chariot of peace
"Their swift hoofs go, and on their necks they bear
"Th' obedient yoke and rein. Therefore a hope
"Of peace is also ours." Then we implored
Minerva's mercy, at her sacred shrine,
The mail-clad goddess who gave welcome there;
And at an altar, mantling well our brows
The Phrygian way, as Helenus ordained,
We paid the honors his chief counsel urged,
With blameless rite, to Juno, Argive Queen.
No tarrying now, but after sacrifice
We twirled the sailyards and shook out all sail,

Leaving the cities of the sons of Greece
And that distrusted land. Tarentum's bay
Soon smiled before us, town of Hercules,
If fame be true; opposing it uptowers
Lacinia's headland unto Juno dear,
The heights of Caulon, and that sailors' bane,
Ship-shattering Scylaceum. Thence half seen,
Trinacrian Ætna cleaves th' horizon line;
We hear from far the crash of shouting seas,
Where lifted billows leap the tide-swept sand.

Father Anchises cried: "'T is none but she —
"Charybdis! Helenus this reef foretold,
"And rocks of dreadful name. O, fly, my men!
"Rise like one man with long, strong sweep of oars!"
Not unobedient they! First Palinure
Veered to the leftward wave the willing keel,
And sails and oars together leftward strove.
We shot to skyward on the arching surge,
Then, as she sank, dropped deeper than the grave;
Thrice bellowed the vast cliffs from vaulted wall;
Thrice saw we spouted foam and showers of stars.

After these things both wind and sun did fail;
And weary, worn, not witting of our way,
We drifted shoreward to the Cyclops' land.
A spreading bay is there, impregnable
To all invading storms; and Ætna's throat
With roar of frightful ruin thunders nigh.
Now to the realm of light it lifts a cloud
Of pitch-black, whirling smoke, and fiery dust,

Shooting out globes of flame, with monster tongues
That lick the stars; now huge crags of itself,
Out of the bowels of the mountain torn,
Its maw disgorges, while the molten rock
Rolls screaming skyward; from the nether deep
The fathomless abyss makes ebb and flow.
Enceladus, his body lightning-scarred,
Lies prisoned under all, so runs the tale:
O'er him gigantic Ætna breathes in fire
From crack and seam; and if he haply turn
To change his wearied side, Trinacria's isle
Trembles and moans, and thick fumes mantle heaven.

That night in screen and covert of a grove
We bore the dire convulsion, unaware
Whence the loud horror came. For not a star
Its lamp allowed, nor burned in upper sky
The constellated fires, but all was gloom,
And frowning night confined the moon in cloud.

When from the eastern waves the light of morn
Began to peer, and from the upper sky
Aurora flamed away the dark and dew,
Out of the forest sprang a startling shape
Of hunger-wasted misery; a man
In wretched guise, who shoreward came with hands
Outstretched in supplication. We turned back
And scanned him well. All grime and foulness he,
With long and tangled beard, his savage garb
Fastened with thorns; but in all else he seemed
A Greek, and in his country's league of arms

Sent to the siege of Troy. When he beheld
The Dardan habit, and our Trojan steel,
He somewhat paused, as if in dread dismay
Such sight to see, and falteringly moved;
But soon with headlong steps he sought the shore,
Ejaculating broken sobs and prayers:
"By stars above! By gods on high! O, hear!
"By this bright heavenly air we mortals breathe,
"Save me, sweet Trojans! Carry me away
"Unto what land ye will! I ask no more.
"I came, I know it, in the ships of Greece;
"And I did war, 't is true, with Ilium's gods.
"O, if the crime deserve it, fling my corse
"On yonder waves, and in the boundless brine
"Sink me forever! Give me in my death
"The comfort that by human hands I die."

He clasped our knees, and writhing on his own
Clung fast. We bid him tell his race and name,
And by what fate pursued. Anchises gave
His own right hand in swift and generous aid,
And by prompt token cheered the exile's heart,
Who, banishing his fears, poured forth this tale:—

"My home was Ithaca, and I partook
"The fortunes of Ulysses evil-starred.
"My name is Achemenides, my sire
"Was Adamastus, and I sailed for Troy,
"Being so poor,—O, that I ne'er had changed
"The lot I bore! In yon vast Cyclops' cave
"My comrades, flying from its gruesome door,

"Left me behind, forgotten. 'T is a house
"Of gory feasts of flesh, 't is deep and dark,
"And vaulted high. He looms as high as heaven;
"I pray the blessèd gods to rid the earth
"Of the vile monster! None can look on him,
"None speak with him. He feeds on clotted gore
"Of disembowelled men. These very eyes
"Saw him seize two of our own company,
"And, as he lolled back in the cave, he clutched
"And dashed them on the stones, fouling the floor
"With torrent of their blood; myself I saw him
"Crunch with his teeth the dripping, bloody limbs
"Still hot and pulsing on his hungry jaw.
"But not without reward! For such a sight
"Ulysses would not brook, and Ithaca
"Forgot not in such strait the name he bore.
"For soon as, gorged with feasting and o'ercome
"With drunken slumber, the foul giant lay
"Sprawled through the cave, his head dropped helpless down,
"Disgorging as he slept thick drool of gore
"And gobbets drenched with bloody wine; then we,
"Calling on Heaven and taking place by lot,
"Drew round him like one man, and with a beam
"Sharpened at end bored out that monster eye,
"Which, huge and sole, lay under the grim brow,
"Round as an Argive shield or Phœbus' star.
"Thus took we joyful vengeance for the shades
"Of our lost mates. But, O ill-fated men!
"Fly, I implore, and cut the cables free
"Along the beach! For in the land abide,

"Like Polyphemus, who in hollow cave
"Kept fleecy sheep, and milked his fruitful ewes,
"A hundred other, huge as he, who rove
"Wide o'er this winding shore and mountains fair:
"Cyclops accursèd, bestial! Thrice the moon
"Has filled her horns with light, while here I dwell
"In lonely woods and lairs of creatures wild;
"Or from tall cliffs out-peering I discern
"The Cyclops, and shrink shuddering from the sound
"Of their vast step and cry. My sorry fare
"Is berries and hard cornels dropped from trees,
"Or herb-roots torn out from the niggard ground.
"Though watching the whole sea, only to-day
"Have I had sight of ships. To you I fled.
"Whate'er ye be, it was my only prayer
"To 'scape that monster brood. I ask no more.
"O, set me free by any death ye will!"

He scarce had said, when moving o'er the crest
Of a high hill a giant shape we saw:
That shepherd Polyphemus, with his flocks
Down-wending to the well-known water-side;
Huge, shapeless, horrible, with blinded eye,
Bearing a lopped pine for a staff, he made
His footing sure, while the white, fleecy sheep,
Sole pleasure now, and solace of his woes,
Ran huddling at his side.
Soon to the vast flood of the level brine
He came, and washed the flowing gore away
From that out-hollowed eye; he gnashed his teeth,
Groaning, and deep into the watery way

Stalked on, his tall bulk wet by scarce a wave.
We fled in haste, though far, and with us bore
The truthful suppliant; cut silently
The anchor-ropes, and, bending to the oar,
Swept on with eager strokes clean out to sea.
Aware he was, and toward our loud halloo
Whirled sudden round; but when no power had he
To seize or harm, nor could his fierce pursuit
O'ertake the Ionian surges as they rolled,
He raised a cry incredible; the sea
With all its billows trembled; the wide shore
Of Italy from glens and gorges moaned,
And Ætna roared from every vaulted cave.
Then rallied from the grove-clad, lofty isle
The Cyclops' clan, and lined the beach and bay.
We saw each lonely eyeball glare in vain,
As side by side those brothers Ætna-born
Stood towering high, a conclave dark and dire:
As when, far up some mountain's famous crest,
Wind-fronting oaks or cone-clad cypresses
Have made assembling in the solemn hills,
Jove's giant wood or Dian's sacred grove.

We, terror-struck, would fly we knew not where,
With loosened sheet and canvas swelling strong
Before a welcome wind; but Helenus
Bade us both Scylla and Charybdis fear,
Where 'twixt the twain death straitly hems the way;
And so the counsel was to veer our bark
The course it came. But lo! a northern gale
Burst o'er us from Pelorus' narrowed side,

And on we rode far past Pantagia's bay
Of unhewn rock, and past the haven strong
Of Megara, and Thapsus lying low.
Such were the names retold, and such the shores
Shown us by Achemenides, whose fate
Made him familiar there, for he had sailed
With evil-starred Ulysses o'er that sea.

Off the Sicilian shore an island lies,
Wave-washed Plemmyrium, called in olden days
Ortygia; here Alpheus, river-god,
From Elis flowed by secret sluice, they say,
Beneath the sea, and mingles at thy mouth,
Fair Arethusa! with Sicilian waves.
Our voices hailed the great gods of the land
With reverent prayer; then skirted we the shore,
Where smooth Helorus floods the fruitful plain.
Under Pachynus' beetling precipice
We kept our course; then Camarína rose
In distant view, firm-seated evermore
By Fate's decree; and that far-spreading vale
Of Gela, with the name of power it takes
From its wide river; and, uptowering far,
The ramparts of proud Acragas appeared,
Where fiery steeds were bred in days of old.
Borne by the winds, along thy coast I fled,
Selinus, green with palm! and past the shore
Of Lilybæum with its treacherous reef;
Till at the last the port of Drepanum
Received me to its melancholy strand.
Here, woe is me! outworn by stormful seas,

My sire, sole comfort of my grievous doom,
Anchises ceased to be. O best of sires!
Here didst thou leave me in the weary way;
Through all our perils — O the bitter loss! —
Borne safely, but in vain. King Helenus,
Whose prophet-tongue of dark events foretold,
Spoke not this woe; nor did Celæno's curse
Of this forebode. Such my last loss and pain;
Such, of my weary way, the destined goal.
From thence departing, the divine behest
Impelled me to thy shores, O listening queen!

Such was, while all gave ear, the tale sublime
Father Æneas, none but he, set forth
Of wanderings and of dark decrees divine:
Silent at last, he ceased, and took repose.

END OF BOOK III

BOOK IV

Now felt the Queen the sharp, slow-gathering pangs
Of love; and out of every pulsing vein
Nourished the wound and fed its viewless fire.
Her hero's virtues and his lordly line
Keep calling to her soul; his words, his glance,
Cling to her heart like lingering, barbèd steel,
And rest and peace from her vexed body fly.

A new day's dawn with Phœbus' lamp divine
Lit up all lands, and from the vaulted heaven
Aurora had dispelled the dark and dew;
When thus unto the ever-answering heart
Of her dear sister spoke the stricken Queen:
"Anna, my sister, what disturbing dreams
"Perplex me and alarm? What guest is this
"New-welcomed to our house? How proud his mien!
"What dauntless courage and exploits of war!
"Sooth, I receive it for no idle tale
"That of the gods he sprang. 'T is cowardice
"Betrays the base-born soul. Ah me! How fate
"Has smitten him with storms! What dire extremes
"Of war and horror in his tale he told!
"O, were it not immutably resolved
"In my fixed heart, that to no shape of man

"I would be wed again (since my first love
"Left me by death abandoned and betrayed);
"Loathed I not so the marriage torch and train,
"I could — who knows? — to this one weakness yield.
"Anna, I hide it not! But since the doom
"Of my ill-starred Sichæus, when our shrines
"Were by a brother's murder dabbled o'er,
"This man alone has moved me; he alone
"Has shaken my weak will. I seem to feel
"The motions of love's lost, familiar fire.
"But may the earth gape open where I tread,
"And may almighty Jove with thunder-scourge
"Hurl me to Erebus' abysmal shade,
"To pallid ghosts and midnight fathomless,
"Before, O Chastity! I shall offend
"Thy holy power, or cast thy bonds away!
"He who first mingled his dear life with mine
"Took with him all my heart. 'T is his alone —
"O, let it rest beside him in the grave!"
She spoke: the bursting tears her breast o'erflowed.

"O dearer to thy sister than her life,"
Anna replied, "wouldst thou in sorrow's weed
"Waste thy long youth alone, nor ever know
"Sweet babes at thine own breast, nor gifts of love?
"Will dust and ashes, or a buried ghost,
"Reck what we do? 'T is true thy grieving heart
"Was cold to earlier wooers, Libya's now,
"And long ago in Tyre. Iarbas knew
"Thy scorn, and many a prince and captain bred
"In Afric's land of glory. Why resist

"A love that makes thee glad? Hast thou no care
"What alien lands are these where thou dost reign?
"Here are Gætulia's cities and her tribes
"Unconquered ever; on thy borders rove
"Numidia's uncurbed cavalry; here too
"Lies Syrtis' cruel shore, and regions wide
"Of thirsty desert, menaced everywhere
"By the wild hordes of Barca. Shall I tell
"Of Tyre's hostilities, the threats and rage
"Of our own brother? Friendly gods, I trow,
"Wafted the Teucrian ships, with Juno's aid,
"To these our shores. O sister, what a throne,
"And what imperial city shall be thine,
"If thus espoused! With Trojan arms allied
"How far may not our Punic fame extend
"In deeds of power? Call therefore on the gods
"To favor thee; and, after omens fair,
"Give queenly welcome, and contrive excuse
"To make him tarry, while yon wintry seas
"Are loud beneath Orion's stormful star,
"And on his battered ships the season frowns."

So saying, she stirred a passion-burning breast
To love more madly still; her words infused
A doubting mind with hope, and bade the blush
Of shame begone. First to the shrines they went
And sued for grace; performing sacrifice,
Choosing an offering of unblemished ewes,
To law-bestowing Ceres, to the god
Of light, to sire Lyæus, lord of wine;
But chiefly unto Juno, patroness

Of nuptial vows. There Dido, beauteous Queen,
Held forth in her right hand the sacred bowl,
And poured it full between the lifted horns
Of the white heifer; or on temple floors
She strode among the richly laden shrines,
The eyes of gods upon her, worshipping
With many a votive gift; or, peering deep
Into the victims' cloven sides, she read
The fate-revealing tokens trembling there.
How blind the hearts of prophets be! Alas!
Of what avail be temples and fond prayers
To change a frenzied mind? Devouring ever,
Love's fire burns inward to her bones; she feels
Quick in her breast the viewless, voiceless wound.
Ill-fated Dido ranges up and down
The spaces of her city, desperate,
Her life one flame — like arrow-stricken doe,
Through Cretan forest rashly wandering,
Pierced by a far-off shepherd, who pursues
With shafts, and leaves behind his light-winged steel,
Not knowing; while she scours the dark ravines
Of Dicte and its woodlands; at her heart
The mortal barb irrevocably clings.
Around her city's battlements she guides
Æneas, to make show of Sidon's gold,
And what her realm can boast; full oft her voice
Essays to speak and trembling dies away:
Or, when the daylight fades, she spreads anew
A royal banquet, and once more will plead,
Mad that she is, to hear the Trojan sorrow;
And with oblivious ravishment once more

Hangs on his lips who tells; or when her guests
Are scattered, and the wan moon's fading horn
Bedims its ray, while many a sinking star
Invites to slumber, there she weeps alone
In the deserted hall, and casts her down
On the cold couch he pressed. Her love from far
Beholds her vanished hero and receives
His voice upon her ears; or to her breasts,
Moved by a father's image in his child,
She clasps Ascanius, seeking to deceive
Her unblest passion so. Her enterprise
Of tower and rampart stops: her martial host
No longer she reviews, nor fashions now
Defensive haven and defiant wall;
But idly all her half-built bastions frown,
And enginery of sieges, high as heaven.

But soon the chosen spouse of Jove perceived
The Queen's infection; and because the voice
Of honor to such frenzy spoke not, she,
Daughter of Saturn, unto Venus turned
And counselled thus: "How noble is the praise,
"How glorious the spoils of victory,
"For thee and for thy boy! Your names should be
"In lasting, vast renown — that by the snare
"Of two great gods in league one woman fell!
"It 'scapes me not that my protected realms
"Have ever been thy fear, and the proud halls
"Of Carthage thy vexation and annoy.
"Why further go? Prithee, what useful end
"Has our long war? Why not from this day forth

"Perpetual peace and nuptial amity?
"Hast thou not worked thy will? Behold and see
"How love-sick Dido burns, and all her flesh
"The madness feels! So let our common grace
"Smile on a mingled people! Let her serve
"A Phrygian husband, while thy hands receive
"Her Tyrian subjects for the bridal dower!"

In answer (reading the dissembler's mind
Which unto Libyan shores were fain to shift
Italia's future throne) thus Venus spoke:
"'T were mad to spurn such favor, or by choice
"Be numbered with thy foes. But can it be
"That fortune on thy noble counsel smiles?
"To me Fate shows but dimly whether Jove
"Unto the Trojan wanderers ordains
"A common city with the sons of Tyre,
"With mingling blood and sworn, perpetual peace.
"His wife thou art; it is thy rightful due
"To plead to know his mind. Go, ask him, then!
"For humbly I obey!"
With instant word
Juno the Queen replied: "Leave that to me!
"But in what wise our urgent task and grave
"May soon be sped, I will in brief unfold
"To thine attending ear. A royal hunt
"In sylvan shades unhappy Dido gives
"For her Æneas, when to-morrow's dawn
"Uplifts its earliest ray and Titan's beam
"Shall first unveil the world. But I will pour
"Black storm-clouds with a burst of heavy hail

"Along their way; and as the huntsmen speed
"To hem the wood with snares, I will arouse
"All heaven with thunder. The attending train
"Shall scatter and be veiled in blinding dark,
"While Dido and her hero out of Troy
"To the same cavern fly. My auspices
"I will declare — if thou alike wilt bless;
"And yield her in true wedlock for his bride.
"Such shall their spousal be!" To Juno's will
Cythéra's Queen inclined assenting brow:
And laughed such guile to see.
Aurora rose,
And left the ocean's rim. The city's gates
Pour forth to greet the morn a gallant train
Of huntsmen, bearing many a woven snare
And steel-tipped javelin; while to and fro
Run the keen-scented dogs and Libyan squires.
The Queen still keeps her chamber; at her doors
The Punic lords await; her palfrey, brave
In gold and purple housing, paws the ground
And fiercely champs the foam-flecked bridle-rein.
At last, with numerous escort, forth she shines:
Her Tyrian pall is bordered in bright hues,
Her quiver, gold; her tresses are confined
Only with gold; her robes of purple rare
Meet in a golden clasp. To greet her come
The noble Phrygian guests; among them smiles
The boy Iulus; and in fair array
Æneas, goodliest of all his train.
In such a guise Apollo (when he leaves
Cold Lycian hills and Xanthus' frosty stream

To visit Delos to Latona dear)
Ordains the song, while round his altars cry
The choirs of many islands, with the pied,
Fantastic Agathyrsi; soon the god
Moves o'er the Cynthian steep; his flowing hair
He binds with laurel garland and bright gold;
Upon his shining shoulder as he goes
The arrows ring: — not less uplifted mien
Æneas wore; from his illustrious brow
Such beauty shone.

Soon to the mountains tall
The cavalcade comes nigh, to pathless haunts
Of woodland creatures; the wild goats are seen,
From pointed crag descending leap by leap
Down the steep ridges; in the vales below
Are routed deer, that scour the spreading plain,
And mass their dust-blown squadrons in wild flight,
Far from the mountain's bound. Ascanius,
Flushed with the sport, spurs on a mettled steed
From vale to vale, and many a flying herd
His chase outspeeds; but in his heart he prays
Among these tame things suddenly to see
A tusky boar, or, leaping from the hills,
A growling mountain-lion, golden-maned.

Meanwhile low thunders in the distant sky
Mutter confusedly; soon bursts in full
The storm-cloud and the hail. The Tyrian troop
Is scattered wide; the chivalry of Troy,
With the young heir of Dardan's kingly line,
Of Venus sprung, seek shelter where they may,

With sudden terror; down the deep ravines
The swollen torrents roar. In that same hour
Queen Dido and her hero out of Troy
To the same cavern fly. Old Mother-Earth
And wedlock-keeping Juno gave the sign;
The flash of lightnings on the conscious air
Lit them the bridal bed; along the hills
The wailing wood-nymphs sobbed a wedding song.
Such was that day of death, the source and spring
Of many a woe. For Dido took no heed
Of honor and good-name; nor did she mean
Her loves to hide; but called the lawless deed
A marriage, and with phrases veiled her shame.

Swift through the Libyan cities Rumor sped.
Rumor! What evil can surpass her speed?
In movement she grows mighty, and achieves
Strength and dominion as she swifter flies.
Small first, because afraid, she soon exalts
Her stature skyward, stalking through the lands
And mantling in the clouds her baleful brow.
The womb of Earth, in anger at high Heaven,
Bore her, they say, last of the Titan spawn,
Sister to Cœus and Enceladus.
Feet swift to run and pinions like the wind
The dreadful monster wears; her carcase huge
Is feathered, and at root of every plume
A peering eye abides; and, strange to tell,
An equal number of vociferous tongues,
Foul, whispering lips, and ears, that catch at all.
At night she spreads midway 'twixt earth and heaven

Her pinions in the darkness, hissing loud,
Nor e'er to happy slumber gives her eyes:
But with the morn she takes her watchful throne
High on the housetops or on lofty towers,
To terrify the nations. She can cling
To vile invention and malignant wrong,
Or mingle with her word some tidings true.

She now with changeful story filled men's ears,
Exultant, whether false or true she sung:
How, Trojan-born Æneas having come,
Dido, the lovely widow, looked his way,
Deigning to wed; how all the winter long
They passed in revel and voluptuous ease,
To dalliance given o'er; naught heeding now
Of crown or kingdom — shameless! lust-enslaved!
Such tidings broadcast on the lips of men
The filthy goddess spread; and soon she hied
To King Iarbas, where her hateful song
To newly-swollen wrath his heart inflamed.
Him the god Ammon got by forced embrace
Upon a Libyan nymph; his kingdoms wide
Possessed a hundred ample shrines to Jove,
A hundred altars whence ascended ever
The fires of sacrifice, perpetual seats
For a great god's abode, where flowing blood
Enriched the ground, and on the portals hung
Garlands of every flower. The angered King,
Half-maddened by malignant Rumor's voice,
Unto his favored altars came, and there,
Surrounded by the effluence divine,

Upraised in prayer to Jove his suppliant hands.
"Almighty Jupiter, to whom each day,
"At banquet on the painted couch reclined,
"Numidia pours libation! Do thine eyes
"Behold us? Or when out of yonder heaven,
"O sire, thou launchest the swift thunderbolt,
"Is it for naught we fear thee? Do the clouds
"Shoot forth blind fire to terrify the soul
"With wild, unmeaning roar? O, look upon
"That woman, who was homeless in our realm,
"And bargained where to build her paltry town,
"Receiving fertile coastland for her farms,
"By hospitable grant! She dares disdain
"Our proffered nuptial vow. She has proclaimed
"Æneas partner of her bed and throne.
"And now that Paris, with his eunuch crew,
"Beneath his chin and fragrant, oozy hair
"Ties the soft Lydian bonnet, boasting well
"His stolen prize. But we to all these fanes,
"Though they be thine, a fruitless offering bring,
"And feed on empty tales our trust in thee."

As thus he prayed and to the altars clung,
Th' Omnipotent gave ear, and turned his gaze
Upon the royal dwelling, where for love
The amorous pair forgot their place and name.
Then thus to Mercury he gave command:
"Haste thee, my son, upon the Zephyrs call,
"And take thy wingèd way! My mandate bear
"Unto that prince of Troy who tarries now
"In Tyrian Carthage, heedless utterly

"Of empire Heaven-bestowed. On wingèd winds
"Hasten with my decrees. Not such the man
"His beauteous mother promised; not for this
"Twice did she shield him from the Greeks in arms:
"But that he might rule Italy, a land
"Pregnant with thrones and echoing with war;
"That he of Teucer's seed a race should sire,
"And bring beneath its law the whole wide world.
"If such a glory and event supreme
"Enkindle not his bosom; if such task
"To his own honor speak not; can the sire
"Begrudge Ascanius the heritage
"Of the proud name of Rome? What plans he now?
"What mad hope bids him linger in the lap
"Of enemies, considering no more
"The land Lavinian and Ausonia's sons.
"Let him to sea! Be this our final word:
"This message let our herald faithful bear."
He spoke. The god a prompt obedience gave
To his great sire's command. He fastened first
Those sandals of bright gold, which carry him
Aloft o'er land or sea, with airy wings
That race the fleeting wind; then lifted he
His wand, wherewith he summons from the grave
Pale-featured ghosts, or, if he will, consigns
To doleful Tartarus; or by its power
Gives slumber or dispels; or quite unseals
The eyelids of the dead: on this relying,
He routs the winds or cleaves th' obscurity
Of stormful clouds. Soon from his flight he spied
The summit and the sides precipitous

Of stubborn Atlas, whose star-pointing peak
Props heaven; of Atlas, whose pine-wreathèd brow
Is girdled evermore with misty gloom
And lashed of wind and rain; a cloak of snow
Melts on his shoulder; from his aged chin
Drop rivers, and ensheathed in stiffening ice
Glitters his great grim beard.
Here first was stayed
The speed of Mercury's well-poising wing;
Here making pause, from hence he headlong flung
His body to the sea; in motion like
Some sea-bird's, which along the levelled shore
Or round tall crags where rove the swarming fish,
Flies low along the waves: o'er-hovering so
Between the earth and skies, Cyllene's god
Flew downward from his mother's mountain-sire,
Parted the winds and skimmed the sandy marge
Of Libya. When first his wingèd feet
Came nigh the clay-built Punic huts, he saw
Æneas building at a citadel,
And founding walls and towers; at his side
Was girt a blade with yellow jaspers starred,
His mantle with the stain of Tyrian shell
Flowed purple from his shoulder, broidered fair
By opulent Dido with fine threads of gold,
Her gift of love; straightway the god began:
"Dost thou for lofty Carthage toil, to build
"Foundations strong? Dost thou, a wife's weak thrall,
"Build her proud city? Hast thou, shameful loss!
"Forgot thy kingdom and thy task sublime?
"From bright Olympus, I. He who commands

"All gods, and by his sovran deity
"Moves earth and heaven — he it was who bade
"Me bear on wingèd winds his high decree.
"What plan is thine? By what mad hope dost thou
"Linger so long in lap of Libyan land?
"If the proud guerdon of thy destined way
"Move not thy heart, if all the arduous toil
"To thine own honor speak not, look upon
"Iulus in his bloom, thy hope and heir
"Ascanius. It is his rightful due
"In Italy o'er Roman lands to reign."
After such word Cyllene's wingèd god
Vanished, and e'er his accents died away,
Dissolved in air before the mortal's eyes.

Æneas at the sight stood terror-dumb
With choking voice and horror-rising hair.
He fain would fly at once and get him gone
From that voluptuous land, much wondering
At Heaven's wrathful word. Alas! how stir?
What cunning argument can plead his cause
Before th' infuriate Queen? How break such news?
Flashing this way and that, his startled mind
Makes many a project and surveys them all.
But, pondering well, his final counsel stopped
At this resolve: he summoned to his side
Mnestheus, Sergestus, and Serestus bold,
And bade them fit the fleet, all silently
Gathering the sailors and collecting gear,
But carefully dissembling what emprise
Such novel stir intends: himself the while

(Since high-born Dido dreamed not love so fond
Could have an end) would seek an audience,
At some indulgent time, and try what shift
Such matters may require. With joy they heard,
And wrought, assiduous, at their prince's plan.

But what can cheat true love? The Queen foreknew
His stratagem, and all the coming change
Perceived ere it began. Her jealous fear
Counted no hour secure. That unclean tongue
Of Rumor told her fevered heart the fleet
Was fitting forth, and hastening to be gone.
Distractedly she raved, and passion-tossed
Roamed through her city, like a Mænad roused
By the wild rout of Bacchus, when are heard
The third year's orgies, and the midnight scream
To cold Cithæron calls the frenzied crew.
Finding Æneas, thus her plaint she poured:
"Didst hope to hide it, false one, that such crime
"Was in thy heart, — to steal without farewell
"Out of my kingdom? Did our mutual joy
"Not move thee; nor thine own true promise given
"Once on a time? Nor Dido, who will die
"A death of sorrow? Why compel thy ships
"To brave the winter stars? Why off to sea
"So fast through stormy skies? O, cruelty!
"If Troy still stood, and if thou wert not bound
"For alien shore unknown, wouldst steer for Troy
"Through yonder waste of waves? Is it from me
"Thou takest flight? O, by these flowing tears,

"By thine own plighted word (for nothing more
"My weakness left to miserable me),
"By our poor marriage of imperfect vow,
"If aught to me thou owest, if aught in me
"Ever have pleased thee — O, be merciful
"To my low-fallen fortunes! I implore,
"If place be left for prayer, thy purpose change!
"Because of thee yon Libyan savages
"And nomad chiefs are grown implacable,
"And my own Tyrians hate me. Yes, for thee
"My chastity was slain and honor fair,
"By which alone to glory I aspired,
"In former days. To whom dost thou in death
"Abandon me? my guest! — since but this name
"Is left me of a husband! Shall I wait
"Till fell Pygmalion, my brother, raze
"My city walls? Or the Gætulian king,
"Iarbas, chain me captive to his car?
"O, if, ere thou hadst fled, I might but bear
"Some pledge of love to thee, and in these halls
"Watch some sweet babe Æneas at his play,
"Whose face should be the memory of thine own —
"I were not so forsaken, lost, undone!"

She said. But he, obeying Jove's decree,
Gazed steadfastly away; and in his heart
With strong repression crushed his cruel pain;
Then thus the silence broke: "O Queen, not one
"Of my unnumbered debts so strongly urged
"Would I gainsay. Elissa's memory
"Will be my treasure long as memory holds,

"Or breath of life is mine. Hear my brief plea!
"'T was not my hope to hide this flight I take,
"As thou hast dreamed. Nay, I did never light
"A bridegroom's torch, nor gave I thee the vow
"Of marriage. Had my destiny decreed,
"That I should shape life to my heart's desire,
"And at my own will put away the weight
"Of toil and pain, my place would now be found
"In Troy, among the cherished sepulchres
"Of my own kin, and Priam's mansion proud
"Were standing still; or these my loyal hands
"Had rebuilt Ilium for her vanquished sons.
"But now to Italy Apollo's power
"Commands me forth; his Lycian oracles
"Are loud for Italy. My heart is there,
"And there my fatherland. If now the towers
"Of Carthage and thy Libyan colony
"Delight thy Tyrian eyes; wilt thou refuse
"To Trojan exiles their Ausonian shore?
"I too by Fate was driven, not less than thou,
"To wander far a foreign throne to find.
"Oft when in dewy dark night hides the world,
"And flaming stars arise, Anchises' shade
"Looks on me in my dreams with angered brow.
"I think of my Ascanius, and the wrong
"To that dear heart, from whom I steal away
"Hesperia, his destined home and throne.
"But now the wingèd messenger of Heaven,
"Sent down by Jove (I swear by thee and me!),
"Has brought on wingèd winds his sire's command.
"My own eyes with unclouded vision saw

"The god within these walls; I have received
"With my own ears his word. No more inflame
"With lamentation fond thy heart and mine.
"'T is not my own free act seeks Italy."

She with averted eyes and glance that rolled
Speechless this way and that, had listened long
To his reply, till thus her rage broke forth:
"No goddess gave thee birth. No Dardanus
"Begot thy sires. But on its breast of stone
"Caucasus bore thee, and the tigresses
"Of fell Hyrcania to thy baby lip
"Their udders gave. Why should I longer show
"A lying smile? What worse can I endure?
"Did my tears draw one sigh? Did he once drop
"His stony stare? or did he yield a tear
"To my lament, or pity this fond heart?
"Why set my wrongs in order? Juno, now,
"And Jove, the son of Saturn, heed no more
"Where justice lies. No trusting heart is safe
"In all this world. That waif and castaway
"I found in beggary and gave him share —
"Fool that I was! — in my own royal glory.
"His lost fleet and his sorry crews I steered
"From death away. O, how my fevered soul
"Unceasing raves! Forsooth Apollo speaks!
"His Lycian oracles! and sent by Jove
"The messenger of Heaven on fleeting air
"The ruthless bidding brings! Proud business
"For gods, I trow, that such a task disturbs
"Their still abodes! I hold thee back no more,

"Nor to thy cunning speeches give the lie.
"Begone! Sail on to Italy, thy throne,
"Through wind and wave! I pray that, if there be
"Any just gods of power, thou mayest drink down
"Death on the mid-sea rocks, and often call
"With dying gasps on Dido's name — while I
"Pursue with vengeful fire. When cold death rends
"The body from the breath, my ghost shall sit
"Forever in thy path. Full penalties
"Thy stubborn heart shall pay. They 'll bring me news
"In yon deep gulf of death of all thy woe."

Abrupt her utterance ceased; and sick at heart
She fled the light of day, as if to shrink
From human eyes, and left Æneas there
Irresolute with horror, while his soul
Framed many a vain reply. Her swooning shape
Her maidens to a marble chamber bore
And on her couch the helpless limbs reposed.

Æneas, faithful to a task divine,
Though yearning sore to remedy and soothe
Such misery, and with the timely word
Her grief assuage, and though his burdened heart
Was weak because of love, while many a groan
Rose from his bosom, yet no whit did fail
To do the will of Heaven, but of his fleet
Resumed command. The Trojans on the shore
Ply well their task and push into the sea
The lofty ships. Now floats the shining keel,
And oars they bring all leafy from the grove,

With oak half-hewn, so hurried was the flight.
Behold them how they haste — from every gate
Forth-streaming! — just as when a heap of corn
Is thronged with ants, who, knowing winter nigh,
Refill their granaries; the long black line
Runs o'er the levels, and conveys the spoil
In narrow pathway through the grass; a part
With straining and assiduous shoulder push
The kernels huge; a part array the file,
And whip the laggards on; their busy track
Swarms quick and eager with unceasing toil.

O Dido, how thy suffering heart was wrung,
That spectacle to see! What sore lament
Was thine, when from the towering citadel
The whole shore seemed alive, the sea itself
In turmoil with loud cries! Relentless Love,
To what mad courses may not mortal hearts
By thee be driven? Again her sorrow flies
To doleful plaint and supplication vain;
Again her pride to tyrant Love bows down,
Lest, though resolved to die, she fail to prove
Each hope of living: "O Anna, dost thou see
"Yon busy shore? From every side they come.
"Their canvas wooes the winds, and o'er each prow
"The merry seamen hang their votive flowers.
"Dear sister, since I did forebode this grief,
"I shall be strong to bear it. One sole boon
"My sorrow asks thee, Anna! Since of thee,
"Thee only, did that traitor make a friend,
"And trusted thee with what he hid so deep —

"The feelings of his heart; since thou alone
"Hast known what way, what hour the man would
yield
"To soft persuasion — therefore, sister, haste,
"And humbly thus implore our haughty foe:
"'I was not with the Greeks what time they swore
"'At Aulis to cut off the seed of Troy;
"'I sent no ships to Ilium. Pray, have I
"'Profaned Anchises' tomb, or vexed his shade?'
"Why should his ear be deaf and obdurate
"To all I say? What haste? May he not make
"One last poor offering to her whose love
"Is only pain? O, bid him but delay
"Till flight be easy and the winds blow fair.
"I plead no more that bygone marriage-vow
"By him forsworn, nor ask that he should lose
"His beauteous Latium and his realm to be.
"Nothing but time I crave! to give repose
"And more room to this fever, till my fate
"Teach a crushed heart to sorrow. I implore
"This last grace. (To thy sister's grief be kind!)
"I will requite with increase, till I die."

Such plaints, such prayers, again and yet again,
Betwixt the twain the sorrowing sister bore.
But no words move, no lamentations bring
Persuasion to his soul; decrees of Fate
Oppose, and some wise god obstructs the way
That finds the hero's ear. Oft-times around
The aged strength of some stupendous oak
The rival blasts of wintry Alpine winds

Smite with alternate wrath: loud is the roar,
And from its rocking top the broken boughs
Are strewn along the ground; but to the crag
Steadfast it ever clings; far as toward heaven
Its giant crest uprears, so deep below
Its roots reach down to Tartarus: — not less
The hero by unceasing wail and cry
Is smitten sore, and in his mighty heart
Has many a pang, while his serene intent
Abides unmoved, and tears gush forth in vain.

Then wretched Dido, by her doom appalled,
Asks only death. It wearies her to see
The sun in heaven. Yet that she might hold fast
Her dread resolve to quit the light of day,
Behold, when on an incense-breathing shrine
Her offering was laid — O fearful tale! —
The pure libation blackened, and the wine
Flowed like polluting gore. She told the sight
To none, not even to her sister's ear.
A second sign was given: for in her house
A marble altar to her husband's shade,
With garlands bright and snowy fleeces dressed,
Had fervent worship; here strange cries were heard
As if her dead spouse called while midnight reigned,
And round her towers its inhuman song
The lone owl sang, complaining o'er and o'er
With lamentation and long shriek of woe.
Forgotten oracles by wizards told
Whisper old omens dire. In dreams she feels
Cruel Æneas goad her madness on,

And ever seems she, friendless and alone,
Some lengthening path to travel, or to seek
Her Tyrians through wide wastes of barren lands.
Thus frantic Pentheus flees the stern array
Of the Eumenides, and thinks to see
Two noonday lights blaze o'er his doubled Thebes;
Or murdered Agamemnon's haunted son,
Orestes, flees his mother's phantom scourge
Of flames and serpents foul, while at his door
Avenging horrors wait.
Now sorrow-crazed
And by her grief undone, resolved on death,
The manner and the time her secret soul
Prepares, and, speaking to her sister sad,
She masks in cheerful calm her fatal will:
"I know a way — O, wish thy sister joy! —
"To bring him back to love, or set me free.
"On Ocean's bound and next the setting sun
"Lies the last Æthiop land, where Atlas tall
"Lifts on his shoulder the wide wheel of heaven,
"Studded with burning stars. From thence is come
"A witch, a priestess, a Numidian crone,
"Who guards the shrine of the Hesperides
"And feeds the dragon; she protects the fruit
"Of that enchanting tree, and scatters there
"Her slumb'rous poppies mixed with honey-dew.
"Her spells and magic promise to set free
"What hearts she will, or visit cruel woes
"On men afar. She stops the downward flow
"Of rivers, and turns back the rolling stars;
"On midnight ghosts she calls: her vot'ries hear

"Earth bellowing loud below, while from the hills
"The ash-trees travel down. But, sister mine,
"Thou knowest, and the gods their witness give,
"How little mind have I to don the garb
"Of sorcery. Depart in secret, thou,
"And bid them build a lofty funeral pyre
"Inside our palace-wall, and heap thereon
"The hero's arms, which that blasphemer hung
"Within my chamber; every relic bring,
"And chiefly that ill-omened nuptial bed,
"My death and ruin! For I must blot out
"All sight and token of this husband vile.
"'T is what the witch commands." She spoke no more,
And pallid was her brow. Yet Anna's mind
Knew not what web of death her sister wove
By these strange rites, nor what such frenzy dares;
Nor feared she worse than when Sichæus died,
But hied her forth the errand to fulfil.

Soon as the funeral pyre was builded high
In a sequestered garden, looming huge
With boughs of pine and faggots of cleft oak,
The queen herself enwreathed it with sad flowers
And boughs of mournful shade; and crowning all
She laid on nuptial bed the robes and sword
By him abandoned; and stretched out thereon
A mock Æneas; — but her doom she knew.
Altars were there; and with loose locks unbound
The priestess with a voice of thunder called
Three hundred gods, Hell, Chaos, the three shapes
Of triple Hecate, the faces three

Of virgin Dian. She aspersed a stream
From dark Avernus drawn, she said; soft herbs
Were cut by moonlight with a blade of bronze,
Oozing black poison-sap; and she had plucked
That philter from the forehead of new foal
Before its dam devours. Dido herself,
Sprinkling the salt meal, at the altar stands;
One foot unsandalled, and with cincture free,
On all the gods and fate-instructed stars,
Foreseeing death, she calls. But if there be
Some just and not oblivious power on high,
Who heeds when lovers plight unequal vow,
To that god first her supplications rise.

Soon fell the night, and peaceful slumbers breathed
On all earth's weary creatures; the loud seas
And babbling forests entered on repose;
Now midway in their heavenly course the stars
Wheeled silent on; the outspread lands below
Lay voiceless; all the birds of tinted wing,
And flocks that haunt the marge of waters wide
Or keep the thorny wold, oblivious lay
Beneath the night so still; the stings of care
Ceased troubling, and no heart its burden knew.
Not so the Tyrian Queen's deep-grieving soul!
To sleep she could not yield; her eyes and heart
Refused the gift of night; her suffering
Redoubled, and in full returning tide
Her love rebelled, while on wild waves of rage
She drifted to and fro. So, ceasing not
From sorrow, thus she brooded on her wrongs:

"What refuge now? Shall I invite the scorn
"Of my rejected wooers, or entreat
"Of some disdainful, nomad blackamoor
"To take me to his bed — though many a time
"Such husbands I made mock of? Shall I sail
"On Ilian ships away, and sink to be
"The Trojans' humble thrall? Do they rejoice
"That once I gave them bread? Lives gratitude
"In hearts like theirs for bygone kindnesses?
"O, who, if so I stooped, would deign to bear
"On yon proud ships the scorned and fallen Queen?
"Lost creature! Woe betide thee! Knowest thou not
"The perjured children of Laomedon?
"What way is left? Should I take flight alone
"And join the revelling sailors? Or depart
"With Tyrians, the whole attending train
"Of my own people? Hard the task to force
"Their hearts from Sidon's towers; how once more
"Compel to sea, and bid them spread the sail?
"Nay, perish! Thou hast earned it. Let the sword
"From sorrow save thee! Sister of my blood —
"Who else but thee, — by my own tears borne down,
"Didst heap disaster on my frantic soul,
"And fling me to this foe? Why could I not
"Pass wedlock by, and live a blameless life
"As wild things do, nor taste of passion's pain?
"But I broke faith! I cast the vows away
"Made at Sichæus' grave." Such loud lament
Burst from her breaking heart with doleful sound.

Meanwhile Æneas on his lofty ship,

Having made ready all, and fixed his mind
To launch away, upon brief slumber fell.
But the god came; and in the self-same guise
Once more in monitory vision spoke, —
All guised as Mercury, — his voice, his hue,
His golden locks, and young limbs strong and fair.
"Hail, goddess-born! Wouldst linger on in sleep
"At such an hour? Nor seest thou the snares
"That hem thee round? Nor hearest thou the voice
"Of friendly zephyrs calling? Senseless man!
"That woman's breast contrives some treachery
"And horrid stroke; for, resolute to die,
"She drifts on swollen floods of wrath and scorn.
"Wilt thou not fly before the hastening hour
"Of flight is gone? To-morrow thou wilt see
"Yon waters thronged with ships, the cruel glare
"Of fire-brands, and yonder shore all flame,
"If but the light of morn again surprise
"Thee loitering in this land. Away! Away!
"Stay not! A mutable and shifting thing
"Is woman ever."

Such command he spoke,
Then melted in the midnight dark away.
Æneas, by that fleeting vision struck
With an exceeding awe, straightway leaped forth
From slumber's power, and to his followers cried:
"Awake, my men! Away! Each to his place
"Upon the thwarts! Unfurl at once the sails!
"A god from heaven a second time sent down
"Urges our instant flight, and bids us cut
"The twisted cords. Whatever be thy name,

"Behold, we come, O venerated Power!
"Again with joy we follow! Let thy grace
"Assist us as we go! And may thy power
"Bring none but stars benign across our sky."
So saying, from its scabbard forth he flashed
The lightning of his sword, with naked blade
Striking the hawsers free. Like ardor seized
On all his willing men, who raced and ran;
And, while their galleys shadowed all the sea,
Clean from the shore they scudded, with strong strokes
Sweeping the purple waves and crested foam.

Aurora's first young beams to earth were pouring
As from Tithonus' saffron bed she sprang;
While from her battlements the wakeful Queen
Watched the sky brighten, saw the mated sails
Push forth to sea, till all her port and strand
Held not an oar or keel. Thrice and four times
She smote her lovely breast with wrathful hand,
And tore her golden hair. "Great Jove," she cries,
"Shall that departing fugitive make mock
"Of me, a queen? Will not my men-at-arms
"Draw sword, give chase, from all my city thronging?
"Down from the docks, my ships! Out, out! Begone!
"Take fire and sword! Bend to your oars, ye slaves!
"What have I said? Where am I? What mad thoughts
"Delude this ruined mind? Woe unto thee,
"Thou wretched Dido, now thy impious deeds
"Strike back upon thee. Wherefore struck they not,
"As was most fit, when thou didst fling away

"Thy sceptre from thy hand? O lying oaths!
"O faith forsworn! of him who brings, they boast,
"His father's gods along, and bowed his back
"To lift an age-worn sire! Why dared I not
"Seize on him, rend his body limb from limb,
"And hurl him piecemeal on the rolling sea?
"Or put his troop of followers to the sword,
"Ascanius too, and set his flesh before
"That father for a feast? Such fearful war
"Had been of doubtful issue. Be it so!
"What fears a woman dying? Would I had
"Attacked their camp with torches, kindled flame
"From ship to ship, until that son and sire,
"With that whole tribe, were unto ashes burned
"In one huge holocaust — myself its crown!
"Great orb of light whose holy beam surveys
"All earthly deeds! Great Juno, patroness
"Of conjugal distress, who knowest all!
"Pale Hecate, whose name the witches cry
"At midnight crossways! O avenging furies!
"O gods that guard Queen Dido's dying breath!
"Give ear, and to my guiltless misery
"Extend your power. Hear me what I pray!
"If it be fated that yon creature curst
"Drift to the shore and happy haven find,
"If Father Jove's irrevocable word
"Such goal decree — there may he be assailed
"By peoples fierce and bold. A banished man,
"From his Iulus' kisses sundered far,
"May his own eyes see miserably slain
"His kin and kind, and sue for alien arms.

"Nor when he basely bows him to receive
"Terms of unequal peace, shall he be blest
"With sceptre or with life; but perish there
"Before his time, and lie without a grave
"Upon the barren sand. For this I pray.
"This dying word is flowing from my heart
"With my spilt blood. And — O ye Tyrians!
"Sting with your hatred all his seed and tribe
"Forevermore. This is the offering
"My ashes ask. Betwixt our nations twain,
"No love! No truce or amity! Arise,
"Out of my dust, unknown Avenger, rise!
"To harry and lay waste with sword and flame
"Those Dardan settlers, and to vex them sore,
"To-day, to-morrow, and as long as power
"Is thine to use! My dying curse arrays
"Shore against shore and the opposing seas
"In shock of arms with arms. May living foes
"Pass down from sire to son insatiate war!"

She said. From point to point her purpose flew,
Seeking without delay to quench the flame
Of her loathed life. Brief bidding she addressed
To Barce then, Sichæus' nurse (her own
Lay dust and ashes in a lonely grave
Beside the Tyrian shore), "Go, nurse, and call
"My sister Anna! Bid her quickly bathe
"Her limbs in living water, and procure
"Due victims for our expiating fires.
"Bid her make haste. Go, bind on thy own brow
"The sacred fillet. For to Stygian Jove

"It is my purpose now to consummate
"The sacrifice ordained, ending my woe,
"And touch with flame the Trojan's funeral pyre."

The aged crone to do her bidding ran
With trembling zeal. But Dido (horror-struck
At her own dread design, unstrung with fear,
Her bloodshot eyes wide-rolling, and her cheek
Twitching and fever-spotted, her cold brow
Blanched with approaching death) — sped past the doors
Into the palace garden; there she leaped,
A frenzied creature, on the lofty pyre
And drew the Trojan's sword; a gift not asked
For use like this! When now she saw the garb
Of Ilian fashion, and the nuptial couch
She knew too well, she lingered yet awhile
For memory and tears, and, falling prone
On that cold bed, outpoured a last farewell:
"Sweet relics! Ever dear when Fate and Heaven
"Upon me smiled, receive my parting breath,
"And from my woe set free! My life is done.
"I have accomplished what my lot allowed;
"And now my spirit to the world of death
"In royal honor goes. The founder I
"Of yonder noble city, I have seen
"Walls at my bidding rise. I was avenged
"For my slain husband: I chastised the crimes
"Of our injurious brother. Woe is me!
"Blest had I been, beyond deserving blest,
"If but the Trojan galleys ne'er had moored

"Upon my kingdom's bound!" So saying, she pressed
One last kiss on the couch. "Though for my death
"No vengeance fall, O, give me death!" she cried.
"O thus! O thus! it is my will to take
"The journey to the dark. From yonder sea
"May his cold Trojan eyes discern the flames
"That make me ashes! Be this cruel death
"His omen as he sails!"
She spoke no more.
But almost ere she ceased, her maidens all
Thronged to obey her cry, and found their Queen
Prone fallen on the sword, the reeking steel
Still in her bloody hands. Shrill clamor flew
Along the lofty halls; wild rumor spread
Through the whole smitten city; loud lament,
Groans and the wail of women echoed on
From roof to roof, and to the dome of air
The noise of mourning rose. Such were the cry
If a besieging host should break the walls
Of Carthage or old Tyre, and wrathful flames
O'er towers of kings and worshipped altars roll.
Her sister heard. Half in a swoon, she ran
With trembling steps, where thickest was the throng,
Beating her breast, while with a desperate hand
She tore at her own face, and called aloud
Upon the dying Queen. "Was it for this
"My own true sister used me with such guile?
"O, was this horrid deed the dire intent
"Of altars, lofty couch, and funeral fires?
"What shall I tell for chiefest of my woes?
"Lost that I am! Why, though in death, cast off

"Thy sister from thy heart? Why not invite
"One mortal stroke for both, a single sword,
"One agony together? But these hands
"Built up thy pyre; and my voice implored
"The blessing of our gods, who granted me
"That thou shouldst perish thus — and I not know!
"In thy self-slaughter, sister, thou hast slain
"Myself, thy people, the grave counsellors
"Of Sidon, and yon city thou didst build
"To be thy throne! — Go, fetch me water, there!
"That I may bathe those gashes! If there be
"One hovering breath that stays, let my fond lips
"Discover and receive!"

So saying, she sprang up
From stair to stair, and, clasping to her breast
Her sister's dying form, moaned grievously,
And staunched the dark blood with her garment's fold.
Vainly would Dido lift her sinking eyes,
But backward fell, while at her heart the wound
Opened afresh; three times with straining arm
She rose; three times dropped helpless, her dimmed eyes
Turned skyward, seeking the sweet light of day, —
Which when she saw, she groaned.

Great Juno then
Looked down in mercy on that lingering pain
And labor to depart: from realms divine
She sent the goddess of the rainbow wing,
Iris, to set the struggling spirit free
And loose its fleshly coil. For since the end

Came not by destiny, nor was the doom
Of guilty deed, but of a hapless wight
To sudden madness stung, ere ripe to die,
Therefore the Queen of Hades had not shorn
The fair tress from her forehead, nor assigned
That soul to Stygian dark. So Iris came
On dewy, saffron pinions down from heaven,
A thousand colors on her radiant way,
From the opposing sun. She stayed her flight
Above that pallid brow: "I come with power
"To make this gift to Death. I set thee free
"From thy frail body's bound." With her right hand
She cut the tress: then through its every limb
The sinking form grew cold; the vital breath
Fled forth, departing on the viewless air.

END OF BOOK IV

BOOK V

MEANWHILE Æneas, now well launched away,
Steered forth with all the fleet to open sea,
On his unswerving course, and ploughed the waves,
Sped by a driving gale; but when his eyes
Looked back on Carthage, they beheld the glare
Of hapless Dido's fire. Not yet was known
What kindled the wild flames; but that the pang
Of outraged love is cruel, and what the heart
Of desperate woman dares, they knew too well,
And sad foreboding shook each Trojan soul.
Soon in mid-sea, beyond all chart of shore,
When only seas and skies were round their way,
Full in the zenith loomed a purple cloud,
Storm-laden, dark as night, and every wave
Grew black and angry; from his lofty seat
The helmsman Palinurus cried, "Alas!
"What means this host of storms encircling heaven?
"What, Neptune, wilt thou now?" He, having said,
Bade reef and tighten, bend to stronger stroke,
And slant sail to the wind; then spake again:
"High-souled Æneas, not if Jove the King
"Gave happy omen, would I have good hope
"Of making Italy through yonder sky.
"Athwart our course from clouded evening-star
"Rebellious winds run shifting, and the air

"Into a cloud-wrack rolls. Against such foes
"Too weak our strife and strain! Since now the hand
"Of Fortune triumphs, let us where she calls
"Obedient go. For near us, I believe,
"Lies Eryx' faithful and fraternal shore:
"Here are Sicilian havens, if my mind
"Of yon familiar stars have knowledge true."
Then good Æneas: "For a friendly wind
"Long have I sued, and watched thee vainly strive.
"Shift sail! What happier land for me and mine,
"Or for our storm-beat ships what safer shore,
"Than where Dardanian Acestes reigns;
"The land whose faithful bosom cherishes
"Anchises' ashes?" Heedful of his word,
They landward steer, while favoring zephyrs fill
The spreading sail. On currents swift and strong
The fleet is wafted, and with thankful soul
They moor on Sicily's familiar strand.

From a far hill-top having seen with joy
The entering ships, and knowing them for friends,
Good King Acestes ran to bid them hail.
Garbed in rough pelt of Libyan bear was he,
And javelins he bore, in sylvan guise:
For him the river-god Crimisus sired
Of Trojan wife. Remembering in his heart
His ancient blood, he greeted with glad words
The wanderers returned; bade welcome to
His rude abundance, and with friendly gifts
Their weariness consoled. The morrow morn,

Soon as the new beams of a golden day
Had banished every star, Æneas called
A council of his followers on the shore,
And from a fair green hillock gave this word:
"Proud sons of Dardanus, whose lofty line
"None but the gods began! This day fulfils
"The annual cycle of revolving time,
"Since the dear relics of my god-like sire
"To earth we gave, and with dark offerings due
"Built altars sorrowful. If now I err not,
"This is my day — ye gods have willed it so! —
"For mourning and for praise. Should it befall
"Me exiled in Gætulia's wilderness,
"Or sailing some Greek sea, or at the walls
"Of dire Mycenæ, still would I renew
"Unfailing vows, and make solemnity
"With thankful rites, and worshipful array,
"At altars rich with gifts. But, lo, we come,
"Beyond all hope, where lie the very bones
"Of my great sire. Nor did it come to pass
"Without divine intent and heavenly power,
"That on these hospitable shores we stand.
"Up, then! For we will make a festal day,
"Imploring lucky winds! O, may his spirit
"Grant me to build my city, where his shrines
"Forever shall receive perpetual vows
"Made in his name! This prince of Trojan line,
"Acestes, upon every ship bestows
"A pair of oxen. To our offerings call
"The powers that bless the altars and the fires
"Of our ancestral hearth; and join with these

"The gods of good Acestes. Presently,
"When the ninth dawn shall bring its beam benign
"To mortal men, and show the radiant world,
"For all my Teucrian people I ordain
"A holiday of games; the flying ships
"Shall first contend; then swiftest runners try
"A foot-race; after that the champions bold
"Who step forth for a cast of javelins,
"Or boast the soaring arrow; or fear not
"The boxing-bout, with gauntlet of thick thongs.
"This summons is for all; let all have hope
"To earn some noble palm! And from this hour
"Speak but well-boding words, and bind your brows
"With garlands green." So saying, he twined a wreath
Of his own mother's myrtle-tree, to shade
His sacred brow; the hero Helymus,
And King Acestes for his tresses gray,
Like coronals took on; Ascanius
And all the warrior youth like emblems wore.
Then in th' attendant throng conspicuous,
With thousands at his side, the hero moved
From place of council to his father's tomb.
There on the ground he poured libation due,
Two beakers of good wine, of sweet milk two,
Two of the victim's blood — and scattered flowers
Of saddest purple stain, while thus he prayed:
"Hail, hallowed sire! And hail, ye ashes dear
"Of him I vainly saved! O soul and shade
"Of my blest father! Heaven to us denied
"To find together that predestined land
"Of Italy, or our Ausonian stream

"Of Tiber — ah! but where?"
He scarce had said,
When from the central shrine a gliding snake,
Coiled seven-fold in seven spirals wide,
Twined round the tomb and trailed innocuous o'er
The very altars; his smooth back was flecked
With green and azure, and his changeful scales
Gleamed golden, as the cloud-born rainbow flings
Its thousand colors from th' opposing sun.
Æneas breathless watched the serpent wind
Among the bowls and cups of polished rim,
Tasting the sacred feast; where, having fed,
Back to the tomb all harmless it withdrew.
Then with new zeal his sacrifice he brings
In honor of his sire; for he must deem
That serpent the kind genius of the place,
Or of his very father's present shade
Some creature ministrant. Two lambs he slew,
The wonted way, two swine, and, sable-hued,
The yoke of bulls; from shallow bowl he poured
Libation of the grape, and called aloud
On great Anchises' spirit, and his shade,
From Acheron set free. Then all the throng,
Each from his separate store, heap up the shrines
With victims slain; some range in order fair
The brazen cauldrons; or along the grass,
Scattered at ease, hold o'er the embers bright
The spitted flesh and roast it in the flames.

Arrived the wished-for day; through cloudless sky
The coursers of the Sun's bright-beaming car

Bore upward the ninth morn. The neighboring folk
Thronged eager to the shore; some hoped to see
Æneas and his warriors, others fain
Would their own prowess prove in bout and game.
Conspicuous lie the guerdons, ranged in sight
In the mid-circus; wreaths of laurel green,
The honored tripod, coronals of palm
For conquerors' brows, accoutrements of war,
Rare robes of purple stain, and generous weight
Of silver and of gold. The trumpet's call
Proclaimed from lofty mound the opening games.
First, side by side, with sturdy, rival oars,
Four noble galleys, pride of all the fleet,
Come forward to contend. The straining crew
Of Mnestheus bring his speedy Pristis on, —
Mnestheus in Italy erelong the sire
Of Memmius' noble line. Brave Gyas guides
His vast Chimæra, a colossal craft,
A floating city, by a triple row
Of Dardan sailors manned, whose banks of oars
In triple order rise. Sergestus, he
Of whom the Sergian house shall after spring,
Rides in his mighty Centaur. Next in line,
On sky-blue Scylla proud Cloanthus rides —
Whence thy great stem, Cluentius of Rome!

Fronting the surf-beat shore, far out at sea
Rises a rock, which under swollen waves
Lies buffeted unseen, when wintry storms
Mantle the stars; but when the deep is calm,
Lifts silently above the sleeping wave

Its level field, — a place where haunt and play
Flocks of the sea-birds, lovers of the sun.
Here was the goal; and here Æneas set
A green-leaved ilex-tree, to be a mark
For every captain's eye, from whence to veer
The courses of their ships in sweeping curves
And speed them home. Now places in the line
Are given by lot. Upon the lofty sterns
The captains ride, in beautiful array
Of Tyrian purple and far-flaming gold;
The crews are poplar-crowned, the shoulders bare
Rubbed well with glittering oil; their straining arms
Make long reach to the oar, as on the thwarts
They sit attentive, listening for the call
Of the loud trumpet; while with pride and fear
Their hot hearts throb, impassioned for renown.

Soon pealed the signal clear; from all the line
Instant the galleys bounded, and the air
Rang to the rowers' shouting, while their arms
Pulled every inch and flung the waves in foam;
Deep cut the rival strokes; the surface fair
Yawned wide beneath their blades and cleaving keels.
Not swifter scour the chariots o'er the plain,
Sped headlong from the line behind their teams
Of mated coursers, while each driver shakes
Loose, rippling reins above his plunging pairs,
And o'er the lash leans far. With loud applause
Vociferous and many an urgent cheer
The woodlands rang, and all the concave shores
Back from the mountains took the Trojan cry

In answering song. Forth-flying from his peers,
While all the crowd acclaims, sped Gyas' keel
Along the outmost wave. Cloanthus next
Pushed hard upon, with stronger stroke of oars
But heavier ship. At equal pace behind
The Pristis and the Centaur fiercely strive
For the third place. Now Pristis seems to lead,
Now mightier Centaur past her flies, then both
Ride on together, prow with prow, and cleave
Long lines of foaming furrow with swift keels.
Soon near the rock they drew, and either ship
Was making goal, — when Gyas, in the lead,
And winner of the half-course, loudly hailed
Menœtes, the ship's pilot: "Why so far
"To starboard, we? Keep her head round this way!
"Hug shore! Let every oar-blade almost graze
"That reef to larboard! Let the others take
"The deep-sea course outside!" But while he spoke,
Menœtes, dreading unknown rocks below,
Veered off to open sea. "Why steer so wide?
"Round to the rock, Menœtes!" Gyas roared, —
Again in vain, for looking back he saw
Cloanthus hard astern, and ever nearer,
Who, in a trice, betwixt the booming reef
And Gyas' galley, lightly forward thrust
The beak of Scylla to the inside course,
And, quickly taking lead, flew past the goal
To the smooth seas beyond. Then wrathful grief
Flamed in the warrior's heart, nor was his cheek
Unwet with tears; and, reckless utterly
Of his own honor and his comrades' lives,

He hurled poor, slack Menœtes from the poop
Headlong upon the waters, while himself,
Pilot and master both, the helm assuming,
Urged on his crew, and landward took his way.
But now, with heavy limbs that hardly won
His rescue from the deep, engulfing wave,
Up the rude rock graybeard Menœtes climbed
With garment dripping wet, and there dropped down
Upon the cliff's dry top. With laughter loud
The Trojan crews had watched him plunging, swimming,
And now to see his drink of bitter brine
Spewed on the ground, the sailors laughed again.
But Mnestheus and Sergestus, coming last,
Have joyful hope enkindled in each heart
To pass the laggard Gyas. In the lead
Sergestus' ship shoots forth; and to the rock
Runs boldly nigh; but not his whole long keel
May pass his rival; the projecting beak
Is followed fast by Pristis' emulous prow.
Then, striding straight amidships through his crew,
Thus Mnestheus urged them on: "O Hector's friends!
"Whom in the dying hours of Troy I chose
"For followers! Now stand ye to your best!
"Put forth the thews of valor that ye showed
"In the Gætulian Syrtes, or that sea
"Ionian, or where the waves race by
"The Malean promontory! Mnestheus now
"Hopes not to be the first, nor do I strive
"For victory. O Father Neptune, give
"That garland where thou wilt! But O, the shame

"If we are last! Endure it not, my men!
"The infamy refuse!" So, bending low,
They enter the home-stretch. Beneath their stroke
The brass-decked galley throbs, and under her
The sea-floor drops away. On, on they fly!
Parched are the panting lips, and sweat in streams
Pours down their giant sides; but lucky chance
Brought the proud heroes what their honor craved.
For while Sergestus furiously drove
His ship's beak toward the rock, and kept inside
The scanty passage, by his evil star
He grounded on the jutting reef; the cliffs
Rang with the blow, and his entangled oars
Grated along the jaggèd granite, while
The prow hung wrecked and helpless. With loud cry
Upsprang the sailors, while the ship stood still,
And pushed off with long poles and pointed iron,
Or snatched the smashed oars from the whirling tide.
Mnestheus exults; and, roused to keener strife
By happy fortune, with a quicker stroke
Of each bright rank of oars, and with the breeze
His prayer implored, skims o'er the obedient wave
And sweeps the level main. Not otherwise
A startled dove, emerging o'er the fields
From secret cavern in the crannied hill
Where her safe house and pretty nestlings lie,
Soars from her nest, with whirring wings — but soon
Through the still sky she takes her path of air
On pinions motionless. So Pristis sped
With Mnestheus, cleaving her last stretch of sea,
By her own impulse wafted. She outstripped

Sergestus first; for he upon the reef
Fought with the breakers, desperately shouting
For help, for help in vain, with broken oars
Contriving to move on. Then Mnestheus ran
Past Gyas, in Chimæra's ponderous hulk,
Of pilot now bereft; at last remains
Cloanthus his sole peer, whom he pursues
With a supreme endeavor. From the shore
Burst echoing cheers that spur him to the chase,
And wild applause makes all the welkin ring.
The leaders now with eager souls would scorn
To lose their glory, and faint-hearted fail
To grasp a prize half-won, but fain would buy
Honor with life itself; the followers too
Are flushed with proud success, and feel them strong
Because their strength is proven. Both ships now
With indistinguishable prows had sped
To share one prize, — but with uplifted hands
Spread o'er the sea, Cloanthus, suppliant,
Called on the gods to bless his votive prayer:
"Ye gods who rule the waves, whose waters be
"My pathway now; for you on yonder strand
"A white bull at the altar shall be slain
"In grateful tribute for a granted vow;
"And o'er the salt waves I will scatter far
"The entrails, and outpour the flowing wine."
He spoke; and from the caverns under sea
Phorcus and virgin Panopea heard,
And all the sea-nymphs' choir; while with strong hand
The kindly God of Havens rose and thrust

The gliding ship along, that swifter flew
Than south wind, or an arrow from the string,
And soon made land in haven safe and sure.

Æneas then, assembling all to hear,
By a far-sounding herald's voice proclaimed
Cloanthus victor, and arrayed his brows
With the green laurel-garland; to the crews
Three bulls, at choice, were given, and plenteous
wine
And talent-weight of silver; to the chiefs
Illustrious gifts beside; the victor had
A gold-embroidered mantle with wide band
Of undulant Melibœan purple rare,
Where, pictured in the woof, young Ganymede
Through Ida's forest chased the light-foot deer
With javelin; all flushed and panting he.
But lo! Jove's thunder-bearing eagle fell,
And his strong talons snatched from Ida far
The royal boy, whose aged servitors
Reached helpless hands to heaven; his faithful
hound
Bayed fiercely at the air. To him whose worth
The second place had won, Æneas gave
A smooth-linked golden corselet, triple-chained,
Of which his own victorious hand despoiled
Demoleos, by the swift, embattled stream
Of Simois, under Troy, — and bade it be
A glory and defence on valor's field;
Scarce might the straining shoulders of two slaves,
Phegeus and Sagaris, the load endure,

Yet oft Demoleos in this armor dressed
Charged down full speed on routed hosts of Troy.
The third gift was two cauldrons of wrought brass,
And bowls of beaten silver, cunningly
Embossed with sculpture fair. Bearing such gifts,
Th' exultant victors onward moved, each brow
Bound with a purple fillet. But behold!
Sergestus, from the grim rock just dragged off
By cunning toil, one halting rank of oars
Left of his many lost, comes crawling in
With vanquished ship, a mockery to all.
As when a serpent, on the highway caught,
Some brazen wheel has crushed, or traveller
With heavy-smiting blow left half alive
And mangled by a stone; in vain he moves
In writhing flight; a part is lifted high
With hissing throat and angry, glittering eyes;
But by the wounded part a captive still
He knots him fold on fold: with such a track
The maimed ship labored slow; but by her sails
She still made way, and with full canvas on
Arrived at land. Æneas then bestowed
A boon upon Sergestus, as was meet
For guerdon of the ship in safety brought
With all its men; a fair slave was the prize,
The Cretan Pholoë, well taught to weave,
And twin boy-babes upon her breast she bore.

Then good Æneas, the ship-contest o'er,
Turned to a wide green valley, circled round
With clasp of wood-clad hills, wherein was made

An amphitheatre; entering with a throng
Of followers, the hero took his seat
In mid-arena on a lofty mound.
For the fleet foot-race, now, his summons flies, —
He offers gifts, and shows the guerdons due.
The mingling youth of Troy and Sicily
Hastened from far. Among the foremost came
The comrades Nisus and Euryalus,
Euryalus for beauty's bloom renowned,
Nisus for loyal love; close-following these
Diores strode, a prince of Priam's line;
Then Salius and Patron, who were bred
In Acarnania and Arcady;
Then two Sicilian warriors, Helymus
And Panopes, both sylvan bred and born,
Comrades of King Acestes; after these
The multitude whom Fame forgets to tell.

Æneas, so surrounded, thus spake forth:
"Hear what I purpose, and with joy receive!
"Of all your company, not one departs
"With empty hand. The Cretan javelins
"Bright-tipped with burnished steel, and battle-axe
"Adorned with graven silver, these shall be
"The meed of all. The three first at the goal
"Shall bind their foreheads with fair olive green,
"And win the guerdons due. The first shall lead,
"Victorious, yon rich-bridled steed away;
"This Amazonian quiver, the next prize,
"Well-stocked with Thracian arrows; round it goes
"A baldrick broad and golden, — in its clasp

"A lustrous gem. The third man goes away
"Taking this helmet from the Argive spoil."

They heard, and took their places. The loud horn
Gave signal, and impetuous from the line,
Swift as a bursting storm they sped away,
Eyes fixed upon the goal. Far in advance
Nisus shot forward, swifter than the winds
Or wingèd thunderbolt; the next in course,
Next, but out-rivalled far, was Salius,
And after him a space, Euryalus
Came third; him Helymus was hard upon;
And, look! Diores follows, heel on heel,
Close at his shoulder — if the race be long
He sure must win, or claim a doubtful prize.
Now at the last stretch, spent and panting, all
Pressed to the goal, when in a slime of blood
Nisus, hard fate! slipped down, where late the death
Of victims slain had drenched the turf below.
Here the young victor, with his triumph flushed,
Lost foothold on the yielding ground, and plunged
Face forward in the pool of filth and gore;
But not of dear Euryalus was he
Forgetful then, nor heedless of his friend;
But rising from the mire he hurled himself
In Salius' way; so he in equal plight
Rolled in the filthy slough. Euryalus
Leaped forth, the winner of the race by gift
Of his true friend, and flying to the goal
Stood first, by many a favoring shout acclaimed.
Next Helymus ran in; and, for the third, last prize,

Diores. But the multitude now heard
The hollowed hill-side ringing with wild wrath
From Salius, clamoring where the chieftains sate
For restitution of his stolen prize,
Lost by a cheat. But general favor smiles
Upon Euryalus, whose beauteous tears
Commend him much, and nobler seems the worth
Of valor clothed in youthful shape so fair.
Diores, too, assists the victor's claim,
With loud appeal — he too has won a prize,
And vainly holds his last place, if the first
To Salius fall. Æneas then replied:
"Your gifts, my gallant youths, remain secure.
"None can re-judge the prize. But to console
"The misadventure of a blameless friend,
"Is in my power." Therewith to Salius
An Afric lion's monstrous pelt he gave,
With ponderous mane, the claws o'erlaid with gold.
But Nisus cried: "If such a gift be found
"For less than victory, and men who fall
"Are worthy so much sorrow, pray, what prize
"Shall Nisus have? For surely I had won
"The proudest of the garlands, if one stroke
"Of inauspicious fortune had not fallen
"On Salius and me." So saying, he showed
His smeared face and his sorry limbs befouled
With mire and slime. Then laughed the gracious sire,
And bade a shield be brought, the cunning work
Of Didymaon, which the Greeks tore down
From Neptune's temple; with this noble gift
He sent the high-born youth upon his way.

The foot-race over and the gifts disbursed,
"Come forth!" he cries, "if any in his heart
"Have strength and valor, let him now pull on
"The gauntlets and uplift his thong-bound arms
"In challenge." For the guerdon of this fight
A two-fold gift he showed: the victor's meed,
A bullock decked and gilded; but a sword
And glittering helmet to console the fallen.
Straightway, in all his pride of giant strength,
Dares loomed up, and wondering murmurs ran
Along the gazing crowd; for he alone
Was wont to match with Paris, he it was
Met Butes, the huge-bodied champion
Boasting the name and race of Amycus,
Bythinian-born; him felled he at a blow,
And stretched him dying on the tawny sand.
Such Dares was, who now held high his head,
Fierce for the fray, bared both his shoulders broad,
Lunged out with left and right, and beat the air.
Who shall his rival be? Of all the throng
Not one puts on the gauntlets, or would face
The hero's challenge. Therefore, striding forth,
Believing none now dare but yield the palm,
He stood before Æneas, and straightway
Seized with his left hand the bull's golden horn,
And cried, "O goddess-born, if no man dares
"To risk him in this fight, how long delay?
"How long beseems it I should stand and wait?
"Bid me bear off my prize." The Trojans all
Murmured assent, and bade the due award
Of promised gift. But with a brow severe

Acestes to Entellus at his side
Addressed upbraiding words, where they reclined
On grassy bank and couch of pleasant green:
"O my Entellus, in the olden days
"Bravest among the mighty, but in vain!
"Endurest thou to see yon guerdon won
"Without a blow? Where, prithee, is that god
"Who taught thee? Are thy tales of Eryx vain?
"Does all Sicilia praise thee? Is thy roof
"With trophies hung?" The other in reply:
"My jealous honor and good name yield not
"To fear. But age, so cold and slow to move,
"Makes my blood laggard, and my ebbing powers
"In all my body are but slack and chill.
"O, if I had what yonder ruffian boasts —
"My own proud youth once more! I would not ask
"The fair bull for a prize, nor to the lists
"In search of gifts come forth." So saying, he threw
Into the mid-arena a vast pair
Of ponderous gauntlets, which in former days
Fierce Eryx for his fights was wont to bind
On hand and arm, with the stiff raw-hide thong.
All marvelled; for a weight of seven bulls' hides
Was pieced with lead and iron. Dares stared
Astonished, and step after step recoiled;
High-souled Anchises' son, this way and that,
Turned o'er the enormous coil of knots and thongs;
Then with a deep-drawn breath the veteran spoke:
"O, that thy wondering eyes had seen the arms
"Of Hercules, and what his gauntlets were!
"Would thou hadst seen the conflict terrible

"Upon this self-same shore! These arms were borne
"By Eryx. Look; thy brother's! — spattered yet
"With blood, with dashed-out brains! In these he stood
"When he matched Hercules. I wore them oft
"When in my pride and prime, ere envious age
"Shed frost upon my brows. But if these arms
"Be of our Trojan Dares disapproved,
"If good Æneas rules it so, and King
"Acestes wills it, let us offer fight
"On even terms. Let Eryx' bull's-hide go.
"Tremble no more! But strip those gauntlets off —
"Fetched here from Troy." So saying, he dropped down
The double-folded mantle from his shoulders,
Stripped bare the huge joints, the huge arms and thews,
And towered gigantic in the midmost ring.
Anchises' son then gave two equal pairs
Of gauntlets, and accoutred with like arms
Both champions. Each lifted him full height
On tiptoe; each with mien unterrified
Held both fists high in air, and drew his head
Far back from blows assailing. Then they joined
In struggle hand to hand, and made the fray
Each moment fiercer. One was light of foot
And on his youth relied; the other strong
In bulk of every limb, but tottering
On sluggish knees, while all his body shook
With labor of his breath. Without avail
They rained their blows, and on each hollow side,

Each sounding chest, the swift, reverberate strokes
Fell without pause; around their ears and brows
Came blow on blow, and with relentless shocks
The smitten jaws cracked loud. Entellus stands
Unshaken, and, the self-same posture keeping,
Only by body-movement or quick eye
Parries attack. Dares (like one in siege
Against a mountain-citadel, who now will drive
With ram and engine at the craggy wall,
Now wait in full-armed watch beneath its towers)
Tries manifold approach, most craftily
Invests each point of vantage, and renews
His unsuccessful, ever various war.
Then, rising to the stroke, Entellus poised
Aloft his ponderous right; but, quick of eye,
The other the descending wrath foresaw
And nimbly slipped away; Entellus so
Wasted his stroke on air, and, self-o'erthrown,
Dropped prone to earth his monstrous length along,
As when on Erymanth or Ida falls
A hollowed pine from giant roots uptorn.
Alike the Teucrian and Trinacrian throng
Shout wildly; while Acestes, pitying, hastes
To lift his gray companion. But, unchecked,
Undaunted by his fall, the champion brave
Rushed fiercer to the fight, his strength now roused
By rage, while shame and courage confident
Kindle his soul; impetuous he drives
Dares full speed all round the ring, with blows
Redoubled right and left. No stop or stay
Gives he, but like a storm of rattling hail

Upon a house-top, so from each huge hand
The champion's strokes on dizzy Dares fall.

Then Sire Æneas willed to make a stay
To so much rage, nor let Entellus' soul
Flame beyond bound, but bade the battle pause,
And, rescuing weary Dares, thus he spoke
In soothing words: "Ill-starred! What mad attempt
"Is in thy mind? Will not thy heart confess
"Thy strength surpassed, and auspices averse?
"Submit, for Heaven decrees!" With such wise words
He sundered the fell strife. But trusty friends
Bore Dares off: his spent limbs helpless trailed,
His head he could not lift, and from his lips
Came blood and broken teeth. So to the ship
They bore him, taking, at Æneas' word,
The helmet and the sword — but left behind
Entellus' prize of victory, the bull.
He, then, elate and glorying, spoke forth:
"See, goddess-born, and all ye Teucrians, see,
"What strength was mine in youth, and from what
death
"Ye have delivered Dares." Saying so,
He turned him full front to the bull, who stood
For guerdon of the fight, and, drawing back
His right hand, poising the dread gauntlet high,
Swung sheer between the horns and crushed the skull;
A trembling, lifeless creature, to the ground
The bull dropped forward dead. Above the fallen
Entellus cried aloud, "This victim due
"I give thee, Eryx, more acceptable

"Than Dares' death to thy benignant shade.
"For this last victory and joyful day,
"My gauntlets and my art I leave with thee."

Forthwith Æneas summons all who will
To contest of swift arrows, and displays
Reward and prize. With mighty hand he rears
A mast within th' arena, from the ship
Of good Sergestus taken; and thereto
A fluttering dove by winding cord is bound
For target of their shafts. Soon to the match
The rival bowmen came and cast the lots
Into a brazen helmet. First came forth
Hippocoön's number, son of Hyrtacus,
By cheers applauded; Mnestheus was the next,
Late victor in the ship-race, Mnestheus crowned
With olive-garland; next Eurytion,
Brother of thee, O bowman most renowned,
Pandarus, breaker of the truce, who hurled
His shaft upon the Achæans, at the word
The goddess gave. Acestes' lot and name
Came from the helmet last, whose royal hand
The deeds of youth dared even yet to try.

Each then with strong arm bends his pliant bow,
Each from the quiver plucks a chosen shaft.
First, with loud arrow whizzing from the string,
The young Hippocoön with skyward aim
Cuts through the yielding air; and lo! his barb
Pierces the very wood, and makes the mast
Tremble; while with a fluttering, frighted wing

The bird tugs hard, — and plaudits fill the sky.
Boldly rose Mnestheus, and with bow full-drawn
Aimed both his eye and shaft aloft; but he
Failing, unhappy man, to bring his barb
Up to the dove herself, just cut the cord
And broke the hempen bond, whereby her feet
Were captive to the tree: she, taking flight,
Clove through the shadowing clouds her path of air.
But swiftly — for upon his waiting bow
He held a shaft in rest — Eurytion
Invoked his brother's shade, and, marking well
The dove, whose happy pinions fluttered free
In vacant sky, pierced her, hard by a cloud;
Lifeless she fell, and left in light of heaven
Her spark of life, as, floating down, she bore
The arrow back to earth. Acestes now
Remained, last rival, though the victor's palm
To him was lost; yet did the aged sire,
To show his prowess and resounding bow,
Hurl forth one shaft in air; then suddenly
All eyes beheld such wonder as portends
Events to be (but when fulfilment came,
Too late the fearful seers its warning sung):
For, soaring through the stream of cloud, his shaft
Took fire, tracing its bright path in flame,
Then vanished on the wind, — as oft a star
Will fall unfastened from the firmament,
While far behind its blazing tresses flow.
Awe-struck both Trojan and Trinacrian stood,
Calling upon the gods. Nor came the sign
In vain to great Æneas. But his arms

Folded the blest Acestes to his heart,
And, loading him with noble gifts, he cried:
"Receive them, sire! The great Olympian King
"Some peerless honor to thy name decrees
"By such an omen given. I offer thee
"This bowl with figures graven, which my sire,
"Good gray Anchises, for proud gift received
"Of Thracian Cisseus, for their friendship's pledge
"And memory evermore." Thereon he crowned
His brows with garland of the laurel green,
And named Acestes victor over all.
Nor could Eurytion, noble youth, think ill
Of honor which his own surpassed, though he,
He only, pierced the bird in upper air.
Next gift was his whose arrow cut the cord;
Last, his whose light shaft clove the lofty pine.

Father Æneas now, not making end
Of game and contest, summoned to his side
Epytides, the mentor and true friend
Of young Iulus, and this bidding gave
To his obedient ear: "Arise and go
"Where my Ascanius has lined his troop
"Of youthful cavalry, and trained the steeds
"To tread in ranks of war. Bid him lead forth
"The squadron in our sire Anchises' name,
"And wear a hero's arms!" So saying, he bade
The course be cleared, and from the whole wide field
Th' insurging, curious multitude withdrew.
In rode the boys, to meet their parents' eyes,
In even lines, a glittering cavalry;

While all Trinacria and the host from Troy
Made loud applause. On each bright brow
A well-trimmed wreath the flowing tresses bound;
Two javelins of cornel tipped with steel
Each bore for arms; some from the shoulder slung
A polished quiver; to each bosom fell
A pliant necklace of fine, twisted gold.
Three bands of horsemen ride, three captains proud
Prance here and there, assiduous in command,
Each of his twelve, who shine in parted lines
Which lesser captains lead. One cohort proud
Follows a little Priam's royal name —
One day, Polites, thy illustrious race
Through him prolonged, shall greater glory bring
To Italy. A dappled Thracian steed
With snow-white spots and fore-feet white as snow
Bears him along, its white face lifted high.
Next Atys rode, young Atys, sire to be
Of th' Atian house in Rome, a boy most dear
Unto the boy Iulus; last in line,
And fairest of the throng, Iulus came,
Astride a steed from Sidon, the fond gift
Of beauteous Dido and her pledge of love.
Close followed him the youthful chivalry
Of King Acestes on Trinacrian steeds.
The Trojans, with exultant, loud acclaim,
Receive the shy-faced boys, and joyfully
Trace in the features of the sons their sires.

After, with smiling eyes, the horsemen proud
Have greeted each his kin in all the throng,

Epytides th' appointed signal calls,
And cracks his lash; in even lines they move,
Then, loosely sundering in triple band,
Wheel at a word and thrust their lances forth
In hostile ranks; or on the ample field
Retreat or charge, in figure intricate
Of circling troop with troop, and swift parade
Of simulated war; now from the field
They flee with backs defenceless to the foe;
Then rally, lance in rest — or, mingling all,
Make common front, one legion strong and fair.
As once in Crete, the lofty mountain-isle,
That fabled labyrinthine gallery
Wound on through lightless walls, with thousand paths
Which baffled every clue, and led astray
In unreturning mazes dark and blind:
So did the sons of Troy their courses weave
In mimic flights and battles fought for play,
Like dolphins tumbling in the liquid waves,
Along the Afric or Carpathian seas.

This game and mode of march Ascanius,
When Alba Longa's bastions proudly rose,
Taught to the Latin people of the prime;
And as the princely Trojan and his train
Were wont to do, so Alba to her sons
The custom gave; so glorious Rome at last
The heritage accepted and revered;
And still we know them for the "Trojan Band,"
And call the lads a "Troy." Such was the end

Of game and contest at Anchises' grave.

Then fortune veered and different aspect wore.
For ere the sacred funeral games are done,
Saturnian Juno from high heaven sent down
The light-winged Iris to the ships of Troy,
Giving her flight good wind — still full of schemes
And hungering to avenge her ancient wrong.
Unseen of mortal eye, the virgin took
Her pathway on the thousand-colored bow,
And o'er its gliding passage earthward flew.
She scanned the vast assemblage; then her gaze
Turned shoreward, where along the idle bay
The Trojan galleys quite unpeopled rode.
But far removed, upon a lonely shore,
A throng of Trojan dames bewailed aloud
Their lost Anchises, and with tears surveyed
The mighty deep. "O weary waste of seas!
"What vast, untravelled floods beyond us roll!"
So cried they with one voice, and prayed the gods
For an abiding city; every heart
Loathed utterly the long, laborious sea.
Then in their midst alighted, not unskilled
In working woe, the goddess; though she wore
Nor garb nor form divine, but made herself
One Beroë, Doryclus' aged wife,
Who in her happier days had lineage fair
And sons of noble name; in such disguise
She called the Trojan dames: "O ye ill-starred,
"That were not seized and slain by Grecian foes
"Under your native walls! O tribe accursed,

"What death is Fate preparing? Since Troy fell
"The seventh summer flies, while still we rove
"O'er cruel rocks and seas, from star to star,
"From alien land to land, as evermore
"We chase, storm-tossed, that fleeting Italy
"Across the waters wide. Behold this land
"Of Eryx, of Acestes, friend and kin;
"What hinders them to raise a rampart here
"And build a town? O city of our sires!
"O venerated gods from haughty foes
"Rescued in vain! Will nevermore a wall
"Rise in the name of Troy? Shall I not see
"A Xanthus or a Simois, the streams
"To Hector dear? Come now! I lead the way.
"Let us go touch their baneful ships with fire!
"I saw Cassandra in a dream. Her shade,
"Prophetic ever, gave me firebrands,
"And cried, 'Find Ilium so! The home for thee
"'Is where thou art.' Behold, the hour is ripe
"For our great act! No longer now delay
"To heed the heavenly omen. Yonder stand
"Four altars unto Neptune. 'T is the god,
"The god himself, gives courage for the deed,
"And swift-enkindling fire." So having said,
She seized a dreadful brand; then, lifting high,
Waved it all flaming, and with furious arm
Hurled it from far. The Ilian matrons gazed,
Bewildered and appalled. But one, of all
The eldest, Pyrgo, venerated nurse
Of Priam's numerous sons, exclaimed, "Nay, nay!
"This is no Beroë, my noble dames.

"Doryclus knew her not. Behold and see
"Her heavenly beauty and her radiant eyes!
"What voice of music and majestic mien,
"What movement like a god! Myself am come
"From Beroë sick, and left her grieving sore
"That she, she only, had no gift to bring
"Of mournful honor to Anchises' shade."
She spoke. The women with ill-boding eyes
Looked on the ships. Their doubting hearts were torn
'Twixt tearful passion for the beauteous isle
Their feet then trod, and that prophetic call
Of Fate to lands unknown. Then on wide wings
Soared Iris into heaven, and through the clouds
Clove a vast arch of light. With wonder dazed,
The women in a shrieking frenzy rose,
Took embers from the hearth-stones, stole the fires
Upon the altars — faggots, branches, brands —
And rained them on the ships. The god of fire,
Through thwarts and oars and bows of painted fir,
Ran in unbridled flame.
Swift to the tomb
Of Sire Anchises, to the circus-seats,
The messenger Eumelus flew, to bring
News of the ships on fire; soon every eye
The clouds of smoke and hovering flame could see.
Ascanius, who had led with smiling brow
His troops of horse, accoutred as he was,
Rode hot-haste to the turmoil of the camp,
Nor could his guards restrain. "What madness now?
"What is it ye would do?" he cried. "Alas!
"Ill-fated women! Not our enemies,

"Nor the dread bulwarks of the Greek ye burn,
"But all ye have to hope for. Look at me,
"Your own Ascanius!" His helmet then
Into their midst he flung, which he had worn
For pageantry of war. Æneas, too,
With Trojan bands sped thither. But far off,
The women, panic-scattered on the shore,
Fled many ways, and deep in caverned crags
Or shadowed forests hid them, for they loathed
Their deed and life itself; their thoughts were changed;
They knew their kin and husbands, and their hearts
From Juno were set free. But none the less
The burning and indomitable flames
Raged without stay; beneath the ships' smeared sides
The hempen fuel puffed a lingering smoke,
As, through the whole bulk creeping, the slow fire
Devoured its way; and little it availed
That strong men fought the fire with stream on stream.

Then good Æneas from his shoulder rent
His garment, and with lifted hands implored
The help of Heaven. "O Jove omnipotent!
"If thou not yet thy wrath implacable
"On every Trojan pourest, if thou still
"Hast pity, as of old, for what men bear,
"O, grant my fleet deliverance from this flame!
"From uttermost destruction, Father, save
"Our desperate Trojan cause! Or even now —
"Last cruelty! thy fatal thunders throw.
"If this be my just meed, let thy dread arm
"Confound us all." But scarce the prayer is said,

When with a bursting deluge a dark storm
Falls, marvellous to see; while hills and plains
With thunder shake, and to each rim of heaven
Spreads swollen cloud-rack, black with copious rain
And multitudinous gales. The full flood pours
On every ship, and all the smouldering beams
Are drenched, until the smoke and flames expire,
And (though four ships be lost) the burning fleet
Rides rescued from its doom.

But smitten sore
By this mischance, Æneas doubtfully
Weighs in his heart its mighty load of cares,
And ponders if indeed he may abide
In Sicily, not heeding prophet-songs,
Or seek Italian shores. Thereon uprose
Nautes, an aged sire, to whom alone
Tritonian Pallas of her wisdom gave
And made his skill renowned; he had the power
To show celestial anger's warning signs,
Or tell Fate's fixed decree. The gifted man
Thus to Æneas comfortably spoke:
"O goddess-born, we follow here or there,
"As Fate compels or stays. But come what may,
"He triumphs over Fortune, who can bear
"Whate'er she brings. Behold, Acestes draws
"From Dardanus his origin divine!
"Make him thy willing friend, to share with thee
"Thy purpose and thy counsel. Leave with him
"The crews of the lost ships, and all whose hearts
"Repine at thy high task and great emprise:
"The spent old men, the women ocean-weary,

"Whate'er is feeble found, or faint of heart
"In danger's hour, — set that apart, and give
"Such weary ones within this friendly isle
"A city called Acesta, — if he will."

Much moved Æneas was by this wise word
Of his gray friend, though still his anxious soul
Was vexed by doubt and care. But when dark night
Had brought her chariot to the middle sky,
The sacred shade of Sire Anchises seemed,
From heaven descending, thus to speak aloud:
"My son, than life more dear, when life was mine!
"O son, upon whose heart the Trojan doom
"Has weighed so long! Beside thy couch I stand,
"At pleasure of great Jove, whose hand dispelled
"The mad fire from thy ships; and now he looks
"From heaven with pitying brow. I bid thee heed
"The noble counsels aged Nautes gave.
"Only with warriors of dauntless breast
"To Italy repair; of hardy breed,
"Of wild, rough life, thy Latin foes will be.
"But first the shores of Pluto and the Shades
"Thy feet must tread, and through the deep abyss
"Of dark Avernus come to me, thy sire:
"For I inhabit not the guilty gloom
"Of Tartarus, but bright Elysian day,
"Where all the just their sweet assemblies hold.
"Hither the virgin Sibyl, if thou give
"Full offerings of the blood of sable kine,
"Shall lead thee down; and visions I will show
"Of cities proud and nations sprung from thee.

"Farewell, for dewy Night has wheeled her way
"Far past her middle course; the panting steeds
"Of orient Morn breathe pitiless upon me."

He spoke, and passed, like fleeting clouds of smoke,
To empty air. "O, whither haste away?"
Æneas cried. "Whom dost thou fly? What god
From my fond yearning and embrace removes?"
Then on the altar of the gods of Troy
He woke the smouldering embers, at the shrine
Of venerable Vesta, worshipping
With hallowed bread and incense burning free.
Straightway he calls assembly of his friends, —
Acestes first in honor, — and makes known
Jove's will, the counsel of his cherished sire,
And his own fresh resolve. With prompt assent
They hear his word, nor does Acestes fail
The task to share. They people the new town
With women; and leave every wight behind
Who wills it — souls not thirsting for high praise.
Themselves re-bench their ships, rebuild, and fit
With rope and oar the flame-swept galleys all;
A band not large, but warriors bold and true.
Æneas, guiding with his hand a plough,
Marks out the city's ground, gives separate lands
By lot, and bids within this space appear
A second Troy. Trojan Acestes takes
The kingly power, and with benignant joy
Appoints a forum, and decrees just laws
Before a gathered senate. Then they raise
On that star-circled Erycinian hill,

The temple to Idalian Venus dear;
And at Anchises' sepulchre ordain
A priesthood and wide groves of hallowed shade.

Now the nine days of funeral pomp are done,
And every altar has had honors due
From all the folk. Now tranquil-breathing winds
Have levelled the great deep, while brisk and free,
A favoring Auster bids them launch away.
But sound of many a wailing voice is heard
Along the winding shore; for ere they go,
In fond embraces for a night and day
They linger still. The women — aye, and men! —
Who hated yesterday the ocean's face
And loathed its name, now clamor to set sail
And bear all want and woe to exiles known.
But good Æneas with benignant words
Their sorrow soothes, and, not without a tear,
Consigns them to Acestes' kindred care.
Then bids he sacrifice to Eryx' shade
Three bulls, and to the wind-gods and the storm
A lamb, then loose the ships in order due.
He, with a garland of shorn olive, stood
Holding aloft the sacrificial bowl
From his own vessel's prow, and scattered far
The sacred entrails o'er the bitter wave,
With gift of flowing wine. Swift at the stern
A fair wind rose and thrust them; while the crews
With rival strokes swept o'er the spreading sea.

Venus, the while, disturbed with grief and care,

To Neptune thus her sorrowing heart outpoured:
"Stern Juno's wrath and breast implacable
"Compel me, Neptune, to abase my pride
"In lowly supplication. Lapse of days,
"Nor prayers, nor virtues her hard heart subdue,
"Nor Jove's command; nor will she rest or yield
"At Fate's decree. Her execrable grudge
"Is still unfed, although she did consume
"The Trojan city, Phrygia's midmost throne,
"And though she has accomplished stroke on stroke
"Of retribution. But she now pursues
"The remnant — aye! the ashes and bare bones
"Of perished Ilium; though the cause and spring
"Of wrath so great none but herself can tell.
"Wert thou not witness on the Libyan wave
"What storm she stirred, immingling sea and sky,
"And with Æolian whirlwinds made her war, —
"In vain and insolent invasion, sire,
"Of thine own realm and power? Behold, but now,
"Goading to evil deeds the Trojan dames,
"She basely burned his ships; he in strange lands
"Must leave the crews of his lost fleet behind.
"O, I entreat thee, let the remnant sail
"In safety o'er thy sea, and end their way
"In Tiber's holy stream; — if this my prayer
"Be lawful, and that city's rampart proud
"Be still what Fate intends."
Then Saturn's son,
The ruler of the seas profound, replied:
"Queen of Cythera, it is meet for thee
"To trust my waves from which thyself art sprung.

"Have I not proved a friend, and oft restrained
"The anger and wild wrath of seas and skies?
"On land, let Simois and Xanthus tell
"If I have loved Æneas! On that day
"Achilles drove the shuddering hosts of Troy
"In panic to the walls, and hurled to death
"Innumerable foes, until the streams
"Were choked with dead, and Xanthus scarce could find
"His wonted path to sea; that self-same day,
"Æneas, spent, and with no help of Heaven,
"Met Peleus' dreadful son: — who else but I
"In cloudy mantle bore him safe afar?
"Though 't was my will to cast down utterly
"The walls of perjured Troy, which my own hands
"Had built beside the sea. And even to-day
"My favor changes not. Dispel thy fear!
"Safe, even as thou prayest, he shall ride
"To Cumæ's haven, where Avernus lies.
"One only sinks beneath th' engulfing seas, —
"One life in lieu of many." Having soothed
And cheered her heart divine, the worshipped sire
Flung o'er his mated steeds a yoke of gold,
Bridled the wild, white mouths, and with strong hand
Shook out long, loosened reins. His azure car
Skimmed light and free along the crested waves;
Before his path the rolling billows all
Were calm and still, and each o'er-swollen flood
Sank 'neath his sounding wheel; while from the skies
The storm-clouds fled away. Behind him trailed
A various company; vast bulk of whales,
The hoary band of Glaucus, Inoüs,
Palæmon and the nimble Tritons all,

The troop of Phorcus; and to leftward ranged
Thalia, Thetis, and fair Melite,
With virgin Panopea, and the nymphs
Nesæa, Spio and Cymodoce.

Now in Æneas' ever-burdened breast
The voice of hope revived. He bade make haste
To raise the masts, spread canvas on the spars;
All hands hauled at the sheets, and left or right
Shook out the loosened sails, or twirled in place
The horn-tipped yards. Before a favoring wind
The fleet sped on. The line in close array
Was led by Palinurus, in whose course
All ships were bid to follow. Soon the car
Of dewy Night drew near the turning-point
Of her celestial round. The oarsmen all
Yielded their limbs to rest, and prone had fallen
On the hard thwarts, in deep, unpillowed slumber.
Then from the high stars on light-moving wings,
The God of Sleep found passage through the dark
And clove the gloom, — to bring upon thy head,
O Palinurus, an ill-boding sleep,
Though blameless thou. Upon thy ship the god
In guise of Phorbas stood, thus whispering:
"Look, Palinurus, how the flowing tides
"Lift on thy fleet unsteered, and changeless winds
"Behind thee breathe! 'T is now a happy hour
"To take thy rest. Lay down the weary head.
"Steal tired eyes from toiling. I will do
"Thine office for thee, just a little space."
But Palinurus, lifting scarce his eyes,
Thus answered him: "Have I not known the face

"Of yonder placid seas and tranquil waves?
"Put faith in such a monster? Could I trust —
"I, oft by ocean's treacherous calm betrayed —
"My lord Æneas to false winds and skies?"
So saying, he grasped his rudder tight, and clung
More firmly, fixing on the stars his eyes.
Then waved the god above his brows a branch
Wet with the dews of Lethe, and imbued
With power of Stygian dark, until his eyes
Wavered and slowly sank. The slumberous snare
Had scarce unbound his limbs, when, leaning o'er,
The god upon the waters flung him forth,
Hands clutching still the helm and ship-rail torn,
And calling on his comrades, but in vain.

Then soared th' immortal into viewless air;
And in swift course across the level sea
The fleet sped safe, protected from all fear
By Neptune's vow. Yet were they drawing nigh
The sirens' island-steep, where oft are seen
White, bleaching bones, and to the distant ear
The rocks roar harshly in perpetual foam.
Then of his drifting fleet and pilot gone
Æneas was aware, and, taking helm,
Steered through the midnight waves, with many a sigh;
And, by his comrade's pitiable death
Sore-smitten, cried, "O, thou didst trust too far
"Fair skies and seas, and liest without a grave,
"My Palinurus, in a land unknown!"

END OF BOOK V

BOOK VI

AFTER such words and tears, he flung free rein
To the swift fleet, which sped along the wave
To old Eubœan Cumæ's sacred shore.
They veer all prows to sea; the anchor fluke
Makes each ship sure, and shading the long strand
The rounded sterns jut o'er. Impetuously
The eager warriors leap forth to land
Upon Hesperian soil. One strikes the flint
To find the seed-spark hidden in its veins;
One breaks the thick-branched trees, and steals away
The shelter where the woodland creatures bide;
One leads his mates where living waters flow.

Æneas, servant of the gods, ascends
The templed hill where lofty Phœbus reigns,
And that far-off, inviolable shrine
Of dread Sibylla, in stupendous cave,
O'er whose deep soul the god of Delos breathes
Prophetic gifts, unfolding things to come.
Here are pale Trivia's golden house and grove.
Here Dædalus, the ancient story tells,
Escaping Minos' power, and having made
Hazard of heaven on far-mounting wings,
Floated to northward, a cold, trackless way,
And lightly poised, at last, o'er Cumæ's towers.

Here first to earth come down, he gave to thee
His gear of wings, Apollo! and ordained
Vast temples to thy name and altars fair.
On huge bronze doors Androgeos' death was done;
And Cecrops' children paid their debt of woe,
Where, seven and seven, — O pitiable sight! —
The youths and maidens wait the annual doom,
Drawn out by lot from yonder marble urn.
Beyond, above a sea, lay carven Crete:
The bull was there; the passion, the strange guile;
And Queen Pasiphaë's brute-human son,
The Minotaur — of monstrous loves the sign.
Here was the toilsome, labyrinthine maze,
Where, pitying love-lorn Ariadne's tears,
The crafty Dædalus himself betrayed
The secret of his work; and gave the clue
To guide the path of Theseus through the gloom.
O Icarus, in such well-graven scene
How proud thy place should be! but grief forbade:
Twice in pure gold a father's fingers strove
To shape thy fall, and twice they strove in vain.

Æneas long the various work would scan;
But now Achates comes, and by his side
Deïphobe, the Sibyl, Glaucus' child.
Thus to the prince she spoke:
"Is this thine hour
"To stand and wonder? Rather go obtain
"From young unbroken herd the bullocks seven,
"And seven yearling ewes, our wonted way."
Thus to Æneas; his attendants haste

To work her will; the priestess, calling loud,
Gathers the Trojans to her mountain-shrine.

Deep in the face of that Eubœan crag
A cavern vast is hollowed out amain,
With hundred openings, a hundred mouths,
Whence voices flow, the Sibyl's answering songs.
While at the door they paused, the virgin cried:
"Ask now thy doom! — the god! the god is nigh!"
So saying, from her face its color flew,
Her twisted locks flowed free, the heaving breast
Swelled with her heart's wild blood; her stature seemed
Vaster, her accent more than mortal man,
As all th' oncoming god around her breathed:
"On with thy vows and prayers, O Trojan, on!
"For only unto prayer this haunted cave
"May its vast lips unclose." She spake no more.
An icy shudder through the marrow ran
Of the bold Trojans; while their sacred King
Poured from his inmost soul this plaint and prayer:
"Phœbus, who ever for the woes of Troy
"Hadst pitying eyes! who gavest deadly aim
"To Paris when his Dardan shaft he hurled
"On great Achilles! Thou hast guided me
"Through many an unknown water, where the seas
"Break upon kingdoms vast, and to the tribes
"Of the remote Massyli, whose wild land
"To Syrtes spreads. But now, because at last
"I touch Hesperia's ever-fleeting bound,
"May Troy's ill fate forsake me from this day!
"O gods and goddesses, beneath whose wrath

"Dardania's glory and great Ilium stood,
"Spare, for ye may, the remnant of my race!
"And thou, most holy prophetess, whose soul
"Foreknows events to come, grant to my prayer
"(Which asks no kingdom save what Fate decrees)
"That I may stablish in the Latin land
"My Trojans, my far-wandering household-gods,
"And storm-tossed deities of fallen Troy.
"Then unto Phœbus and his sister pale
"A temple all of marble shall be given,
"And festal days to Phœbus evermore.
"Thee also in my realms a spacious shrine
"Shall honor; thy dark books and holy songs
"I there will keep, to be my people's law;
"And thee, benignant Sibyl, for all time
"A company of chosen priests shall serve.
"O, not on leaves, light leaves, inscribe thy songs!
"Lest, playthings of each breeze, they fly afar
"In swift confusion! Sing thyself, I pray."

So ceased his voice; the virgin through the cave,
Scarce bridled yet by Phœbus' hand divine,
Ecstatic swept along, and vainly strove
To fling its potent master from her breast;
But he more strongly plied his rein and curb
Upon her frenzied lips, and soon subdued
Her spirit fierce, and swayed her at his will.
Free and self-moved the cavern's hundred doors
Swung open wide, and uttered to the air
The oracles the virgin-priestess sung:
"Thy long sea-perils thou hast safely passed;

"But heavier woes await thee on the land.
"Truly thy Trojans to Lavinian shore
"Shall come — vex not thyself thereon — but, oh!
"Shall rue their coming thither! war, red war!
"And Tiber stained with bloody foam I see.
"Simois, Xanthus, and the Dorian horde
"Thou shalt behold; a new Achilles now
"In Latium breathes, — he, too, of goddess born;
"And Juno, burden of the sons of Troy,
"Will vex them ever; while thyself shalt sue
"In dire distress to many a town and tribe
"Through Italy; the cause of so much ill
"Again shall be a hostess-queen, again
"A marriage-chamber for an alien bride.
"Oh! yield not to thy woe, but front it ever,
"And follow boldly whither Fortune calls.
"Thy way of safety, as thou least couldst dream,
"Lies through a city of the Greeks, thy foes."

Thus from her shrine Cumæa's prophetess
Chanted the dark decrees; the dreadful sound
Reverberated through the bellowing cave,
Commingling truth with ecstasies obscure.
Apollo, as she raged, flung loosened rein,
And thrust beneath her heart a quickening spur.
When first her madness ceased, and her wild lips
Were still at last, the hero thus began:
"No tribulations new, O Sibyl blest,
"Can now confront me; every future pain
"I have foretasted; my prophetic soul
"Endured each stroke of fate before it fell.

"One boon I ask. If of th' infernal King
"This be the portal where the murky wave
"Of swollen Acheron o'erflows its bound,
"Here let me enter and behold the face
"Of my loved sire. Thy hand may point the way;
"Thy word will open wide yon holy doors.
"My father through the flames and falling spears,
"Straight through the centre of our foes, I bore
"Upon these shoulders. My long flight he shared
"From sea to sea, and suffered at my side
"The anger of rude waters and dark skies, —
"Though weak — O task too great for old and gray!
"Thus as a suppliant at thy door to stand,
"Was his behest and prayer. On son and sire,
"O gracious one, have pity, — for thy rule
"Is over all; no vain authority
"Hadst thou from Trivia o'er th' Avernian groves.
"If Orpheus could call back his loved one's shade,
"Emboldened by the lyre's melodious string:
"If Pollux by the interchange of death
"Redeemed his twin, and oft repassed the way:
"If Theseus — but why name him? why recall
"Alcides' task? I, too, am sprung from Jove."

Thus, to the altar clinging, did he pray:
The Sibyl thus replied: "Offspring of Heaven,
"Anchises' son, the downward path to death
"Is easy; all the livelong night and day
"Dark Pluto's door stands open for a guest.
"But O! remounting to the world of light,
"This is a task indeed, a strife supreme.

"Few, very few, whom righteous Jove did bless,
"Or quenchless virtue carried to the stars,
"Children of gods, have such a victory won.
"Grim forests stop the way, and, gliding slow,
"Cocytus circles through the sightless gloom.
"But if it be thy dream and fond desire
"Twice o'er the Stygian gulf to travel, twice
"On glooms of Tartarus to set thine eyes,
"If such mad quest be now thy pleasure — hear
"What must be first fulfilled. A certain tree
"Hides in obscurest shade a golden bough,
"Of pliant stems and many a leaf of gold,
"Sacred to Proserpine, infernal Queen.
"Far in the grove it hides; in sunless vale
"Deep shadows keep it in captivity.
"No pilgrim to that underworld can pass
"But he who plucks this burgeoned, leafy gold;
"For this hath beauteous Proserpine ordained
"Her chosen gift to be. Whene'er 't is culled,
"A branch out-leafing in like golden gleam,
"A second wonder-stem, fails not to spring.
"Therefore go seek it with uplifted eyes!
"And when by will of Heaven thou findest it,
"Reach forth and pluck; for at a touch it yields,
"A free and willing gift, if Fate ordain;
"But otherwise no mortal strength avails,
"Nor strong, sharp steel, to rend it from the tree.
"Another task awaits; thy friend's cold clay
"Lies unentombed. Alas! thou art not ware
"(While in my house thou lingerest, seeking light)
"That all thy ships are by his death defiled.

"Unto his resting-place and sepulchre,
"Go, carry him! And sable victims bring,
"In expiation, to his mournful shade.
"So at the last on yonder Stygian groves,
"And realms to things that breathe impassable,
"Thine eye shall gaze." So closed her lips inspired.
Æneas then drew forth, with downcast eyes,
From that dark cavern, pondering in his heart
The riddle of his fate. His faithful friend
Achates at his side, with paces slow,
Companioned all his care, while their sad souls
Made mutual and oft-renewed surmise
What comrade dead, what cold and tombless clay,
The Sibyl's word would show.
But as they mused,
Behold Misenus on the dry sea-sands,
By hasty hand of death struck guiltless down!
A son of Æolus, none better knew
To waken heroes by the clarion's call,
With war-enkindling sound. Great Hector's friend
In happier days, he oft at Hector's side
Strode to the fight with glittering lance and horn.
But when Achilles stripped his fallen foe,
This dauntless hero to Æneas gave
Allegiance true, in not less noble cause.
But, on a day, he chanced beside the sea
To blow his shell-shaped horn, and wildly dared
Challenge the gods themselves to rival song;
Till jealous Triton, if the tale be true,
Grasped the rash mortal, and out-flung him far
'Mid surf-beat rocks and waves of whirling foam.

Now from all sides, with tumult and loud cry,
The Trojans came, — Æneas leading all
In faithful grief; they hasten to fulfil
The Sibyl's mandate, and with many a tear
Build, altar-wise, a pyre, of tree on tree
Heaped high as heaven: then they penetrate
The tall, old forest, where wild creatures bide,
And fell pitch-pines, or with resounding blows
Of axe and wedge, cleave oak and ash-tree through,
Or logs of rowan down the mountains roll.
Æneas oversees and shares the toil,
Cheers on his mates, and swings a woodman's steel.
But, sad at heart with many a doubt and care,
O'erlooks the forest wide; then prays aloud:
"O, that the Golden Bough from this vast grove
"Might o'er me shine! For, O Æolides,
"The oracle foretold thy fate, too well!"
Scarce had he spoken, when a pair of doves
Before his very eyes flew down from heaven
To the green turf below; the prince of Troy
Knew them his mother's birds, and joyful cried,
"O, guide me on, whatever path there be!
"In airy travel through the woodland fly,
"To where yon rare branch shades the blessed ground.
"Fail thou not me, in this my doubtful hour,
"O heavenly mother!" So saying, his steps he stayed,
Close watching whither they should signal give;
The lightly-feeding doves flit on and on,
Ever in easy ken of following eyes,
Till over foul Avernus' sulphurous throat
Swiftly they lift them through the liquid air,

In silent flight, and find a wished-for rest
On a twy-natured tree, where through green boughs
Flames forth the glowing gold's contrasted hue.
As in the wintry woodland bare and chill,
Fresh-budded shines the clinging mistletoe,
Whose seed is never from the parent tree
O'er whose round limbs its tawny tendrils twine, —
So shone th' out-leafing gold within the shade
Of dark holm-oak, and so its tinsel-bract
Rustled in each light breeze. Æneas grasped
The lingering bough, broke it in eager haste,
And bore it straightway to the Sibyl's shrine.

Meanwhile the Trojans on the doleful shore
Bewailed Misenus, and brought tribute there
Of grief's last gift to his unheeding clay.
First, of the full-sapped pine and well-hewn oak
A lofty pyre they build; then sombre boughs
Around it wreathe, and in fair order range
Funereal cypress; glittering arms are piled
High over all; on blazing coals they lift
Cauldrons of brass brimmed o'er with waters pure;
And that cold, lifeless clay lave and anoint
With many a moan and cry; on their last couch
The poor, dead limbs they lay, and mantle o'er
With purple vesture and familiar pall.
Then in sad ministry the chosen few,
With eyes averted, as our sires did use,
Hold the enkindling torch beneath the pyre:
They gather up and burn the gifts of myrrh,
The sacred bread and bowls of flowing oil;

And when in flame the dying embers fall,
On thirsty ash they pour the streams of wine.
Good Corynæus, in an urn of brass
The gathered relics hides; and three times round,
With blessed olive branch and sprinkling dew,
Purges the people with ablution cold,
In lustral rite; oft chanting, "Hail! Farewell!"
Faithful Æneas for his comrade built
A mighty tomb, and dedicated there
Trophy of arms, with trumpet and with oar,
Beneath a windy hill, which now is called
"Misenus," — for all time the name to bear.

After these toils, they hasten to fulfil
What else the Sibyl said. Straightway they find
A cave profound, of entrance gaping wide,
O'erhung with rock, in gloom of sheltering grove,
Near the dark waters of a lake, whereby
No bird might ever pass with scathless wing,
So dire an exhalation is breathed out
From that dark deep of death to upper air: —
Hence, in the Grecian tongue, Aornos called.
Here first four youthful bulls of swarthy hide
Were led for sacrifice; on each broad brow
The priestess sprinkled wine; 'twixt the two horns
Outplucked the lifted hair, and cast it forth
Upon the holy flames, beginning so
Her offerings; then loudly sued the power
Of Hecate, a Queen in heaven and hell.
Some struck with knives, and caught in shallow bowls
The smoking blood. Æneas' lifted hand

Smote with a sword a sable-fleecèd ewe
To Night, the mother of th' Eumenides,
And Earth, her sister dread; next unto thee,
O Proserpine, a curst and barren cow;
Then unto Pluto, Stygian King, he built
An altar dark, and piled upon the flames
The ponderous entrails of the bulls, and poured
Free o'er the burning flesh the goodly oil.
Then lo! at dawn's dim, earliest beam began
Beneath their feet a groaning of the ground:
The wooded hill-tops shook, and, as it seemed,
She-hounds of hell howled viewless through the shade,
To hail their Queen. "Away, O souls profane!
"Stand far away!" the priestess shrieked, "nor dare
"Unto this grove come near! Æneas, on!
"Begin thy journey! Draw thy sheathèd blade!
"Now, all thy courage! now, th' unshaken soul!"
She spoke, and burst into the yawning cave
With frenzied step; he follows where she leads,
And strides with feet unfaltering at her side.

Ye gods! who rule the spirits of the dead!
Ye voiceless shades and silent lands of night!
O Phlegethon! O Chaos! let my song,
If it be lawful, in fit words declare
What I have heard; and by your help divine
Unfold what hidden things enshrouded lie
In that dark underworld of sightless gloom.

They walked exploring the unpeopled night,
Through Pluto's vacuous realms, and regions void,

As when one's path in dreary woodlands winds
Beneath a misty moon's deceiving ray,
When Jove has mantled all his heaven in shade,
And night seals up the beauty of the world.
In the first courts and entrances of Hell
Sorrows and vengeful Cares on couches lie:
There sad Old Age abides, Diseases pale,
And Fear, and Hunger, temptress to all crime;
Want, base and vile, and, two dread shapes to see,
Bondage and Death: then Sleep, Death's next of kin;
And dreams of guilty joy. Death-dealing War
Is ever at the doors, and hard thereby
The Furies' beds of steel, where wild-eyed Strife
Her snaky hair with blood-stained fillet binds.
There in the middle court a shadowy elm
Its ancient branches spreads, and in its leaves
Deluding visions ever haunt and cling.
Then come strange prodigies of bestial kind:
Centaurs are stabled there, and double shapes
Like Scylla, or the dragon Lerna bred,
With hideous scream; Briareus clutching far
His hundred hands, Chimæra girt with flame,
A crowd of Gorgons, Harpies of foul wing,
And giant Geryon's triple-monstered shade.
Æneas, shuddering with sudden fear,
Drew sword and fronted them with naked steel;
And, save his sage conductress bade him know
These were but shapes and shadows sweeping by,
His stroke had cloven in vain the vacant air.
Hence the way leads to that Tartarean stream
Of Acheron, whose torrent fierce and foul

Disgorges in Cocytus all its sands.
A ferryman of gruesome guise keeps ward
Upon these waters, — Charon, foully garbed,
With unkempt, thick gray beard upon his chin,
And staring eyes of flame; a mantle coarse,
All stained and knotted, from his shoulder falls,
As with a pole he guides his craft, tends sail,
And in the black boat ferries o'er his dead; —
Old, but a god's old age looks fresh and strong.

To those dim shores the multitude streams on —
Husbands and wives, and pale, unbreathing forms
Of high-souled heroes, boys and virgins fair,
And strong youth at whose graves fond parents mourned.
As numberless the throng as leaves that fall
When autumn's early frost is on the grove;
Or like vast flocks of birds by winter's chill
Sent flying o'er wide seas to lands of flowers.
All stood beseeching to begin their voyage
Across that river, and reached out pale hands,
In passionate yearning for its distant shore.
But the grim boatman takes now these, now those,
Or thrusts unpitying from the stream away.

Æneas, moved to wonder and deep awe,
Beheld the tumult; "Virgin seer!" he cried,
"Why move the thronging ghosts toward yonder stream?
"What seek they there? Or what election holds
"That these unwilling linger, while their peers

"Sweep forward yonder o'er the leaden waves?"
To him, in few, the aged Sibyl spoke:
"Son of Anchises, offspring of the gods,
"Yon are Cocytus and the Stygian stream,
"By whose dread power the gods themselves do fear
"To take an oath in vain. Here far and wide
"Thou seest the hapless throng that hath no grave.
"That boatman Charon bears across the deep
"Such as be sepulchred with holy care.
"But over that loud flood and dreadful shore
"No trav'ler may be borne, until in peace
"His gathered ashes rest. A hundred years
"Round this dark borderland some haunt and roam,
"Then win late passage o'er the longed-for wave."

Æneas lingered for a little space,
Revolving in his soul with pitying prayer
Fate's partial way. But presently he sees
Leucaspis and the Lycian navy's lord,
Orontes; both of melancholy brow,
Both hapless and unhonored after death,
Whom, while from Troy they crossed the wind-swept
 seas,
A whirling tempest wrecked with ship and crew.
There, too, the helmsman Palinurus strayed:
Who, as he whilom watched the Libyan stars,
Had fallen, plunging from his lofty seat
Into the billowy deep. Æneas now
Discerned his sad face through the blinding gloom,
And hailed him thus: "O Palinurus, tell
"What god was he who ravished thee away

"From me and mine, beneath the o'erwhelming wave?
"Speak on! for he who ne'er had spoke untrue,
"Apollo's self, did mock my listening mind,
"And chanted me a faithful oracle
"That thou shouldst ride the seas unharmed, and touch
"Ausonian shores. Is this the pledge divine?"
Then he, "O chieftain of Anchises' race,
"Apollo's tripod told thee not untrue.
"No god did thrust me down beneath the wave,
"For that strong rudder unto which I clung,
"My charge and duty, and my ship's sole guide,
"Wrenched from its place, dropped with me as I fell.
"Not for myself — by the rude seas I swear —
"Did I have terror, but lest thy good ship,
"Stripped of her gear, and her poor pilot lost,
"Should fail and founder in that rising flood.
"Three wintry nights across the boundless main
"The south wind buffeted and bore me on;
"At the fourth daybreak, lifted from the surge,
"I looked at last on Italy, and swam
"With weary stroke on stroke unto the land.
"Safe was I then. Alas! but as I climbed
"With garments wet and heavy, my clenched hand
"Grasping the steep rock, came a cruel horde
Upon me with drawn blades, accounting me —
"So blind they were! — a wrecker's prize and spoil.
"Now are the waves my tomb, and wandering winds
"Toss me along the coast. O, I implore,
"By heaven's sweet light, by yonder upper air,
"By thy lost father, by Iulus dear,

"Thy rising hope and joy, that from these woes,
"Unconquered chieftain, thou wilt set me free!
"Give me a grave where Velia's haven lies,
"For thou hast power! Or if some path there be,
"If thy celestial mother guide thee here
"(For not, I ween, without the grace of gods
"Wilt cross yon rivers vast, yon Stygian pool)
"Reach me a hand! and bear with thee along!
"Until (least gift!) death bring me peace and calm."

Such words he spoke: the priestess thus replied:
"Why, Palinurus, these unblest desires?
"Wouldst thou, unsepulchred, behold the wave
"Of Styx, stern river of th' Eumenides?
"Wouldst thou, unbidden, tread its fearful strand?
"Hope not by prayer to change the laws of Heaven!
"But heed my words, and in thy memory
"Cherish and keep, to cheer this evil time.
"Lo, far and wide, led on by signs from Heaven,
"Thy countrymen from many a templed town
"Shall consecrate thy dust, and build thy tomb,
"A tomb with annual feasts and votive flowers,
"To Palinurus a perpetual fame!"
Thus was his anguish stayed, from his sad heart
Grief ebbed awhile, and even to this day,
Our land is glad such noble name to wear.

The twain continue now their destined way
Unto the river's edge. The Ferryman,
Who watched them through still groves approach his
shore,

Hailed them, at distance, from the Stygian wave,
And with reproachful summons thus began:
"Whoe'er thou art that in this warrior guise
"Unto my river comest, — quickly tell
"Thine errand! Stay thee where thou standest now!
"This is ghosts' land, for sleep and slumbrous dark.
"That flesh and blood my Stygian ship should bear
"Were lawless wrong. Unwillingly I took
"Alcides, Theseus, and Pirithous,
"Though sons of gods, too mighty to be quelled.
"One bound in chains yon warder of Hell's door,
"And dragged him trembling from our monarch's throne:
"The others, impious, would steal away
"Out of her bride-bed Pluto's ravished Queen."

Briefly th' Amphrysian priestess made reply:
"Not ours, such guile: Fear not! This warrior's arms
"Are innocent. Let Cerberus from his cave
"Bay ceaselessly, the bloodless shades to scare;
"Let Proserpine immaculately keep
"The house and honor of her kinsman King.
"Trojan Æneas, famed for faithful prayer
"And victory in arms, descends to seek
"His father in this gloomy deep of death.
"If loyal goodness move not such as thee,
"This branch at least" (she drew it from her breast)
"Thou knowest well."

Then cooled his wrathful heart;
With silent lips he looked and wondering eyes
Upon that fateful, venerable wand,

Seen only once an age. Shoreward he turned,
And pushed their way his boat of leaden hue.
The rows of crouching ghosts along the thwarts
He scattered, cleared a passage, and gave room
To great Æneas. The light shallop groaned
Beneath his weight, and, straining at each seam,
Took in the foul flood with unstinted flow.

At last the hero and his priestess-guide
Came safe across the river, and were moored
'Mid sea-green sedges in the formless mire.
Here Cerberus, with triple-throated roar,
Made all the region ring, as there he lay
At vast length in his cave. The Sibyl then,
Seeing the serpents writhe around his neck,
Threw down a loaf with honeyed herbs imbued
And drowsy essences: he, ravenous,
Gaped wide his three fierce mouths and snatched the
bait,
Crouched with his large backs loose upon the ground,
And filled his cavern floor from end to end.
Æneas through hell's portal moved, while sleep
Its warder buried; then he fled that shore
Of Stygian stream, whence travellers ne'er return.
Now hears he sobs, and piteous, lisping cries
Of souls of babes upon the threshold plaining;
Whom, ere they took their portion of sweet life,
Dark Fate from nursing bosoms tore, and plunged
In bitterness of death. Nor far from these,
The throng of dead by unjust judgment slain.
Not without judge or law these realms abide:

Wise Minos there the urn of justice moves,
And holds assembly of the silent shades,
Hearing the stories of their lives and deeds.
Close on this place those doleful ghosts abide,
Who, not for crime, but loathing life and light
With their own hands took death, and cast away
The vital essence. Willingly, alas!
They now would suffer need, or burdens bear,
If only life were given! But Fate forbids.
Around them winds the sad, unlovely wave
Of Styx: nine times it coils and interflows.
Not far from hence, on every side outspread,
The Fields of Sorrow lie, — such name they bear;
Here all whom ruthless love did waste away
Wander in paths unseen, or in the gloom
Of a dark myrtle grove: not even in death
Have they forgot their griefs of long ago.
Here impious Phædra and poor Procris bide;
Lorn Eriphyle bares the vengeful wounds
Her own son's dagger made; Evadne here,
And foul Pasiphaë are seen; hard by,
Laodamia, nobly fond and fair;
And Cæneus, not a boy, but maiden now,
By Fate remoulded to her native seeming.
Here Tyrian Dido, too, her wound unhealed,
Roamed through a mighty wood. The Trojan's eyes
Beheld her near him through the murky gloom,
As when, in her young month and crescent pale,
One sees th' o'er-clouded moon, or thinks he sees.
Down dropped his tears, and thus he fondly spoke:

"O suffering Dido! Were those tidings true
"That thou didst fling thee on the fatal steel?
"Thy death, ah me! I dealt it. But I swear
"By stars above us, by the powers in Heaven,
"Or whatsoever oath ye dead believe,
"That not by choice I fled thy shores, O Queen!
"Divine decrees compelled me, even as now
"Among these ghosts I pass, and thread my way
"Along this gulf of night and loathsome land.
"How could I deem my cruel taking leave
"Would bring thee at the last to all this woe?
"O, stay! Why shun me? Wherefore haste away?
"Our last farewell! Our doom! I speak it now!"
Thus, though she glared with fierce, relentless gaze,
Æneas, with fond words and tearful plea,
Would soothe her angry soul. But on the ground
She fixed averted eyes. For all he spoke
Moved her no more than if her frowning brow
Were changeless flint or carved in Parian stone.
Then, after pause, away in wrath she fled,
And refuge took within the cool, dark grove,
Where her first spouse, Sichæus, with her tears
Mingled his own in mutual love and true.
Æneas, none the less, her guiltless woe
With anguish knew, watched with dimmed eyes her way,
And pitied from afar the fallen Queen.
But now his destined way he must be gone;
Now the last regions round the travellers lie,
Where famous warriors in the darkness dwell:
Here Tydeus comes in view, with far-renowned

Parthenopæus and Adrastus pale;
Here mourn in upper air with many a moan,
In battle fallen, the Dardanidæ,
Whose long defile Æneas groans to see:
Glaucus and Medon and Thersilochus,
Antenor's children three, and Ceres' priest,
That Polypœtes, and Idæus still
Keeping the kingly chariot and spear.
Around him left and right the crowding shades
Not only once would see, but clutch and cling
Obstructive, asking on what quest he goes.
Soon as the princes of Argolic blood,
With line on line of Agamemnon's men,
Beheld the hero and his glittering arms
Flash through the dark, they trembled with amaze,
Or turned in flight, as if once more they fled
To shelter of the ships; some raised aloft
A feeble shout, or vainly opened wide
Their gaping lips in mockery of sound.

Here Priam's son, with body rent and torn,
Deïphobus, is seen, — his mangled face,
His face and bloody hands, his wounded head
Of ears and nostrils infamously shorn.
Scarce could Æneas know the shuddering shade
That strove to hide its face and shameful scar;
But, speaking first, he said, in their own tongue:
"Deïphobus, strong warrior, nobly born
"Of Teucer's royal stem, what ruthless foe
"Could wish to wreak on thee this dire revenge?
"Who ventured, unopposed, so vast a wrong?

"The rumor reached me how, that deadly night,
"Wearied with slaying Greeks, thyself didst fall
"Prone on a mingled heap of friends and foes.
"Then my own hands did for thy honor build
"An empty tomb upon the Trojan shore,
"And thrice with echoing voice I called thy shade.
"Thy name and arms are there. But, O my friend,
"Thee could I nowhere find, but launched away,
"Nor o'er thy bones their native earth could fling."

To him the son of Priam thus replied:
"Nay, friend, no hallowed rite was left undone,
"But every debt to death and pity due
"The shades of thy Deïphobus received.
"My fate it was, and Helen's murderous wrong,
"Wrought me this woe; of her these tokens tell.
"For how that last night in false hope we passed,
"Thou knowest, — ah, too well we both recall!
"When up the steep of Troy the fateful horse
"Came climbing, pregnant with fierce men-at-arms,
"'T was she, accurst, who led the Phrygian dames
"In choric dance and false bacchantic song,
"And, waving from the midst a lofty brand,
"Signalled the Greeks from Ilium's central tower.
"In that same hour on my sad couch I lay,
"Exhausted by long care and sunk in sleep,
"That sweet, deep sleep, so close to tranquil death.
"But my illustrious bride from all the house
"Had stolen all arms; from 'neath my pillowed head
"She stealthily bore off my trusty sword;
"Then loud on Menelaus did she call,

"And with her own false hand unbarred the door;
"Such gift to her fond lord she fain would send
"To blot the memory of his ancient wrong!
"Why tell the tale, how on my couch they broke,
"While their accomplice, vile Æolides,
"Counselled to many a crime. O heavenly Powers!
"Reward these Greeks their deeds of wickedness,
"If with clean lips upon your wrath I call!
"But, friend, what fortunes have thy life befallen?
"Tell point by point. Did waves of wandering seas
"Drive thee this way, or some divine command?
"What chastisement of fortune thrusts thee on
"Toward this forlorn abode of night and cloud?"

While thus they talked, the crimsoned car of Morn
Had wheeled beyond the midmost point of heaven,
On her ethereal road. The princely pair
Had wasted thus the whole brief gift of hours;
But Sibyl spoke the warning: "Night speeds by,
"And we, Æneas, lose it in lamenting.
"Here comes the place where cleaves our way in twain.
"Thy road, the right, toward Pluto's dwelling goes,
"And leads us to Elysium. But the left
"Speeds sinful souls to doom, and is their path
"To Tartarus th' accurst." Deïphobus
Cried out: "O priestess, be not wroth with us!
"Back to the ranks with yonder ghosts I go.
"O glory of my race, pass on! Thy lot
"Be happier than mine!" He spoke, and fled.

Æneas straightway by the leftward cliff

Beheld a spreading rampart, high begirt
With triple wall, and circling round it ran
A raging river of swift floods of flame,
Infernal Phlegethon, which whirls along
Loud-thundering rocks. A mighty gate is there
Columned in adamant; no human power,
Nor even the gods, against this gate prevail.
Tall tower of steel it has; and seated there
Tisiphone, in blood-flecked pall arrayed,
Sleepless forever, guards the entering way.
Hence groans are heard, fierce cracks of lash and
scourge,
Loud-clanking iron links and trailing chains.
Æneas motionless with horror stood
O'erwhelmed at such uproar. "O virgin, say
"What shapes of guilt are these? What penal woe
"Harries them thus? What wailing smites the air?"
To whom the Sibyl, "Far-famed prince of Troy,
"The feet of innocence may never pass
"Into this house of sin. But Hecate,
"When o'er th' Avernian groves she gave me power,
"Taught me what penalties the gods decree,
"And showed me all. There Cretan Rhadamanth
"His kingdom keeps, and from unpitying throne
"Chastises and lays bare the secret sins
"Of mortals who, exulting in vain guile,
"Elude, till death, their expiation due.
"There, armed forever with her vengeful scourge,
"Tisiphone, with menace and affront,
"The guilty swarm pursues; in her left hand
"She lifts her angered serpents, while she calls

"A troop of sister-furies fierce as she.
"Then, grating loud on hinge of sickening sound,
"Hell's portals open wide. O, dost thou see
"What sentinel upon that threshold sits,
"What shapes of fear keep guard upon that gloom?
"Far, far within the dragon Hydra broods
"With half a hundred mouths, gaping and black;
"And Tartarus slopes downward to the dark
"Twice the whole space that in the realms of light
"Th' Olympian heaven above our earth aspires.
"Here Earth's first offspring, the Titanic brood,
"Roll lightning-blasted in the gulf profound;
"The twin Aloïdæ, colossal shades,
"Came on my view; their hands made stroke at Heaven
"And strove to thrust Jove from his seat on high.
"I saw Salmoneus his dread stripes endure,
"Who dared to counterfeit Olympian thunder
"And Jove's own fire. In chariot of four steeds,
"Brandishing torches, he triumphant rode
"Through throngs of Greeks, o'er Elis' sacred way,
"Demanding worship as a god. O fool!
"To mock the storm's inimitable flash
"With crash of hoofs and roll of brazen wheel!
"But mightiest Jove from rampart of thick cloud
"Hurled his own shaft, no flickering, mortal flame,
"And in vast whirl of tempest laid him low.
"Next unto these, on Tityos I looked,
"Child of old Earth, whose womb all creatures bears:
"Stretched o'er nine roods he lies; a vulture huge
"Tears with hooked beak at his immortal side,
"Or deep in entrails ever rife with pain

"Gropes for a feast, making his haunt and home
"In the great Titan bosom; nor will give
"To ever new-born flesh surcease of woe.
"Why name Ixion and Pirithous,
"The Lapithæ, above whose impious brows
"A crag of flint hangs quaking to its fall,
"As if just toppling down, while couches proud,
"Propped upon golden pillars, bid them feast
"In royal glory: but beside them lies
"The eldest of the Furies, whose dread hands
"Thrust from the feast away, and wave aloft
"A flashing firebrand, with shrieks of woe.
"Here in a prison-house awaiting doom
"Are men who hated, long as life endured,
"Their brothers, or maltreated their gray sires,
"Or tricked a humble friend; the men who grasped
"At hoarded riches, with their kith and kin
"Not sharing ever — an unnumbered throng;
"Here slain adulterers be; and men who dared
"To fight in unjust cause, and break all faith
"With their own lawful lords. Seek not to know
"What forms of woe they feel, what fateful shape
"Of retribution hath o'erwhelmed them there.
"Some roll huge boulders up; some hang on wheels,
"Lashed to the whirling spokes; in his sad seat
"Theseus is sitting, nevermore to rise;
"Unhappy Phlegyas uplifts his voice
"In warning through the darkness, calling loud,
"'O, ere too late, learn justice and fear God!'
"Yon traitor sold his country, and for gold
"Enchained her to a tyrant, trafficking

"In laws, for bribes enacted or made void;
"Another did incestuously assail
"His daughter's bed with infamous embrace.
"All ventured some unclean, prodigious crime;
"And what they dared, achieved. I could not tell,
"Not with a hundred mouths, a hundred tongues,
"Or iron voice, their divers shapes of sin,
"Nor call by name the myriad pangs they bear."

So spake Apollo's aged prophetess.
"Now up and on!" she cried. "Thy task fulfil!
"We must make speed. Behold yon arching doors,
"Yon walls in furnace of the Cyclops forged!
"'T is there we are commanded to lay down
"Th' appointed offering." So, side by side,
Swift through the intervening dark they strode,
And, drawing near the portal-arch, made pause.
Æneas, taking station at the door,
Pure, lustral waters o'er his body threw,
And hung for garland there the Golden Bough.
Now, every rite fulfilled, and tribute due
Paid to the sovereign power of Proserpine,
At last within a land delectable
Their journey lay, through pleasurable bowers
Of groves where all is joy, — a blest abode!
An ampler sky its roseate light bestows
On that bright land, which sees the cloudless beam
Of suns and planets to our earth unknown.
On smooth green lawns, contending limb with limb,
Immortal athletes play, and wrestle long
'Gainst mate or rival on the tawny sand;

With sounding footsteps and ecstatic song,
Some thread the dance divine: among them moves
The bard of Thrace, in flowing vesture clad,
Discoursing seven-noted melody,
Who sweeps the numbered strings with changeful hand,
Or smites with ivory point his golden lyre.
Here Trojans be of eldest, noblest race,
Great-hearted heroes, born in happier times,
Ilus, Assaracus, and Dardanus,
Illustrious builders of the Trojan town.
Their arms and shadowy chariots he views,
And lances fixed in earth, while through the fields
Their steeds without a bridle graze at will.
For if in life their darling passion ran
To chariots, arms, or glossy-coated steeds,
The self-same joy, though in their graves, they feel.
Lo! on the left and right at feast reclined
Are other blessed souls, whose chorus sings
Victorious pæans on the fragrant air
Of laurel groves; and hence to earth outpours
Eridanus, through forests rolling free.
Here dwell the brave who for their native land
Fell wounded on the field; here holy priests
Who kept them undefiled their mortal day;
And poets, of whom the true-inspired song
Deserved Apollo's name; and all who found
New arts, to make man's life more blest or fair;
Yea! here dwell all those dead whose deeds bequeath
Deserved and grateful memory to their kind.
And each bright brow a snow-white fillet wears.
Unto this host the Sibyl turned, and hailed

Musæus, midmost of a numerous throng,
Who towered o'er his peers a shoulder higher:
"O spirits blest! O venerable bard!
"Declare what dwelling or what region holds
"Anchises, for whose sake we twain essayed
"Yon passage over the wide streams of hell."
And briefly thus the hero made reply:
"No fixed abode is ours. In shadowy groves
"We make our home, or meadows fresh and fair,
"With streams whose flowery banks our couches be.
"But you, if thitherward your wishes turn,
"Climb yonder hill, where I your path may show."

So saying, he strode forth and led them on,
Till from that vantage they had prospect fair
Of a wide, shining land; thence wending down,
They left the height they trod; for far below
Father Anchises in a pleasant vale
Stood pondering, while his eyes and thought surveyed
A host of prisoned spirits, who there abode
Awaiting entrance to terrestrial air.
And musing he reviewed the legions bright
Of his own progeny and offspring proud —
Their fates and fortunes, virtues and great deeds.
Soon he discerned Æneas drawing nigh
O'er the green slope, and, lifting both his hands
In eager welcome, spread them swiftly forth.
Tears from his eyelids rained, and thus he spoke:
"Art here at last? Hath thy well-proven love
"Of me thy sire achieved yon arduous way?

"Will Heaven, belovèd son, once more allow
"That eye to eye we look? and shall I hear
"Thy kindred accent mingling with my own?
"I cherished long this hope. My prophet-soul
"Numbered the lapse of days, nor did my thought
"Deceive. O, o'er what lands and seas wast driven
"To this embrace! What perils manifold
"Assailed thee, O my son, on every side!
"How long I trembled, lest that Libyan throne
"Should work thee woe!"
Æneas thus replied:
"Thine image, sire, thy melancholy shade,
"Came oft upon my vision, and impelled
"My journey hitherward. Our fleet of ships
"Lies safe at anchor in the Tuscan seas.
"Come, clasp my hand! Come, father, I implore,
"And heart to heart this fond embrace receive!"
So speaking, all his eyes suffused with tears;
Thrice would his arms in vain that shape enfold.
Thrice from the touch of hand the vision fled,
Like wafted winds or likest hovering dreams.

After these things Æneas was aware
Of solemn groves in one deep, distant vale,
Where trees were whispering, and forever flowed
The river Lethe, through its land of calm.
Nations unnumbered roved and haunted there:
As when, upon a windless summer morn,
The bees afield among the rainbow flowers
Alight and sip, or round the lilies pure
Pour forth in busy swarm, while far diffused

Their murmured songs from all the meadows rise.
Æneas in amaze the wonder views,
And fearfully inquires of whence and why;
What yonder rivers be; what people press,
Line after line, on those dim shores along.
Said Sire Anchises: "Yonder thronging souls
"To reincarnate shape predestined move.
"Here, at the river Lethe's wave, they quaff
"Care-quelling floods, and long oblivion.
"Of these I shall discourse, and to thy soul
"Make visible the number and array
"Of my posterity; so shall thy heart
"In Italy, thy new-found home, rejoice."
"O father," said Æneas, "must I deem
"That from this region souls exalted rise
"To upper air, and shall once more return
"To cumbering flesh? O, wherefore do they feel,
"Unhappy ones, such fatal lust to live?"
"I speak, my son, nor make thee longer doubt,"
Anchises said, and thus the truth set forth,
In ordered words from point to point unfolding:

"Know first that heaven and earth and ocean's plain,
"The moon's bright orb, and stars of Titan birth
"Are nourished by one Life; one primal Mind,
"Immingled with the vast and general frame,
"Fills every part and stirs the mighty whole.
"Thence man and beast, thence creatures of the air,
"And all the swarming monsters that be found
"Beneath the level of the marbled sea;
"A fiery virtue, a celestial power,

"Their native seeds retain; but bodies vile,
"With limbs of clay and members born to die,
"Encumber and o'ercloud; whence also spring
"Terrors and passions, suffering and joy;
"For from deep darkness and captivity
"All gaze but blindly on the radiant world.
"Nor when to life's last beam they bid farewell
"May sufferers cease from pain, nor quite be freed
"From all their fleshly plagues; but by fixed law,
"The strange, inveterate taint works deeply in.
"For this, the chastisement of evils past
"Is suffered here, and full requital paid.
"Some hang on high, outstretched to viewless winds;
"For some their sin's contagion must be purged
"In vast ablution of deep-rolling seas,
"Or burned away in fire. Each man receives
"His ghostly portion in the world of dark;
"But thence to realms Elysian we go free,
"Where for a few these seats of bliss abide,
"Till time's long lapse a perfect orb fulfils,
"And takes all taint away, restoring so
"The pure, ethereal soul's first virgin fire.
"At last, when the millennial æon strikes,
"God calls them forth to yon Lethæan stream,
"In numerous host, that thence, oblivious all,
"They may behold once more the vaulted sky,
"And willingly to shapes of flesh return."

So spoke Anchises; then led forth his son,
The Sibyl with him, to the assembled shades
(A voiceful throng), and on a lofty mound

His station took, whence plainly could be seen
The long procession, and each face descried.
"Hark now! for of the glories I will tell
"That wait our Dardan blood; of our sons' sons
"Begot upon the old Italian breed,
"Who shall be mighty spirits, and prolong
"Our names, their heritage. I will unfold
"The story, and reveal the destined years.
"You princeling, thou beholdest leaning there
"Upon a royal lance, shall next emerge
"Into the realms of day. He is the first
"Of half-Italian strain, the last-born heir
"To thine old age by fair Lavinia given,
"Called Silvius, a royal Alban name
"(Of sylvan birth and sylvan nurture he),
"A king himself and sire of kings to come,
"By whom our race in Alba Longa reign.
"Next Procas stands, our Trojan people's boast;
"Capys and Numitor, and, named like thee,
"Æneas Sylvius, like thee renowned
"For faithful honor and for deeds of war,
"When he ascends at last his Alban throne.
"Behold what warrior youth they be! How strong
"Their goodly limbs! Above their shaded brows
"The civic oak they wear! For thee they build
"Nomentum, and the walls of Gabii,
"Fidena too, and on the mountains pile
"Collatia's citadels, Pometii,
"Bola and Cora, Castrum-Inui —
"Such be the names the nameless lands shall bear.
"See, in that line of sires the son of Mars,

"Great Romulus, of Ilian mother born,
"From far-descended line of Trojan kings!
"See from his helm the double crest uprear,
"While his celestial father in his mien
"Shows forth his birth divine! Of him, my son,
"Great Rome shall rise, and, favored of his star,
"Have power world-wide, and men of godlike mind.
"She clasps her seven hills in single wall,
"Proud mother of the brave! So Cybele,
"The Berecynthian goddess, castle-crowned,
"On through the Phrygian kingdoms speeds her car,
"Exulting in her hundred sons divine,
"All numbered with the gods, all throned on high.

"Let now thy visionary glance look long
"On this thy race, these Romans that be thine.
"Here Cæsar, of Iulus' glorious seed,
"Behold ascending to the world of light!
"Behold, at last, that man, for this is he,
"So oft unto thy listening ears foretold,
"Augustus Cæsar, kindred unto Jove.
"He brings a golden age; he shall restore
"Old Saturn's sceptre to our Latin land,
"And o'er remotest Garamant and Ind
"His sway extend; the fair dominion
"Outruns th' horizon planets, yea, beyond
"The sun's bright path, where Atlas' shoulder bears
"Yon dome of heaven set thick with burning stars.
"Against his coming the far Caspian shores
"Break forth in oracles; the Mæotian land
"Trembles, and all the seven-fold mouths of Nile.

"Not o'er domain so wide Alcides passed,
"Although the brazen-footed doe he slew
"And stilled the groves of Erymanth, and bade
"The beast of Lerna at his arrows quail.
"Nor half so far triumphant Bacchus drove,
"With vine-entwisted reins, his frolic team
"Of tigers from the tall-topped Indian hill.

"Still do we doubt if heroes' deeds can fill
"A realm so wide? Shall craven fear constrain
"Thee or thy people from Ausonia's shore?
"Look, who is he I may discern from far
"By olive-branch and holy emblems known?
"His flowing locks and hoary beard, behold!
"Fit for a Roman king! By hallowed laws
"He shall found Rome anew — from mean estate
"In lowly Cures led to mightier sway.
"But after him arises one whose reign
"Shall wake the land from slumber: Tullus then
"Shall stir slack chiefs to battle, rallying
"His hosts which had forgot what triumphs be.
"Him boastful Ancus follows hard upon,
"O'erflushed with his light people's windy praise.
"Wilt thou see Tarquins now? And haughty hand
"Of vengeful Brutus seize the signs of power?
"He first the consul's name shall take; he first
"Th' inexorable fasces sternly bear.
"When his own sons in rash rebellion join,
"The father and the judge shall sentence give
"In beauteous freedom's cause — unhappy he!
"Howe'er the age to come the story tell,

"'T will bless such love of honor and of Rome.
"See Decius, sire and son, the Drusi, see!
"Behold Torquatus with his axe! Look where
"Camillus brings the Gallic standards home!

"But who are these in glorious armor clad
"And equal power? In this dark world of cloud
"Their souls in concord move; — but woe is me!
"What duel 'twixt them breaks, when by and by
"The light of life is theirs, and forth they call
"Their long-embattled lines to carnage dire!
"Allied by nuptial truce, the sire descends
"From Alpine rampart and that castled cliff,
"Monœcus by the sea; the son arrays
"His hostile legions in the lands of morn.
"Forbear, my children! School not your great souls
"In such vast wars, nor turn your giant strength
"Against the bowels of your native land!
"But be thou first, O first in mercy! thou
"Who art of birth Olympian! Fling away
"Thy glorious sword, mine offspring and mine heir!

"Yonder is one whose chariot shall ascend
"The laurelled Capitolian steep; he rides
"In glory o'er Achæa's hosts laid low,
"And Corinth overthrown. There, too, is he
"Who shall uproot proud Argos and the towers
"Of Agamemnon; vanquishing the heir
"Even of Æacus, the warrior seed
"Of Peleus' son; such vengeance shall be wrought
"For Troy's slain sires, and violated shrines!

"Or who could fail great Cato's name to tell?
"Or, Cossus, thine? or in oblivion leave
"The sons of Gracchus? or the Scipios,
"Twin thunderbolts of war, and Libya's bane?
"Or, more than kingly in his mean abode,
"Fabricius? or Serranus at the plough?
"Ye Fabii, how far would ye prolong
"My weary praise? But see! 't is Maximus,
"Who by wise waiting saves his native land.

"Let others melt and mould the breathing bronze
"To forms more fair, — aye! out of marble bring
"Features that live; let them plead causes well;
"Or trace with pointed wand the cycled heaven,
"And hail the constellations as they rise;
"But thou, O Roman, learn with sovereign sway
"To rule the nations. Thy great art shall be
"To keep the world in lasting peace, to spare
"The humbled foe, and crush to earth the proud."

So did Anchises speak, then, after pause,
Thus to their wondering ears his word prolonged:
"Behold Marcellus, bright with glorious spoil,
"In lifted triumph through his warriors move!
"The Roman power in tumultuous days
"He shall establish; he rides forth to quell
"Afric and rebel Gaul; and to the shrine
"Of Romulus the third-won trophy brings."
Then spoke Æneas, for he now could see
A beauteous youth in glittering dress of war,
Though of sad forehead and down-dropping eyes:

"Say, father, who attends the prince? a son?
"Or of his greatness some remoter heir?
"How his friends praise him, and how matchless he!
"But mournful night rests darkly o'er his brow."
With brimming eyes Anchises answer gave:
"Ask not, O son, what heavy weight of woe
"Thy race shall bear, when fate shall just reveal
"This vision to the world, then yield no more.
"O gods above, too glorious did ye deem
"The seed of Rome, had this one gift been sure?
"The lamentation of a multitude
"Arises from the field of Mars, and strikes
"The city's heart. O Father Tiber, see
"What pomp of sorrow near the new-made tomb
"Beside thy fleeting stream! What Ilian youth
"Shall e'er his Latin kindred so advance
"In hope of glory? When shall the proud land
"Of Romulus of such a nursling boast?
"Ah, woe is me! O loyal heart and true!
"O brave, right arm invincible! What foe
"Had 'scaped his onset in the shock of arms,
"Whether on foot he strode, or if he spurred
"The hot flanks of his war-horse flecked with foam?
"O lost, lamented child! If thou evade
"Thy evil star, Marcellus thou shalt be.
"O bring me lilies! Bring with liberal hand!
"Sad purple blossoms let me throw — the shade
"Of my own kin to honor, heaping high
"My gifts upon his grave! So let me pay
"An unavailing vow!"

Then, far and wide

Through spacious fields of air, they wander free,
Witnessing all; Anchises guides his son
From point to point, and quickens in his mind
Hunger for future fame. Of wars he tells
Soon imminent; of fair Laurentum's tribes;
Of King Latinus' town; and shows what way
Each task and hardship to prevent, or bear.

Now Sleep has portals twain, whereof the one
Is horn, they say, and easy exit gives
To visions true; the other, gleaming white
With polished ivory, the dead employ
To people night with unsubstantial dreams.
Here now Anchises bids his son farewell;
And with Sibylla, his companion sage,
Up through that ivory portal lets him rise.
Back to his fleet and his dear comrades all
Æneas hastes. Then hold they their straight course
Into Caieta's bay. An anchor holds
Each lofty prow; the sterns stand firm on shore.

END OF BOOK VI

BOOK VII

ONE more immortal name thy death bequeathed,
Nurse of Æneas, to Italian shores,
Caieta; there thy honor hath a home;
Thy bones a name: and on Hesperia's breast
Their proper glory. When Æneas now
The tribute of sepulchral vows had paid
Beside the funeral mound, and o'er the seas
Stillness had fallen, he flung forth his sails,
And leaving port pursued his destined way.
Freshly the night-winds breathe; the cloudless moon
Outpours upon his path unstinted beam,
And with far-trembling glory smites the sea.

Close to the lands of Circe soon they fare,
Where the Sun's golden daughter in far groves
Sounds forth her ceaseless song; her lofty hall
Is fragrant every night with flaring brands
Of cedar, giving light the while she weaves
With shrill-voiced shuttle at her linens fine.
From hence are heard the loud lament and wrath
Of lions, rebels to their linkèd chains
And roaring all night long; great bristly boars
And herded bears, in pinfold closely kept,
Rage horribly, and monster-wolves make moan;
Whom the dread goddess with foul juices strong
From forms of men drove forth, and bade to wear

The mouths and maws of beasts in Circe's thrall.
But lest the sacred Trojans should endure
Such prodigy of doom, or anchor there
On that destroying shore, kind Neptune filled
Their sails with winds of power, and sped them on
In safety past the perils of that sea.

Now morning flushed the wave, and saffron-garbed
Aurora from her rose-red chariot beamed
In highest heaven; the sea-winds ceased to stir;
A sudden calm possessed the air, and tides
Of marble smoothness met the laboring oar.
Then, gazing from the deep, Æneas saw
A stretch of groves, whence Tiber's smiling stream,
Its tumbling current rich with yellow sands,
Burst seaward forth: around it and above
Shore-haunting birds of varied voice and plume
Flattered the sky with song, and, circling far
O'er river-bed and grove, took joyful wing.
Thither to landward now his ships he steered,
And sailed, high-hearted, up the shadowy stream.

Hail, Erato! while olden kings and thrones
And all their sequent story I unfold!
How Latium's honor stood, when alien ships
Brought war to Italy, and from what cause
The primal conflict sprang, O goddess, breathe
Upon thy bard in song. Dread wars I tell,
Array of battle, and high-hearted kings
Thrust forth to perish, when Etruria's host
And all Hesperia gathered to the fray.

Events of grander march impel my song,
And loftier task I try.
Latinus, then
An aged king, held long-accepted sway
O'er tranquil vales and towns. He was the son
Of Faunus, so the legend tells, who wed
The nymph Marica of Laurentian stem.
Picus was Faunus' father, whence the line
To Saturn's loins ascends. O heavenly sire,
From thee the stem began! But Fate had given
To King Latinus' body no heirs male:
For taken in the dawning of his day
His only son had been; and now his home
And spacious palace one sole daughter kept,
Who was grown ripe to wed and of full age
To take a husband. Many suitors hied
From all Ausonia and Latium's bounds;
But comeliest in all their princely throng
Came Turnus, of a line of mighty sires.
Him the queen mother chiefly loved, and yearned
To call him soon her son. But omens dire
And menaces from Heaven withstood her will.
A laurel-tree grew in the royal close,
Of sacred leaf and venerated age,
Which, when he builded there his wall and tower,
Father Latinus found, and hallowed it
To Phœbus' grace and power, wherefrom the name
Laurentian, which his realm and people bear.
Unto this tree-top, wonderful to tell,
Came hosts of bees, with audible acclaim
Voyaging the stream of air, and seized a place

On the proud, pointing crest, where the swift swarm,
With interlacement of close-clinging feet,
Swung from the leafy bough. "Behold, there comes,"
The prophet cried, "a husband from afar!
"To the same region by the self-same path
"Behold an arm'd host taking lordly sway
"Upon our city's crown!" Soon after this,
When, coming to the shrine with torches pure,
Lavinia kindled at her father's side
The sacrifice, swift seemed the flame to burn
Along her flowing hair — O sight of woe!
Over her broidered snood it sparkling flew,
Lighting her queenly tresses and her crown
Of jewels rare: then, wrapt in flaming cloud,
From hall to hall the fire-god's gift she flung.
This omen dread and wonder terrible
Was rumored far: for prophet-voices told
Bright honors on the virgin's head to fall
By Fate's decree, but on her people, war.

The King, sore troubled by these portents, sought
Oracular wisdom of his sacred sire,
Faunus, the fate-revealer, where the groves
Stretch under high Albunea, and her stream
Roars from its haunted well, exhaling through
Vast, gloomful woods its pestilential air.
Here all Œnotria's tribes ask oracles
In dark and doubtful days: here, when the priest
Has brought his gifts, and in the night so still,
Couched on spread fleeces of the offered flock,
Awaiting slumber lies, then wondrously

A host of flitting shapes he sees, and hears
Voices that come and go: with gods he holds
High converse, or in deep Avernian gloom
Parleys with Acheron. Thither drew near
Father Latinus, seeking truth divine.
Obedient to the olden rite, he slew
A hundred fleecy sheep, and pillowed lay
Upon their outstretched skins. Straightway a voice
Out of the lofty forest met his prayer.
"Seek not in wedlock with a Latin lord
"To join thy daughter, O my son and seed!
"Beware this purposed marriage! There shall come
"Sons from afar, whose blood shall bear our name
"Starward; the children of their mighty loins,
"As far as eve and morn enfold the seas,
"Shall see a subject world beneath their feet
"Submissive lie."

This admonition given
Latinus hid not. But on restless wing
Rumor had spread it, when the men of Troy
Along the river-bank of mounded green
Their fleet made fast. Æneas and his chiefs,
With fair Iulus, under spreading boughs
Of one great tree made resting-place, and set
The banquet on. Thin loaves of altar-bread
Along the sward to bear their meats were laid
(Such was the will of Jove), and wilding fruits
Rose heaping high, with Ceres' gift below.
Soon, all things else devoured, their hunger turned
To taste the scanty bread, which they attacked
With tooth and nail audacious, and consumed

Both round and square of that predestined leaven.
"Look, how we eat our tables even!" cried
Iulus, in a jest. Such was the word
Which bade their burdens fall. From his boy's lip
The father caught this utterance of Fate,
Silent with wonder at the ways of Heaven;
Then swift he spoke: "Hail! O my destined shore,
"Protecting deities of Ilium, hail!
"Here is our home, our country here! This day
"I publish the mysterious prophecy
"By Sire Anchises given: 'My son,' said he,
"'When hunger in strange lands shall bid devour
"'The tables of thy banquet gone, then hope
"'For home, though weary, and take thought to build
"'A dwelling and a battlement.' Behold!
"This was our fated hunger! This last proof
"Will end our evil days. Up, then! For now
"By morning's joyful beam we will explore
"What men, what cities, in this region be,
"And, leaving ship, our several errands ply.
"Your gift to Jove outpour! Make thankful prayer
"Unto Anchises' shade! To this our feast
"Bring back the flowing wine!" Thereat he bound
His forehead with green garland, calling loud
Upon the Genius of that place, and Earth,
Eldest of names divine; the Nymphs he called,
And river-gods unknown; his voice invoked
The night, the omen-stars through night that roll:
Jove, Ida's child, and Phrygia's fertile Queen:
He called his mother from Olympian skies,
And sire from Erebus. Lo, o'er his head

Three times unclouded Jove omnipotent
In thunder spoke, and, with effulgent ray
From his ethereal tract outreaching far,
Shook visibly the golden-gleaming air.
Swift, through the concourse of the Trojans, spread
News of the day at hand when they should build
Their destined walls. So, with rejoicing heart
At such vast omen, they set forth a feast
With zealous emulation, ranging well
The wine-cups fair with many a garland crowned.

Soon as the morrow with the lamp of dawn
Looked o'er the world, they took their separate ways,
Exploring shore and towns; here spread the pools
And fountain of Numicius; here they see
The river Tiber, where bold Latins dwell.
Anchises' son chose out from his brave band
A hundred envoys, bidding them depart
To the King's sacred city, each enwreathed
With Pallas' silver leaf; and gifts they bear
To plead for peace and friendship at his throne.
While on this errand their swift steps are sped,
Æneas, by a shallow moat and small,
His future city shows, breaks ground, and girds
With mound and breastwork like a camp of war
The Trojans' first abode. Soon, making way
To where the Latin citadel uprose,
The envoys scanned the battlements, and paused
Beneath its wall. Outside the city gates
Fair youths and striplings in life's early bloom
Course with swift steeds, or steer through dusty cloud

The whirling chariot, or stretch stout bows,
Or hurl the seasoned javelin, or strive
In boxing-bout and foot-race: one of these
Made haste on horseback to the aged King,
With tidings of a stranger company
In foreign garb approaching. The good King
Bade call them to his house, and took his seat
In mid-court on his high, ancestral throne.
Large and majestical the castle rose:
A hundred columns lifted it in air
Upon the city's crown — the royal keep
Of Picus of Laurentum; round it lay
Deep, gloomy woods by olden worship blest.
Here kings took sceptre and the fasces proud
With omens fair; the selfsame sacred place
Was senate-house and temple; here was found
A hall for hallowed feasting, where a ram
Was offered up, and at long banquet-boards
The nation's fathers sat in due array.
Here ranged ancestral statues roughly hewn
Of ancient cedar-wood: King Italus;
Father Sabinus, planter of the vine,
A curving sickle in his sculptured hand;
Gray-bearded Saturn; and the double brow
Of Janus' head; and other sires and kings
Were wardens of the door, with many a chief
Wounded in battle for his native land.
Trophies of arms in goodly order hung
Along the columns: chariots of war
From foeman taken, axes of round blade,
Plumed helmets, bolts and barriers of steel

From city-gates, shields, spears, and beaks of bronze
From captured galleys by the conqueror torn.
Here, wielding his Quirinal augur-staff,
Girt in scant shift, and bearing on his left
The sacred oval shield, appeared enthroned
Picus, breaker of horses, whom his bride,
Enamoured Circe, smote with golden wand,
And, raining o'er him potent poison-dew,
Changed to a bird of pied and dappled wings.

In such a temple of his gods did Sire
Latinus, on hereditary throne,
Welcome the Trojans to his halls, and thus
With brow serene gave greeting as they came:
"O sons of Dardanus, think not unknown
"Your lineage and city! Rumored far
"Your venturous voyage has been. What seek ye here?
"What cause, what quest, has brought your barks and
you
"O'er the blue waters to Ausonia's hills?
"What way uncharted, or wild stress of storm,
"Or what that sailors suffer in mid-sea,
"Unto this river bank and haven bore?
"Doubt not our welcome! We of Latin land
"Are Saturn's sons, whose equitable minds,
"Not chained by statute or compulsion, keep
"In freedom what the god's good custom gave.
"Now I bethink me our Ausonian seers
"Have dark, dim lore that 't was this land gave birth
"To Dardanus, who after took his way
"Through Phrygian Ida's towns and Samothrace.

"Once out of Tuscan Corythus he fared;
"But now in golden house among the stars
"He has a throne, and by his altars blest
"Adds to the number of the gods we praise."

He spoke; Ilioneus this answer made:
"O King, great heir of Faunus! No dark storm
"Impelled us o'er the flood thy realm to find.
"Nor star deceived, nor strange, bewildering shore
"Threw out of our true course; but we are come
"By our free choice and with deliberate aim
"To this thy town, though exiled forth of realms
"Once mightiest of all the sun-god sees
"When moving from his utmost eastern bound.
"From Jove our line began; the sons of Troy
"Boast Jove to be their sire, and our true King
"Is of Olympian seed. To thine abode
"Trojan Æneas sent us. How there burst
"O'er Ida's vales from dread Mycenæ's kings
"A tempest vast, and by what stroke of doom
"All Asia's world with Europe clashed in war,
"That lone wight hears whom earth's remotest isle
"Has banished to the Ocean's rim, or he
"Whose dwelling is the ample zone that burns
"Betwixt the changeful sun-god's milder realms,
"Far severed from the world. We are the men
"From war's destroying deluge safely borne
"Over the waters wide. We only ask
"Some low-roofed dwelling for our fathers' gods,
"Some friendly shore, and, what to all is free,
"Water and air. We bring no evil name

"Upon thy people; thy renown will be
"But wider spread; nor of a deed so fair
"Can grateful memory die. Ye ne'er will rue
"That to Ausonia's breast ye gathered Troy.
"I swear thee by the favored destinies
"Of great Æneas, by his strength of arm
"In friendship or in war, that many a tribe
"(O, scorn us not, that, bearing olive green,
"With suppliant words we come), that many a throne
"Has sued us to be friends. But Fate's decree
"To this thy realm did guide. Here Dardanus
"Was born; and with reiterate command
"This way Apollo pointed to the stream
"Of Tiber and Numicius' haunted spring.
"Lo, these poor tributes from his greatness gone
"Æneas sends, these relics snatched away
"From Ilium burning: with this golden bowl
"Anchises poured libation when he prayed;
"And these were Priam's splendor, when he gave
"Laws to his gathered states; this sceptre his,
"This diadem revered, and beauteous pall,
"Handwork of Asia's queens."
So ceased to speak
Ilioneus. But King Latinus gazed
Unanswering on the ground, all motionless
Save for his musing eyes. The broidered pall
Of purple, and the sceptre Priam bore,
Moved little on his kingly heart, which now
Pondered of giving to the bridal bed
His daughter dear. He argues in his mind
The oracle of Faunus: — might this be

That destined bridegroom from an alien land,
To share his throne, to get a progeny
Of glorious valor, which by mighty deeds
Should win the world for kingdom? So at last
With joyful brow he spoke: "Now let the gods
"Our purpose and their own fair promise bless!
"Thou hast, O Trojan, thy desire. Thy gifts
"I have not scorned; nor while Latinus reigns
"Shall ye lack riches in my plenteous land,
"Not less than Trojan store. But where is he,
"Æneas' self? If he our royal love
"So much desire, and have such urgent mind
"To be our guest and friend, let him draw near,
"Nor turn him from well-wishing looks away!
"My offering and pledge of peace shall be
"To clasp your monarch's hand. Bear back, I pray,
"This answer to your King: my dwelling holds
"A daughter, whom with husband of her blood
"Great signs in heaven and from my father's tomb
"Forbid to wed. A son from alien shores
"They prophesy for Latium's heir, whose seed
"Shall lift our glory to the stars divine.
"I am persuaded this is none but he,
"That man of destiny; and if my heart
"Be no false prophet, I desire it so."

Thus having said, the sire took chosen steeds
From his full herd, whereof, well-groomed and fair,
Three hundred stood within his ample pale.
Of these to every Teucrian guest he gave
A courser swift and strong, in purple clad

And broidered housings gay; on every breast
Hung chains of gold; in golden robes arrayed,
They champed the red gold curb their teeth between.
For offering to Æneas, he bade send
A chariot, with chargers twain of seed
Ethereal, their nostrils breathing fire:
The famous kind which guileful Circe bred,
Cheating her sire, and mixed the sun-god's team
With brood-mares earthly born. The sons of Troy,
Such gifts and greetings from Latinus bearing,
Rode back in pomp his words of peace to bring.

But lo! from Argos on her voyage of air
Rides the dread spouse of Jove. She, sky-enthroned
Above the far Sicilian promontory,
Pachynus, sees Dardania's rescued fleet,
And all Æneas' joy. The prospect shows
Houses a-building, lands of safe abode,
And the abandoned ships. With bitter grief
She stands at gaze: then with storm-shaken brows,
Thus from her heart lets loose the wrathful word:
"O hated race! O Phrygian destinies —
"To mine forevermore (unhappy me!)
"A scandal and offense! Did no one die
"On Troy's embattled plain? Could captured slaves
"Not be enslaved again? Was Ilium's flame
"No warrior's funeral pyre? Did they walk safe
"Through serried swords and congregated fires?
"At last, methought, my godhead might repose,
"And my full-fed revenge in slumber lie.
"But nay! Though flung forth from their native land,

"I o'er the waves, with enmity unstayed,
"Dared give them chase, and on that exiled few
"Hurled the whole sea. I smote the sons of Troy
"With ocean's power and heaven's. But what availed
"Syrtes, or Scylla, or Charybdis' waves?
"The Trojans are in Tiber; and abide
"Within their prayed-for land delectable,
"Safe from the seas and me! Mars once had power
"The monstrous Lapithæ to slay; and Jove
"To Dian's honor and revenge gave o'er
"The land of Calydon. What crime so foul
"Was wrought by Lapithæ or Calydon?
"But I, Jove's wife and Queen, who in my woes
"Have ventured each bold stroke my power could find,
"And every shift essayed, — behold me now
"Outdone by this Æneas! If so weak
"My own prerogative of godhead be,
"Let me seek strength in war, come whence it will!
"If Heaven I may not move, on Hell I call.
"To bar him from his Latin throne exceeds
"My fated power. So be it! Fate has given
"Lavinia for his bride. But long delays
"I still can plot, and to the high event
"Deferment and obstruction. I can smite
"The subjects of both kings. Let sire and son
"Buy with their people's blood this marriage-bond!
"Let Teucrian and Rutulian slaughter be
"Thy virgin dower, and Bellona's blaze
"Light thee the bridal bed! Not only teemed
"The womb of Hecuba with burning brand,

"And brought forth nuptial fires; but Venus, too,
"Such offspring bore, a second Paris, who
"To their new Troy shall fatal wedlock bring."

So saying, with aspect terrible she sped
Earthward her way; and called from gloom of hell
Alecto, woeful power, from cloudy throne
Among the Furies, where her heart is fed
With horrid wars, wrath, vengeance, treason foul,
And fatal feuds. Her father Pluto loathes
The creature he engendered, and with hate
Her hell-born sister-fiends the monster view.
A host of shapes she wears, and many a front
Of frowning black brows viper-garlanded.
Juno to her this goading speech addressed:
"O daughter of dark Night, arouse for me
"Thy wonted powers and our task begin!
"Lest now my glory fail, my royal name
"Be vanquished, while Æneas and his crew
"Cheat with a wedlock bond the Latin King
"And seize Italia's fields. Thou canst thrust on
"Two loving brothers to draw sword and slay,
"And ruin homes with hatred, calling in
"The scourge of Furies and avenging fires.
"A thousand names thou bearest, and thy ways
"Of ruin multiply a thousand-fold.
"Arouse thy fertile breast! Go, rend in twain
"This plighted peace! Breed calumnies and sow
"Causes of battle, till yon warrior hosts
"Cry out for swords and leap to gird them on."

Straightway Alecto, through whose body flows
The Gorgon poison, took her viewless way
To Latium and the lofty walls and towers
Of the Laurentian King. Crouching she sate
In silence on the threshold of the bower
Where Queen Amata in her fevered soul
Pondered, with all a woman's wrath and fear,
Upon the Trojans and the marriage-suit
Of Turnus. From her Stygian hair the fiend
A single serpent flung, which stole its way
To the Queen's very heart, that, frenzy-driven,
She might on her whole house confusion pour.
Betwixt her smooth breast and her robe it wound
Unfelt, unseen, and in her wrathful mind
Instilled its viper soul. Like golden chain
Around her neck it twined, or stretched along
The fillets on her brow, or with her hair
Enwrithing coiled; then on from limb to limb
Slipped tortuous. Yet though the venom strong
Thrilled with its first infection every vein,
And touched her bones with fire, she knew it not,
Nor yielded all her soul, but made her plea
In gentle accents such as mothers use;
And many a tear she shed, about her child,
Her darling, destined for a Phrygian's bride:
"O father! can we give Lavinia's hand
"To Trojan fugitives? why wilt thou show
"No mercy on thy daughter, nor thyself;
"Nor unto me, whom at the first fair wind
"That wretch will leave deserted, bearing far
"Upon his pirate ship my stolen child?

"Was it not thus that Phrygian shepherd came
"To Lacedæmon, ravishing away
"Helen, the child of Leda, whom he bore
"To those false Trojan lands? Hast thou forgot
"Thy plighted word? Where now thy boasted love
"Of kith and kin, and many a troth-plight given
"Unto our kinsman Turnus? If we need
"An alien son, and Father Faunus' words
"Irrevocably o'er thy spirit brood,
"I tell thee every land not linked with ours
"Under one sceptre, but distinct and free,
"Is alien; and 't is thus the gods intend.
"Indeed, if Turnus' ancient race be told,
"It sprang of Inachus, Acrisius,
"And out of mid-Mycenæ."

But she sees
Her lord Latinus resolute, her words
An effort vain; and through her body spreads
The Fury's deeply venomed viper-sting.
Then, woe-begone, by dark dreams goaded on,
She wanders aimless, fevered and unstrung
Along the public ways; as oft one sees
Beneath the twisted whips a leaping top
Sped in long spirals through a palace-close
By lads at play: obedient to the thong,
It weaves wide circles in the gaping view
Of its small masters, who admiring see
The whirling boxwood made a living thing
Under their lash. So fast and far she roved
From town to town among the clansmen wild.
Then to the wood she ran, feigning to feel

The madness Bacchus loves; for she essays
A fiercer crime, by fiercer frenzy moved.
Now in the leafy dark of mountain vales
She hides her daughter, ravished thus away
From Trojan bridegroom and the wedding-feast.
"Hail, Bacchus! Thou alone," she shrieked and raved,
"Art worthy such a maid. For thee she bears
"The thyrsus with soft ivy-clusters crowned,
"And trips ecstatic in thy beauteous choir.
"For thee alone my daughter shall unbind
"The glory of her virgin hair." Swift runs
The rumor of her deed; and, frenzy-driven,
The wives of Latium to the forests fly,
Enkindled with one rage. They leave behind
Their desolated hearths, and let rude winds
O'er neck and tresses blow; their voices fill
The welkin with convulsive shriek and wail;
And, with fresh fawn-skins on their bodies bound,
They brandish vine-clad spears. The Queen herself
Lifts high a blazing pine tree, while she sings
A wedding-song for Turnus and her child.
With bloodshot glance and anger wild, she cries:
"Ho! all ye Latin wives, if e'er ye knew
"Kindness for poor Amata, if ye care
"For a wronged mother's woes, O, follow me!
"Cast off the matron fillet from your brows,
"And revel to our mad, voluptuous song."

Thus, through the woodland haunt of creatures wild,
Alecto urges on the raging Queen
With Bacchus' cruel goad. But when she deemed

The edge of wrath well whetted, and the house
Of wise Latinus of all reason reft,
Then soared the black-winged goddess to the walls
Of the bold Rutule, to the city built
(So runs the tale) by beauteous Danaë
And her Acrisian people, shipwrecked there
By south wind strong. Its name was Ardea
In language of our sires, and that proud name
Of Ardea still it wears, though proud no more.
Here Turnus in the gloom of midnight lay
Half-sleeping in his regal hall. For him
Alecto her grim fury-guise put by,
And wore an old crone's face, her baleful brow
Delved deep with wrinkled age, her hoary hair
In sacred fillet bound, and garlanded
With leaf of olive: Calybe she seemed,
An aged servitress of Juno's shrine,
And in this seeming thus the prince addressed:—
"O Turnus, wilt thou tamely see thy toil
"Lavished in vain? and thy true throne consigned
"To Trojan wanderers? The King repels
"Thy noble wooing and thy war-won dower.
"He summons him a son of alien stem
"To take his kingdom. Rouse thee now, and front,
"Scorned and without reward, these perilous days.
"Tread down that Tuscan host! Protect the peace
"Of Latium from its foe! Such is the word
"Which, while in night and slumber thou wert laid,
"Saturnia's godhead, visibly revealed,
"Bade me declare. Up, therefore, and array
"Thy warriors in arms! Swift sallying forth

"From thy strong city-gates, on to the fray
"Exultant go! Assail the Phrygian chiefs
"Who tent them by thy beauteous river's marge,
"And burn their painted galleys! 't is the will
"Of gods above that speaks. Yea, even the King
"Latinus, if he will not heed thy plea,
"Nor hear thy wooing, shall be taught too late
"What Turnus is in panoply of war."

In mocking answer to the prophetess
The warrior thus replied: "That stranger fleet
"In Tiber moored, not, as thy folly prates,
"Of me unnoted lies. Vex me no more
"With thy fantastic terror. Juno's power
"Is watchful of my cause. 'T is mere old age,
"Gone to decay and dotage, fills thy breast
"With vain foreboding, and, while kings contend,
"Scares and deceives thy visionary eye.
"Guard thou in yonder temple's holy shade
"The images divine! Of peace and war
"Let men and warriors the burden bear!"
So kindled he Alecto's wrath to flame;
And even as he spoke a shudder thrilled
The warrior's body, and his eyeballs stood
Stonily staring at the hydra hair
Which hissed and writhed above the grisly head
Of the large-looming fiend. With eyes of fire
Horribly rolling, she repelled him far,
While he but faltered speechless. She upraised
Two coiling snakes out of her tresses, cracked
The lashes of her scourge, and wrathfully,

With raving lips replied: "Look well on me,
"Gone to decay and dotage of old age!
"And mocked with foolish fear while kings contend!
"Wilt hearken now! Behold me, hither flown
"From where my sister-furies dwell! My hands
"Bring bloody death and war." She spoke, and hurled
Her firebrand at the hero, thrusting deep
Beneath his heart her darkly smouldering flame.
Then horror broke his sleep, and fearful sweat
Dripped from his every limb. He shrieked aloud
For arms; and seized the ready arms that lay
Around his couch and hall. Then o'er his soul
The lust of battle and wild curse of war
Broke forth in angry power, as when the flames
Of faggots round the bubbling cauldron sing,
And up the waters leap; the close-kept flood
Brims over, streaming, foaming, breaking bound,
And flings thick clouds in air.
He, summoning
His chieftains, bade them on Latinus move,
Break peace, take arms, and, over Italy
Their shields extending, to thrust forth her foe:
Himself for Teucrian with Latin joined
Was more than match. He called upon the gods
In witness of his vows: while, nothing loth,
Rutulia's warriors rushed into array;
Some by his youth and noble beauty moved,
Some by his kingly sires and fame in arms.

While Turnus stirred Rutulia's valiant souls,
Alecto on her Stygian pinions sped

To where the Teucrians lay. She scanned the ground
With eager guile, where by the river's marge
Fair-browed Iulus with his nets and snares
Rode fiercely to the chase. Then o'er his hounds
That hell-born virgin breathed a sudden rage,
And filled each cunning nostril with the scent
Of stags, till forth in wild pursuit they flew.
Here all the woe began, and here awoke
In rustic souls the swift-enkindling war.
For a fair stag, tall-antlered, stolen away
Even from its mother's milk, had long been kept
By Tyrrhus and his sons — the shepherd he
Of all the royal flocks, and forester
Of a wide region round. With fondest care
Their sister Silvia entwined its horns
With soft, fresh garlands, tamed it to run close,
And combed the creature, or would bring to bathe
At a clear, crystal spring. It knew the hands
Of all its gentle masters, and would feed
From their own dish; or wandering through the wood,
Come back unguided to their friendly door,
Though deep the evening shade. Iulus' dogs
Now roused this wanderer in their ravening chase,
As, drifted down-stream far from home it lay,
On a green bank a-cooling. From bent bow
Ascanius, eager for a hunter's praise,
Let go his shaft; nor did Alecto fail
His aim to guide: but, whistling through the air,
The light-winged reed pierced deep in flank and side.
Swift to its cover fled the wounded thing,

And crept loud-moaning to its wonted stall,
Where, like a blood-stained suppliant, it seemed
To fill that shepherd's house with plaintive prayer.

Then Silvia the sister, smiting oft
On breast and arm, made cry for help, and called
The sturdy rustics forth in gathering throng.
These now (for in the silent forest crouched
The cruel Fury) swift to battle flew.
One brandished a charred stake, another swung
A knotted cudgel, as rude anger shapes
Its weapon of whate'er the searching eye
First haps to fall on. Tyrrhus roused his clans,
Just when by chance he split with blows of wedge
An oak in four; and, panting giant breath,
Shouldered his woodman's axe. Alecto then,
Prompt to the stroke of mischief, soared aloft
From where she spying sate, to the steep roof
Of a tall byre, and from its peak of straw
Blew a wild signal on a shepherd's horn,
Outflinging her infernal note so far
That all the forest shuddered, and the grove
Throbbed to its deepest glen. Cold Trivia's lake
From end to end gave ear, and every wave
Of the white stream of Nar, the lonely pools
Of still Velinus heard: while at the sound
Pale mothers to their breasts their children drew.
Swift to the signal of the dreadful horn,
Snatching their weapons rude, the freeborn swains
Assembled for the fray; the Trojan bands
Poured from their bivouac with instant aid

For young Ascanius. In array of war
Both stand confronting. Not mere rustic brawl
With charred oak-staff and cudgel is the fight,
But with the two-edged steel; the naked swords
Wave like dark-bladed harvest-field, while far
The brazen arms flash in the smiting sun,
And skyward fling their beam: so some wide sea,
At first but whitened in the rising wind,
Swells its slow-rolling mass and ever higher
Its billows rears, until the utmost deep
Lifts in one surge to heaven.
The first to fall
Was Almo, eldest-born of Tyrrhus' sons,
Whom, striding in the van, a loud-winged shaft
Laid low in death; deep in his throat it clung,
And silenced with his blood the dying cry
Of his frail life. Around him fell the forms
Of many a brave and strong; among them died
Gray-haired Galæsus pleading for a truce:
Righteous he was, and of Ausonian fields
A prosperous master; five full flocks had he
Of bleating sheep, and from his pastures came
Five herds of cattle home; his busy churls
Turned with a hundred ploughs his fruitful glebe.

While o'er the battle-field thus doubtful swung
The scales of war, the Fury (to her task
Now equal proven) having dyed the day
A deep-ensanguined hue, and opened fight
With death and slaughter, made no tarrying
Within Hesperia, but skyward soared,

And, loud in triumph, insolently thus
To Juno called: "See, at thy will, their strife
"Full-blown to war and woe! Could even thyself
"Command them now to truce and amity?
"But I, that with Ausonia's blood befoul
"Their Trojan hands, yet more can do, if thou
"Shift not thy purpose. For with dire alarms
"I will awake the bordering states to war,
"Enkindling in their souls the frenzied lust
"The war-god breathes; till from th' horizon round
"The reinforcement pours — I scattering seeds
"Of carnage through the land."
In answer spoke
Juno: "Enough of artifice and fear!
"Thy provocation works. Now have they joined
"In close and deadly combat, and warm blood
"Those sudden-leaping swords incarnadines,
"Which chance put in their hands. Such nuptial joys,
"Such feast of wedlock, let the famous son
"Of Venus with the King Latinus share!
"But yon Olympian Sire and King no more
"Permits thee freely in our skies to roam.
"Go, quit the field! Myself will take control
"Of hazards and of labors yet to be."
Thus Saturn's daughter spoke. Alecto then,
Unfolding far her hissing, viperous wings,
Turned toward her Stygian home, and took farewell
Of upper air. Deep in Italia lies
A region mountain-girded, widely famed,
And known in olden songs from land to land:
The valley of Amsanctus; deep, dark shades

Enclose it between forest-walls, whereby
Through thunderous stony channel serpentines
A roaring fall. Here in a monstrous cave
Are breathing-holes of hell, a vast abyss
Where Acheron opes wide its noisome jaws:
In this Alecto plunged, concealing so
Her execrable godhead, while the air
Of earth and heaven felt the curse removed.

Forthwith the sovereign hands of Juno haste
To consummate the war. The shepherds bear
Back from the field of battle to the town
The bodies of the slain: young Almo's corse
And gray Galæsus' bleeding head. They call
Just gods in heaven to look upon their wrong,
And bid Latinus see it. Turnus comes,
And, while the angry mob surveys the slain,
Adds fury to the hour. "Shall the land
"Have Trojan lords? Shall Phrygian marriages
"Debase our ancient, royal blood — and I
"Be spurned upon the threshold?" Then drew near
The men whose frenzied women-folk had held
Bacchantic orgies in the pathless grove,
Awed by Amata's name: these, gathering,
Sued loud for war. Yea, all defied the signs
And venerable omens; all withstood
Divine decrees, and clamored for revenge,
Prompted by evil powers. They besieged
The house of King Latinus, shouting loud
With emulous rage. But like a sea-girt rock
Unmoved he stood; like sea-girt rock when surge

Of waters o'er it sweeps, or howling waves
Surround; it keeps a ponderous front of power,
Though foaming cliffs around it vainly roar;
From its firm base the broken sea-weeds fall.
But when authority no whit could change
Their counsels blind, and each event fulfilled
Dread Juno's will, then with complaining prayer
The aged sire cried loud upon his gods
And on th' unheeding air: "Alas," said he,
"My doom is shipwreck, and the tempest bears
"My bark away! O wretches, your own blood
"Shall pay the forfeit for your impious crime.
"O Turnus! O abominable deed!
"Avenging woes pursue thee; to deaf gods
"Thy late and unavailing prayer shall rise.
"Now was my time to rest. But as I come
"Close to my journey's end, thou spoilest me
"Of comfort in my death." With this the King
Fled to his house and ceased his realm to guide.

A sacred custom the Hesperian land
Of Latium knew, by all the Alban hills
Honored unbroken, which wide-ruling Rome
Keeps to this day, when to new stroke she stirs
The might of Mars; if on the Danube's wave
Resolved to fling the mournful doom of war,
Or on the Caspian folk or Arabs wild;
Or chase the morning far as India's verge,
And from the Parthian despot wrest away
Our banners lost. Twin Gates of War there be,
Of fearful name, to Mars' fierce godhead vowed:

A hundred brass bars shut them, and the strength
Of uncorrupting steel; in sleepless watch
Janus the threshold keeps. 'T is here, what time
The senate's voice is war, the consul grave
In Gabine cincture and Quirinal shift
Himself the griding hinges backward moves,
And bids the Romans arm; obedient then
The legionary host makes loud acclaim,
And hoarse consent the brazen trumpets blow.
Thus King Latinus on the sons of Troy
Was urged to open war, and backward roll
Those gates of sorrow: but the aged King
Recoiled, refused the loathsome task, and fled
To solitary shades. Then from the skies
The Queen of gods stooped down, and her sole hand
The lingering portal moved; Saturnia
Swung on their hinges the barred gates of war.

Ausonia from its old tranquillity
Bursts forth in flame. Foot-soldiers through the field
Run to and fro; and mounted on tall steeds
The cavaliers in clouds of dust whirl by.
All arm in haste. Some oil the glittering shield
Or javelin bright, or on the whetstone wear
Good axes to an edge, while joyful bands
Uplift the standards or the trumpets blow.
Five mighty cities to their anvils bring
New-tempered arms: Atina — martial name —
Proud Tibur, Ardea, Crustumium,
And river-walled Antemnæ, crowned with towers.
Strong hollow helmets on their brows they draw,

And weave them willow-shields; or melt and mould
Corselets of brass or shining silver greaves;
None now for pruning-hook or sacred plough
Have love or care: but old, ancestral swords
For hardier tempering to the smith they bring.
Now peals the clarion; through the legions pass
The watchwords: the impatient yeoman takes
His helmet from the idle roof-tree hung;
While to his chariot the master yokes
The mettled war-horse, dons a shining shield
And golden mail, and buckles his good sword.

Virgins of Helicon, renew my song!
Instruct me what proud kings to battle flown
With following legions throng the serried plain.
Tell me what heroes and illustrious arms
Italia's bosom in her dawning day
Benignant bore: for your celestial minds
Have memory of the past, but faint and low
Steals glory's whisper on a mortal ear.

Foremost in fight, from shores Etrurian came
Mezentius, scornful rebel against Heaven,
His people all in arms; and at his side
Lausus his heir (no fairer youth than he,
Save Turnus of Laurentum), Lausus, skilled
To break proud horses and wild beasts to quell;
Who from Agylla's citadel in vain
Led forth his thousand warriors: worthy he
To serve a nobler sire, and happier far
If he had ne'er been born Mezentius' son.

Next after these, conspicuous o'er the plain,
With palm-crowned chariot and victorious steeds,
Rode forth well-moulded Aventinus, sprung
From shapely Hercules; upon the shield
His blazon was a hundred snakes, and showed
His father's hydra-cincture serpentine;
Him deep in Aventine's most secret grove
The priestess Rhea bore — a mortal maid
Clasped in a god's embrace the wondrous day
When, flushed with conquest of huge Geryon,
The lord of Tiryns to Laurentum drove,
And washed in Tiber's wave th' Iberian kine.
His followers brandished pointed pikes and staves,
Or smooth Sabellian bodkin tipped with steel;
But he, afoot, swung round him as he strode
A monstrous lion-skin, its bristling mane
And white teeth crowning his ferocious brow:
For garbed as Hercules he sought his King.

Then came twin brethren, leaving Tibur's keep
(Named from Tiburtus, brother of them twain)
Catillus and impetuous Coras, youth
Of Argive seed, who foremost in the van
Pressed ever where the foemen densest throng:
As when two centaurs, children of the cloud,
From mountain-tops descend in swift career,
The snows of Homole and Othrys leaving,
While crashing thickets in their pathway fall.
Nor was Præneste's founder absent there,
By Vulcan sired, among the herds and hinds,
And on a hearth-stone found (so runs the tale

Each pious age repeats) King Cæculus
With rustic legions gathered from afar:
From steep Præneste and the Gabian vale
To Juno dear, from Anio's cold stream,
From upland Hernic rocks and foaming rills,
From rich Anagnia's pastures, and the plain
Whence Amasenus pours his worshipped wave.
Not all of armor boast, and seldom sound
The chariot and shield; but out of slings
They hurl blue balls of lead, or in one hand
A brace of javelins bear; pulled o'er their brows
Are hoods of tawny wolf-skin; as they march
The left foot leaves a barefoot track behind,
A rawhide sandal on the right they wear.

Messapus came, steed-tamer, Neptune's son,
By sword and fire invincible: this day,
Though mild his people and unschooled in war,
He calls them to embattled lines, and draws
No lingering sword. Fescennia musters there,
Æqui Falisci, and what clans possess
Soracte's heights, Flavinia's fruitful farms,
Ciminian lake and mountain, and the groves
About Capena. Rank on rank they move,
Loud singing of their chieftain's praise: as when
A flock of snowy swans through clouded air
Return from feeding, and make tuneful cry
From their long throats, while Asia's rivers hear,
And lone Caÿster's startled moorland rings:
For hardly could the listening ear discern
The war-cry of a mail-clad host; the sound

Was like shrill-calling birds, when home from sea
Their soaring flock moves shoreward like a cloud.

Then, one of far-descended Sabine name,
Clausus advanced, the captain of a host,
And in himself an equal host he seemed;
From his proud loins the high-born Claudian stem
Through Latium multiplies, since Roman power
With Sabine first was wed. A cohort came
From Amiternum and the olden wall
Of Cures, called Quirites even then;
Eretum answered and Mutusca's hill
With olives clad, Velinus' flowery field,
Nomentum's fortress, the grim precipice
Of Tetrica, Severus' upland fair,
Casperia, Foruli, Himella's waves,
Tiber and Fabaris, and wintry streams
Of Nursia; to the same proud muster sped
Tuscan with Latin tribes, and loyal towns
Beside whose walls ill-omened Allia flows.
As numerous they moved as rolling waves
That stir smooth Libyan seas, when in cold floods
Sinks grim Orion's star; or like the throng
Of clustering wheat-tops in the summer sun,
Near Hermus or on Lycia's yellowing plain:
Shields clashed; their strong tramp smote the trembling ground.

Now Agamemnon's kinsman, cruel foe
To the mere name of Troy, Halæsus, yokes
The horses of his car and summons forth

A thousand savage clans at Turnus' call:
Rude men whose mattocks to the Massic hills
Bring Bacchus' bounty, or by graybeard sires
Sent from Auruncan upland and the mead
Of Sidicinum; out of Cales came
Its simple folk; and dwellers by the stream
Of many-shoaled Volturnus, close-allied
With bold Saticulan or Oscan swains.
Their arms are tapered javelins, which they wear
Bound by a coiling thong; a targe conceals
The left side, and they fight with crooked swords.

Nor shalt thou, Œbalus, depart unsung,
Whom minstrels say the nymph Sebethis bore
To Telon, who in Capri was a king
When old and gray; but that disdaining son
Quitted so small a seat, and conquering sway
Among Sarrastian folk and those wide plains
Watered by Sarnus' wave, became a king
Over Celenna, Rufræ, Batulum,
And where among her apple-orchards rise
Abella's walls. All these, as Teutons use,
Hurl a light javelin; for helm they wear
Stripped cork-tree bark; the crescent of their shields
Is gleaming bronze, and gleaming bronze the sword.

Next Ufens, mountain-bred, from Nersæ came
To join the war; of goodly fame was he
For prosperous arms: his Æquian people show
No gentle mien, but scour the woods for prey,
Or, ever-armed, across the stubborn glebe

Compel the plough; though their chief pride and joy
Are rapine, violence, and plundered store.

Next after these, his brows and helmet bound
With noble olive, from Marruvium came
A priest, brave Umbro, ordered to the field
By King Archippus: o'er the viper's brood,
And venomed river-serpents he had power
To scatter slumber with wide-waving hands
And wizard-songs. His potent arts could soothe
Their coiling rage and heal the mortal sting:
But 'gainst a Trojan sword no drug had he,
Nor could his drowsy spells his flesh repair,
Nor gathered simples from the Marsic hills.
Thee soon in wailing woods Anguitia mourned,
Thee, Lake Fucinus and its crystal wave,
Thee, many a mountain-tarn!

Next, Virbius in martial beauty rode,
Son of Hippolytus, whose mother, proud
Aricia, sent him in his flower of fame
Out of Egeria's hills and cloudy groves
Where lies Diana's gracious, gifted fane.
For legend whispers that Hippolytus,
By step-dame's plot undone, his life-blood gave
To sate his vengeful father, and was rent
In sunder by wild horses; but the grave
To air of heaven and prospect of the stars
Restored him; — for Diana's love and care
Poured out upon him Pæon's healing balm.
But Jove, almighty Sire, brooked not to see

A mortal out of death and dark reclimb
To light of life, and with a thunderbolt
Hurled to the Stygian river Phœbus' son,
Who dared such good elixir to compound.
But pitying Trivia hid Hippolytus
In her most secret cave, and gave in ward
To the wise nymph Egeria in her grove;
Where he lived on inglorious and alone,
Ranging the woods of Italy, and bore
The name of Virbius. 'T is for this cause
The hallowed woods to Trivia's temple vowed
Forbid loud-footed horses, such as spilled
Stripling and chariot on the fatal shore,
Scared by the monsters peering from the sea.
Yet did the son o'er that tumultuous plain
His battle-chariot guide and plunging team.

Lo, Turnus strides conspicuous in the van,
Full-armed, of mighty frame, his lordly head
High o'er his peers emerging! His tall helm
With flowing triple crest for ensign bears
Chimæra, whose terrific lips outpour
Volcanic fires; where'er the menace moves
Of her infernal flames and wrathful frown,
There wildest flows the purple flood of war.
On his smooth shield deep graven in the gold
Is hornèd Io — wondrous the device! —
A shaggy heifer-shape the maiden shows;
Argus is watching her, while Inachus
Pours forth his river from the pictured urn.
A storm of tramping troops, to Turnus sworn,

Throngs all the widespread plain with serried shields:
Warriors of Argos, and Auruncan bands,
Sicani, Rutuli, Sacranian hosts,
Labicum's painted targes; all who till
Thy woodland vales, O Tiber! or the shore
Numicius hallows; all whose ploughs upturn
Rutulia's hills, or that Circæan range
Where Jove of Anxur guards, and forests green
Make fair Feronia glad; where lie the fens
Of Satura, and Ufens' icy wave
Through lowland valleys seeks his seaward way.

Last came Camilla, of the Volscians bred,
Leading her mail-clad, radiant chivalry;
A warrior-virgin, of Minerva's craft
Of web and distaff, fit for woman's toil,
No follower she; but bared her virgin breast
To meet the brunt of battle, and her speed
Left even the winds behind; for she would skim
An untouched harvest ere the sickle fell,
Nor graze the quivering wheat-tops as she ran;
Or o'er the mid-sea billows' swollen surge
So swiftly race, she wet not in the wave
Her flying feet. For sight of her the youth
From field and fortress sped, and matrons grave
Stood wondering as she passed, well-pleased to see
Her royal scarf in many a purple fold
Float off her shining shoulder, her dark hair
In golden clasp caught fast, and how she bore
For arms a quiver of the Lycian mode,
And shepherd's shaft of myrtle tipped with steel.

BOOK VIII

WHEN Turnus from Laurentum's bastion proud
Published the war, and roused the dreadful note
Of the harsh trumpet's song; when on swift steeds
The lash he laid and clashed his sounding arms:
Then woke each warrior soul; all Latium stirred
With tumult and alarm; and martial rage
Enkindled youth's hot blood. The chieftains proud,
Messapus, Ufens, and that foe of Heaven,
Mezentius, compel from far and wide
Their loyal hosts, and strip the field and farm
Of husbandmen. To seek auxiliar arms
They send to glorious Diomed's domain
The herald Venulus, and bid him cry:
"Troy is to Latium come; Æneas' fleet
"Has come to land. He brings his vanquished gods,
"And gives himself to be our destined King.
"Cities not few accept him, and his name
"Through Latium waxes large. But what the foe
"By such attempt intends, what victory
"Is his presumptuous hope, if Fortune smile,
"Ætolia's lord will not less wisely fear
"Than royal Turnus or our Latin King."

Thus Latium's cause moved on. Meanwhile the heir
Of great Laomedon, who knew full well
The whole wide land astir, was vexed and tossed

In troubled seas of care. This way and that
His swift thoughts flew, and scanned with like dismay
Each partial peril or the general storm.
Thus the vexed waters at a fountain's brim,
Smitten by sunshine or the silver sphere
Of a reflected moon, send forth a beam
Of flickering light that leaps from wall to wall,
Or, skyward lifted in ethereal flight,
Glances along some rich-wrought, vaulted dome.

Now night had fallen, and all weary things,
All shapes of beast or bird, the wide world o'er,
Lay deep in slumber. So beneath the arch
Of a cold sky Æneas laid him down
Upon the river-bank, his heart sore tried
By so much war and sorrow, and gave o'er
His body to its long-delayed repose.
There, 'twixt the poplars by the gentle stream,
The River-Father, genius of that place,
Old Tiberinus visibly uprose;
A cloak of gray-green lawn he wore, his hair
O'erhung with wreath of reeds. In soothing words
Thus, to console Æneas' cares, he spoke:
"Seed of the gods! who bringest to my shore
"Thy Trojan city wrested from her foe,
"A stronghold everlasting, Latium's plain
"And fair Laurentum long have looked for thee.
"Here truly is thy home. Turn not away.
"Here the true guardians of thy hearth shall be.
"Fear not the gathering war. The wrath of Heaven
"Has stilled its swollen wave. A sign I tell:

"Lest thou shouldst deem this message of thy sleep
"A vain, deluding dream, thou soon shalt find
"In the oak-copses on my margent green,
"A huge sow, with her newly-littered brood
"Of thirty young; along the ground she lies,
"Snow-white, and round her udders her white young.
"There shall thy city stand, and there thy toil
"Shall find untroubled rest. After the lapse
"Of thrice ten rolling years, Ascanius
"Shall found a city there of noble name,
"White-City, Alba; 't is no dream I sing!
"But I instruct thee now by what wise way
"Th' impending wars may bring thee victory:
"Receive the counsel, though the words be few:
"Within this land are men of Arcady,
"Of Pallas' line, who, following in the train
"Of King Evander and his men-at-arms,
"Built them a city in the hills, and chose
"(Honoring Pallas, their Pelasgian sire),
"The name of Pallanteum. They make war
"Incessant with the Latins. Therefore call
"This people to thy side and bind them close
"In federated power. My channel fair
"And shaded shore shall guide thee where they dwell,
"And thy strong oarsmen on my waters borne
"Shall mount my falling stream. Rise, goddess-born,
"And ere the starlight fade give honor due
"To Juno, and with supplicating vow
"Avert her wrath and frown. But unto me
"Make offering in thy victorious hour,
"In time to come. I am the copious flood

"Which thou beholdest chafing at yon shores
"And parting fruitful fields: cerulean stream
"Of Tiber, favored greatly of high Heaven.
"Here shall arise my house magnificent,
"A city of all cities chief and crown."
So spake the river-god, and sank from view
Down to his deepest cave; then night and sleep
Together from Æneas fled away.

He rose, and to the orient beams of morn
His forehead gave; in both his hollowed palms
He held the sacred waters of the stream,
And called aloud: "O ye Laurentian nymphs,
"Whence flowing rills be born, and chiefly thou,
"O Father Tiber, worshipped stream divine,
"Accept Æneas, and from peril save!
"If in some hallowed lake or haunted spring
"Thy power, pitying my woes, abides,
"Or wheresoe'er the blessed place be found
"Whence first thy beauty flows, there evermore
"My hands shall bring thee gift and sacrifice.
"O chief and sovereign of Hesperian streams,
"O river-god that hold'st the plenteous horn,
"Protect us, and confirm thy words divine!"

He spoke; then chose twin biremes from the fleet,
Gave them good gear and armed their loyal crews.
But, lo! a sudden wonder met his eyes:
White gleaming through the grove, with all her brood
White like herself, on the green bank the Sow
Stretched prone. The good Æneas slew her there,

Great Juno, for a sacrifice to thee,
Himself the priest, and with the sucklings all
Beside thine altar stood. So that whole night
The god of Tiber calmed his swollen wave,
Ebbing or lingering in silent flow,
Till like some gentle lake or sleeping pool
His even waters lay, and strove no more
Against the oarsmen's toil. Upon their way
They speed with joyful sound; the well-oiled wood
Slips through the watery floor; the wondering waves,
And all the virgin forests wondering,
Behold the warriors in far-shining arms
Their painted galleys up the current drive.
O'er the long reaches of the winding flood
Their sturdy oars outweary the slow course
Of night and day. Fair groves of changeful green
Arch o'er their passage, and they seem to cleave
Green forests in the tranquil wave below.
Now had the flaming sun attained his way
To the mid-sphere of heaven, when they discerned
Walls and a citadel in distant view,
With houses few and far between; 't was there,
Where sovran Rome to-day has rivalled Heaven,
Evander's realm its slender strength displayed:
Swiftly they turned their prows and neared the town.
It chanced th' Arcadian King had come that day
To honor Hercules, Amphitryon's son,
And to the powers divine pay worship due
In groves outside the wall. Beside him stood
Pallas his son, his noblest men-at-arms,
And frugal senators, who at the shrines

Burnt incense, while warm blood of victims flowed.
But when they saw the tall ships in the shade
Of that dark forest plying noiseless oars,
The sudden sight alarmed, and all the throng
Sprang to its feet and left the feast divine.
But dauntless Pallas bade them give not o'er
The sacred festival, and spear in hand
Flew forward to a bit of rising ground,
And cried from far: "Hail, warriors! what cause
"Drives you to lands unknown, and whither bound?
"Your kin, your country? Bring ye peace or war?"
Father Æneas then held forth a bough
Of peaceful olive from the lofty ship,
Thus answering: "Men Trojan-born are we,
"Foes of the Latins, who have driven us forth
"With insolent assault. We fain would see
"Evander. Pray, deliver this, and say
"That chosen princes of Dardania
"Sue for his help in arms." So wonder fell
On Pallas, awestruck at such mighty name.
"O, come, whoe'er thou art," he said, "and speak
"In presence of my father. Enter here,
"Guest of our hearth and altar." He put forth
His right hand in true welcome, and they stood
With lingering clasp; then hand in hand advanced
Up the steep woodland, leaving Tiber's wave.

Æneas to Evander speaking fair,
These words essayed: "O best of Grecian-born!
"Whom Fortune's power now bids me seek and sue,
"Lifting this olive-branch with fillets bound,

"I have not feared thee, though I know thou art
"A Greek, and an Arcadian king, allied
"To the two sons of Atreus. For behold,
"My conscious worth, great oracles from Heaven,
"The kinship of our sires, thy own renown
"Spread through the world — all knit my cause with
thine,
"All make me glad my fates have so decreed.
"The sire and builder of the Trojan town
"Was Dardanus; but he, Electra's child,
"Came over sea to Teucria; the sire
"Of fair Electra was great Atlas, he
"Whose shoulder carries the vast orb of heaven.
"But thy progenitor was Mercury,
"And him conceiving, Maia, that white maid,
"On hoar Cyllene's frosty summit bore.
"But Maia's sire, if aught of truth be told,
"Was Atlas also, Atlas who sustains
"The weight of starry skies. Thus both our tribes
"Are one divided stem. Secure in this,
"No envoys have I sent, nor tried thy mind
"With artful first approaches, but myself,
"Risking my person and my life, have come
"A suppliant here. For both on me and thee
"The house of Daunus hurls insulting war.
"If us they quell, they doubt not to obtain
"Lordship of all Hesperia, and subdue
"Alike the northern and the southern sea.
"Accept good faith, and give! Behold, our hearts
"Quail not in battle; souls of fire are we,
"And warriors proved in many an action brave."

Æneas ceased. The other long had scanned
The hero's face, his eyes, and wondering viewed
His form and mien divine; in answer now
He briefly spoke: "With hospitable heart,
"O bravest warrior of all Trojan-born,
"I know and welcome thee. I well recall
"Thy sire Anchises, how he looked and spake.
"For I remember Priam, when he came
"To greet his sister, Queen Hesione,
"In Salamis, and thence pursued his way
"To our cool uplands of Arcadia.
"The bloom of tender boyhood then was mine,
"And with a wide-eyed wonder I did view
"Those Teucrian lords, Laomedon's great heir,
"And, towering highest in their goodly throng,
"Anchises, whom my warm young heart desired
"To speak with and to clasp his hand in mine.
"So I approached, and joyful led him home
"To Pheneus' olden wall. He gave me gifts
"The day he bade adieu; a quiver rare
"Filled with good Lycian arrows, a rich cloak
"Inwove with thread of gold, and bridle reins
"All golden, now to youthful Pallas given.
"Therefore thy plea is granted, and my hand
"Here clasps in loyal amity with thine.
"To-morrow at the sunrise thou shalt have
"My tribute for the war, and go thy way
"My glad ally. But now this festival,
"Whose solemn rite 't were impious to delay,
"I pray thee celebrate, and bring with thee
"Well-omened looks and words. Allies we are!

"Use this our sacred feast as if your own."

So saying, he bade his followers renew
Th' abandoned feast and wine; and placed each guest
On turf-built couch of green, most honoring
Æneas by a throne of maple fair
Decked with a lion's pelt and flowing mane.
Then high-born pages, with the altar's priest,
Bring on the roasted beeves and load the board
With baskets of fine bread; and wine they bring —
Of Ceres and of Bacchus gift and toil.
While good Æneas and his Trojans share
The long whole ox and meats of sacrifice.

When hunger and its eager edge were gone,
Evander spoke: "This votive holiday,
"Yon tables spread and altar so divine,
"Are not some superstition dark and vain,
"That knows not the old gods, O Trojan King!
"But as men saved from danger and great fear
"This thankful sacrifice we pay. Behold,
"Yon huge rock, beetling from the mountain wall,
"Hung from the cliff above. How lone and bare
"The hollowed mountain looks! How crag on crag
"Tumbled and tossed in huge confusion lie!
"A cavern once it was, which ran deep down
"Into the darkness. There th' half-human shape
"Of Cacus made its hideous den, concealed
"From sunlight and the day. The ground was wet
"At all times with fresh gore; the portal grim
"Was hung about with heads of slaughtered men,

"Bloody and pale — a fearsome sight to see.
"Vulcan begat this monster, which spewed forth
"Dark-fuming flames from his infernal throat,
"And vast his stature seemed. But time and tide
"Brought to our prayers the advent of a god
"To help us at our need. For Hercules,
"Divine avenger, came from laying low
"Three-bodied Geryon, whose spoils he wore
"Exultant, and with hands victorious drove
"The herd of monster bulls, which pastured free
"Along our river-valley. Cacus gazed
"In a brute frenzy, and left not untried
"Aught of bold crime or stratagem, but stole
"Four fine bulls as they fed, and heifers four,
"All matchless; but, lest hoof-tracks point his way,
"He dragged them cave-wards by the tails, confusing
"The natural trail, and hid the stolen herd
"In his dark den; and not a mark or sign
"Could guide the herdsmen to that cavern-door.
"But after, when Amphitryon's famous son,
"Preparing to depart, would from the meads
"Goad forth the full-fed herd, his lingering bulls
"Roared loud, and by their lamentable cry
"Filled grove and hills with clamor of farewell:
"One heifer from the mountain-cave lowed back
"In answer, so from her close-guarded stall
"Foiling the monster's will. Then hadst thou seen
"The wrath of Hercules in frenzy blaze
"From his exasperate heart. His arms he seized,
"His club of knotted oak, and climbed full-speed
"The wind-swept hill. Now first our people saw

"Cacus in fear, with panic in his eyes.
"Swift to the black cave like a gale he flew,
"His feet by terror winged. Scarce had he passed
"The cavern door, and broken the big chains,
"And dropped the huge rock which was pendent there
"By Vulcan's well-wrought steel; scarce blocked and barred
"The guarded gate: when there Tirynthius stood,
"With heart aflame, surveying each approach,
"Rolling this way and that his wrathful eyes,
"Gnashing his teeth. Three times his ire surveyed
"The slope of Aventine; three times he stormed
"The rock-built gate in vain; and thrice withdrew
"To rest him in the vale. But high above
"A pointed peak arose, sheer face of rock
"On every side, which towered into view
"From the long ridge above the vaulted cave,
"Fit haunt for birds of evil-boding wing.
"This peak, which leftward toward the river leaned,
"He smote upon its right — his utmost blow —
"Breaking its bases loose; then suddenly
"Thrust at it: as he thrust, the thunder-sound
"Filled all the arching sky, the river's banks
"Asunder leaped, and Tiber in alarm
"Reversed his flowing wave. So Cacus' lair
"Lay shelterless, and naked to the day
"The gloomy caverns of his vast abode
"Stood open, deeply yawning, just as if
"The riven earth should crack, and open wide
"Th' infernal world and fearful kingdoms pale,
"Which gods abhor; and to the realms on high

"The measureless abyss should be laid bare,
"And pale ghosts shrink before the entering sun.
"Now upon Cacus, startled by the glare,
"Caged in the rocks and howling horribly,
"Alcides hurled his weapons, raining down
"All sorts of deadly missiles — trunks of trees,
"And monstrous boulders from the mountain torn.
"But when the giant from his mortal strait
"No refuge knew, he blew from his foul jaws
"A storm of smoke — incredible to tell —
"And with thick darkness blinding every eye,
"Concealed his cave, uprolling from below
"One pitch-black night of mingled gloom and fire.
"This would Alcides not endure, but leaped
"Headlong across the flames, where densest hung
"The rolling smoke, and through the cavern surged
"A drifting and impenetrable cloud.
"With Cacus, who breathed unavailing flame,
"He grappled in the dark, locked limb with limb,
"And strangled him, till o'er the bloodless throat
"The starting eyeballs stared. Then Hercules
"Burst wide the doorway of the sooty den,
"And unto Heaven and all the people showed
"The stolen cattle and the robber's crimes,
"And dragged forth by the feet the shapeless corpse
"Of the foul monster slain. The people gazed
"Insatiate on the grewsome eyes, the breast
"Of bristling shag, the face both beast and man,
"And that fire-blasted throat whence breathed no more
"The extinguished flame.

"'T is since that famous day

"We celebrate this feast, and glad of heart
"Each generation keeps the holy time.
"Potitius began the worship due,
"And our Pinarian house is vowed to guard
"The rites of Hercules. An altar fair
"Within this wood they raised; 't is called 'the Great,'
"And *Ara Maxima* its name shall be.
"Come now, my warriors, and bind your brows
"With garlands worthy of the gift of Heaven.
"Lift high the cup in every thankful hand,
"And praise our people's god with plenteous wine."
He spoke; and of the poplar's changeful sheen,
Sacred to Hercules, wove him a wreath
To shade his silvered brow. The sacred cup
He raised in his right hand, while all the rest
Called on the gods and pure libation poured.

Soon from the travelling heavens the western star
Glowed nearer, and Potitius led forth
The priest-procession, girt in ancient guise
With skins of beasts and carrying burning brands.
New feasts are spread, and altars heaped anew
With gifts and laden chargers. Then with song
The Salian choir surrounds the blazing shrine,
Their foreheads wreathed with poplar. Here the youth,
The elders yonder, in proud anthem sing
The glory and the deeds of Hercules:
How first he strangled with strong infant hand
Two serpents, Juno's plague; what cities proud,
Troy and Œchalia, his famous war

In pieces broke; what labors numberless
As King Eurystheus' bondman he endured,
By cruel Juno's will. "Thou, unsubdued,
"Didst strike the twy-formed, cloud-bred centaurs
down,
"Pholus and tall Hylæus. Thou hast slain
"The Cretan horror, and the lion huge
"Beneath the Nemean crag. At sight of thee
"The Stygian region quailed, and Cerberus,
"Crouching o'er half-picked bones in gory cave.
"Nothing could bid thee fear. Typhœus towered
"In his colossal Titan-panoply
"O'er thee in vain; nor did thy cunning fail
"When Lerna's wonder-serpent round thee drew
"Its multitudinous head. Hail, Jove's true son!
"New glory to the gods above, come down,
"And these thine altars and thy people bless!"
Such hymns they chanted, telling oft the tale
Of Cacus' cave and blasting breath of fire:
While hills and sacred grove the note prolong.

Such worship o'er, all take the homeward way
Back to the town. The hospitable King,
Though bowed with weight of years, kept at his side
Æneas and his son, and as they fared,
With various discourse beguiled the way.
Æneas scanned with quick-admiring eyes
The region wide, and lingered with delight
Now here, now there, inquiring eagerly
Of each proud monument of heroes gone.
Then King Evander, he who builded first

On Palatine, spoke thus: "These groves erewhile
"Their native nymphs and fauns enjoyed, with men
"From trees engendered and stout heart of oak.
"Nor laws nor arts they knew; nor how to tame
"Bulls to the yoke, nor fill great barns with store
"And hoard the gathered grain; but rudely fared
"On wild fruits and such food as hunters find.
"Then Saturn from Olympian realms came down,
"In flight from Jove's dread arms, his sceptre lost,
"And he an exiled King. That savage race
"He gathered from the mountain slopes; and gave
"Wise laws and statutes; so that latent land
"Was Latium, 'hid land', where he hid so long.
"The golden centuries by legends told
"Were under that good King, whose equal sway
"Untroubled peace to all his peoples gave.
"But after slow decline arrived an age
"Degenerate and of a darker hue,
"Prone to insensate war and greed of gain.
"Then came Sicanian and Ausonian tribes,
"And oft the land of Saturn lost its name.
"New chieftains rose, and Thybris, giant King
"And violent, from whom th' Italians named
"The flooding Tiber, which was called no more
"The Albula, its true and ancient style.
"Myself, in exile from my fatherland
"Sailing uncharted seas, was guided here
"By all-disposing Chance and iron laws
"Of Destiny. With prophecy severe
"Carmentis, my nymph-mother, thrust me on,
"Warned by Apollo's word."

He scarce had said,
When near their path he showed an altar fair
And the Carmental gate, where Romans see
Memorial of Carmentis, nymph divine,
The prophetess of fate, who first foretold
What honors on Æneas' sons should fall
And lordly Pallanteum, where they dwell.
Next the vast grove was seen, where Romulus
Ordained inviolable sanctuary;
Then the Lupercal under its cold crag,
Wolf-hill, where old Arcadians revered
Their wolf-god, the Lycæan Pan. Here too
The grove of Argiletum, sacred name,
Where good Evander told the crime and death
Of Argus, his false guest. From this they climbed
The steep Tarpeian hill, the Capitol,
All gold to-day, but then a tangled wild
Of thorny woodland. Even then the place
Woke in the rustics a religious awe,
And bade them fear and tremble at the view
Of that dread rock and grove. "This leafy wood,
"Which crowns the hill-top, is the favored seat
"Of some great god," said he, "but of his name
"We know not surely. The Arcadians say
"Jove's dread right hand here visibly appears
"To shake his ægis in the darkening storm,
"The clouds compelling. Yonder rise in view
"Two strongholds with dismantled walls, which now
"Are but a memory of great heroes gone:
"One father Janus built, and Saturn one;
"Their names, Saturnia and Janiculum."

'Mid such good parley to the house they came
Of King Evander, unadorned and plain,
Whence herds of browsing cattle could be seen
Ranging the Forum, and loud-bellowing
In proud Carinæ. As they entered there,
"Behold," said he, "the threshold that received
"Alcides in his triumph! This abode
"He made his own. Dare, O illustrious guest,
"To scorn the pomp of power. Shape thy soul
"To be a god's fit follower. Enter here,
"And free from pride our frugal welcome share."
So saying, 'neath his roof-tree scant and low
He led the great Æneas, offering him
A couch of leaves with Libyan bear-skin spread.

Now night drew near, enfolding the wide world
In shadowy wings. But Venus, sore disturbed,
Vexed not unwisely her maternal breast,
Fearing Laurentum's menace and wild stir
Of obstinate revolt, and made her plea
To Vulcan in their nuptial bower of gold,
Outbreathing in the music of her words
Celestial love: "When warring Argive kings
"Brought ruin on Troy's sacred citadel
"And ramparts soon to sink in hostile flames,
"I asked not thee to help that hopeless woe,
"Nor craved thy craft and power. For, dearest lord,
"I would not tax in vain thine arduous toil,
"Though much to Priam's children I was bound,
"And oft to see Æneas burdened sore
"I could but weep. But now by will of Jove

"He has found foothold in Rutulian lands.
"Therefore I come at last with lowly suit
"Before a godhead I adore, and pray
"For gift of arms, — a mother for her son.
"Thou wert not unrelenting to the tears
"Of Nereus' daughter or Tithonus' bride.
"Behold what tribes conspire, what cities strong
"Behind barred gates now make the falchion keen
"To ruin and blot out both me and mine!"

So spake the goddess, as her arms of snow
Around her hesitating spouse she threw
In tender, close embrace. He suddenly
Knew the familiar fire, and o'er his frame
Its wonted ardor unresisted ran,
Swift as the glittering shaft of thunder cleaves
The darkened air and on from cloud to cloud
The rift of lightning runs. She, joyful wife,
Felt what her beauty and her guile could do;
As, thralled by love unquenchable, her spouse
Thus answered fair: "Why wilt thou labor so
"With far-fetched pleas? my goddess, hast thou lost
"Thy faith in me? Had such a prayer been thine,
"I could have armed the Teucrians. Neither Jove
"Nor Destiny had grudged ten added years
"Of life to Troy and Priam. If to-day
"Thou hast a war in hand, and if thy heart
"Determine so, I willingly engage
"To lend thee all my cunning; whatsoe'er
"Molten alloy or welded iron can,
"Whate'er my roaring forge and flames achieve,

"I offer thee. No more in anxious prayer
"Distrust thy beauty's power." So saying, he gave
Embrace of mutual desire, and found
Deep, peaceful sleep, on her fond heart reclined.

Night's course half run, soon as the first repose
Had banished sleep, — what time some careful wife
Whose distaff and Minerva's humble toil
Must earn her bread, rekindling her warm hearth,
Adds a night-burden to her laboring day,
And by the torch-light cheers her maidens on
To their long tasks; that so her husband's bed
She may in honor keep, and train to power
Her dear men-children — at such prime of morn,
With not less eager mind the Lord of Fire
Fled his soft couch and to his forges hied.

An island near Æolian Lipara
Not far from a Sicilian headland lies,
Where smoking rocks precipitously tower
Above a vast vault, which the Cyclops' skill
Outhollowed large as Ætna's thunderous caves.
There ring the smitten anvils, and the roof
Re-echoes, roaring loud. Chalybian ores
Hiss in the gloom, and from the furnace mouths
Puff the hot-panting fires. 'T is Vulcan's seat,
And all that island is Vulcania.
Thither descended now the god of fire
From height of heaven. At their task were found
The Cyclops in vast cavern forging steel,

Naked Pyracmon and gigantic-limbed
Brontes and Steropes; beneath their blows
A lightning-shaft, half-shaped, half-burnished lay,
Such as the Thunderer is wont to fling
In numbers from the sky, but formless still.
Three strands of whirling storm they wove with three
Of bursting cloud, and three did interfuse
Of ruddy-gleaming fires and wingèd winds;
Then fearful lightnings on the skilful forge
They welded with loud horror, and with flames
That bear swift wrath from Jove. Elsewhere a crew
Toiled at the chariot and wingèd wheel
Wherewith the war-god wakens from repose
Heroes and peopled cities. Others wrought
The awful Ægis, herald of dismay,
By angry Pallas worn; they burnished bright
The golden serpent-scales and wreathing snakes,
Till from the corselet of the goddess glared
The Gorgon's severed head and rolling eyes.
"Cyclops of Ætna," Vulcan cried, "have done!
"Leave ev'ry task unfinished, and receive
"My new command! Good armor must be forged
"For warrior brave. For this I need to use
"Your utmost sinew and your swiftest hand,
"With all your master skill. No lingering now!"

Swift the command, and swiftly they divide
To each his portion, and united urge
The common task. Forth flow the molten streams
Of brass and gold, and, melted in fierce flame,
The deeply-wounding steel like liquid flows.

A mighty shield took shape, its single orb
Sufficient to withstand the gathered shock
Of all the Latin arms; for seven times
They welded ring with ring. Some deftly ply
The windy bellows, which receive and give
The roaring blasts; some plunge in cooling pond
The hissing metal, while the smithy floor
Groans with the anvil's weight, as side by side
They lift their giant arms in numbered blows
And roll with gripe of tongs the ponderous bars.

While thus the Lemnian god his labor sped
In far Æolian isle, the cheerful morn
With voice of swallows round his lowly eaves
Summoned Evander. From his couch arose
The royal sire, and o'er his aged frame
A tunic threw, tying beneath his feet
The Tuscan sandals: an Arcadian sword,
Girt at his left, was o'er one shoulder slung,
His cloak of panther trailing from behind.
A pair of watch-dogs from the lofty door
Ran close, their lord attending, as he sought
His guest Æneas; for his princely soul
Remembered faithfully his former word,
And promised gift. Æneas with like mind
Was stirring early. King Evander's son
Pallas was at his side; Achates too
Accompanied his friend. All these conjoin
In hand-clasp and good-morrow, taking seats
In midcourt of the house, and give the hour
To converse unrestrained.

First spoke the King:
"Great leader of the Teucrians, while thy life
"In safety stands, I call not Trojan power
"Vanquished or fallen. But to help thy war
"My small means match not thy redoubted name.
"Yon Tuscan river is my bound. That way
"Rutulia thrusts us hard and chafes our wall
"With loud, besieging arms. But I propose
"To league with thee a numerous array
"Of kings and mighty tribes, which fortune strange
"Now brings to thy defence. Thou comest here
"Because the Fates intend. Not far from ours
"A city on an ancient rock is seen,
"Agylla, which a warlike Lydian clan
"Built on the Tuscan hills. It prospered well
"For many a year, then under the proud yoke
"Of King Mezentius it came and bore
"His cruel sway. Why tell the loathsome deeds
"And crimes unspeakable the despot wrought?
"May Heaven requite them on his impious head
"And on his children! For he used to chain
"Dead men to living, hand on hand was laid
"And face on face,—torment incredible!
"Till, locked in blood-stained, horrible embrace,
"A lingering death they found. But at the last
"His people rose in furious despair,
"And while he blasphemously raged, assailed
"His life and throne, cut down his guards
"And fired his regal dwellings; he, the while,
"Escaped immediate death and fled away
"To the Rutulian land, to find defence

"In Turnus' hospitality. To-day
"Etruria, to righteous anger stirred,
"Demands with urgent arms her guilty King.
"To their large host, Æneas, I will give
"An added strength, thyself. For yonder shores
"Re-echo with the tumult and the cry
"Of ships in close array; their eager lords
"Are clamoring for battle. But the song
"Of the gray omen-giver thus declares
"Their destiny: 'O goodly princes born
"'Of old Mæonian lineage! Ye that are
"'The bloom and glory of an ancient race,
"'Whom just occasions now and noble rage
"'Enflame against Mezentius your foe,
"'It is decreed that yonder nation proud
"'Shall ne'er submit to chiefs Italian-born.
"'Seek ye a king from far!' So in the field
"Inert and fearful lies Etruria's force,
"Disarmed by oracles. Their Tarchon sent
"Envoys who bore a sceptre and a crown
"Even to me, and prayed I should assume
"The sacred emblems of Etruria's king,
"And lead their host to war. But unto me
"Cold, sluggish age, now barren and outworn,
"Denies new kingdoms, and my slow-paced powers
"Run to brave deeds no more. Nor could I urge
"My son, who by his Sabine mother's line
"Is half Italian-born. Thyself art he,
"Whose birth illustrious and manly prime
"Fate favors and celestial powers approve.
"Therefore go forth, O bravest chief and King

"Of Troy and Italy! To thee I give
"The hope and consolation of our throne,
"Pallas, my son, and bid him find in thee
"A master and example, while he learns
"The soldier's arduous toil. With thy brave deeds
"Let him familiar grow, and reverence thee
"With youthful love and honor. In his train
"Two hundred horsemen of Arcadia,
"Our choicest men-at-arms, shall ride; and he
"In his own name an equal band shall bring
"To follow only thee." Such the discourse.
With meditative brows and downcast eyes
Æneas and Achates, sad at heart,
Mused on unnumbered perils yet to come.

But out of cloudless sky Cythera's Queen
Gave sudden signal: from th' ethereal dome
A thunder-peal and flash of quivering fire
Tumultuous broke, as if the world would fall,
And bellowing Tuscan trumpets shook the air.
All eyes look up. Again and yet again
Crashed the terrific din, and where the sky
Looked clearest hung a visionary cloud,
Whence through the brightness blazed resounding arms.
All hearts stood still. But Troy's heroic son
Knew that his mother in the skies redeemed
Her pledge in sound of thunder: so he cried,
"Seek not, my friend, seek not thyself to read
"The meaning of the omen. 'T is to me
"Olympus calls. My goddess-mother gave

"Long since her promise of a heavenly sign
"If war should burst; and that her power would bring
"A panoply from Vulcan through the air,
"To help us at our need. Alas, what deaths
"Over Laurentum's ill-starred host impend!
"O Turnus, what a reckoning thou shalt pay
"To me in arms! O Tiber, in thy wave
"What helms and shields and mighty soldiers slain
"Shall in confusion roll! Yea, let them lead
"Their lines to battle, and our league abjure!"

He said: and from the lofty throne uprose.
Straightway he roused anew the slumbering fire
Sacred to Hercules, and glad at heart
Adored, as yesterday, the household gods
Revered by good Evander, at whose side
The Trojan company made sacrifice
Of chosen lambs, with fitting rites and true.
Then to his ships he hied him, and rejoined
His trusty followers, of whom he took
The best for valor known, to lend him aid
In deeds of war. Others he bade return
Down stream in easy course, and tidings bear
To young Ascanius of the new event,
And of his father. Horses then were brought
For all the Teucrians to Etruria bound;
And for Æneas one of rarest breed,
O'er whom a tawny robe descended low,
Of lion-skin, with claws of gleaming gold.

Noised swiftly through the little town it flies

That to the precinct of the Tuscan King
Armed horsemen speed. Pale mothers in great fear
Unceasing pray; for panic closely runs
In danger's steps; the war-god drawing nigh
Looms larger; and good sire Evander now
Clings to the hand of his departing son
And, weeping without stay, makes sad farewell:
"O, that great Jove would give me once again
"My vanished years! O, if such man I were,
"As when beneath Præneste's wall I slew
"The front ranks of her sons, and burned for spoil
"Their gathered targes on my triumph day;
"Or when this right hand hurled king Erulus
"To shades below, though — terrible to tell —
"Feronia bore him with three lives, that thrice
"He might arise from deadly strife o'erthrown,
"And thrice be slain — yet all these lives took I,
"And of his arms despoiled him o'er and o'er:
"Not now, sweet son (if such lost might were mine),
"Should I from thy beloved embrace be torn;
"Nor could Mezentius with insulting sword
"Do murder in my sight and make my land
"Depopulate and forlorn. O gods in Heaven,
"And chiefly thou whom all the gods obey,
"Have pity, Jove, upon Arcadia's King,
"And hear a father's prayer: if your intent
"Be for my Pallas a defence secure,
"If it be writ that long as I shall live,
"My eyes may see him, and my arms enfold,
"I pray for life, and all its ills I bear.
"But if some curse, too dark to tell, impend

"From thee, O Fortune blind! I pray thee break
"My thread of miserable life to-day;
"To-day, while fear still doubts and hope still smiles
"On the unknown to-morrow, as I hold
"Thee to my bosom, dearest child, who art
"My last and only joy; to-day, before
"Th' intolerable tidings smite my ears."
Such grief the royal father's heart outpoured
At this last parting; the strong arms of slaves
Lifted him, fallen in swoon, and bore him home.

Now forth beneath the wide-swung city-gates
The mounted squadron poured; Æneas rode,
Companioned of Achates, in the van;
Then other lords of Troy. There Pallas shone
Conspicuous in the midmost line, with cloak
And blazoned arms, as when the Morning-star
(To Venus dearest of all orbs that burn),
Out of his lucent bath in ocean wave
Lifts to the skies his countenance divine,
And melts the shadows of the night away.
Upon the ramparts trembling matrons stand
And follow with dimmed eyes the dusty cloud
Whence gleam the brazen arms. The warriors ride
Straight on through brake and fell, the nearest way;
Loud ring the war-cries, and in martial line
The pounding hoof-beats shake the crumbling ground.

By Cære's cold flood lies an ample grove
Revered from age to age. The hollowing hills
Enclasp it in wide circles of dark fir,

And the Pelasgians, so the legends tell,
Primæval settlers of the Latin plains,
Called it the haunt of Silvan, kindly god
Of flocks and fields, and honoring the grove
Gave it a festal day. Hard by this spot
Had Tarchon with the Tuscans fortified
His bivouac, and from the heights afar
His legions could be seen in wide array
Outstretching through the plain. To meet them there
Æneas and his veteran chivalry
Made sure advance, and found repose at eve
For warrior travel-worn and fainting steed.

But now athwart the darkening air of heaven
Came Venus gleaming bright, to bring her son
The gifts divine. In deep, sequestered vale
She found him by a cooling rill retired,
And hailed him thus: "Behold the promised gift,
"By craft and power of my Olympian spouse
"Made perfect, that my son need never fear
"Laurentum's haughty host, nor to provoke
"Fierce Turnus to the fray." Cythera's Queen
So saying, embraced her son, and hung the arms,
All glittering, on an oak that stood thereby.
The hero, with exultant heart and proud,
Gazing unwearied at his mother's gift,
Surveys them close, and poises in his hands
The helmet's dreadful crest and glancing flame,
The sword death-dealing, and the corselet strong,
Impenetrable brass, blood-red and large,
Like some dark-lowering, purple cloud that gleams

Beneath the smiting sun and flashes far
Its answering ray; and burnished greaves were there,
Fine gold and amber; then the spear and shield —
The shield — of which the blazonry divine
Exceeds all power to tell.
Thereon were seen
Italia's story and triumphant Rome,
Wrought by the Lord of Fire, who was not blind
To lore inspired and prophesying song,
Fore-reading things to come. He pictured there
Iulus' destined line of glorious sons
Marshalled for many a war. In cavern green,
Haunt of the war-god, lay the mother-wolf;
The twin boy-sucklings at her udders played,
Nor feared such nurse; with long neck backward thrown
She fondled each, and shaped with busy tongue
Their bodies fair. Near these were pictured well
The walls of Rome and ravished Sabine wives
In the thronged theatre violently seized,
When the great games were done; then, sudden war
Of Romulus against the Cures grim
And hoary Tatius; next, the end of strife
Between the rival kings, who stood in arms
Before Jove's sacred altar, cup in hand,
And swore a compact o'er the slaughtered swine.

Hard by, behold, the whirling chariots tore
Mettus asunder (would thou hadst been true,
False Alban, to thy vow!); and Tullus trailed
The traitor's mangled corse along the hills,

The wild thorn dripping gore. Porsenna, next,
Sent to revolted Rome his proud command
To take her Tarquin back, and with strong siege
Assailed the city's wall; while unsubdued
Æneas' sons took arms in freedom's name.
There too the semblance of the frustrate King,
A semblance of his wrath and menace vain,
When Cocles broke the bridge, and Clœlia burst
Her captive bonds and swam the Tiber's wave.
Lo, on the steep Tarpeian citadel
Stood Manlius at the sacred doors of Jove,
Holding the capitol, whereon was seen
The fresh-thatched house of Romulus the King.
There, too, all silver, through arcade of gold
Fluttered the goose, whose monitory call
Revealed the foeman at the gate: outside
Besieging Gauls the thorny pathway climbed,
Ambushed in shadow and the friendly dark
Of night without a star; their flowing hair
Was golden, and their every vesture gold;
Their cloaks were glittering plaid; each milk-white
neck
Bore circlet of bright gold; in each man's hand
Two Alpine javelins gleamed, and for defence
Long targes the wild northern warriors bore.
There, graven cunningly, the Salian choir
Went leaping, and in Lupercalian feast
The naked striplings ran; while others, crowned
With peakèd cap, bore shields that fell from heaven;
And, bearing into Rome their emblems old,
Chaste priestesses on soft-strewn litters passed.

But far from these th' artificer divine
Had wrought a Tartarus, the dreadful doors
Of Pluto, and the chastisements of sin;
Swung o'er a threatening precipice, was seen
Thy trembling form, O Catiline, in fear
Of fury-faces nigh: and distant far
Th' assemblies of the righteous, in whose midst
Was Cato, giving judgment and decree.

Encircled by these pictures ran the waves
Of vast, unrestful seas in flowing gold,
Where seemed along the azure crests to fly
The hoary foam, and in a silver ring
The tails of swift, emerging dolphins lashed
The waters bright, and clove the tumbling brine.
For the shield's central glory could be seen
Great fleets of brazen galleys, and the fight
At Actium; where, ablaze with war's array,
Leucate's peak glowed o'er the golden tide.
Cæsar Augustus led Italia's sons
To battle: at his side concordant moved
Senate and Roman People, with their gods
Of hearth and home, and all Olympian Powers.
Uplifted on his ship he stands; his brows
Beneath a double glory smile, and bright
Over his forehead beams the Julian star.
In neighboring region great Agrippa leads,
By favor of fair winds and friendly Heaven,
His squadron forth: upon his brows he wears
The peerless emblem of his rostral crown.
Opposing, in barbaric splendor shine

The arms of Antony: in victor's garb
From nations in the land of morn he rides,
And from the Red Sea, bringing in his train
Egypt and Syria, utmost Bactria's horde,
And last — O shameless! — his Egyptian Queen.
All to the fight make haste; the slanted oars
And triple beaks of brass uptear the waves
To angry foam, as to the deep they speed
Like hills on hill-tops hurled, or Cyclades
Drifting and clashing in the sea: so vast
That shock of castled ships and mighty men!
Swift, arrowy steel and balls of blazing tow
Rain o'er the waters, till the sea-god's world
Flows red with slaughter. In the midst, the Queen,
Sounding her native timbrel, wildly calls
Her minions to the fight, nor yet can see
Two fatal asps behind. Her monster-gods,
Barking Anubis, and his mongrel crew,
On Neptune, Venus, and Minerva fling
Their impious arms; the face of angry Mars,
Carved out of iron, in the centre frowns;
Grim Furies fill the air; Discordia strides
In rent robe, mad with joy; and at her side,
Bellona waves her sanguinary scourge.

There Actian Apollo watched the war,
And o'er it stretched his bow; which when they knew,
Egyptian, Arab, and swart Indian slave,
And all the sons of Saba fled away
In terror of his arm. The vanquished Queen
Made prayer to all the winds, and more and more

Flung out the swelling sail: on wind-swept wave
She fled through dead and dying; her white brow
The Lord of Fire had cunningly portrayed
Blanched with approaching doom. Beyond her lay
The large-limbed picture of the mournful Nile,
Who from his bosom spread his garments wide,
And offered refuge in his sheltering streams
And broad, blue breast, to all her fallen power.
But Cæsar in his triple triumph passed
The gates of Rome, and gave Italia's gods,
For grateful offering and immortal praise,
Three hundred temples; all the city streets
With game and revel and applauding song
Rang loud; in all the temples altars burned
And Roman matrons prayed; the slaughtered herds
Strewed well the sacred ground. The hero, throned
At snow-white marble threshold of the fane
To radiant Phœbus, views the gift and spoil
The nations bring, and on the portals proud
Hangs a perpetual garland: in long file
The vanquished peoples pass, of alien tongues,
Of arms and vesture strange. Here Vulcan showed
Ungirdled Afric chiefs and Nomads bold,
Gelonian bowmen, men of Caria,
And Leleges. Euphrates seemed to flow
With humbler wave; the world's remotest men,
Morini came, with double-hornèd Rhine,
And Dahæ, little wont to bend the knee,
And swift Araxes, for a bridge too proud.

Such was the blazoned shield his mother gave

From Vulcan's forge; which with astonished eyes
Æneas viewed, and scanned with joyful mind
Such shadows of an unknown age to be;
Then on his shoulder for a burden bore
The destined mighty deeds of all his sons.

END OF BOOK VIII

BOOK IX

While thus in distant region moves the war,
Down to bold Turnus Saturn's daughter sends
Celestial Iris. In a sacred vale,
The seat of worship at his grandsire's tomb,
Pilumnus, Faunus' son, the hero mused.
And thus the wonder-child of Thaumas called
With lips of rose: "O Turnus, what no god
"Dared give for guerdon of thy fondest vow,
"Has come unbidden on its destined day.
"Behold, Æneas, who has left behind
"The city with his fleet and followers,
"Is gone to kingly Palatine, the home
"Of good Evander. Yea, his march invades
"The far Etrurian towns, where now he arms
"The Lydian rustics. Wilt thou longer muse?
"Call for thy chariot and steeds! Away!
"Take yonder tents by terror and surprise!"
She spoke; and heavenward on poising wings
Soared, cleaving as she fled from cloud to cloud
A vast, resplendent bow. The warrior saw,
And, lifting both his hands, pursued with prayer
The fading glory: "Beauteous Iris, hail!
"Proud ornament of heaven! who sent thee here
"Across yon cloud to earth, and unto me?
"Whence may this sudden brightness fall? I see
"The middle welkin lift, and many a star,

"Far-wandering in the sky. Such solemn sign
"I shall obey, and thee, O god unknown!"
So saying, he turned him to a sacred stream,
Took water from its brim, and offered Heaven
Much prayer, with many an importuning vow.

Soon o'er the spreading fields in proud array
The gathered legions poured; no lack was there
Of steeds all fire, and broidered pomp and gold.
Messapus led the van; in rearguard rode
The sons of Tyrrheus; kingly Turnus towered
From the mid-column eminent: the host
Moved as great Ganges lifting silently
His seven peaceful streams, or when the flood
Of fructifying Nile from many a field
Back to his channel flows.
A swift-blown cloud
Of black, uprolling dust the Teucrians see
O'ershadowing the plain; Caïcus calls
From lofty outpost: "O my countrymen,
"I see a huge, black ball of rolling smoke.
"Your swords and lances! Man the walls! To arms!
"The foe is here! What ho!" With clamors loud
The Teucrians through the city-gates retire,
And muster on the walls. For, wise in war,
Æneas, ere he went, had left command
They should not range in battle-line, nor dare,
Whate'er might hap, to risk in open plain
The bold sortie, but keep them safe entrenched
In mounded walls. So now, though rage and shame
Prick to a close fight, they defensive bar

Each portal strong, and, patient of control,
From hollow towers expect th' encircling foe.

Turnus, at full speed, had outridden far
His laggard host, and, leading in his train
A score of chosen knights, dashed into view
Hard by the walls. A barb of Thracian breed
Dappled with white he rode; a crimson plume
Flamed o'er his golden helmet. "Who," he cries,
"Is foremost at the foe? Who follows me?
"Behold!" And, with the word, he hurled in air
A javelin, provoking instant war:
And, towering from his horse, charged o'er the field.
With answering shout his men-at-arms pursue,
And war-cries terrible. They laugh to scorn
"The craven hearts of Troy, that cannot give
"Fair, equal vantage, matching man to man,
"But cuddle into camp." This way and that
Turnus careers, and stormily surveys
The frowning rampart, and where way is none
Some entering breach would find: so prowls a wolf
Nigh the full sheepfold, and through wind and rain
Stands howling at the postern all night long;
Beneath the ewes their bleating lambs lie safe;
But he, with undesisting fury, more
Rages from far, made frantic for his prey
By hunger of long hours, his foaming jaws
Athirst for blood: not less the envy burned
Of the Rutulian, as he scanned in vain
The stronghold of his foe. Indignant scorn
Thrilled all his iron frame. But how contrive

To storm the fortress or by force expel
The Trojans from the rampart, and disperse
Along the plain? Straightway he spied the ships,
In hiding near the camp, defended well
By mounded river-bank and fleeting wave.
On these he fell; while his exultant crew
Brought firebrands, and he with heart aflame
Grasped with a vengeful hand the blazing pine.
To the wild work his followers sped; for who
Could prove him craven under Turnus' eye?
The whole troop for the weapon of their rage
Seized smoking coals, of many a hearth the spoil;
Red glare of fuming torches burned abroad,
And Vulcan starward flung a sparkling cloud.

What god, O Muses, saved the Trojans then
From wrathful flame? Who shielded then the fleet,
I pray you tell, from bursting storm of fire?
From hoary eld the tale, but its renown
Sings on forever. When Æneas first
On Phrygian Ida hewed the sacred wood
For rib and spar, and soon would put to sea,
That mighty mother of the gods, they say,
The Berecynthian goddess, thus to Jove
Addressed her plea: "Grant, O my son, a boon,
"Which thy dear mother asks, who aided thee
"To quell Olympian war. A grove I have
"Of sacred pine, long-loved from year to year.
"On lofty hill it grew, and thither came
"My worshippers with gifts, in secret gloom
"Of pine-trees dark and shadowing maple-boughs;

"These on the Dardan warrior at his need
"I, not unwilling, for his fleet bestowed.
"But I have fears. O, let a parent's prayer
"In this prevail, and bid my care begone!
"Let not rude voyages nor the shock of storm
"My ships subdue, but let their sacred birth
"On my charmed hills their strength and safety be!"
Then spake her son, who guides the wheeling spheres:
"Wouldst thou, my mother, strive to oversway
"The course of Fate? What means this prayer of thine?
"Can it be granted ships of mortal mould
"To wear immortal being? Wouldst thou see
"Æneas pass undoubting and secure
"Through doubtful strait and peril? On what god
"Was e'er such power bestowed? Yet will I grant
"A different boon. Whatever ships shall find
"A safe Ausonian haven, and convey
"Safe through the seas to yon Laurentian plain
"The Dardan King, from such I will remove
"Their perishable shapes, and bid them be
"Sea-nymphs divine, like Nereus' daughters fair,
"Doto and Galatea, whose white breasts
"Divide the foaming wave." He said, and swore
By his Tartarean brother's mournful stream,
The pitch-black floods and dark engulfing shore
Of Styx; then great Jove bowed his head, and all
Olympus quaked at his consenting brow.

Now was the promised day at hand (for Fate
Had woven the web so far) when Turnus' rage
Stirred the divine progenitress to save

Her sacred ships from fire. Then sudden shone
A strange effulgence in the eastern air;
And in a storm-cloud wafted o'er the sky
Were Corybantic choirs, whose dreadful song
Smote both on Teucrian and Rutulian ear:
"O Teucrians, fear not for the sure defence
"Of all the ships, nor arm your mortal hands.
"Yon impious Turnus shall burn up the seas
"Before my pine-trees blest. Arise! Be free,
"Ye goddesses of ocean, and obey
"Your mother's mighty word." Then instant broke
The hawsers of the sterns; the beakèd prows
Went plunging like great dolphins from the shore
Down to the deeps, and, wonderful to tell,
The forms of virgin goddesses uprose,
One for each ship, and seaward sped away.

The hearts of the Rutulian host stood still
In panic, and Messapus terrified
His trembling horses reined; the sacred stream
Of Father Tiber, harshly murmuring,
Held back his flood and checked his seaward way.
But Turnus' courage failed not; he alone
His followers roused, and with reproachful words
Alone spoke forth: "These signs and prodigies
"Threaten the Trojan only. Jove himself
"Has stripped them of their wonted strength: no more
"Can they abide our deadly sword and fire.
"The Trojan path to sea is shut. What hope
"Of flight is left them now? The half their cause
"Is fallen. The possession of this land

"Is ours already; thousands of sharp swords
"Italia's nations bring. Small fear have I
"Of Phrygia's boasted omens. What to me
"Their oracles from heaven? The will of Fate
"And Venus have achieved their uttermost
"In casting on Ausonia's fruitful shore
"Yon sons of Troy. I too have destinies:
"And mine, good match for theirs, with this true blade
"Will spill the blood of all the baneful brood,
"In vengeance for my stolen wife. Such wrongs
"Move not on Atreus' sons alone, nor rouse
"Only Mycenæ to a righteous war.
"Say you, 'Troy falls but once?' One crime, say I,
"Should have contented them; and now their souls
"Should little less than loathe all womankind.
"These are the sort of soldiers that be brave
"Behind entrenchment, where the moated walls
"May stem the foe and make a little room
"Betwixt themselves and death. Did they not see
"How Troy's vast bulwark built by Neptune's hand
"Crumbled in flame? Forward, my chosen brave!
"Who follows me to cleave his deadly way
"Through yonder battlement, and leap like storm
"Upon its craven guard? I have no need
"Of arms from Vulcan's smithy; nor of ships
"A thousand strong against our Teucrian foes,
"Though all Etruria's league enlarge their power.
"Let them not fear dark nights, nor coward theft
"Of Pallas' shrine, nor murdered sentinels
"On their acropolis. We shall not hide
"In blinding belly of a horse. But I

"In public eye and open day intend
"To compass their weak wall with siege and fire.
"I'll prove them we be no Pelasgic band,
"No Danaan warriors, such as Hector's arm
"Ten years withstood. But look! this day hath spent
"Its better part. In what remains, rejoice
"In noble deeds well done; let weary flesh
"Have rest and food. My warriors, husband well
"Your strength against to-morrow's hopeful war."
Meanwhile to block their gates with wakeful guard
Is made Messapus' work, and to gird round
Their camp with watchfires. Then a chosen band,
Twice seven Rutulian chieftains, man the walls
With soldiery; each leads a hundred men
Crested with crimson, armed with glittering gold.
Some post to separate sentries, and prepare
Alternate vigil; others, couched on grass,
Laugh round the wine and lift the brazen bowls.
The camp-fires cheerly burn; the jovial guard
Spend the long, sleepless night in sport and game.

The Trojans peering from the lofty walls
Survey the foe, and arm for sure defence
Of every point exposed. They prove the gates
With fearful care, bind bridge with tower, and bring
Good store of javelins. Serestus bold
And Mnestheus to their labors promptly fly,
Whom Sire Æneas bade in time of stress
To have authority and free command
Over his warriors. Along the walls
The legions, by the cast of lots, divide

The pain and peril, giving each his due
Of alternating vigil and repose.

Nisus kept sentry at the gate: a youth
Of eager heart for noble deeds, the son
Of Hyrtacus, whom in Æneas' train
Ida the huntress sent; swift could he speed
The spear or light-winged arrow to its aim.
Beside him was Euryalus, his friend:
Of all th' Æneadæ no youth more fair
Wore Trojan arms; upon his cheek unshorn
The tender bloom of boyhood lingered still.
Their loving hearts were one, and oft in war
They battled side by side, as in that hour
A common sentry at the gate they shared.
Said Nisus: "Is it gods above that breathe
"This fever in my soul, Euryalus?
"Or is the tyrant passion of each breast
"The god it serves? Me now my urgent mind
"To battles or some mighty deed impels,
"And will not give me rest. Look yonder, where
"The Rutuli in dull security
"The siege maintain. Yet are their lights but few.
"They are asleep or drunk, and in their line
"Is many a silent space. O, hear my thought,
"And what my heart is pondering. To recall
"Æneas is the dearest wish to-night
"Of all, both high and low. They need true men
"To find him and bring tidings. If our chiefs
"But grant me leave to do the thing I ask
"(Claiming no guerdon save what honor gives),

"Methinks I could search out by yonder hill
"A path to Pallanteum." The amazed
Euryalus, flushed warm with eager love
For deeds of glory, instantly replied
To his high-hearted friend: "Dost thou refuse,
"My Nisus, to go with me hand in hand
"When mighty deeds are done? Could I behold
"Thee venturing alone on danger? Nay!
"Not thus my sire Opheltes, schooled in war,
"Taught me his true child, 'mid the woes of Troy
"And Argive terrors reared; not thus with thee
"Have I proved craven, since we twain were leal
"To great Æneas, sharing all his doom.
"In this breast also is a heart which knows
"Contempt of life, and deems such deeds, such praise,
"Well worth a glorious death." Nisus to him:
"I have not doubted thee, nor e'er could have
"One thought disloyal. May almighty Jove,
"Or whatsoe'er good power my purpose sees,
"Bring me triumphant to thy arms once more!
"But if, as oft in doubtful deeds befalls,
"Some stroke of chance, or will divine, should turn
"To adverse, 't is my fondest prayer that thou
"Shouldst live the longer of us twain. Thy years
"Suit better with more life. Oh! let there be
"One mourner true to carry to its grave
"My corpse, recaptured in the desperate fray,
"Or ransomed for a price. Or if this boon
"Should be — 't is Fortune's common way — refused,
"Then pay the debt of grief and loyal woe
"Unto my far-off dust, and garlands leave

"Upon an empty tomb. No grief I give
"To any sorrowing mother; one alone,
"Of many Trojan mothers, had the heart
"To follow thee, her child, and would not stay
"In great Acestes' land." His friend replied:
"Thou weavest but a web of empty words
"And reasons vain, nor dost thou shake at all
"My heart's resolve. Come, let us haste away!"
He answered so, and summoned to the gate
A neighboring watch, who, bringing prompt relief,
The sentry-station took; then quitted he
His post assigned; at Nisus' side he strode,
And both impatient sped them to the King.

Now in all lands all creatures that have breath
Lulled care in slumber, and each heart forgot
Its load of toil and pain. But they who led
The Teucrian cause, with all their chosen brave,
Took counsel in the kingdom's hour of need
What action to command or whom dispatch
With tidings to Æneas. In mid-camp
On long spears leaning and with ready shield
To leftward slung, th' assembled warriors stood.
Thither in haste arrived the noble pair,
Brave Nisus with Euryalus his friend,
And craved a hearing, for their suit, they said,
Was urgent and well-worth a patient ear.
Iulus to the anxious striplings gave
A friendly welcome, bidding Nisus speak.
The son of Hyrtacus obeyed: "O, hear,
"Princes of Teucria, with impartial mind,

"Nor judge by our unseasoned youth the worth
"Of what we bring. Yon Rutule watch is now
"In drunken sleep, and all is silent there.
"With our own eyes we picked out a good place
"To steal a march, that cross-road by the gate
"Close-fronting on the bridge. Their lines of fire
"Are broken, and a murky, rolling smoke
"Fills all the region. If ye grant us leave
"By this good luck to profit, we will find
"Æneas and the walls of Palatine,
"And after mighty slaughter and huge spoil
"Ye soon shall see us back. Nor need ye fear
"We wander from the way. Oft have we seen
"That city's crest loom o'er the shadowy vales,
"Where we have hunted all day long and know
"Each winding of yon river." Then uprose
Aged Aletes, crowned with wisdom's years:
"Gods of our fathers, who forevermore
"Watch over Troy, ye surely had no mind
"To blot out Teucria's name, when ye bestowed
"Such courage on young hearts, and bade them be
"So steadfast and so leal." Joyful he clasped
Their hands in his, and on their shoulders leaned,
His aged cheek and visage wet with tears.
"What guerdon worthy of such actions fair,
"Dear heroes, could be given? Your brightest prize
"Will come from Heaven and your own hearts. The rest
"Æneas will right soon bestow; nor will
"Ascanius, now in youth's unblemished prime,
"Ever forget your praise." Forthwith replied

Æneas' son, "By all our household gods,
"By great Assaracus, and every shrine
"Of venerable Vesta, I confide
"My hopes, my fortunes, and all future weal
"To your heroic hearts. O, bring me back
"My father! Set him in these eyes once more!
"That day will tears be dry; and I will give
"Two silver wine-cups graven and o'erlaid
"With clear-cut figures, which my father chose
"Out of despoiled Arisbe; also two
"Full talents of pure gold, and tripods twain,
"And ancient wine-bowl, Tyrian Dido's token.
"But if indeed our destiny shall be
"To vanquish Italy in prosperous war,
"To seize the sceptre and divide the spoil, —
"Saw you that steed of Turnus and the arms
"In which he rode, all golden? That same steed,
"That glittering shield and haughty crimson crest
"I will reserve thee, e'er the lots are cast,
"And, Nisus, they are thine. Hereto my sire
"Will add twelve captive maids of beauty rare,
"And slaves in armor; last, thou hast the fields
"Which now Latinus holds. But as for thee,
"To whom my youth but binds me closer still,
"Thee, kingly boy, my whole heart makes my own,
"And through all changeful fortune we shall be
"Inseparable peers: nor will I seek
"Renown and glory, or in peace or war,
"Forgetting thee: but trust thee from this day
"In deed and word." To him in answer spoke
Euryalus, "O, may no future show

"This heart unworthy thy heroic call!
"And may our fortune ever prosperous prove,
"Not adverse. But I now implore of thee
"A single boon worth all beside. I have
"A mother, from the venerated line
"Of Priam sprung, whom not the Trojan shore
"Nor King Acestes' city could detain,
"Alas! from following me. I leave her now
"Without farewell; nor is her love aware
"Of my supposèd peril. For I swear
"By darkness of this night and thy right hand,
"That all my courage fails me if I see
"A mother's tears. O, therefore, I implore,
"Be thou her sorrow's comfort and sustain
"Her solitary day. Such grace from thee
"Equip me for my war, and I shall face
"With braver heart whatever fortune brings."

With sudden sorrow thrilled, the veteran lords
Of Teucria showed their tears. But most of all
Such likeness of his own heart's filial love
On fair Iulus moved, and thus he spoke:
"Promise thyself what fits thy generous deeds.
"Thy mother shall be mine, Creüsa's name
"Alone not hers; nor is the womb unblest
"That bore a child like thee. Whate'er success
"May follow, I make oath immutable
"By my own head, on which my father swore,
"That all I promise thee of gift or praise
"If home thou comest triumphing, shall be
"The glory of thy mother and thy kin."

Weeping he spoke, and from his shoulder drew
The golden sword, well-wrought and wonderful,
Which once in Crete Lycaon's cunning made
And sheathed in ivory. On Nisus then
Mnestheus bestowed a shaggy mantle torn
From a slain lion; good Aletes gave
Exchange of crested helms. In such array
They hastened forth; and all the princely throng,
Young men and old, ran with them to the gates,
Praying all gods to bless. Iulus then,
A fair youth, but of grave, heroic soul
Beyond his years, gave them in solemn charge
Full many a message for his sire, but these
The hazard of wild winds soon scattered far,
And flung them fruitless on the darkening storm.

Forth through the moat they climb, and steal away
Through midnight shades, to where their foemen lie
Encamped in arms; of whom, before these fall,
A host shall die. Along the turf were seen,
Laid low in heavy slumber and much wine,
A prostrate troop; the horseless chariots
Stood tilted on the shore, 'twixt rein and wheel
The drivers dozed, wine-cups and idle swords
Strewn round them without heed. The first to speak
Was Nisus. "Look, Euryalus," he cried,
"Now boldly strike. The hour to do the deed
"Is here, the path this way. Keep wide-eyed watch
"That no man smite behind us. I myself
"Will mow the mighty field, and lead thee on
"In a wide swath of slaughter." With this word

He shut his lips; and hurled him with his sword
On haughty Rhamnes, who lay propped at ease
On pillows huge, and from his heaving breast
Poured slumber loud: of royal stem was he
And honored of King Turnus for his skill
In augury; yet could no augur's charm
That bloody stroke forefend. And Nisus slew
Three slaves near by, that lay in reckless sleep
Upon their spears; then him that bore the shield
Of Remus, then the driver of his car
Close to the horses caught; his sword cut through
Their prostrate necks; then their great master's head
He lifted high, and left decapitate
The huge corpse spilling forth its crimson gore
O'er couch and ground. Like stroke on Lamus fell
And Lamyrus, with young Serranus, who
Had gamed the midnight through and sleeping lay,
His fair young body to the wine-god given;
But happier now had that long-revelling night
Been merry till the dawn! Thus round full folds
Of sheep a famished lion fiercely prowls;
Mad hunger moves him; he devours and rends
With bloody, roaring mouth, the feeble flock
That trembles and is dumb.

Nor was the sword
Of fair Euryalus less fatal found;
But fiercely raging on his path of death,
He pressed on through a base and nameless throng,
Rhœtus, Herbesus, Fadus, Abaris;
Surprising all save Rhœtus, who awake

Saw every stroke, and crouched in craven fear
Behind a mighty wine-bowl; but not less
Clean through his bare breast as he started forth
The youth thrust home his sword, then drew it back
Death-dripping, while the bursting purple stream
Of life outflowed, with mingling blood and wine.
Then, flushed with stealthy slaughter, he crept near
The followers of Messapus, where he saw
Their camp-fire dying down, and tethered steeds
Upon the meadow feeding. Nisus then
Knew the hot lust of slaughter had swept on
Too far, and cried, "Hold off! For, lo,
"The monitory dawn is nigh. Revenge
"Has fed us to the full. We have achieved
"Clean passage through the foe."

Full many a prize
Was left untaken: princely suits of mail
Enwrought with silver pure, huge drinking-bowls,
And broideries fair. Yet grasped Euryalus
The blazonry at Rhamnes' corselet hung,
And belt adorned with gold: which were a gift
To Remulus of Tibur from the store
Of opulent Cædicus, who sued from far
To be a friend; and these in death he gave
To his son's son, who slain in battle fell,
And proud Rutulians seized them with the spoil.
Euryalus about his shoulder strong
This booty slung — unprofitable gain! —
And fitted on a gorgeous, crested helm
Which once Messapus wore. So from the camp,
Escaping danger, the two champions ran.

But horsemen from the Latin city sent
To join the serried legions of the plain
Had come at Turnus' call, three hundred strong,
All bearing shields, and under the command
Of Volscens. Nigh the camp and walls they drew;
And soon they spied upon the leftward path
Th' heroic pair, where in dim shades of night
The helmet of Euryalus betrayed
The heedless boy, and with a glancing beam
Flashed on the foe. Nor was it seen in vain.
Loud from the line the voice of Volscens called:
"Stand, gentlemen! What business brings you here?
"Whose your allegiance? Whither speed so fast?"
No answer gave they save to fly in haste
To cover of the forest and deep gloom
Of the defensive night. The horsemen then
Blocked every crossway known, and, scattering wide,
Kept sentry at the entrance. The great wood
Was all of tangled brush and blinding shade
Of ilex-boughs. Impenetrable thorns
Had thickly overgrown, and seldom showed
A pathway through the maze. Euryalus,
By the black branches and his ponderous spoil
Impeded, groped along in fearful doubt,
Deceived and quite astray. Nisus his friend
Had quit him, and incautiously had forced
A sally through the close-encircling foe,
Into that region which should after bear
The name of Alba — a rude shelter then
For King Latinus' herds. He stayed him there
And looked, but vainly, for the comrade gone.

"Euryalus, ill-fated boy!" he cried,
"Where have I lost thee in the pathless wild?
"How find thee? How retrace the blinding maze
"Of yonder treacherous wood?"
Yet ere he said,
On his own path he turns him back, and scans
His own light footprints through the tangled thorn,
So dark and still. But suddenly he hears
The tread of horses, with confusing din
And tumult of pursuit. Nor was it long
He tarried ere upon his anguished ear
Smote a great cry: and, lo! Euryalus,
Trapped by the dark night, the deceptive ground,
Faced the whole onset, and fell back o'erwhelmed
By a loud mob of foes, while his sole sword
Tried many a thrust in vain. O, what defence
May Nisus bring? With what audacious arms
His chosen comrade save? Shall he make bare
His dying breast to all their swords, and run
To honorable death that bloody way?
He swung his spear with lifted arm, then looked
To the still moon in heaven, and thus implored:
"O goddess, aid me in my evil case.
"O glory of the stars, Latona's child!
"O guardian of groves, if in my name
"My father Hyrtacus made offerings
"On burning altars, if my own right hand,
"Successful in the chase, ere hung its gift
"Beneath thy dome or on thy sacred wall,
"Grant me yon troop to scatter. Guide my spear
"Along its path in air." He spoke, and hurled

With all his gathered strength the shaft of steel.
The swift spear clove the shades of night, and struck
Full in the back of Sulmo, where it split,
But tore through to his very heart. The breast
Poured forth life's glowing stream, and he, o'erthrown,
Lay cold in death, while his huge, heaving sides
Gave lingering throes. The men about him stared
This way and that. But Nisus, fiercer still,
Poised level with his ear a second shaft,
And, while the foeman paused, the whizzing spear
Straight through the brows of Tagus drove, and clung
Deep in the cloven brain. In frenzy rose
Volscens, but nowhere could espy what hand
The shaft had hurled, nor whither his wild rage
Could make reply. "But thou," he cried, "shalt feed
"With thy hot blood my honor and revenge
"For both the slain." Then with a sword unsheathed
Upon Euryalus he fell. Loud shrieked
Nisus, of reason reft, who could not bear
Such horror, nor in sheltering gloom of night
Longer abide: "'T is I, 't is I!" he said.
"Look on the man who slew them! Draw on me
"Your swords, Rutulians! The whole stratagem
"Was mine, mine only, and the lad ye slay
"Dared not, and could not. O, by Heaven above
"And by the all-beholding stars I swear,
"He did but love his hapless friend too well."

But while he spoke, the furious-thrusting sword
Had pierced the tender body, and run through

The bosom white as snow. Euryalus
Sank prone in death; upon his goodly limbs
The life-blood ran unstopped, and low inclined
The drooping head; as when some purpled flower,
Cut by the ploughshare, dies, or poppies proud
With stem forlorn their ruined beauty bow
Before the pelting storm.
Then Nisus flew
Straight at his foes; but in their throng would find
Volscens alone, for none but Volscens stayed:
They gathered thickly round and grappled him
In shock of steel with steel. But on he plunged,
Swinging in ceaseless circles round his head
His lightning-sword, and thrust it through the face
Of shrieking Volscens, with his own last breath
Striking his foeman down; then cast himself
Upon his fallen comrade's breast; and there,
Stabbed through, found tranquil death and sure repose.

Heroic pair and blest! If aught I sing
Have lasting music, no remotest age
Shall blot your names from honor's storied scroll:
Not while the altars of Æneas' line
Shall crown the Capitol's unshaken hill,
Nor while the Roman Father's hand sustains
Its empire o'er the world.

The Rutules seized the spoils of victory,
And slowly to their camp, with wail and cry,
Bore Volscens' corse; and in the camp they made

Like wailing over Rhamnes lifeless found,
O'er Numa and Serranus, and a throng
Of princes dead. The gazing people pressed
Around the slain, the dying, where the earth
Ran red with slaughter and full many a stream
Of trickling gore; nor did they fail to know
Messapus' glittering helm, his baldric fair,
Recaptured now with lavish sweat and pain.

Now, from Tithonus' saffron couch set free,
Aurora over many a land outpoured
The rising morn; the sun's advancing beam
Unveiled the world; and Turnus to his host
Gave signal to stand forth, while he arrayed
Himself in glorious arms. Then every chief
Awoke his mail-clad company, and stirred
Their slumbering wrath with tidings from the foe.
Tumultuously shouting, they impaled
On lifted spears — O pitiable sight! —
The heads of Nisus and Euryalus.
Th' undaunted Trojans stood in battle-line
Along the wall to leftward (for the right
The river-front defended) keeping guard
On the broad moat; upon the ramparts high
Sad-eyed they stood, and shuddered as they saw
The hero-faces thrust aloft; too well
Their loyal grief the blood-stained features knew.

On restless pinions to the trembling town
Had voiceful Rumor hied, and to the ears
Of that lone mother of Euryalus

Relentless flown. Through all her feeble frame
The chilling sorrow sped. From both her hands
Dropped web and shuttle; she flew shrieking forth,
Ill-fated mother! and with tresses torn,
To the wide ramparts and the battle-line
Ran frantic, heeding naught of men-at-arms,
Nor peril nor the rain of falling spears;
And thus with loud and lamentable cry
Filled all the air: "Is it in yonder guise,
"Euryalus, thou comest? Art thou he,
"Last comfort of my life? O cruel one!
"Couldst thou desert me? When they thrust thee forth
"To death and danger, did they dare refuse
"A wretched mother's last embrace? But now —
"O woe is me! — upon this alien shore
"Thou liest for a feast to Latin dogs
"And carrion birds. Nor did thy mother lead
"The mourners to thy grave, nor shut those eyes,
"Nor wash the dreadful wounds, nor cover thee
"With the fair shroud, which many a night and day
"I swiftly wove, and at my web and loom
"Forgot my years and sorrows. Whither now
"To seek and follow thee? What spot of earth
"Holds the torn body and the mangled limbs?
"Is all the gift thou bringest home, dear child,
"This? O, was this the prize for which I came
"O'er land and sea? O, stab me very deep,
"If ye have any pity; hurl on me
"Your every spear, Rutulians; make of me
"Your swords' first work. Or, Father of the gods!
"Show mercy, thou! and with thy lightning touch

"This head accurst, and let it fall by thee
"Down to the dark. For else what power is mine
"My tortured life to end?" Her agony
Smote on their listening souls; a wail of woe
Along the concourse ran. Stern men-at-arms
Felt valor for a moment sleep, and all
Their rage of battle fail. But while she stirred
The passion of her grief, Ilioneus
And young Iulus, weeping filial tears,
Bade Actor and Idæus, lifting her
In both their reverent arms, to bear her home.

But now the brazen trumpet's fearsome song
Blares loud, and startled shouts of soldiery
Spread through the roaring sky. The Volscian band
Press to the siege, and, locking shield with shield,
Fill the great trenches, tear the palisades,
Or seek approach by ladders up the walls,
Where'er the line of the defenders thins, and light
Through their black circle shines. The Trojans pour
Promiscuous missiles down, and push out hard
With heavy poles — so well have they been schooled
To fight against long sieges. They fling down
A crushing weight of rocks, in hope to break
Th' assailing line, where roofed in serried shields
The foe each charge repels. But not for long
The siegers stand; along their dense array
The crafty Teucrians down the rampart roll
A boulder like a hill-top, laying low
The Rutule troop and crashing through their shields.
Nor may the bold Rutulian longer hope

To keep in cover, but essays to storm
Only with far-flung shafts the bastion strong.

Here grim Mezentius, terrible to see,
Waved an Etrurian pine, and made his war
With smoking firebrands; there, in equal rage,
Messapus, the steed-tamer, Neptune's son,
Ripped down the palisade, and at the breach
Strung a steep path of ladders up the wall.

Aid, O Calliope, the martial song!
Tell me what carnage and how many deaths
The sword of Turnus wrought: what peer in arms
Each hero to the world of ghosts sent down.
Unroll the war's great book before these eyes.

A tower was there, well-placed and looming large,
With many a lofty bridge, which desperately
Th' Italians strove to storm, and strangely plied
Besieging enginery to cast it down:
The Trojans hurled back stones, or, standing close,
Flung through the loopholes a swift shower of spears.
But Turnus launched a firebrand, and pierced
The wooden wall with flame, which in the wind
Leaped larger, and devoured from floor to floor,
Burning each beam away. The trembling guards
Sought flight in vain; and while they crowded close
Into the side unkindled yet, the tower
Bowed its whole weight and fell, with sudden crash
That thundered through the sky. Along the ground
Half dead the warriors fell (the crushing mass

Piled over them) by their own pointed spears
Pierced to the heart, or wounded mortally
By cruel splinters of the wreck. Two men,
Helenor one, and Lycus at his side,
Alone get free. Helenor of the twain
Was a mere youth; the slave Lycymnia
Bore him in secret to the Lydian King,
And, arming him by stealth, had sent away
To serve the Trojan cause. One naked sword
For arms had he, and on his virgin shield
No blazon of renown; but when he saw
The hosts of Turnus front him, and the lines
This way and that of Latins closing round, —
As a fierce, forest-creature, brought to bay
In circling pack of huntsmen, shows its teeth
Against the naked spears, and scorning death
Leaps upward on the javelins, — even so,
Not loth to die, the youthful soldier flew
Straight at the centre of his foes, and where
The shining swords looked thickest, there he sprung.
But Lycus, swifter-footed, forced his way
Past the opposing spears and made escape
Far as the city-wall, where he would fain
Clutch at the coping and climb up to clasp
Some friend above: but Turnus, spear in hand,
Had hotly followed, and exulting loud
Thus taunted him, "Hadst thou the hope, rash fool,
"Beyond this grasp to fly?" So, as he clung,
He tore him down; and with him broke and fell
A huge piece of the wall: not otherwise
A frail hare, or a swan of snow-white wing,

Is clutched in eagle-talons, when the bird
Of Jove soars skyward with his prey; or tender lamb
From bleating mother and the broken fold
Is stolen by the wolf of Mars. Wild shouts
On every side resound. In closer siege
The foe press on, and heap the trenches full,
Or hurl hot-flaming torches at the towers.

Ilioneus with mountain-mass of stone
Struck down Lucetius, as he crept with fire
Too near the city-gate. Emathion fell
By Liger's hand, and Corynæus' death
Asilas dealt: one threw the javelin well;
Th' insidious arrow was Asilas' skill.
Ortygius was slain by Cæneus, then
Victorious Cæneus fell by Turnus' ire.
Then smote he Dioxippus, and laid low
Itys and Promolus and Sagaris
And Clonius, and from the lofty tower
Shot Idas down. The shaft of Capys pierced
Privernus, whom Themilla's javelin
But now had lightly grazed, and he, too bold,
Casting his shield far from him, had outspread
His left hand on the wound: then sudden flew
The feathered arrow, and the hand lay pinned
Against his left side, while the fatal barb
Was buried in his breathing life.

The son
Of Arcens now stood forth in glittering arms.
His broidered cloak was red Iberian stain,
And beautiful was he. Arcens his sire

Had sent him to the war; but he was bred
In a Sicilian forest by a stream
To his nymph-mother dear, where rose the shrine
Of merciful Palicus, blest and fair.
But, lo! Mezentius his spear laid by,
And whirled three times about his head the thong
Of his loud sling: the leaden bullet clove
The youth's mid-forehead, and his towering form
Fell prostrate its full length along the ground.

'T was then Ascanius first shot forth in war
The arrow swift from which all creatures wild
Were wont to fly in fear: and he struck down
With artful aim Numanus, sturdy foe,
Called Remulus, who lately was espoused
To Turnus' younger sister. He had stalked
Before the van, and made vociferous noise
Of truths and falsehoods foul and base, his heart
Puffed up with new-found greatness. Up and down
He strode, and swelled his folly with loud words:
"No shame have ye this second time to stay
"Cooped close within a rampart's craven siege,
"O Phrygians twice-vanquished? Is a wall
"Your sole defence from death? Are such the men
"Who ask our maids in marriage? Say what god,
"What doting madness, rather, drove ye here
"To Italy? This way ye will not find
"The sons of Atreus nor the trickster tongue
"Of voluble Ulysses. Sturdy stock
"Are we; our softest new-born babes we dip
"In chilling rivers, till they bear right well

"The current's bitter cold. Our slender lads
"Hunt night and day and rove the woods at large,
"Or for their merriment break stubborn steeds,
"Or bend the horn-tipped bow. Our manly prime
"In willing labor lives, and is inured
"To poverty and scantness; we subdue
"Our lands with rake and mattock, or in war
"Bid strong-walled cities tremble. Our whole life
"Is spent in use of iron; and we goad
"The flanks of bullocks with a javelin's end.
"Nor doth old age, arriving late, impair
"Our brawny vigor, nor corrupt the soul
"To frail decay. But over silvered brows
"We bind the helmet. Our unfailing joy
"Is rapine, and to pile the plunder high.
"But ye! your gowns are saffron needlework
"Or Tyrian purple; ye love shameful ease,
"Or dancing revelry. Your tunics flow
"Long-sleeved, and ye have soft caps ribbon-bound.
"Aye, Phrygian girls are ye, not Phrygian men!
"Hence to your hill of Dindymus! Go hear
"The twy-mouthed piping ye have loved so long.
"The timbrel, hark! the Berecynthian flute
"Calls you away, and Ida's goddess calls.
"Leave arms to men, true men! and quit the sword!"

Of such loud insolence and words of shame
Ascanius brooked no more, but laid a shaft
Athwart his bowstring, and with arms stretched wide
Took aim, first offering suppliant vow to Jove:
"Almighty Jupiter, thy favor show

"To my bold deed! So to thy shrine I bear
"Gifts year by year, and to thine altars lead
"A bull with gilded brows, snow-white, and tall
"As his own dam, what time his youth begins
"To lower his horns and fling the sand in air."
The Father heard, and from a cloudless sky
Thundered to leftward, while the deadly bow
Resounded and the arrow's fearful song
Hissed from the string; it struck unswervingly
The head of Remulus and clove its way
Deep in the hollows of his brow. "Begone!
"Proud mocker at the brave! Lo, this reply
"Twice-vanquished Phrygians to Rutulia send."
Ascanius said no more. The Teucrians
With deep-voiced shout of joy applaud, and lift
Their exultation starward. Then from heaven
The flowing-haired Apollo bent his gaze
Upon Ausonia's host, and cloud-enthroned
Looked downward o'er the city, speaking thus
To fair Iulus in his victory:
"Hail to thy maiden prowess, boy! This way
"The starward path to dwelling-place divine.
"O sired of gods and sire of gods to come,
"All future storms of war by Fate ordained
"Shall into peace and lawful calm subside
"Beneath the offspring of Assaracus.
"No Trojan destinies thy glory bound."

So saying, from his far, ethereal seat
He hied him down, and, cleaving the quick winds
Drew near Ascanius. He wore the guise

Of aged Butes, who erewhile had borne
Anchises' armor and kept trusty guard
Before his threshold, but attended now
Ascanius, by commandment of his sire.
Clad in this graybeard's every aspect, moved
Apollo forth, — his very voice and hue,
His hoary locks and grimly sounding shield, —
And to the flushed Iulus spoke this word:
"Child of Æneas, be content that now
"Numanus unavenged thine arrows feels.
"Such dawn of glory great Apollo's will
"Concedes, nor envies thee the fatal shaft
"So like his own. But, tender youth, refrain
"Hereafter from this war!" So said divine
Apollo, who, while yet he spoke, put by
His mortal aspect, and before their eyes
Melted to viewless air. The Teucrians knew
The vocal god with armament divine
Of arrows; for his rattling quiver smote
Their senses as he fled. Obedient
To Phœbus' voice they held back from the fray
Iulus' fury, and their eager souls
Faced the fresh fight and danger's darkest frown.

From tower to tower along the bastioned wall
Their war-cry flew: they bend with busy hand
The cruel bow, or swing the whirling thong
Of javelins. The earth on every side
Is strewn with spent shafts, the reverberant shield
And hollow helmet ring with blows; the fight
More fiercely swells; not less the bursting storm

From watery Kid-stars in the western sky
Lashes the plain, or multitudinous hail
Beats upon shallow seas, when angry Jove
Flings forth tempestuous and boundless rain,
And splits the bellied clouds in darkened air.

The brothers Pandarus and Bitias,
Of whom Alcanor was the famous sire,
On Ida born, and whom Iæra bred
In sacred wood of Jove, an oread she,
Twin warriors, like their native hills and trees
Of stature proud, now burst those portals wide
To them in ward consigned, and sword in hand
Challenge the foe to enter. Side by side,
Steel-clad, their tall heads in bright crested helms,
To left and right, like towers, the champions stand:
As when to skyward, by the gliding waves
Of gentle Athesis or Padus wide,
A pair of oaks uprise, and lift in air
Their shaggy brows and nodding crests sublime.
In burst the Rutules where the onward way
Seemed open wide; Quercens no tarrying knows,
Nor proud Aquiculus in well-wrought arms;
Tmarus sweeps on impetuous, and the host
Of Hæmon, child of Mars. Some routed fly;
Some lay their lives down at the gate. Wild rage
O'erflows each martial breast, and gathered fast
The Trojans rally to one point, and dare
Close conflict, or long sallies o'er the plain.

To Turnus, who upon a distant field
Was storming with huge havoc, came the news
That now his foe, before a gate thrown wide,
Was red with slaughter. His own fight he stays,
And speeds him, by enormous rage thrust on,
To those proud brethren at the Dardan wall.
There first Antiphates, who made his war
Far in the van (a Theban captive's child
To great Sarpedon out of wedlock born),
He felled to earth with whirling javelin:
Th' Italic shaft of cornel lightly flew
Along the yielding air, and through his throat
Pierced deep into the breast; a gaping wound
Gushed blood; the hot shaft to his bosom clung.
Then Erymas and Merops his strong hand
Laid low: Aphidnus next, then came the turn
Of Bitias, fiery-hearted, furious-eyed:
But not by javelin, — such cannot fall
By flying javelin, — the ponderous beam
Of a phalaric spear, with mighty roar,
Like thunderbolt upon him fell; such shock
Neither the bull's-hides of his double shield
Nor twofold corselet's golden scales could stay
But all his towering frame in ruin fell.
Earth groaned, and o'er him rang his ample shield.
So crashes down from Baiæ's storied shore
A rock-built mole, whose mighty masonry,
Piled up with care, men cast into the sea;
It trails its wreckage far, and fathoms down
Lies broken in the shallows, while the waves
Whirl every way, and showers of black sand

Are scattered on the air: with thunder-sound
Steep Prochyta is shaken, and that bed
Of cruel stone, Inárimë, which lies
Heaped o'er Typhœus by revenge of Jove.

Now to the Latins Mars, the lord of war,
Gave might and valor, and to their wild hearts
His spur applied, but on the Teucrians breathed
Dark fear and flight. From every quarter came
Auxiliar hosts, where'er the conflict called,
And in each bosom pulsed the god of war.
When Pandarus now saw his brother's corse
Low lying, and which way the chance and tide
Of battle ran, he violently moved
The swinging hinges of the gate, and strained
With both his shoulders broad. He shut outside
Not few of his own people, left exposed
In fiercest fight: but others with himself
He barred inside and saved them as they fled;
Nor noted, madman, how the Rutule King
Had burst in midmost of the line, and now
Stood prisoned in their wall, as if he were
Some monstrous tiger among helpless kine.
His eyeballs strangely glared; his armor rang
Terrific, his tall crest shook o'er his brows
Blood-red, and lightnings glittered from his shield.
Familiar loomed that countenance abhorred
And frame gigantic on the shrinking eyes
Of the Æneadæ. Then Pandarus
Sprang towering forth, all fever to revenge
His brother's slaughter. "Not this way," he cried,

"Amata's marriage-gift! No Ardea here
"Mews Turnus in his fathers' halls. Behold
"Thy foeman's castle! Thou art not allowed
"To take thy leave." But Turnus looked his way,
And smiled with heart unmoved. "Begin! if thou
"Hast manhood in thee, and meet steel with steel!
"Go tell dead Priam thou discoverest here
"Achilles!" For reply, the champion tall
Hurled with his might and main along the air
His spear of knotted wood and bark untrimmed.
But all it wounded was the passing wind,
For Saturn's daughter turned its course awry,
And deep in the great gate the spear-point drove.
"Now from the stroke this right arm means for thee
"Thou shalt not fly. Not such the sender of
"This weapon and this wound." He said, and towered
Aloft to his full height; the lifted sword
Clove temples, brows, and beardless cheeks clean through
With loudly ringing blow; the ground beneath
Shook with the giant's ponderous fall, and, lo,
With nerveless limbs, and brains spilt o'er his shield,
Dead on the earth he lay! in equal halves
The sundered head from either shoulder swung.
In horror and amaze the Trojans all
Dispersed and fled; had but the conqueror thought
To break the barriers of the gates and call
His followers through, that fatal day had seen
An ending of the Teucrians and their war.

But frenzied joy of slaughter urged him on,

Infuriate, to smite the scattering foe.
First Phaleris he caught; then cut the knees
Of Gyges; both their spears he snatched away
And hurled them at the rout; 't was Juno roused
His utmost might of rage. Now Halys fell,
And Phegeus, whom he pierced right through the shield:
Next, at the walls and urging reckless war,
Alcander, Halius, and Noëmon gave
Their lives, and Prytanis went down. In vain
Lynceus made stand and called his comrades brave:
For Turnus from the right with waving sword
Caught at him and lopped off with one swift blow
The head, which with its helmet rolled away.
Next Amycus, destroyer of wild beasts,
Who knew full well to smear a crafty barb
With venomed oil; young Clytius he slew,
Son of the wind-god; then on Cretheus fell,
A follower of the muses and their friend:
Cretheus, whose every joy it was to sing,
And fit his numbers to the chorded lyre;
Steeds, wars, armed men were his perpetual song.

At last the Teucrian chiefs had heard the tale
Of so much slaughter; and in council met
Are Mnestheus and Serestus bold, who see
Their comrades routed and the conquering foe
Within the gates. Cries Mnestheus, "Whither fly?
"What open way is yonder or what wall?
"Beyond these ramparts lost what stronger lie?
"Shall one lone man here in your walls confined,

"Make havoc unavenged and feed the grave
"With your best warriors? O cowards vile!
"For your sad country and her ancient gods
"And for renowned Æneas, can ye feel
"No pity and no shame?" Enflamed to fight
By words like these, they close the line, and stand
In strong array. So Turnus for a space
Out of the battle step by step withdrew
To make the river-bank his rearguard strong;
Whereat the Teucrians, shouting loud, swept on
The fiercer, and in solid mass pressed round.

As when a troop of hunters with keen spears
Encircle a wild lion, who in fear,
But glaring grim and furious, backward falls,
Valor and rage constrain him ne'er to cease
Fronting the foe; yet not for all his ire
Can he against such serried steel make way:
So Turnus backward with a lingering step
Unwilling drew, and wrath his heart o'erflowed.
For twice already had he cloven a path
Into the foe's mid-press, and twice had driven
Their flying lines in panic through the town.

But now the whole throng from the camp he sees
Massed to the onset. Nor will Juno now
Dare give him vigor to withstand, for Jove
Had sent aerial Iris out of heaven
With stern commandment to his sister-queen
That Turnus from the Teucrian walls retire.
Therefore the warrior's shield avails no more,

Nor his strong arm; but he is overthrown
By general assault. Around his brows
His smitten helmet rings; the ponderous mail
Cracks under falling stones; the haughty plumes
Are scattered from his head, nor can the boss
Of his stout shield endure; the Trojans hurl
Redoubled rain of spears; and with them speeds
Mnestheus like thunderbolt. The hero's flesh
Dissolves in sweat; no room to breathe has he;
His limbs are spent and weary; his whole frame
Shakes with his gasping breath: then bounding forth
With all his harness on, headlong he plunged
Into the flowing stream; its yellow tide
Embraced him as he fell, and gentle waves
Restored him smiling to his friends in arms,
With all the gore and carnage washed away.

END OF BOOK IX

BOOK X

MEANWHILE Olympus, seat of sovereign sway,
Threw wide its portals, and in conclave fair
The Sire of gods and King of all mankind
Summoned th' immortals to his starry court,
Whence, high-enthroned, the spreading earth he views —
And Teucria's camp and Latium's fierce array.

Beneath the double-gated dome the gods
Were sitting; Jove himself the silence broke:
"O people of Olympus, wherefore change
"Your purpose and decree, with partial minds
"In mighty strife contending? I refused
"Such clash of war 'twixt Italy and Troy.
"Whence this forbidden feud? What fears
"Seduced to battles and injurious arms
"Either this folk or that? Th' appointed hour
"For war shall be hereafter — speed it not! —
"When cruel Carthage to the towers of Rome
"Shall bring vast ruin, streaming fiercely down
"The opened Alp. Then hate with hate shall vie,
"And havoc have no bound. Till then, give o'er,
"And smile upon the concord I decree!"

Thus briefly, Jove. But golden Venus made
Less brief reply. "O Father, who dost hold

"O'er Man and all things an immortal sway!
"Of what high throne may gods the aid implore
"Save thine? Behold of yonder Rutuli
"Th' insulting scorn! Among them Turnus moves
"In chariot proud, and boasts triumphant war
"In mighty words. Nor do their walls defend
"My Teucrians now. But in their very gates,
"And on their mounded ramparts, in close fight
"They breast their foes and fill the moats with blood.
"Æneas knows not, and is far away.
"Will ne'er the siege have done? A second time
"Above Troy's rising walls the foe impends;
"Another host is gathered, and once more
"From his Ætolian Arpi wrathful speeds
"A Diomed. I doubt not that for me
"Wounds are preparing. Yea, thy daughter dear
"Awaits a mortal sword! If by thy will
"Unblest and unapproved the Trojans came
"To Italy, for such rebellious crime
"Give them their due, nor lend them succor, thou,
"With thy strong hand! But if they have obeyed
"Unnumbered oracles from gods above
"And sacred shades below, who now has power
"To thwart thy bidding, or to weave anew
"The web of Fate? Why speak of ships consumed
"Along my hallowed Erycinian shore?
"Or of the Lord of Storms, whose furious blasts
"Were summoned from Æolia? Why tell
"Of Iris sped from heaven? Now she moves
"The region of the shades (one kingdom yet
"From her attempt secure) and thence lets loose

"Alecto on the world above, who strides
"In frenzied wrath along th' Italian hills.
"No more my heart now cherishes its hope
"Of domination, though in happier days
"Such was thy promise. Let the victory fall
"To victors of thy choice! If nowhere lies
"The land thy cruel Queen would deign accord
"Unto the Teucrian people, — O my sire,
"I pray thee by yon smouldering wreck of Troy
"To let Ascanius from the clash of arms
"Escape unscathed. Let my own offspring live!
"Yea, let Æneas, tossed on seas unknown,
"Find some chance way; let my right hand avail
"To shelter him and from this fatal war
"In safety bring. For Amathus is mine,
"Mine are Cythera and the Paphian hills
"And temples in Idalium. Let him drop
"The sword, and there live out inglorious days.
"By thy decree let Carthage overwhelm
"Ausonia's power; nor let defence be found
"To stay the Tyrian arms! What profits it
"That he escaped the wasting plague of war
"And fled Argolic fires? or that he knew
"So many perils of wide wilderness
"And waters rude? The Teucrians seek in vain
"A new-born Troy in Latium. Better far
"Crouched on their country's ashes to abide,
"And keep that spot of earth where once was Troy!
"Give back, O Father, I implore thee, give
"Xanthus and Simois back! Let Teucer's sons
"Unfold once more the tale of Ilium's woe!"

Then sovereign Juno, flushed with solemn scorn,
Made answer. "Dost thou bid me here profane
"The silence of my heart, and gossip forth
"Of secret griefs? What will of god or man
"Impelled Æneas on his path of war,
"Or made him foeman of the Latin King?
"Fate brought him to Italia? Be it so!
"Cassandra's frenzy he obeyed. What voice —
"Say, was it mine? — urged him to quit his camp,
"Risk life in storms, or trust his war, his walls,
"To a boy-captain, or stir up to strife
"Etruria's faithful, unoffending sons?
"What god, what pitiless behest of mine,
"Impelled him to such harm? Who traces here
"The hand of Juno, or of Iris sped
"From heaven? Is it an ignoble stroke
"That Italy around the new-born Troy
"Makes circling fire, and Turnus plants his heel
"On his hereditary earth, the son
"Of old Pilumnus and the nymph divine,
"Venilia? For what offence would Troy
"Bring sword and fire on Latium, or enslave
"Lands of an alien name, and bear away
"Plunder and spoil? Why seek they marriages,
"And snatch from arms of love the plighted maids?
"An olive-branch is in their hands; their ships
"Make menace of grim steel. Thy power one day
"Ravished Æneas from his Argive foes,
"And gave them shape of cloud and fleeting air
"To strike at for a man. Thou hast transformed
"His ships to daughters of the sea. What wrong

"If I, not less, have lent the Rutuli
"Something of strength in war? Æneas, then,
"Is far away and knows not! Far away
"Let him remain, not knowing! If thou sway'st
"Cythera, Paphos, and Idalium,
"Why rouse a city pregnant with loud wars,
"And fiery hearts provoke? That fading power
"Of Phrygia, do I, forsooth, essay
"To ruin utterly? O, was it I
"Exposed ill-fated Troy to Argive foe?
"For what offence in vast array of arms
"Did Europe rise and Asia, for a rape
"Their peace dissolving? Was it at my word
"Th' adulterous Dardan shepherd came to storm
"The Spartan city? Did my hand supply
"His armament, or instigate a war
"For Cupid's sake? Then was thy decent hour
"To tremble for thy children; now too late
"The folly of thy long lament to Heaven,
"And objurgation vain." Such Juno's plea;
The throng of gods with voices loud or low
Gave various reply: as gathering winds
Sing through the tree-tops in dark syllables,
And fling faint murmur on the far-off sea,
To tell some pilot of to-morrow's storm.

Then Jupiter omnipotent, whose hands
Have governance supreme, began reply;
Deep silence at his word Olympus knew,
Earth's utmost cavern shook; the realms of light
Were silent; the mild zephyrs breathed no more,

And perfect calm o'erspread the levelled sea.
"Give ear, ye gods, and in your hearts record
"My mandate and decree. Fate yet allows
"No peace 'twixt Troy and Italy, nor bids
"Your quarrel end. Therefore, what Chance this day
"To either foe shall bring, whatever hope
"Either may cherish, — the Rutulian cause
"And Trojan have like favor in my eyes.
"The destinies of Italy constrain
"The siege; which for the fault of Troy fulfils
"An oracle of woe. Yon Rutule host
"I scatter not. But of his own attempt
"Let each the triumph and the burden bear;
"For Jove is over all an equal King.
"The Fates will find the way."
The god confirmed
His sentence by his Stygian brother's wave,
The shadowy flood and black, abysmal shore.
He nodded; at the bending of his brow
Olympus shook. It is the council's end.
Now from the golden throne uprises Jove;
The train of gods attend him to the doors.

Meanwhile at every gate the Rutule foe
Urges the slaughter on, and closes round
The battlements with ring of flame. The host
Of Trojans, prisoned in the palisades,
Lies in strict siege and has no hope to fly.
In wretched plight they man the turrets tall,
To no avail, and with scant garrison
The ramparts crown. In foremost line of guard

Are Asius Imbrasides, the twin
Assaraci, and Hicetaon's son
Thymœtes, and with Castor at his side
The veteran Thymbris; then the brothers both
Of slain Sarpedon, and from Lycian steep
Clarus and Themon. With full-straining thews
Lifting a rock, which was of some huge hill
No fragment small, Lyrnesian Acmon stood;
Nor less than Clytius his sire he seemed,
Nor Mnestheus his great brother. Some defend
The wall with javelins; some hurl down stones
Or firebrands, or to the sounding string
Fit arrows keen. But lo! amid the throng,
Well worth to Venus her protecting care,
The Dardan boy, whose princely head shone forth
Without a helm, like radiant jewel set
In burnished gold for necklace or for crown;
Or like immaculate ivory inclosed
In boxwood or Orician terebinth;
His tresses o'er his white neck rippled down,
Confined in circlet of soft twisted gold.
Thee, too, the warrior nations gaze upon,
High-nurtured Ismarus, inflicting wounds
With shafts of venomed reed: Mæonia's vale
Thy cradle was, where o'er the fruitful fields
Well-tilled and rich, Pactolus pours his gold.
Mnestheus was there, who, for his late repulse
Of Turnus from the rampart, towered forth
In glory eminent; there Capys stood,
Whose name the Capuan citadel shall bear.

While these in many a shock of grievous war
Hotly contend, Æneas cleaves his way
At midnight through the waters. He had fared
From old Evander to th' Etruscan folk,
Addressed their King, and to him told the tale
Of his own race and name, his suit, his powers;
Of what allies Mezentius had embraced,
And Turnus' lawless rage. He bids him know
How mutable is man, and warning gives,
With supplication joined. Without delay
Tarchon made amity and sacred league,
Uniting with his cause. The Lydian tribe,
Now destined from its tyrant to be free,
Embarked, obedient to the gods, and gave
Allegiance to the foreign King. The ship
Æneas rode moved foremost in the line:
Its beak a pair of Phrygian lions bore;
Above them Ida rose, an emblem dear
To exiled Trojans. On his lofty seat
Was great Æneas, pondering the events
Of changeful war; and clinging to his side
The youthful Pallas fain would learn the lore
Of stars, the highway of dark night, and asks
The story of his toils on land and sea.

Now open Helicon and move my song,
Ye goddesses, to tell what host in arms
Followed Æneas from the Tuscan shore,
And manned his ships and travelled o'er the sea!
First Massicus his brazen Tigress rode,
Cleaving the brine; a thousand warriors

Were with him out of Clusium's walls, or from
The citadel of Cosæ, who for arms
Had arrows, quivers from the shoulder slung,
And deadly bows. Grim Abas near him sailed;
His whole band wore well-blazoned mail; his ship
Displayed the form of Phœbus, all of gold:
To him had Populonia consigned
(His mother-city, she) six hundred youth
Well-proven in war; three hundred Elba gave,
An island rich in unexhausted ores
Of iron, like the Chalybes. Next came
Asilas, who betwixt the gods and men
Interprets messages and reads clear signs
In victims' entrails, or the stars of heaven,
Or bird-talk, or the monitory flames
Of lightning: he commands a thousand men
Close lined, with bristling spears, of Pisa all,
That Tuscan city of Alpheus sprung.
Then Astur followed, a bold horseman he,
Astur in gorgeous arms, himself most fair:
Three hundred are his men, one martial mind
Uniting all: in Cære they were bred
And Minio's plain, and by the ancient towers
Of Pyrgo or Gravisca's storm-swept hill.

Nor thy renown may I forget, brave chief
Of the Ligurians, Cinyrus; nor thine,
Cupavo, with few followers, thy crest
The tall swan-wings, of love unblest the sign
And of a father fair: for legends tell
That Cycnus, for his Phaëthon so dear

Lamenting loud beneath the poplar shade
Of the changed sisters, made a mournful song
To soothe his grief and passion: but erewhile,
In his old age, there clothed him as he sang
Soft snow-white plumes, and spurning earth he soared
On high, and sped in music through the stars.
His son with bands of youthful peers urged on
A galley with a Centaur for its prow,
Which loomed high o'er the waves, and seemed to hurl
A huge stone at the water, as the keel
Ploughed through the deep.
Next Ocnus summoned forth
A war-host from his native shores, the son
Of Tiber, Tuscan river, and the nymph
Manto, a prophetess: he gave good walls,
O Mantua, and his mother's name, to thee,—
To Mantua so rich in noble sires,
But of a blood diverse, a triple breed,
Four stems in each; and over all enthroned
She rules her tribes: her strength is Tuscan born.
Hate of Mezentius armed against his name
Five hundred men: upon their hostile prow
Was Mincius in a cloak of silvery sedge,—
Lake Benacus the river's source and sire.

Last good Aulestes smites the depths below,
With forest of a hundred oars: the flood
Like flowing marble foams; his Triton prow
Threatens the blue waves with a trumpet-shell;
Far as the hairy flanks its form is man,

But ends in fish below — the parting waves
Beneath the half-brute bosom break in foam.
Such chosen chiefs in thirty galleys ploughed
The salt-wave, bringing help to Trojan arms.

Day now had left the sky. The moon benign
Had driven her night-wandering chariot
To the mid-arch of heaven. Æneas sate,
For thought and care allowed him no repose,
Holding the helm and tending his own sails.
But, as he sped, behold, the beauteous train,
Lately his own, of nymphs, anon transformed
By kind Cybebe to sea-ruling powers.
In even ranks they swam the cloven wave, —
Nymphs now, but once as brazen galleys moored
Along the sandy shore. With joy they knew
Their King from far, and with attending train
Around him drew. Cymodocea then,
Best skilled in mortal speech, sped close behind,
With her right hand upon the stern, uprose
Breast-high, and with her left hand deeply plied
The silent stream, as to the wondering King
She called: "So late on watch, O son of Heaven,
"Æneas? Slack thy sail, but still watch on!
"We were the pine-trees on the holy top
"Of Ida's mountain. Sea-nymphs now are we,
"And thine own fleet. When, as we fled, the flames
"Rained o'er us from the false Rutulian's hand
"'T was all unwillingly we cast away
"Thy serviceable chains: and now once more
"We follow thee across the sea. These forms

"Our pitying mother bade us take, with power
"To haunt immortally the moving sea.
"Lo, thy Ascanius lies close besieged
"In moated walls, assailed by threatening arms
"And Latium's front of war. Arcadia,
"Her horsemen with the bold Etruscan joined,
"Stands at the place appointed. Turnus means,
"With troop opposing, their advance to bar
"And hold them from the camp. Arouse thee, then,
"And with the rising beams of dawn call forth
"Thy captains and their followers. Take that shield
"Victorious, which for thee the Lord of Fire
"Forged for a gift and rimmed about with gold.
"To-morrow's light—deem not my words be vain!—
"Shall shine on huge heaps of Rutulia's dead."
So saying, she pushed with her right hand the stern
With skilful thrust, and vanished. The ship sped
Swift as a spear, or as an arrow flies
No whit behind the wind: and all the fleet
Quickened its course. Anchises' princely son,
Dumb and bewildered stood, but took good heart
At such an omen fair. Then in few words
With eyes upturned to heaven he made his prayer:
"Mother of gods, O Ida's Queen benign,
"Who lovest Dindymus and towns with towers,
"And lion-yokes obedient to thy rein,
"Be thou my guide in battle, and fulfil
"Thine augury divine. In Phrygia's cause
"Be present evermore with favoring power!"

He spoke no more. For now the wheels of day

Had sped full circle into perfect light,
The dark expelling. Then, for his first care,
He bade his captains heed the signal given,
Equip their souls for war, and wait in arms
The coming fray. Now holds he full in view
His Trojans and their fortress, as he stands
Upon his towering ship. With his left hand
He lifts his radiant shield; then from the wall
The Dardan warriors send a battle-cry
That echoes to the stars, as kindling hope
Their rage renews. A flight of spears they hurl:
'T was like the cranes of Strymon, through dark clouds
Each other calling, when they cleave the skies
Vociferous, outwinging as they fly
The swift south winds — loud music them pursues.
Amazement on Ausonia's captains fell
And Turnus, as they gazed. But soon they saw
Ships pointing shoreward and the watery plain
All stirring with a fleet. Æneas' helm
Uplifted its bright peak, — like streaming flame
The crimson crest; his shield of orbèd gold
Poured forth prodigious fire: it seemed as when
In cloudless night a comet's blood-red beam
Makes mournful splendor, or the Dog-star glows,
Which rises to bring drought and pestilence
To hapless men, and with ill-omened ray
Saddens the sky.

But Turnus, undismayed,
Trusted not less to hurl th' invaders back
And hold the shore against them. "Look!" he cried,
"Your prayer is come to pass, — that sword in hand

"Ye now may shatter them. The might of Mars
"Is in a true man's blow. Remember well
"Each man his home and wife! Now call to mind
"The glory and great deeds of all your sires!
"Charge to yon river-bank, while yet they take
"With weak and fearful steps their shoreward way!
"Fortune will help the brave."
With words like these,
He chose, well-weighing, who should lead the charge,
Who at the leaguered walls the fight sustain.

Æneas straightway from his lofty ships
Lets down his troop by bridges. Some await
The ebbing of slack seas, and boldly leap
Into the shallows; others ply the oar.
Tarchon a beach discovers, where the sands
Sing not, nor waves with broken murmur fall,
But full and silent swells the gentle sea.
Steering in haste that way, he called his crews:
"Now bend to your stout oars, my chosen brave.
"Lift each ship forward, till her beak shall cleave
"Yon hostile shore; and let her keel's full weight
"The furrow drive. I care not if we break
"Our ship's side in so sure an anchorage,
"If once we land." While Tarchon urged them thus,
The crews bent all together to their blades
And sped their foaming barks to Latium's plain,
Till each beak gripped the sand and every keel
Lay on dry land unscathed: — all save thine own,
O Tarchon! dashed upon a sand-bar, she!
Long poised upon the cruel ridge she hung,

Tilted this way or that and beat the waves,
Then split, and emptied forth upon the tide
Her warriors; and now the drifting wreck
Of shattered oars and thwarts entangles them,
Or ebb of swirling waters sucks them down.
Turnus no lingering knows, but fiercely hurls
His whole line on the Teucrians, and makes stand
Along the shore. Now peals the trumpet's call.
Æneas in the van led on his troop
Against the rustic foe, bright augury
For opening war, and laid the Latins low,
Slaughtering Theron, a huge chief who dared
Offer Æneas battle; through the scales
Of brazen mail and corselet stiff with gold
The sword drove deep, and gored the gaping side.
Then smote he Lichas, from his mother's womb
Ripped in her dying hour, and unto thee,
O Phœbus, vowed, because his infant days
Escaped the fatal steel. Hard by him fell
Stout Cisseus and gigantic Gyas; these
To death were hurled, while with their knotted clubs
They slew opposing hosts; but naught availed
Herculean weapons, nor their mighty hands,
Nor that Melampus was their sire, a peer
Of Hercules, what time in heavy toils
Through earth he roved. See next how Pharon boasts!
But while he vainly raves, the whirling spear
Smites full on his loud mouth. And also thou,
Cydon, wast by the Trojan stroke o'erthrown,
While following in ill-omened haste the steps
Of Clytius, thy last joy, whose round cheek wore

Its youthful golden down: soon hadst thou lain
In death, unheeding of thy fancies fond
Which ever turned to youth; — but now arose
The troop of all thy brothers, Phorcus' sons,
A close array of seven, and seven spears
They hurled: some from Æneas' helm or shield
Glanced off in vain; some Venus' kindly power,
Just as they touched his body, turned away.

Æneas then to true Achates cried:
"Bring on my spears: not one shall fruitless fly
"Against yon Rutules, even as they pierced
"The breasts of Greeks upon the Ilian plain."
Then one great shaft he seized and threw; it sped
Straight into Mæon's brazen shield, and clove
His mail-clad heart. Impetuous to his aid
Brother Alcanor came, and lifted up
With strong right hand his brother as he fell:
But through his arm a second skilful shaft
Made bloody way, and by the sinews held
The lifeless right hand from the shoulder swung.
Then from his brother's body Numitor
The weapon plucked and hurled it, furious,
Upon Æneas; but it could not strike
The hero's self, and grazed along the thigh
Of great Achates. Next into the fight
Clausus of Cures came, in youthful bloom
Exulting, and with far-thrown javelin
Struck Dryops at the chin, and took away
From the gashed, shrieking throat both life and voice;
The warrior's fallen forehead smote the dust;

His lips poured forth thick blood. There also fell
Three Thracians, offspring of the lordly stem
Of Boreas, and three of Idas' sons
From Ismara, by various doom struck down.
Halæsus here his wild Auruncans brings;
And flying to the fight comes Neptune's son,
Messapus, famous horseman. On both sides
Each charges on the foe. Ausonia's strand
Is one wide strife. As when o'er leagues of air
The envious winds give battle to their peers,
Well-matched in rage and power; and neither they,
Nor clouds above, nor plunging seas below
Will end the doubtful war, but each withstands
The onset of the whole — in such wild way
The line of Trojans on the Latian line
Hurls itself, limb on limb and man on man.

But at a distance where the river's flood
Had scattered rolling boulders and torn trees
Uprooted from the shore, young Pallas spied
Th' Arcadian band, unused to fight on foot,
In full retreat, the Latins following close —
Who also for the roughness of the ground
Were all unmounted: he (the last resource
Of men in straits) to wild entreaty turned
And taunts, enkindling their faint hearts anew:
"Whither, my men! O, by your own brave deeds,
"O, by our lord Evander's happy wars,
"By the proud hopes I had to make my name
"A rival glory, — think not ye can fly!
"Your swords alone can carve ye the safe way

"Straight through your foes. Where yonder warrior-throng
"Is fiercest, thickest, there and only there
"Your country's honor calls for men like you,
"And for your captain Pallas. Nay, no gods
"Against us fight; we are but mortal men
"Pressed by a mortal foe. Not more than ours
"The number of their lives or swords. Behold,
"The barrier of yonder spreading sea
"Emprisons us, and for a craven flight
"Yon lands are all too small. Ha! Shall we steer
"Across the sea to Troy?"
He said, and sprang
Full in the centre of his gathered foes.
First in his path was Lagus, thither led
By evil stars; whom, as he tried to lift
A heavy stone, the shaft of Pallas pierced
Where ribs and spine divide: backward he drew
The clinging spear. But Hisbo from above
Surprised him not, though meaning it; for while
(In anger blind for friend unpitying slain)
At Pallas' face he flew: — he, standing firm,
Plunged deep into that swelling breast the sword.
Then Sthenius he slew; and next Anchemolus
Of Rhœtus' ancient line, who dared defile
His step-dame's bridal bed. And also ye,
Fair Thymber and Larides, Daucus' twins,
Fell on that Rutule field; so like were ye,
Your own kin scarce discerned, and parents proud
Smiled at the dear deceit; but now in death
Cruel unlikeness Pallas wrought; thy head

Fell, hapless Thymber, by Evander's sword;
And thy right hand, Larides, shorn away,
Seemed feeling for its lord; the fingers cold
Clutched, trembling, at the sword. Now all the troop
Of Arcady, their chief's great action seen,
And by his warning roused, made at their foes,
Spurred on by grief and shame. Next Pallas pierced
The flying Rhœtus in his car; this gained
For Ilus respite and delay, for him
The stout spear aimed at; but its flight was stopped
By Rhœtus, as in swift retreat he rode,
By the two high-born brothers close pursued,
Teuthras and Tyres: from his car he rolled,
Making deep furrows with his lifeless heels
Along the Rutule plain. Oft when the winds
Of summer, long awaited, rise and blow,
A shepherd fires the forest, and the blaze
Devours the dense grove, while o'er the fields,
In that one moment, swift and sudden spread
Grim Vulcan's serried flames; from some high seat
On distant hill, the shepherd peering down
Sees, glad at heart, his own victorious fires:
So now fierce valor spreads, uniting all
In one confederate rage, 'neath Pallas' eyes.

But the fierce warrior Halæsus next
Led on the charge, behind his skilful shield
Close-crouching. Ladon and Demodocus
And Pheres he struck down; his glittering blade
Cut Strymon's hand, which to his neck was raised,
Sheer off; with one great stone he crushed the brows

Of Thoas, scattering wide the broken skull,
Bones, brains, and gore. Halæsus' prophet-sire,
Foreseeing doom, had hid him in dark groves;
But when the old man's fading eyes declined
In death, the hand of Fate reached forth and doomed
The young life to Evander's sword; him now
Pallas assailed, first offering this prayer:
"O Father Tiber, give my poising shaft
"Through stout Halæsus' heart its lucky way!
"The spoil and trophy of the hero slain
"On thine own oak shall hang."
The god received
The vow, and while Halæsus held his shield
Over Imaon, his ill-fated breast
Lay naked to th' Arcadian's hungry spear.
But Lausus, seeing such a hero slain,
Bade his troop have no fear, for he himself
Was no small strength in war; and first he slew
Abas, who fought hard, and had ever seemed
Himself the sticking-point and tug of war.
Down went Arcadia's warriors, and slain
Etruscans fell, with many a Trojan brave
The Greek had spared. Troop charges upon troop
Well-matched in might, with chiefs of like renown;
The last rank crowds the first; — so fierce the press
Scarce hand or sword can stir. Here Pallas stands,
And pushes back the foe; before him looms
Lausus, his youthful peer, conspicuous both
In beauty; but no star will them restore
To home and native land. Yet would the King
Of high Olympus suffer not the pair

To close in battle, but each hero found
A later doom at hands of mightier foes.

Now Turnus' goddess-sister bids him haste
To Lausus' help. So he, in wheeling car,
Cut through the lines; and when his friends he saw,
"Let the fight stop!" he cried, "for none but I
"May strike at Pallas; unto me alone
"The prize of Pallas falls. I would his sire
"Stood by to see." He spake: his troop withdrew
A fitting space. But as they made him room,
The young prince, wondering at the scornful words,
Looked upon Turnus, glancing up and down
That giant frame, and with fierce-frowning brows
Scanned him from far, hurling defiant words
In answer to the King's. "My honor now
"Shall have the royal trophy of this war,
"Or glorious death. For either fortune fair
"My sire is ready. Threaten me no more!"
So saying, to the midmost space he strode,
And in Arcadian hearts the blood stood still.
Swift from his chariot Turnus leaped, and ran
To closer fight. As when some lion sees
From his far mountain-lair a raging bull
That sniffs the battle from the grassy field,
And down the steep he flies — such picture showed
Grim Turnus as he came. But when he seemed
Within a spear's cast, Pallas opened fight,
Expecting Fortune's favor to the brave
In such unequal match; and thus he prayed:
"O, by my hospitable father's roof,

"Where thou didst enter as a stranger-guest,
"Hear me, Alcides, and give aid divine
"To this great deed. Let Turnus see these hands
"Strip from his half-dead breast the bloody spoil!
"And let his eyes in death endure to see
'His conqueror!" Alcides heard the youth:
But prisoned in his heart a deep-drawn sigh,
And shed vain tears; for Jove, the King and Sire,
Spoke with benignant accents to his son:
"To each his day is given. Beyond recall
"Man's little time runs by: but to prolong
"Life's glory by great deeds is virtue's power.
"Beneath the lofty walls of fallen Troy
"Fell many a son of Heaven. Yea, there was slain
"Sarpedon, my own offspring. Turnus too
"Is summoned to his doom, and nears the bounds
"Of his appointed span." So speaking, Jove
Turned from Rutulia's war his eyes away.

But Pallas hurled his lance with might and main,
And from its hollow scabbard flashed his sword.
The flying shaft touched where the plated steel
Over the shoulders rose, and worked its way
Through the shield's rim — then falling, glanced aside
From Turnus' giant body. Turnus then
Poised, without haste, his iron-pointed spear,
And, launching it on Pallas, cried, "Look now
"Will not this shaft a good bit deeper drive?"
He said: and through the mid-boss of the shield,
Steel scales and brass with bull's-hide folded round,

The quivering spear-point crashed resistlessly,
And through the corselet's broken barrier
Pierced Pallas' heart. The youth plucked out in vain
The hot shaft from the wound; his life and blood
Together ebbed away, as sinking prone
On his rent side he fell; above him rang
His armor; and from lips with blood defiled
He breathed his last upon his foeman's ground.

Over him Turnus stood: "Arcadians all,"
He cried, "take tidings of this feat of arms
"To King Evander. With a warrior's wage
"His Pallas I restore, and freely grant
"What glory in a hero's tomb may lie,
"Or comfort in a grave. They dearly pay
"Who bid Æneas welcome at their board."
So saying, with his left foot he held down
The lifeless form, and raised the heavy weight
Of graven belt, which pictured forth that crime
Of youthful company by treason slain,
All on their wedding night, in bridal bowers
To horrid murder given, — which Clonus, son
Of Eurytus, had wrought in lavish gold;
This Turnus in his triumph bore away,
Exulting in the spoil. O heart of man,
Not knowing doom, nor of events to be!
Nor, being lifted up, to keep thy bounds
In prosperous days! To Turnus comes the hour
When he would fain a prince's ransom give
Had Pallas passed unscathed, and will bewail
Such spoil of victory.

With weeping now
And lamentations loud his comrades lay
Young Pallas on his shield, and thronging close
Carry him homeward with a mournful song:
"Alas! the sorrow and the glorious gain
"Thy sire shall have in thee. For one brief day
"Bore thee to battle and now bears away;
"Yet leavest thou full tale of foemen slain.

No doubtful rumor to Æneas breaks
The direful news, but a sure messenger
Tells him his followers' peril, and implores
Prompt help for routed Troy. His ready sword
Reaped down the nearest foes, and through their line
Clove furious path and broad; the valiant blade
Through oft-repeated bloodshed groped its way,
Proud Turnus, unto thee! His heart beholds
Pallas and Sire Evander, their kind board
In welcome spread, their friendly league of peace
Proffered and sealed with him, the stranger-guest.
So Sulmo's sons, four warriors, and four
Of Ufens sprung, he took alive — to slay
As victims to the shades, and pour a stream
Of captives' blood upon a flaming pyre.

Next from afar his hostile shaft he threw
At Mago, who with wary motion bowed
Beneath the quivering weapon, as it sped
Clean over him; then at Æneas' knees
He crouched and clung with supplicating cry:
"O, by thy father's spirit, by thy hope

"In young Iulus, I implore thee, spare
"For son and father's sake this life of mine.
"A lofty house have I, where safely hid
"Are stores of graven silver and good weight
"Of wrought and unwrought gold. The fate of war
"Hangs not on me; nor can one little life
"Thy victory decide." In answer spoke
Æneas: "Hoard the silver and the gold
"For thy own sons. Such bartering in war
"Finished with Turnus, when fair Pallas fell.
"Thus bids Anchises' shade, Iulus — thus!"
He spoke: and, grasping with his mighty left
The helmet of the vainly suppliant foe,
Bent back the throat and drove hilt-deep his sword.

A little space removed, Hæmonides,
A priest of Phœbus and pale Trivia, stood,
Whose ribboned brows a sacred fillet bound:
In shining vesture he, and glittering arms.
Him too the Trojan met, repelled, and towered
Above the fallen form, o'ermantling it
In mortal shade; Serestus bore away
Those famous arms a trophy vowed to thee,
Gradivus, lord of war! Soon to fresh fight
Came Cæculus, a child of Vulcan's line,
And Umbro on the Marsic mountains bred:
These met the Trojan's wrath. His sword shore off
Anxur's left hand, and the whole orbèd shield
Dropped earthward at the stroke: though Anxur's tongue
Had boasted mighty things, as if great words

Would make him strong, and lifting his proud heart
As high as heaven, had hoped perchance to see
Gray hairs and length of days. Then Tarquitus
Strode forth, exulting in his burnished arms
(Him Dryope, the nymph, to Faunus bore),
And dared oppose Æneas' rage. But he
Drew back his lance and, charging, crushed at once
Corselet and ponderous shield; then off he struck
The supplicating head, which seemed in vain
Preparing speech; while o'er the reeking corpse
The victor stood, and thrusting it away
Spoke thus with wrathful soul: "Now lie thou there,
"Thou fearsome sight! No noble mother's hand
"Shall hide thee in the ground, or give those limbs
"To their ancestral tomb. Thou shalt be left
"To birds of ravin; or go drifting far
"Along yon river to engulfing seas,
"Where starving fishes on those wounds shall feed."

Antæus next and Lucas he pursues,
Though all in Turnus' van; and Numa bold
And Camers tawny-tressed, the son and heir
Of Volscens the stout-hearted, whose domain
Surpassed the richest of Ausonia's lords,
When over hushed Amyclæ he was king.
Like old Ægæon of the hundred arms,
The hundred-handed, from whose mouths and breasts
Blazed fifty fiery blasts, as he made war
With fifty sounding shields and fifty swords
Against Jove's thunder; — so Æneas raged

Victorious o'er the field, when once his steel
Warmed to its work.
But lo, he turns him now
Where come Niphæus' bold-advancing wheels
And coursers four, who, when at furious speed
They faced his giant stride and dreadful cry,
Upreared in panic, and reversing spilled
Their captain to the ground, and bore away
The chariot to the river's distant shore.

Meanwhile, with two white coursers to their car,
The brothers Lucagus and Liger drove
Into the heart of battle: Liger kept
With skilful hand the manage of the steeds;
Bold Lucagus swung wide his naked sword.
Æneas, by their wrathful brows defied,
Brooked not the sight, but to the onset flew,
Huge-looming, with adverse and threatening spear.
Cried Liger, "Not Achilles' chariot, ours!
"Nor team of Diomed on Phrygia's plain!
"The last of life and strife shall be thy meed
"Upon this very ground." Such raving word
Flowed loud from Liger's lip: not with a word
The Trojan hero answered him, but flung
His whirling spear; and even as Lucagus
Leaned o'er the horses, goading them with steel,
And, left foot forward, gathered all his strength
To strike — the spear crashed through the under rim
Of his resplendent shield and entered deep
In the left groin; then from the chariot fallen,
The youth rolled dying on the field, while thus

Pious Æneas paid him taunting words:
"O Lucagus, thy chariot did not yield
"Because of horses slow to fly, or scared
"By shadows of a foe. It was thyself
"Leaped o'er the wheel and fled." So saying, he grasped
The horses by the rein. The brother then,
Spilled also from the car, reached wildly forth
His helpless hands: "O, by thy sacred head,
"And by the parents who such greatness gave,
"Good Trojan, let me live! Some pity show
"To prostrate me!" But ere he longer sued,
Æneas cried, "Not so thy language ran
"A moment gone! Die thou! Nor let this day
"Brother from brother part!" Then where the life
Hides in the bosom, he thrust deep his sword.
Thus o'er the field of war the Dardan King
Moved on, death-dealing: like a breaking flood
Or cloudy whirlwind seemed his wrath. Straightway
The boy Ascanius from the ramparts came,
His warriors with him; for the siege had failed.

Now Jupiter to Juno thus began:
"O ever-cherished spouse and sister dear,
"Surely 't is Venus — as thy mind misgave —
"Whose favor props — O, what discernment thine! —
"Yon Trojan power; not swift heroic hands,
"Nor souls of fury facing perilous war!"
Juno made meek reply: "O noblest spouse!
"Why vex one sick at heart, who humbly fears
"Thy stern command? If I could claim to-day

"What once I had, my proper right and due,
"Love's influence, I should not plead in vain
"To thee, omnipotent, to give me power
"To lead off Turnus from the fight unscathed,
"And save him at his father Daunus' prayer.
"Aye, let him die! And with his loyal blood
"The Teucrians' vengeance feed! Yet he derives
"From our Saturnian stem, by fourth remove
"Sprung from Pilumnus. Oft his liberal hands
"Have heaped unstinted offering at thy shrine."
Thus in few words th' Olympian King replied:
"If for the fated youth thy prayer implores
"Delay and respite of impending doom,
"If but so far thou bidst me interpose,—
"Go, favor Turnus' flight, and keep him safe
"In this imperilled hour; I may concede
"Such boon. But if thy pleading words intend
"Some larger grace, and fain would touch or change
"The issue of the war, then art thou fed
"On expectation vain." With weeping eyes
Juno made answer: "Can it be thy mind
"Gives what thy words refuse, and Turnus' life,
"If rescued, may endure? Yet afterward
"Some cruel close his guiltless day shall see —
"Or far from truth I stray! O, that I were
"The dupe of empty fears! and O, that thou
"Wouldst but refashion to some happier end
"The things by thee begun — for thou hast power!"
She ceased; and swiftly from the peak of heaven
Moved earthward, trailing cloud-wrack through the air,

And girdled with the storm. She took her way
To where Troy's warriors faced Laurentum's line.
There of a hollow cloud the goddess framed
A shape of airy, unsubstantial shade,
Æneas' image, wonderful to see,
And decked it with a Dardan lance and shield,
A crested helmet on the godlike head;
And windy words she gave of soulless sound,
And motion like a stride — such shapes, they say,
The hovering phantoms of the dead put on,
Or empty dreams which cheat our slumbering eyes.
Forth to the front of battle this vain shade
Stalked insolent, and with its voice and spear
Challenged the warrior. At it Turnus flew,
And hurled a hissing spear with distant aim;
The thing wheeled round and fled. The foe forthwith,
Thinking Æneas vanquished, with blind scorn
Flattered his own false hope: "Where wilt thou fly,
"Æneas? Wilt thou break a bridegroom's word?
"This sword will give thee title to some land
"Thou hast sailed far to find!" So clamoring loud
He followed, flashing far his naked sword;
Nor saw the light winds waft his dream away.

By chance in covert of a lofty crag
A ship stood fastened and at rest; her sides
Showed ready bridge and stairway; she had brought
Osinius, king of Clusium. Thither came
Æneas' counterfeit of flight and fear,
And dropped to darkness. Turnus, nothing loth,

Gave close chase, overleaping every bar,
And scaling the high bridge; but scarce he reached
The vessel's prow, when Juno cut her loose,
The cables breaking, and along swift waves
Pushed her to sea. Yet in that very hour
Æneas to the battle vainly called
The vanished foe, and round his hard-fought path
Stretched many a hero dead. No longer now
The mocking shadow sought to hide, but soared
Visibly upward and was lost in cloud,
While Turnus drifted o'er the waters wide
Before the wind. Bewildered and amazed
He looked around him; little joy had he
In his own safety, but upraised his hands
In prayer to Heaven: "O Sire omnipotent!
"Didst thou condemn me to a shame like this?
"Such retribution dire? Whither now?
"Whence came I here? What panic wafts away
"This Turnus — if 't is he? Shall I behold
"Laurentum's towers once more? But what of those
"My heroes yonder, who took oath to me,
"And whom — O sin and shame! — I have betrayed
"To horrible destruction? Even now
"I see them routed, and my ears receive
"Their dying groans. What is this thing I do?
"Where will the yawning earth crack wide enough
"Beneath my feet? Ye tempests, pity me!
"On rocks and reef — 't is Turnus' faithful prayer,
"Let this bark founder; fling it on the shoals
"Of wreckful isles, where no Rutulian eye
"Can follow me, or Rumor tell my shame."

With such wild words his soul tossed to and fro,
Not knowing if to hide his infamy
With his own sword and madly drive its blade
Home to his heart, or cast him in the sea,
And, swimming to the rounded shore, renew
His battle with the Trojan foe. Three times
Each fatal course he tried; but Juno's power
Three times restrained, and with a pitying hand
The warrior's purpose barred. So on he sped
O'er yielding waters and propitious tides,
Far as his father Daunus' ancient town.

At Jove's command Mezentius, breathing rage,
Now takes the field and leads a strong assault
Against victorious Troy. The Tuscan ranks
Meet round him, and press hard on him alone,
On him alone with vengeance multiplied
Their host of swords they draw. As some tall cliff,
Projecting to the sea, receives the rage
Of winds and waters, and untrembling bears
Vast, frowning enmity of seas and skies, —
So he.

First Dolichaon's son he slew,
Hebrus; then Latagus and Palmus, though
They fled amain; he smote with mighty stone
Torn from the mountain, full upon the face
Of Latagus; and Palmus he let lie
Hamstrung and rolling helpless; he bestowed
The arms on his son Lausus for a prize,
Another proud crest in his helm to wear;
He laid the Phrygian Euanthus low;

And Mimas, Paris' comrade, just his age,—
Born of Theano's womb to Amycus
His sire, that night when royal Hecuba,
Teeming with firebrand, gave Paris birth:
One in the city of his fathers sleeps;
And one, inglorious, on Laurentian strand.

As when a wild boar, harried from the hills
By teeth of dogs (one who for many a year
Was safe in pine-clad Vesulus, or roamed
The meres of Tiber, feeding in the reeds)
Falls in the toils at last, and stands at bay,
Raging and bristling, and no hunter dares
Defy him or come near, but darts are hurled
From far away, with cries unperilous:
Not otherwise, though righteous is their wrath
Against Mezentius, not a man so bold
As face him with drawn sword, but at long range
They throw their shafts and with loud cries assail;
He, all unterrified, makes frequent stand,
Gnashing his teeth, and shaking off their spears.

From ancient Corythus had Acron come,
A Greek, who left half-sung his wedding-song,
And was an exile; him Mezentius saw
Among long lines of foes, with flaunting plumes
And purple garments from his plighted spouse.
Then as a starving lion when he prowls
About high pasture-lands, urged on his way
By maddening hunger (if perchance he see

A flying she-goat or tall-antlered stag)
Lifts up his shaggy mane, and gaping wide
His monstrous jaws, springs at the creature's side,
Feeding foul-lipped, insatiable of gore:
So through his gathered foes Mezentius
Flew at his prey. He stretched along the ground
Ill-fated Acron, who breathed life away,
Beating the dark dust with his heels, and bathed
His broken weapons in his blood. Nor deigned
Mezentius to strike Orodes down
As he took flight, nor deal a wound unseen
With far-thrown spear; but ran before his face,
Fronting him man to man, nor would he win
By sleight or trick, but by a mightier sword.
Soon on the fallen foe he set his heel,
And, pushing hard, with heel and spear, cried out:
"Look ye, my men, where huge Orodes lies,
"Himself a dangerous portion of this war!"
With loyal, loud acclaim his peers reply;
But thus the dying hero: "Victor mine,
"Whoe'er thou art, I fall not unavenged!
"Thou shalt but triumph for a fleeting hour.
"Like doom for thee is written. Speedily
"Thou shalt this dust inhabit, even as I!"
Mezentius answered him with wrathful smile:
"Now die! What comes on me concerns alone
"The Sire of gods and Sovereign of mankind."
So saying, from the wounded breast he plucked
His javelin: and on those eyes there fell
Inexorable rest and iron slumber,
And in unending night their vision closed.

Then Cædicus cut down Alcathous,
Sacrator slew Hydaspes, Rapo smote
Parthenius and Orses stout and strong;
Messapus' good blade cut down Clonius
And Ericetes, fierce Lycaon's child;
The one from an unbridled war-horse thrown,
The other slain dismounted. Then rode forth
Agis the Lycian, but bold Valerus,
True to his valiant breeding, hurled him down;
Having slain Thronius, Salius was slain
By skilled Nealces, of illustrious name
For spear well cast and far-surprising bow.

Thus Mars relentless holds in equal scale
Slaughters reciprocal and mutual woe;
The victors and the vanquished kill or fall
In equal measure; neither knows the way
To yield or fly. Th' Olympians look down
Out of Jove's house, and pity as they see
The unavailing wrath of either foe,
And burdens measureless on mortals laid.
Lo! Venus here, Saturnian Juno yon,
In anxious watch; while pale Tisiphone
Moves on infuriate through the battling lines.

On strode Mezentius o'er the gory plain,
And swollen with rage waved wide his awful spear.
Like tall Orion when on foot he goes
Through the deep sea and lifts his shoulders high
Above the waves; or when he takes his path
Along the mountain-tops, and has for staff

An aged ash-tree, as he fixes firm
His feet in earth and hides his brows in cloud;—
So loomed Mezentius with his ponderous arms.

To match him now, Æneas, looking down
The long array of war, came forth in arms
To challenge and defy. But quailing not,
A mass immovable, the other stood
Waiting his noble foe, and with a glance
Measured to cast his spear the space between.
"May this right hand," he said, "and this swift spear
"Which here I poise, be favoring gods for me!
"The spoils from yonder robber's carcase stripped
"I vow to hang on thee, my Lausus, thou
"Shalt stand for trophy of Æneas slain."
He said, and hurled from far the roaring spear,
Which from the shield glanced off, and speeding still
Smote famed Antores 'twixt the loin and side —
Antores, friend of Hercules, who came
From Argos, and had joined Evander's cause,
Abiding in Italia. Lo, a wound
Meant for another pierced him, and he lay,
Ill-fated! looking upward to the light,
And dreaming of dear Argos as he died.

Then good Æneas hurled his spear; it passed
Through hollow orb of triple bronze, and through
Layers of flax and triple-twisted hides;
Then in the lower groin it lodged, but left
Its work undone. Æneas, not ill-pleased
To see the Tuscan wounded, swiftly drew

The falchion from his thigh, and hotly pressed
His startled foe. But Lausus at the sight
Groaned loud, so much he loved his father dear,
And tears his cheek bedewed. O storied youth!
If olden worth may win believing ear,
Let not my song now fail of thee to sing,
Thy noble deeds, thy doom of death and pain!
Mezentius, now encumbered and undone,
Fell backward, trailing from the broken shield
His foeman's spear. His son leaped wildly forth
To join the fray; and where Æneas' hand
Lifted to strike, he faced the thrusting sword
And gave the hero pause. His comrades raised
Applauding cries, as shielded by his son
The father made retreat; their darts they hurl,
And vex with flying spears the distant foe:
Æneas, wrathful, stands beneath his shield.
As when the storm-clouds break in pelting hail,
The swains and ploughmen from the furrows fly,
And every traveller cowers in sure defence
Of river-bank or lofty shelving crag,
While far and wide it pours; and by and by,
Each, when the sun returns, his task pursues:
So great Æneas, by assault o'erwhelmed,
Endured the cloud of battle, till its rage
Thundered no more; then with a warning word
To Lausus with upbraiding voice he called:
"Why, O death-doomed, rush on to deeds too high
"For strength like thine. Thou art betrayed, rash boy,
"By thine own loyal heart!" But none the less

The youth made mad defence; while fiercer burned
The Trojan's anger; and of Lausus' days
The loom of Fate spun forth the last thin thread;
For now Æneas thrust his potent blade
Deep through the stripling's breast and out of sight;
Through the light shield it passed—a frail defence
To threaten with!—and through the tunic fine
His mother's hand had wrought with softest gold:
Blood filled his bosom, and on path of air
Down to the shades the mournful soul withdrew,
Its body quitting. As Anchises' son
Beheld the agonizing lips and brow
So wondrous white in death, he groaned aloud
In pity, and reached o'er him his right hand,
Touched to the heart such likeness to behold
Of his own filial love. "Unhappy boy!
"What guerdon worthy of heroic deeds
"Can I award thee now? Wear still those arms
"So proudly worn! And I will send thee home
"(Perhaps thou carest!) to the kindred shades
"And ashes of thy sires. But let it be
"Some solace in thy pitiable doom
"That none but great Æneas wrought thy fall."
Then to the stripling's tardy followers
He sternly called, and lifted from the earth
With his own hand the fallen foe: dark blood
Defiled those princely tresses braided fair.
Meanwhile Mezentius by the Tiber's wave
With water staunched his wound, and propped his weight
Against a tree; upon its limbs above

His brazen helmet hung, and on the sward
His ponderous arms lay resting. Round him watched
His chosen braves. He, gasping and in pain,
Clutched at his neck and let his flowing beard
Loose on his bosom fall; he questions oft
Of Lausus, and sends many a messenger
To bid him back, and bear him the command
Of his sore-grieving sire. But lo! his peers
Bore the dead Lausus back upon his shield,
And wept to see so strong a hero quelled
By stroke so strong. From long way off the sire,
With soul prophetic of its woe, perceived
What meant their wail and cry. On his gray hairs
The dust he flung, and, stretching both his hands
To heaven, he cast himself the corpse along.

"O son," he cried, "was life to me so sweet,
"That I to save myself surrendered o'er
"My own begotten to a foeman's steel?
"Saved by these gashes shall thy father be,
"And living by thy death? O wretched me,
"How foul an end have I! Now is my wound
"Deep! deep! 't was I, dear son, have stained
"Thy name with infamy — to exile driven
"From sceptre and hereditary throne
"By general curse. Would that myself had borne
"My country's vengeance and my nation's hate!
"Would my own guilty life my debt had paid —
"Yea, by a thousand deaths! But, see, I live!
"Not yet from human kind and light of day
"Have I departed. But depart I will."

So saying, he raised him on his crippled thigh,
And though by reason of the grievous wound
His forces ebbed, yet with unshaken mien
He bade them lead his war-horse forth, his pride,
His solace, which from every war
Victorious bore him home. The master then
To the brave beast, which seemed to know his pain,
Spoke thus: "My Rhœbus, we have passed our days
"Long time together, if long time there be
"For mortal creatures. Either on this day
"Thou shalt his bloody spoils in triumph bear
"And that Æneas' head, — and so shalt be
"Avenger of my Lausus' woe; or else,
"If I be vanquished, thou shalt sink and fall
"Beside me. For, my bravest, thou wouldst spurn
"A stranger's will, and Teucrian lords to bear."
He spoke and, mounting to his back, disposed
His limbs the wonted way and filled both hands
With pointed javelins; a helm of brass
With shaggy horse-hair crest gleamed o'er his brow.
Swift to the front he rode: a mingled flood
Surged in his heart of sorrow, wrath, and shame;
And thrice with loud voice on his foe he called.

Æneas heard and made exulting vow:
"Now may the Father of the gods on high,
"And great Apollo hear! Begin the fray!"
He said, and moved forth with a threatening spear.
The other cried: "Hast robbed me of my son,
"And now, implacable, wouldst fright me more?
"That way, that only, was it in thy power

"To cast me down. No fear of death I feel.
"Nor from thy gods themselves would I refrain.
"Give o'er! For fated and resolved to die
"I come thy way: but bring thee as I pass
These offerings." With this he whirled a spear
Against his foe, and after it drove deep
Another and another, riding swift
In wide gyration round him. But the shield,
The golden boss, broke not. Three times he rode
In leftward circles, hurling spear on spear
Against th' unmoved Æneas: and three times
The Trojan hero in his brazen targe
The sheaf of spears upbore. But such slow fight,
Such plucking of spent shafts from out his shield,
The Trojan liked not, vexed and sorely tried
In duel so ill-matched. With wrathful soul
At length he strode forth, and between the brows
Of the wild war-horse planted his long spear.
Up reared the creature, beating at the air
With quivering feet, then o'er his fallen lord
Entangling dropped, and prone above him lay,
Pinning with ponderous shoulder to the ground.
The Trojans and the Latins rouse the skies
With clamor loud. Æneas hastening forth
Unsheathes his sword, and looming o'er him cries:
"Where now is fierce Mezentius, and his soul's
"Wild pulse of rage?" The Tuscan in reply
With eyes uprolled, and gasping as he gave
Long looks at heaven, recalled his fading mind:
"Why frown at me and fume, O bitterest foe?
"Why threaten death? To slay me is no sin.

"Not to take quarter came I to this war,
"Not truce with thee did my lost Lausus crave,
"Yet this one boon I pray,—if mercy be
"For fallen foes: O, suffer me when dead
"In covering earth to hide! Full well I know
"What curses of my people ring me round.
"Defend me from that rage! I pray to be
"My son's companion in our common tomb."
He spoke: then offered with unshrinking eye
His veined throat to the sword. O'er the bright mail
His vital breath gushed forth in streaming gore.

END OF BOOK X

BOOK XI

Up from the sea now soared the dawning day:
Æneas, though his sorrow bids him haste
To burial of the slain, and his sad soul
Is clouded with the sight of death, fulfils,
For guerdon to his gods, a conqueror's vow,
At morning's earliest beam. A mighty oak
Shorn of its limbs he sets upon a hill
And clothes it o'er with glittering arms, the spoil
Of King Mezentius, and a trophy proud
To thee, great lord of war. The hero's plumes
Bedewed with blood are there, and splintered spears;
There hangs the corselet, by the thrusting steel
Twelve times gored through; upon the left he binds
The brazen shield, and from the neck suspends
The ivory-hilted sword. Æneas thus,
As crowding close his train of captains throng,
Addressed his followers: "Ye warriors mine,
"Our largest work is done. Bid fear begone
"Of what is left to do. Behold the spoils!
"Yon haughty King was firstfruits of our war.
"See this Mezentius my hands have made!
"Now to the Latin town and King we go.
"Arm you in soul! With heart of perfect hope
"Prepare the war! So when the gods give sign
"To open battle and lead forth our brave
"Out of this stronghold, no bewilderment,

"Nor tarrying, nor fearful, faltering mind
"Shall slack our march. Meanwhile in earth we lay
"Our comrades fallen; for no honor else
"In Acheron have they. Go forth," said he,
"Bring gifts of honor and of last farewell
"To those high hearts by shedding of whose blood
"Our country lives. To sad Evander's town
"Bear Pallas first; who, though he did not fail
"Of virtue's crown, was seized by doom unblest,
"And to the bitterness of death consigned."

Weeping he spoke, and slowly backward drew
To the tent-door, where by the breathless clay
Of Pallas stood Acœtes, aged man,
Once bearer of Evander's arms, but now
Under less happy omens set to guard
His darling child. Around him is a throng
Of slaves, with all the Trojan multitude,
And Ilian women, who the wonted way
Let sorrow's tresses loosely flow. When now
Æneas to the lofty doors drew near,
All these from smitten bosoms raised to heaven
A mighty moaning, till the King's abode
Was loud with anguish. There Æneas viewed
The pillowed head of Pallas cold and pale,
The smooth young breast that bore the gaping wound
Of that Ausonian spear, and weeping said:
"Did Fortune's envy, smiling though she came,
"Refuse me, hapless boy, that thou shouldst see
"My throne established, and victorious ride
"Beside me to thy father's house? Not this

"My parting promise to thy King and sire,
"Evander, when with friendly, fond embrace
"To win imperial power he bade me go;
"Yet warned me anxiously I must resist
"Bold warriors and a stubborn breed of foes.
"And haply even now he cheats his heart
"With expectation vain, and offers vows,
"Heaping with gifts the altars of his gods.
"But we with unavailing honors bring
"This lifeless youth, who owes the gods of heaven
"No more of gift and vow. O ill-starred King!
"Soon shalt thou see thy son's unpitying doom!
"What a home-coming! This is glory's day
"So long awaited; this the solemn pledge
"I proudly gave. But fond Evander's eyes
"Will find no shameful wounding on the slain,
"Nor for a son in coward safety kept
"Wilt thou, the sire, crave death. But woe is me!
"How strong a bulwark in Ausonia falls!
"What loss is thine, Iulus!"

Thus lamenting,

He bids them lift the body to the bier,
And sends a thousand heroes from his host
To render the last tributes, and to share
A father's tears: — poor solace and too small
For grief so great, but due that mournful sire.
Some busy them to build of osiers fine
The simple litter, twining sapling oaks
With evergreen, till o'er death's lofty bed
The branching shade extends. Upon it lay,
As if on shepherd's couch, the youthful dead,

Like fairest flower by virgin fingers culled,
Frail violet or hyacinth forlorn,
Of color still undimmed and leaf unmarred;
But from the breast of mother-earth no more
Its life doth feed. Then good Æneas brought
Two broidered robes of scarlet and fine gold,
Which with the gladsome labor of her hands
Sidonian Dido wrought him long ago,
The thin-spun gold inweaving. One of these
The sad prince o'er the youthful body threw
For parting gift; and with the other veiled
Those tresses from the fire; he heaped on high
Laurentum's spoils of war, and bade to bring
Much tribute forth: horses and arms he gave,
Seized from the fallen enemy; with hands
Fettered behind them filed a captive train
Doomed to appease the shades, and with the flames
To mix their flowing blood. He bade his chiefs
Set up the trunks of trees and clothe them well
With captured arms, inscribing on each one
Some foeman's name. Then came Acœtes forth,
A wretched, worn old man, who beat his breast
With tight-clenched hands, and tore his wrinkled face
With ruthless fingers; oft he cast him down
Full length along the ground. Then lead they forth
The blood-stained Rutule chariots of war;
Æthon, the war-horse, of his harness bare,
Walks mournful by; big teardrops wet his cheek.
Some bear the lance and helm; for all the rest
Victorious Turnus seized. Then filed along

A mournful Teucrian cohort; next the host
Etrurian and the men of Arcady
With trailing arms reversed. Æneas now,
When the long company had passed him by,
Spoke thus and groaned aloud: "Ourselves from hence
"Are summoned by the same dread doom of war
"To other tears. Farewell forevermore!
"Heroic Pallas! be forever blest!
"I bid thee hail, farewell!" In silence then
Back to the stronghold's lofty walls he moved.

Now envoys from the Latin citadel
Came olive-crowned, to plead for clemency:
Would he not yield those bodies of the dead
Sword-scattered o'er the plain, and let them lie
Beneath an earth-built tomb? Who wages war
Upon the vanquished, the unbreathing slain?
To people once his hosts and kindred called,
Would he not mercy show? To such a prayer,
Deemed not unworthy, good Æneas gave
The boon, and this benignant answer made:
"Ye Latins, what misfortune undeserved
"Has snared you in so vast a war, that now
"You shun our friendship? Have you here implored
"Peace for your dead, by chance of battle fallen?
"Fain would I grant it for the living too.
"I sailed not hither save by Heaven's decree,
"Which called me to this land. I wage no war
"With you, the people; 't was your King refused
"Our proffered bond of peace, and gave his cause

"To Turnus' arms. More meet and just it were
"Had Turnus met this death that makes you mourn.
"If he would end our quarrel sword in hand,
"Thrusting us Teucrians forth, 't was honor's way
"To cross his blade with mine; that man to whom
"The gods, or his own valor, had decreed
"The longer life, had lived. But now depart!
"Beneath your lost friends light the funeral fires!"

So spoke Æneas; and with wonder mute
All stood at gaze, each turning to behold
His neighbor's face. Then Drances, full of years,
And ever armed with spite and slanderous word
Against young Turnus, made this answering plea:
"O prince of mighty name, whose feats of arms
"Are even mightier! Trojan hero, how
"Shall my poor praise exalt thee to the skies?
"Is it thy rectitude or strenuous war
"Most bids me wonder? We will bear thy word
"Right gladly to the city of our sires;
"And there, if Fortune favor it, contrive
"A compact with the Latin King Henceforth
"Let Turnus find his own allies! Ourselves
"Will much rejoice to see thy destined walls,
"And our own shoulders will be proud to bear
"The stone for building Troy."
Such speech he made,
And all the common voice consented loud.
So twelve days' truce they swore, and safe from harm
Latins and Teucrians unmolested roved
Together o'er the wooded hills. Now rang

Loud steel on ash-tree bole; enormous pines,
Once thrusting starward, to the earth they threw;
And with industrious wedge asunder clove
Stout oak and odorous cedar, piling high
Harvest of ash-trees on the creaking wain.

Now Rumor, herald of prodigious woe,
To King Evander hied, Evander's house
And city filling, where, but late, her word
Had told in Latium Pallas' victory.
Th' Arcadians thronging to the city-gates
Bear funeral torches, the accustomed way;
In lines of flame the long street flashes far,
Lighting the fields beyond. To meet them moves
A Phrygian company, to join with theirs
Its lamentation loud. The Latin wives,
Soon as they saw them entering, aroused
The whole sad city with shrill songs of woe.
No hand could stay Evander. Forth he flew
Into the midmost tumult, and fell prone
On his dead Pallas, on the resting bier;
He clung to the pale corse with tears, with groans,
Till anguish for a space his lips unsealed:
"Not this thy promise, Pallas, to thy sire,
"To walk not rashly in the war-god's way.
"I knew too well how honor's morning-star,
"And sweet, foretasted glory tempt and woo
"In a first battle. O first-fruit forlorn
"Of youth so fair! O prelude pitiless
"Of war approaching! O my vows and prayers,
"Which not one god would hear! My blessèd wife,

"How happy was the death that spared thee not
"To taste this bitterness! But I, the while,
"By living longer lived to meet my doom, —
"A father sole-surviving. Would I myself
"Had perished by the Rutule's cruel spear,
"The Trojan's cause espousing! This breath of life
"How gladly had I given! And O, that now
"Yon black solemnity were bearing home
"Myself, not Pallas, dead! Yet blame I not,
"O Teucrians, the hallowed pact we made,
"Nor hospitable bond and clasp of hands.
"This doom ye bring me was writ long ago,
"For my old age. And though my child is fallen
"Untimely, I take comfort that he fell
"Where thousands of the Volscians slaughtered lie,
"And into Latium led the Teucrian arms.
"What brighter glory could I crave in death
"For thee, my Pallas, than Æneas brings,
"And Phrygian princes, and Etrurian lords
"With all Etruria's legions? Lo, they bear
"Yon glittering spoils of victims of thy sword!
"Thou, Turnus, too, wert now an effigy
"In giant armor clad, if but his years
"And strength full ripe had been fair match for thine!
"But now my woes detain the Trojan host
"From battle. I beseech ye haste away,
"And bear this faithful message to your King:
"Since I but linger out a life I loathe,
"Without my Pallas, nothing but thy sword
"Can bid me live. Then let thy sword repay
"Its debt to sire and son by Turnus slain!

"Such deed alone may with thy honor fit,
"And happier fortunes. But my life to me
"Has no joy left to pray for, save to bring
"My son that solace in the shadowy land."

Meanwhile o'er sorrowing mortals the bright morn
Had lifted her mild beam, renewing so
The burden of man's toil. Æneas now
Built funeral pyres along the winding shore,
King Tarchon at his side. Each thither brought
The bodies of his kin, observing well
All ancient ritual. The fuming fires
Burned from beneath, till highest heaven was hid
In blackest, overmantling cloud. Three times
The warriors, sheathed in proud, resplendent steel,
Paced round the kindling pyres; and three times
Fair companies of horsemen circled slow,
With loud lamenting, round the doleful flame.
The wail of warriors and the trumpets' blare
The very welkin rend. Cast on the flames
Are spoils of slaughtered Latins,—helms and blades,
Bridles and chariot-wheels. Yet others bring
Gifts to the dead familiar, their own shields
And unavailing spears. Around them slain
Great herds of kine give tribute unto death:
Swine, bristly-backed, from many a field are borne,
And slaughtered sheep bleed o'er the sacred fire.
So on the shore the wailing multitude
Behold their comrades burning, and keep guard
O'er the consuming pyres, nor turn away

Till cooling night re-shifts the globe of heaven,
Thick-strewn with numberless far-flaming stars.

Likewise the mournful Latins far away
Have built their myriad pyres. Yet of the slain
Not few in graves are laid, and borne with tears
To neighboring country-side or native town;
The rest — promiscuous mass of dead unknown —
To nameless and unhonored ashes burn;
With multitude of fires the far-spread fields
Blaze forth unweariedly. But when from heaven
The third morn had dispelled the dark and cold,
The mournful bands raked forth the mingled bones
And plenteous ashes from the smouldering pyres,
Then heaped with earth the one sepulchral mound.

Now from the hearth-stones of the opulent town
Of old Latinus a vast wail burst forth,
For there was found the chief and bitterest share
Of all the woe. For mothers in their tears,
Lone brides, and stricken souls of sisters fond,
And boys left fatherless, fling curses loud
On Turnus' troth-plight and the direful war:
"Let him, let Turnus, with his single sword
"Decide the strife," — they cry, — "and who shall claim
"Lordship of Italy and power supreme."
Fierce Drances whets their fury, urging all
That Turnus singly must the challenge hear,
And singly wage the war; but others plead
In Turnus' favor; the Queen's noble name

Protects him, and his high renown in arms
Defends his cause with well-won trophies fair.

Amid these tumults of the wrathful throng,
Lo, the ambassadors to Diomed
Arrive with cloudy forehead from their quest
In his illustrious town; for naught availed
Their toilsome errand, nor the gifts and gold,
Nor strong entreaty. Other help in war
The Latins now must find, or humbly sue
Peace from the Trojan. At such tidings dire
Even Latinus trembles: Heaven's decrees
And influence of gods too visible
Sustain Æneas; so the wrath divine
And new-filled sepulchres conspicuous
Give warning clear. Therefore the King convenes
A general council of his captains brave
Beneath the royal towers. They, gathering,
Throng the approaches thither, where their lord,
Gray-haired Latinus, takes the central throne,
Wearing authority with mournful brow.
He bids the envoys from Ætolia's King
Sent back, to speak and tell the royal words
In order due. Forthwith on every tongue
Fell silence, while the princely Venulus,
Heeding his lord's behest, began the parle:

"My countrymen," he said, "our eyes have seen
"Strongholds of Greeks and Diomed the King.
"We braved all perils to our journey's end
"And clasped that hand whereof the dreadful stroke

"Wrought Ilium's fall. The hero built a town,
"Argyripa, hereditary name,
"Near mount Garganus in Apulian land:
"Passing that city's portal and the King's,
"We found free audience, held forth thy gifts,
"And told our names and fatherland. We showed
"What conflict was enkindled, and what cause
"Brought us to Arpi's King. He, hearing all,
"With brow benign made answer to our plea:
"'O happy tribes in Saturn's kingdom born,
"'Ausonia's ancient stem! What fortune blind
"'Tempts ye from peace away, and now ensnares
"'In wars unknown? Look how we men that dared
"'Lay Ilium waste (I speak not of what woes
"'In battling neath her lofty walls we bore,
"'Nor of dead warriors sunk in Simois' wave)
"'Have paid the penalty in many a land
"'With chastisement accurst and changeful woe,
"'Till Priam's self might pity. Let the star
"'Of Pallas tell its tale of fatal storm,
"'Off grim Caphereus and Eubœa's crags.
"'Driven asunder from one field of war,
"'Atrides unto farthest Egypt strayed,
"'And wise Ulysses saw from Ætna's caves
"'The Cyclops gathering. Why name the throne
"'Of Pyrrhus, or the violated hearth
"'Whence fled Idomeneus? Or Locri cast
"'On Libya's distant shore? For even he,
"'Lord of Mycenæ by the Greeks obeyed,
"'Fell murdered on his threshold by the hand
"'Of that polluted wife, whose paramour

"'Trapped Asia's conqueror. The envious gods
"'Withheld me also from returning home
"'To see once more the hearth-stone of my sires,
"'The wife I yearn for, and my Calydon,
"'The beauteous land. For wonders horrible
"'Pursue me still. My vanished followers
"'Through upper air take wing, or haunt and rove
"'In forms of birds the island waters o'er:
"'Ah me! what misery my people feel!
"'The tall rocks ring with their lament and cry.
"'Naught else had I to hope for from that day
"'When my infatuate sword on gods I drew,
"'And outraged with abominable wound
"'The hand of Venus. Urge me not, I pray,
"'To conflicts in this wise. No more for me
"'Of war with Trojans after Ilium's fall!
"'I take no joy in evils past, nor wish
"'Such memory to renew. Go, lay these gifts,
"'Brought to my honor from your ancient land,
"'At great Æneas' feet. We twain have stood
"'Confronting close with swords implacable
"'In mortal fray. Believe me, I have known
"'The stature of him when he lifts his shield,
"'And swings the whirlwind of his spear. If Troy
"'Two more such sons had bred, the Dardan horde
"'Had stormed at Argos' gates, and Greece to-day
"'Were for her fallen fortunes grieving sore.
"'Our lingering at Ilium's stubborn wall,
"'Our sluggard conquest halting ten years long,
"'Was his and Hector's work. Heroic pair!
"'Each one for valor notable, and each

"'Famous in enterprise of arms, — but he
"'Was first in piety. Enclasp with his
"'Your hands in plighted peace as best ye may:
"'But shock of steel on steel ye well may shun.'
"Now hast thou heard, good King, a king's reply,
"And how his wisdom sits in this vast war."

Soon as the envoys ceased, an answering sound
Of troubled voices through the council flowed
Of various note, as when its rocky bed
Impedes an arrowy stream, and murmurs break
From the strait-channelled flood; the fringing shores
Repeat the tumult of the clamorous wave.

But when their hearts and troublous tongues were still,
The King, invoking first the gods in heaven,
Thus from a lofty throne his sentence gave:
"Less evil were our case, if long ago
"Ye had provided for your country's weal,
"O Latins, as I urged. It is no time
"To hold dispute, while, compassing our walls,
"The foeman waits. Ill-omened war is ours
"Against a race of gods, my countrymen,
"Invincible, unwearied in the fray,
"And who, though lost and fallen, clutch the sword.
"If hope ye cherished of Ætolia's power,
"Dismiss it! For what hope ye have is found
"In your own bosoms only. But ye know
"How slight it is and small. What ruin wide
"Has fallen, is now palpable and clear.

"No blame I cast. What valor's uttermost
"May do was done; our kingdom in this war
"Strained its last thews. Now therefore I will tell
"Such project as my doubtful mind may frame,
"And briefly, if ye give good heed, unfold:
"An ancient tract have I, close-bordering
"The river Tiber; it runs westward far
"Beyond Sicania's bound, and tilth it bears
"To Rutule and Auruncan husbandmen,
"Who furrow its hard hills or feed their flocks
"Along the stonier slopes. Let this demesne,
"Together with its pine-clad mountain tall,
"Be given the Teucrian for our pledge of peace,
"Confirmed by free and equitable league,
"And full alliance with our kingly power.
"Let them abide there, if it please them so,
"And build their city's wall. But if their hearts
"For other land or people yearn, and fate
"Permits them hence to go, then let us build
"Twice ten good galleys of Italian oak,
"Or more, if they can man them. All the wood
"Lies yonder on the shore. Let them but say
"How numerous and large the ships they crave;
"And we will give the brass, the artisans,
"And ship-supplies. Let us for envoys choose
"A hundred of the Latins noblest born
"To tell our message and arrange the peace,
"Bearing mild olive-boughs and weighty gifts
"Of ivory and gold, with chair of state
"And purple robe, our emblems as a king.
"But freely let this council speak; give aid

"To our exhausted cause."
Then Drances rose,
That foe inveterate, whom Turnus' fame
To stinging hate and envy double-tongued
Ever pricked on. Of liberal wealth was he
And flowing speech, but slack of hand in war
At council board accounted no weak voice,
In quarrels stronger still; of lofty birth
In the maternal line, but by his sire's
Uncertain and obscure. He, claiming place,
Thus multiplies with words the people's ire:
"A course most clear, nor needing voice of mine,
"Thy council is, good King; for all men see
"The way of public weal, but smother close
"The telling of it. Turnus must concede
"Freedom to speak, and his own arrogance
"Diminish! Under his ill-boding star
"And fatal conduct — yea, I speak it plain,
"Though with his naked steel my death he swear —
"Yon host of princes fell, and we behold
"The whole land bowed with grief; while he assails
"The Trojan camp (beating such bold retreats!)
"And troubles Heaven with war. One gift the more,
"Among the many to the Trojans given,
"One chiefly, best of kings, thy choice should be.
"Let not wild violence thy will restrain
"From granting, sire, thy virgin daughter's hand
"To son-in-law illustrious, in a match
"Worthy of both, — and thus the lasting bond
"Of peace establish. But if verily
"Our hearts and souls be weak with craven fear,

"Let us on Turnus call, and grace implore
"Even of him. Let him no more oppose;
"But to his country and his King concede
"Their natural right. Why wilt thou o'er and o'er
"Fling thy poor countrymen in danger's way,
"O chief and fountain of all Latium's pain?
"War will not save us. Not a voice but sues
"For peace, O Turnus! and, not less than peace,
"Its one inviolable pledge. Behold,
"I lead in this petition! even I
"Whom thou dost feign thy foe — (I waste no words
"Denying) — look! I supplicate of thee,
"Take pity on thy kindred; drop thy pride,
"And get thee home defeated. We have seen
"Slaughter enough, enough of funeral flames,
"And many a wide field waste and desolate.
"If glory move thee, if thy martial breast
"So swell with strength, and if a royal dower
"Be thy dear dream, go, pluck thy courage up,
"And front thy own brave bosom to the foe.
"For, lo, that Turnus on his wedding day
"May win a princess, our cheap, common lives —
"We the mere mob, unwept, unsepulchred —
"Must be spilled forth in battle! Thou, I say,
"If there be mettle in thee and some drops
"Of thy undaunted sires, look yonder where
"The Trojan chieftain waits thee in the field."

By such discourse he stirred the burning blood
Of Turnus, who groaned loud and from his heart
This utterance hurled: "O Drances, thou art rich

"In large words, when the day of battle calls
"For actions. If our senators convene
"Thou comest early. But the council hall
"Is not for swollen talk, such as thy tongue
"In safety tosses forth; so long as walls
"Hold back thy foes, and ere the trenches flow
"With blood of brave men slain. O, rattle on
"In fluent thunder — thy habitual style!
"Brand me a coward, Drances, when thy sword
"Has heaped up Trojan slain, and on the field
"Thy shining trophies rise. Now may we twain
"Our martial prowess prove. Our foe, forsooth,
"Is not so far to seek; around yon wall
"He lies in siege: to front him let us fly!
"Why art thou tarrying? Wilt thou linger here,
"A soldier only in thy windy tongue,
"And thy swift, coward heels? Defeated, I?
"Foul wretch, what tongue that honors truth can tell
"Of my defeat, while Tiber overflows
"With Trojan blood? while King Evander's house
"In ruin dies, and his Arcadians lie
"Stripped naked on the field? O, not like thee
"Did Bitias or the giant Pandarus
"Misprize my honor; nor those men of Troy
"Whom this good sword to death and dark sent down,
"A thousand in a day, — though I was penned
"A prisoner in the ramparts of my foe.
"War will not save us? Fling that prophecy
"On the doomed Dardan's head, or on thy own,
"Thou madman! Aye, with thy vile, craven soul
"Disturb the general cause. Extol the power

"Of a twice-vanquished people, and decry
"Latinus' rival arms. From this time forth
"Let all the Myrmidonian princes cower
"Before the might of Troy; let Diomed
"And let Achilles tremble; let the stream
"Of Aufidus in panic backward flow
"From Hadria's wave. But hear me when I say
"That though his guilt and cunning feign to feel
"Fear of my vengeance, much embittering so
"His taunts and insult — such a life as his
"My sword disdains. O Drances, be at ease!
"In thy vile bosom let thy breath abide!

"But now of thy grave counsel and thy cause,
"O royal sire, I speak. If from this hour
"Thou castest hope of armed success away,
"If we be so unfriended that one rout
"O'erwhelms us utterly, if Fortune's feet
"Never turn backward, let us, then, for peace
"Offer petition, lifting to the foe
"Our feeble, suppliant hands. Yet would I pray
"Some spark of manhood such as once we knew
"Were ours once more! I count him fortunate,
"And of illustrious soul beyond us all,
"Who, rather than behold such things, has fallen
"Face forward, dead, his teeth upon the dust.
"But if we still have power, and men-at-arms
"Unwasted and unscathed, if there survive
"Italian tribes and towns for help in war,
"Aye! if the Trojans have but won success
"At bloody cost, — for they dig graves, I ween,

"Storm-smitten not less than we, — O, wherefore now
"Stand faint and shameful on the battle's edge?
"Why quake our knees before the trumpet call?
"Time and the toil of shifting, changeful days
"Restore lost causes; ebbing tides of chance
"Deceive us oft, which after at their flood
"Do lift us safe to shore. If aid come not
"From Diomed in Arpi, our allies
"Shall be Mezentius and Tolumnius,
"Auspicious name, and many a chieftain sent
"From many a tribe; not all inglorious
"Are Latium's warriors from Laurentian land!
"Hither the noble Volscian stem sends down
"Camilla with her beauteous cavalry
"In glittering brass arrayed. But if, forsooth,
"The Trojans call me singly to the fight,
"If this be what ye will, and I so much
"The public weal impair — when from this sword
"Has victory seemed to fly away in scorn?
"I should not hopeless tread in honor's way
"Whate'er the venture. Dauntless will I go
"Though equal match for great Achilles, he,
"And though he clothe him in celestial arms
"In Vulcan's smithy wrought. I, Turnus, now,
"Not less than equal with great warriors gone,
"Vow to Latinus, father of my bride,
"And to ye all, each drop of blood I owe.
"Me singly doth Æneas call? I crave
"That challenge. Drances is not called to pay
"The debt of death, if wrath from Heaven impend;
"Nor his a brave man's name and fame to share."

Thus in their doubtful cause the chieftains strove.
Meanwhile Æneas his assaulting line
Moved forward. The ill tidings wildly sped
From royal hall to hall, and filled the town
With rumors dark: for now the Trojan host
O'er the wide plains from Tiber's wave was spread
In close array of war. The people's soul
Was vexed and shaken, and its martial rage
Rose to the stern compulsion. Now for arms
Their terror calls; the youthful soldiery
Clamor for arms; the sires of riper days
Weep or repress their tears. On every side
Loud shouts and cries of dissonant acclaim
Trouble the air, as when in lofty grove
Legions of birds alight, or by the flood
Of Padus' fishy stream the shrieking swans
Far o'er the vocal marish fling their song.

Then, seizing the swift moment, Turnus cried:
"Once more, my countrymen, ye sit in parle,
"Lazily praising peace, while yonder foe
"Speeds forth in arms our kingdom to obtain."
He spoke no more, but hied him in hot haste,
And from the housetop called, "Volusus, go!
"Equip the Volscian companies! Lead forth
"My Rutules also! O'er the spreading plain,
"Ye brothers Coras and Messapus range
"Our host of cavalry! Let others guard
"The city's gates and hold the walls and towers:
"I and my followers elsewhere oppose
"The shock of arms." Now to and fro they run

To man the walls. Father Latinus quits
The place of council and his large design,
Vexed and bewildered by the hour's distress.
He blames his own heart that he did not ask
Trojan Æneas for his daughter's lord,
And gain him for his kingdom's lasting friend.

They dig them trenches at the gates, or lift
Burden of stakes and stones. The horn's harsh note
Sounds forth its murderous signal for the war;
Striplings and women, in a motley ring,
Defend the ramparts; the decisive hour
Lays tasks on all. Upon the citadel
A train of matrons, with the doleful Queen,
Toward Pallas' temple moves, and in their hand
Are gifts and offerings. See, at their side
The maid Lavinia, cause of all these tears,
Drops down her lovely eyes! The incense rolls
In clouds above the altar; at the doors
With wailing voice the women make this prayer:
"Tritonian virgin, arbitress of war!
"Break of thyself yon Phrygian robber's spear!
"Hurl him down dying in the dust! Spill forth
"His evil blood beneath our lofty towers!"

Fierce Turnus girds him, emulous to slay:
A crimson coat of mail he wears, with scales
Of burnished bronze; beneath his knees are bound
The golden greaves; upon his naked brow
No helm he wears; but to his thigh is bound
A glittering sword. Down from the citadel

Runs he, a golden glory, in his heart
Boldly exulting, while impatient hope
Fore-counts his fallen foes. He seemed as when,
From pinfold bursting, breaking his strong chain,
Th' untrammelled stallion ranges the wide field,
Or hies him to a herd of feeding mares,
Or to some cooling river-bank he knows,
Most fierce and mettlesome; the streaming mane
O'er neck and shoulder flies.

Across his path
Camilla with her Volscian escort came,
And at the city-gate the royal maid
Down from her charger leaped; while all her band
At her example glided to the ground,
Their horses leaving. Thus the virgin spoke:
"Turnus, if confidence beseem the brave,
"I have no fear; but of myself do vow
"To meet yon squadrons of Æneadæ
"Alone, and front me to the gathered charge
"Of Tuscan cavalry. Let me alone
"The war's first venture prove. Take station, thou,
"Here at the walls, this rampart to defend."
With fixed eyes on the terror-striking maid,
Turnus replied, "O boast of Italy,
"O virgin bold! What praise, what gratitude
"Can words or deeds repay? But since thy soul
"So large of stature shows, I bid thee share
"My burden and my war. Our spies bring news
"That now Æneas with pernicious mind
"Sends light-armed horse before him, to alarm
"The plains below, while through the wilderness

"He climbs the steep hills, and approaches so
"Our leaguered town. But I in sheltered grove
"A stratagem prepare, and bid my men
"In ambush at a mountain cross-road lie.
"Meet thou the charge of Tuscan cavalry
"With all thy banners. For auxiliar strength
"Take bold Messapus with his Latin troop
"And King Tiburtus' men: but the command
"Shall be thy task and care."
He spoke, and urged
With like instruction for the coming fray
Messapus and his captains; then advanced
To meet the foe. There is a winding vale
For armed deception and insidious war
Well fashioned, and by interlacing leaves
Screened darkly in; a small path thither leads,
Through strait defile — a passage boding ill.
Above it, on a mountain's lofty brow,
Are points of outlook, level spaces fair,
And many a safe, invisible retreat
From whence on either hand to challenge war,
Or, standing on the ridges, to roll down
Huge mountain boulders. Thither Turnus fared,
And, ranging the familiar tract, chose out
His cunning ambush in the dangerous grove.

But now in dwellings of the gods on high,
Diana to fleet-footed Opis called,
A virgin from her consecrated train,
And thus in sorrow spoke: "O maiden mine!
"Camilla now to cruel conflict flies;

"With weapons like my own she girds her side,
"In vain, though dearest of all nymphs to me.
"Nor is it some new love that stirs to-day
"With sudden sweetness in Diana's breast:
"For long ago, when from his kingdom driven,
"For insolent and envied power, her sire
"King Metabus, from old Privernum's wall
"Was taking flight amidst opposing foes,
"He bore a little daughter in his arms
"To share his exile; and he called the child
"(Changing Casmilla, her queen-mother's name)
"Camilla. Bearing on his breast the babe,
"He fled to solitary upland groves.
"But hovering round him with keen lances, pressed
"The Volscian soldiery. Across his path,
"Lo, Amasenus with full-foaming wave
"O'erflowed its banks — so huge a rain had burst
"But lately from the clouds. There would he fain
"Swim over, but the love of that sweet babe
"Restrained him, trembling for his burden dear.
"In his perplexed heart suddenly arose
"A firm resolve. It chanced the warrior bore
"A huge spear in his brawny hand, strong shaft
"Of knotted, seasoned oak; to this he lashed
"His little daughter with a withe of bark
"Pulled from a cork-tree, and with skilful bonds
"Fast bound her to the spear; then, poising it
"High in his right hand, thus he called on Heaven:
"'Latona's daughter, whose benignant grace
"'Protects this grove, behold, her father now
"'Gives thee this babe for handmaid! Lo, thy spear

"'Her infant fingers hold, as from her foes
"'She flies a suppliant to thee! Receive,
"'O goddess, I implore, what now I cast
"'Upon the perilous air.'—He spoke, and hurled
"With lifted arm the whirling shaft. The waves
"Roared loud, as on the whistling javelin
"Hapless Camilla crossed th' impetuous flood.
"But Metabus, his foes in hot pursuit,
"Dared plunge him in mid-stream, and, triumphing,
"Soon plucked from grass-grown river-bank the spear,
"The child upon it,— now to Trivia vowed,
"A virgin offering. Him nevermore
"Could cities hold, nor would his wild heart yield
"Its sylvan freedom, but his days were passed
"With shepherds on the solitary hills.
"His daughter too in tangled woods he bred:
"A brood-mare from the milk of her fierce breast
"Suckled the child, and to its tender lips
"Her udders moved; and when the infant feet
"Their first firm steps had taken, the small palms
"Were armed with a keen javelin; her sire
"A bow and quiver from her shoulder slung.
"Instead of golden combs and flowing pall,
"She wore, from her girl-forehead backward thrown,
"The whole skin of a tigress; with soft hands
"She made her plaything of a whirling spear,
"Or, swinging round her head the polished thong
"Of her good sling, she fetched from distant sky
"Strymonian cranes or swans of spotless wing.
"From Tuscan towns proud matrons oft in vain
"Sought her in marriage for their sons; but she

"To Dian only turned her stainless heart,
"Her virgin freedom and her huntress' arms
"With faithful passion serving. Would that now
"This love of war had ne'er seduced her mind
"The Teucrians to provoke! So might she be
"One of our wood-nymphs still. But haste, I pray,
"For bitter is her now impending doom.
"Descend, dear nymph, from heaven, and explore
"The country of the Latins, where the fight
"With unpropitious omens now begins.
"These weapons take, and from this quiver draw
"A vengeful arrow, wherewith he who dares
"To wound her sacred body, though he be
"A Trojan or Italian, shall receive
"Bloody and swift reward at my command.
"Then, in a cloud concealed, I will consign
"Her corpse, ill-fated but inviolate,
"Unto the sepulchre, restoring so
"The virgin to her native land." Thus spake
The goddess; but her handmaid, gliding down,
Took her loud pathway on the moving winds,
And mantled in dark storm her shape divine.

Meanwhile the Teucrian legions to the wall
Draw near, with Tuscan lords and cavalry
In numbered troops arrayed. Loud-footed steeds
Prance o'er the field, to manage of the rein
Rebellious, but turned deftly here or there.
The iron harvest of keen spears spreads far,
And all the plain burns bright with lifted steel.
Messapus and swift Latin cavalry,

Coras his brother, and th' attending train
Of the fair maid Camilla, form their lines
In the opposing field. Their poised right hands
Point the long lances forward, and light shafts
Are brandished in the air; the warrior hosts
On steeds of fire come kindling as they ride.
One instant, at a spear-throw's space, each line
Its motion stays; then with one sudden cry
They rush forth, spurring on each frenzied steed.
From every side the multitudinous spears
Pour down like snowflakes, mantling heaven in shade.
Now with contending spears and straining thews,
Tyrrhenus, and Aconteus, champion bold,
Ride forward; with the onset terrible
Loudly their armor rings; their chargers twain
Crash breast to breast, and like a thunderbolt
Aconteus drops, or like a ponderous stone
Hurled from a catapult; full length he falls,
Surrend'ring to the winds his fleeting soul.

Now all is panic: holding their light shields
Behind their backs, the Latin horse wheel round,
Retreating to the wall, the Trojan foe
In close pursuit. Asilas, chieftain proud,
Led on th' assault. Hard by the city gates
The Latins wheeled once more and pressed the rein
Strong on the yielding neck; the charging foe
Took flight and hurried far with loose-flung rein.
'T was like the shock and onset of the sea
That landward hurls the alternating flood
And hides high cliffs in foam,—the tawny sands

Upflinging as it rolls; then, suddenly
Whirled backward on the reingulfing waves,
It quits the ledges, and with ebbing flow
Far from the shore retires. The Tuscans twice
Drive back the flying Rutules to the town;
And twice repulsed, with shields to rearward thrown,
Glare back at the pursuer; but conjoined
In the third battle-charge, both armies merge
Confusedly together in grim fight
Of man to man; then follow dying groans,
Armor blood-bathed and corpses, and strong steeds
Inextricably with their masters slain,
So fierce the fray. Orsilochus — afraid
To front the warrior's arms — launched forth a spear
At Remulus' horse, and left the fatal steel
Clinging below its ear; the charger plunged
Madly, and tossed its trembling hoofs in air,
Sustaining not the wound; the rider fell,
Flung headlong to the ground. Catillus slew
Iollas; and then struck Herminius down,
Great-bodied and great-hearted, who could wield
A monster weapon, and whose yellow hair
From naked head to naked shoulder flowed.
By wounds unterrified he dared oppose
His huge bulk to the foe: the quivering spear
Pierced to his broad back, and with throes of pain
Bowed the man double and clean clove him through.
Wide o'er the field th' ensanguined horror flowed,

Where fatal swords were crossed and cut their way
Through many a wound to famous death and fair.

Swift through the midmost slaughter proudly strides
The quiver-girt Camilla, with one breast
Thrust naked to the fight, like Amazon.
Oft from her hand her pliant shafts she rains,
Or whirls with indefatigable arm
A doughty battle-axe; her shoulder bears
Diana's sounding arms and golden bow.
Sometimes retreating and to flight compelled,
The maiden with a rearward-pointing bow
Shoots arrows as she flies. Around her move
Her chosen peers, Larina, virgin brave,
Tarpeia, brandishing an axe of bronze,
And Tulla, virgins out of Italy
Whom the divine Camilla chose to be
Her glory, each a faithful servitress
In days of peace or war. The maids of Thrace
Ride thus along Thermodon's frozen flood,
And fight with blazoned Amazonian arms
Around Hippolyta; or when returns
Penthesilea in triumphal car
'Mid acclamations shrill, and all her host
Of women clash in air the moon-shaped shield.

What warrior first, whom last, did thy strong spear,
Fierce virgin, earthward fling? Or what thy tale
Of prostrate foes laid gasping on the ground?
Eunæus first, the child of Clytius' loins,
Whose bared breast, as he faced his foe, she pierced

With fir-tree javelin; from his lips outpoured
The blood-stream as he fell; and as he bit
The gory dust, he clutched his mortal wound.
Then Liris, and upon him Pagasus
She slew: the one clung closer to the reins
Of his stabbed horse, and rolled off on the ground;
The other, flying to his fallen friend,
Reached out a helpless hand; so both of these
Fell on swift death together. Next in line
She smote Amastrus, son of Hippotas;
Then, swift-pursuing, pierced with far-flung spear
Tereus, Harpalycus, Demophoön,
And Chromis; every shaft the virgin threw
Laid low its Phrygian warrior. From afar
Rode Ornytus on his Apulian steed,
Bearing a hunter's uncouth arms; for cloak
He wore upon his shoulders broad a hide
From some wild bull stripped off; his helmet was
A wolf's great, gaping mouth, with either jaw
Full of white teeth; the weapon in his hand,
A farmer's pole. He strode into the throng,
Head taller than them all. But him she seized
And clove him through (his panic-stricken troop
Gave her advantage), and with wrathful heart
She taunted thus the fallen: "Didst thou deem
"This was a merry hunting in the wood
"In chase of game? Behold, thy fatal day
"Befalls thee at a woman's hand, and thus
"Thy boasting answers. No small glory thou
"Unto the ghosts of thy dead sires wilt tell,
"That 't was Camilla's javelin struck thee down."

The turn of Butes and Orsilochus
Came next, who were the Trojans' hugest twain:
Yet Butes with her javelin-point she clove
From rearward, 'twixt the hauberk and the helm,
Just where the horseman's neck showed white, and where
From shoulder leftward slung the light-weight shield.
From swift Orsilochus she feigned to fly,
Through a wide circle sweeping, craftily
Taking the inside track, pursuing so
Her own pursuer; then she raised herself
To her full height, and through the warrior's helm
Drove to his very skull with doubling blows
Of her strong battle-axe,—while he implored
Her mercy with loud prayers: his cloven brain
Spilt o'er his face. Next in her pathway came—
But shrank in startled fear — the warrior son
Of Aunus, haunter of the Apennine,
Not least of the Ligurians ere his doom
Cut short a life of lies. He, knowing well
No flight could save him from the shock of arms
Nor turn the royal maid's attack, began
With words of cunning and insidious guile:
"What glory is it if a girl be bold,
"On sturdy steed depending? Fly me not!
"But, venturing with me on this equal ground,
"Gird thee to fight on foot. Soon shalt thou see
"Which one of us by windy boast achieves
"A false renown." He spoke; but she, to pangs
Of keenest fury stung, gave o'er her steed
In charge of a companion, and opposed

Her foe at equal vantage, falchion drawn,
On foot, and, though her shield no blazon bore,
Of fear incapable. But the warrior fled,
Thinking his trick victorious, and rode off
Full speed, with reins reversed, — his iron heel
Goading his charger's flight. Camilla cried:
"Ligurian cheat! In vain thy boastful heart
"Puffs thee so large; in vain thou hast essayed
"Thy father's slippery ways; nor shall thy trick
"Bring thee to guileful Aunus safely home."
Herewith on wingèd feet that virgin bold
Flew past the war-horse, seized the streaming rein,
And, fronting him, took vengeance on her foe
In bloody strokes: with not less ease a hawk,
Dark bird of omen, from his mountain crag
Pursues on pinions strong a soaring dove
To distant cloud, and, clutching with hooked claws,
Holds tight and rips,— while through celestial air
The torn, ensanguined plumage floats along.

But now not blindly from Olympian throne
The Sire of gods and men observant saw
How sped the day. Then to the conflict dire
The god thrust Tarchon forth, the Tyrrhene King,
Goading the warrior's rage. So Tarchon rode
Through slaughter wide and legions in retreat,
And roused the ranks with many a wrathful cry:
He called each man by name, and toward the foe
Drove back the routed lines. "What terrors now,

"O Tuscan cowards, dead to noble rage,
"Have seized ye? or what laggard sloth and vile
"Unmans your hearts, that now a woman's arm
"Pursues ye and this scattered host confounds?
"Why dressed in steel, or to what purpose wear
"Your futile swords? Not slackly do ye join
"The ranks of Venus in a midnight war;
"Or when fantastic pipes of Bacchus call
"Your dancing feet, right venturesome ye fly
"To banquets and the flowing wine — what zeal,
"What ardor then! Or if your flattering priest
"Begins the revel, and to lofty groves
"Fat flesh of victims bids ye haste away!"
So saying, his steed he spurred, and scorning death
Dashed into the mid-fray, where, frenzy-driven,
He sought out Venulus, and, grappling him
With one hand, from the saddle snatched his foe,
And, clasping strongly to his giant breast,
Exultant bore away. The shouting rose
To heaven, and all the Latins gazed his way,
As o'er the plain the fiery Tarchon flew
Bearing the full-armed man; then, breaking off
The point of his own spear, he pried a way
Through the seam'd armor for the mortal wound;
The other, struggling, thrust back from his throat
The griping hand, full force to force opposing.
As when a golden eagle high in air
Knits to a victim-snake his clinging feet
And deeply-thrusting claws; but, coiling back,
The wounded serpent roughens his stiff scales
And stretches high his hissing head; whereat

The eagle with hooked beak the more doth rend
Her writhing foe, and with swift stroke of wing
Lashes the air: so Tarchon, from the ranks
Of Tibur's sons, triumphant snatched his prey.

The Tuscans rallied now, well pleased to view
Their king's example and successful war.
Then Arruns, marked for doom, made circling line
Around Camilla's path, his crafty spear
Seeking its lucky chance. Where'er the maid
Sped furious to the battle, Arruns there
In silence dogged her footsteps and pursued;
Or where triumphant from her fallen foes
She backward drew, the warrior stealthily
Turned his swift reins that way: from every side
He circled her, and scanned his vantage here
Or vantage there, his skilful javelin
Stubbornly shaking. But it soon befell
That Chloreus, once a priest of Cybele,
Shone forth in far-resplendent Phrygian arms,
And urged a foaming steed, which wore a robe
O'erwrought with feathery scales of bronze and gold;
While he, in purples of fine foreign stain,
Bore light Gortynian shafts and Lycian bow;
His bow was gold; a golden casque he wore
Upon his priestly brow; the saffron cloak,
All folds of rustling cambric, was enclasped
In glittering gold; his skirts and tunics gay
Were broidered, and the oriental garb
Swathed his whole leg. Him when the maiden spied,
(Perchance she fain on temple walls would hang

The Trojan prize, or in such captured gold
Her own fair shape array), she gave mad chase,
And reckless through the ranks her prey pursued,
Desiring, woman-like, the splendid spoil.
Then from his ambush Arruns seized at last
The fatal moment and let speed his shaft,
Thus uttering his vow to heavenly powers:
"Chief of the gods, Apollo, who dost guard
"Soracte's hallowed steep, whom we revere
"First of thy worshippers, for thee is fed
"The heap of burning pine; for thee we pass
"Through the mid-blaze in sacred zeal secure,
"And deep in glowing embers plant our feet.
"O Sire Omnipotent, may this my spear
"Our foul disgrace put by. I do not ask
"For plunder, spoils, or trophies in my name,
"When yonder virgin falls; let honor's crown
"Be mine for other deeds. But if my stroke
"That curse and plague destroy, may I unpraised
"Safe to the cities of my sires return."

Apollo heard and granted half the prayer,
But half upon the passing breeze he threw:
Granting his votary he should confound
Camilla by swift death; but 't was denied
The mountain-fatherland once more to see,
Or safe return,— that prayer th' impetuous winds
Swept stormfully away. Soon as the spear
Whizzed from his hand, straight-speeding on the air,
The Volscians all turned eager thought and eyes
Toward their Queen. She only did not heed

That windy roar, nor weapon dropped from heaven,
Till in her bare, protruded breast the spear
Drank, deeply driven, of her virgin blood.
Her terror-struck companions swiftly throng
Around her, and uplift their sinking Queen.

But Arruns, panic-stricken more than all,
Makes off, half terror and half joy, nor dares
Hazard his lance again, nor dares oppose
A virgin's arms. As creeps back to the hills
In pathless covert ere his foes pursue,
From shepherd slain or mighty bull laid low,
Some wolf, who, now of his bold trespass ware,
Curls close against his paunch a quivering tail
And to the forest hies: so Arruns speeds
From sight of men in terror, glad to fly,
And hides him in the crowd. But his keen spear
Dying Camilla from her bosom drew,
Though the fixed barb of deeply-wounding steel
Clung to the rib. She sank to earth undone,
Her cold eyes closed in death, and from her cheeks
The roses fled. With failing breath she called
On Acca — who of all her maiden peers
Was chiefly dear and shared her heart's whole pain —
And thus she spoke: "O Acca, sister mine,
"I have been strong till now. The cruel wound
"Consumes me, and my world is growing dark.
"Haste thee to Turnus! Tell my dying words!
"'T is he must bear the battle and hold back
"The Trojan from our city wall. Farewell!"

So saying, her fingers from the bridle-rein
Unclasped, and helpless to the earth she fell;
Then, colder grown, she loosed her more and more
Out of the body's coil; she gave to death
Her neck, her drooping head, and ceased to heed
Her war-array. So fled her spirit forth
With wrath and moaning to the world below.
Then clamor infinite uprose and smote
The golden stars, as round Camilla slain
The battle newly raged. To swifter charge
The gathered Trojans ran, with Tuscan lords
And King Evander's troops of Arcady.

Fair Opis, keeping guard for Trivia
In patient sentry on a lofty hill, beheld
Unterrified the conflict's rage. Yet when,
Amid the frenzied shouts of soldiery,
She saw from far Camilla pay the doom
Of piteous death, with deep-drawn voice of sight
She thus complained: "O virgin, woe is me!
"Too much, too much, this agony of thine,
"To expiate that thou didst lift thy spear
"For wounding Troy. It was no shield in war,
"Nor any vantage to have kept thy vow
"To chaste Diana in the thorny wild.
"Our maiden arrows at thy shoulder slung
"Availed thee not! Yet will our Queen divine
"Not leave unhonored this thy dying day,
"Nor shall thy people let thy death remain
"A thing forgot, nor thy bright name appear
"A glory unavenged. Whoe'er he be

"That marred thy body with the mortal wound
"Shall die as he deserves."
Beneath that hill
An earth-built mound uprose, the tomb
Of King Dercennus, a Laurentine old,
By sombre ilex shaded: thither hied
The fair nymph at full speed, and from the mound
Looked round for Arruns. When his shape she saw
In glittering armor vainly insolent,
"Whither so fast?" she cried. "This way, thy path!
"This fatal way approach, and here receive
"Thy guerdon for Camilla! Thou shalt fall,
"Vile though thou art, by Dian's shaft divine."
She said; and one swift-coursing arrow took
From golden quiver, like a maid of Thrace,
And stretched it on her bow with hostile aim,
Withdrawing far, till both the tips of horn
Together bent, and, both hands poising well,
The left outreached to touch the barb of steel,
The right to her soft breast the bowstring drew:
The hissing of the shaft, the sounding air,
Arruns one moment heard, as to his flesh
The iron point clung fast. But his last groan
His comrades heeded not, and let him lie,
Scorned and forgotten, on the dusty field,
While Opis soared to bright Olympian air.

Camilla's light-armed troop, its virgin chief
Now fallen, were the first to fly; in flight
The panic-stricken Rutule host is seen

And Acer bold; his captains in dismay
With shattered legions from the peril fly,
And goad their horses to the city wall.
Not one sustains the Trojan charge, or stands
In arms against the swift approach of death.
Their bows unstrung from drooping shoulder fall,
And clatter of hoof-beats shakes the crumbling ground.
On to the city in a blinding cloud
The dust uprolls. From watch-towers looking forth,
The women smite their breasts and raise to heaven
Shrill shouts of fear. Those fliers who first passed
The open gates were followed by the foe,
Routed and overwhelmed. They could not fly
A miserable death, but were struck down
In their own ancient city, or expired
Before the peaceful shrines of hearth and home.
Then some one barred the gates. They dared not now
Give their own people entrance, and were deaf
To all entreaty. Woeful deaths ensued,
Both of the armed defenders of the gate,
And of the foe in arms. The desperate band,
Barred from the city in the face and eyes
Of their own weeping parents, either dropped
With headlong and inevitable plunge
Into the moat below; or, frantic, blind,
Battered with beams against the stubborn door
And columns strong. Above in conflict wild
Even the women (who for faithful love

Of home and country schooled them to be brave
Camilla's way) rained weapons from the walls,
And used oak-staves and truncheons shaped in
flame,
As if, well-armed in steel, each bosom bold
Would fain in such defence be first to die.

Meanwhile th' unpitying messenger had flown
To Turnus in the wood; the warrior heard
From Acca of the wide confusion spread,
The Volscian troop destroyed, Camilla slain,
The furious foe increasing, and, with Mars
To help him, grasping all, till in that hour
Far as the city-gates the panic reigned.
Then he in desperate rage (Jove's cruel power
Decreed it) from the ambushed hills withdrew
And pathless wild. He scarce had passed beyond
To the bare plain, when forth Æneas marched
Along the wide ravine, climbed up the ridge,
And from the dark, deceiving grove stood clear.

Then swiftly each with following ranks of war
Moved to the city-wall, nor wide the space
That measured 'twixt the twain. Æneas saw
The plain with dust o'erclouded, and the lines
Of the Laurentian host extending far;
Turnus, as clearly, saw the war array
Of dread Æneas, and his ear perceived
Loud tramp of mail-clad men and snorting steeds.
Soon had they sped to dreadful shock of arms,
Hazard of war to try; but Phœbus now,

Glowing rose-red, had dipped his wearied wheel
Deep in Iberian seas, and brought back night
Above the fading day. So near the town
Both pitch their camps and make their ramparts strong.

END OF BOOK XI

BOOK XII

When Turnus marks how much the Latins quail
In adverse war, how on himself they call
To keep his pledge, and with indignant eyes
Gaze all his way, fierce rage implacable
Swells his high heart. As when on Libyan plain
A lion, gashed along his tawny breast,
By the huntsman's grievous thrust, awakens him
Unto his last grim fight, and gloriously
Shaking the great thews of his manèd neck,
Shrinks not, but crushes the despoiler's spear
With blood-sprent, roaring mouth, — not less than so
Burns the wild soul of Turnus and his ire.
Thus to the King he spoke with stormful brow:
"The war lags not for Turnus' sake. No cause
"Constrains the Teucrian cowards and their King
"To eat their words and what they pledged refuse.
"On his own terms I come. Bring forward, sire,
"The sacrifice, and seal the pact I swear:
"Either to deepest hell this hand shall fling
"Yon Trojan runaway — the Latins all
"May sit at ease and see! — and my sole sword
"Efface the general shame; or let him claim
"The conquest, and Lavinia be his bride."

To him Latinus with unruffled mind
Thus made reply: "O youth surpassing brave!

"The more thy sanguinary valor burns
"Beyond its wont, the more with toilsome care
"I ponder with just fear what chance may fall,
"Weighing it well. Thy father Daunus' throne,
"And many a city by thy sword subdued,
"Are still thy own. Latinus also boasts
"Much golden treasure and a liberal hand.
"Other unwedded maids of noble stem
"In Latium and Laurentine land are found.
"Permit me, then, to tell thee without guile
"Things hard to utter; let them deeply fill
"Thy listening soul. My sacred duty 'twas
"To plight my daughter's hand to nonesoe'er
"Of all her earlier wooers—so declared
"The gods and oracles; but overcome
"By love of thee, by thy dear, kindred blood,
"And by the sad eyes of my mournful Queen,
"I shattered every bond; I snatched away
"The plighted maiden from her destined lord,
"And took up impious arms. What evil case
"Upon that deed ensued, what hapless wars,
"Thou knowest, since thyself dost chiefly bear
"The cruel burden. In wide-ranging fight
"Twice-conquered, our own city scarce upholds
"The hope of Italy. Yon Tiber's wave
"Still runs warm with my people's blood; the plains
"Far round us glisten with their bleaching bones.
"Why tell it o'er and o'er? What maddening dream
"Perverts my mind? If after Turnus slain
"I must for friendship of the Trojan sue,
"Were it not better to suspend the fray

"While Turnus lives? For what will be the word
"Of thy Rutulian kindred—yea, of all
"Italia, if to death I give thee o'er—
"(Which Heaven avert!) because thou fain wouldst win
"My daughter and be sworn my friend and son?
"Bethink thee what a dubious work is war;
"Have pity on thy father's reverend years,
"Who even now thy absence daily mourns
"In Ardea, his native land and thine."

But to this pleading Turnus' frenzied soul
Yields not at all, but rather blazes forth
More wildly, and his fever fiercer burns
Beneath the healer's hand. In answer he,
Soon as his passion gathered voice, began:
"This keen solicitude for love of me,
"I pray, good sire, for love of me put by!
"And let me traffic in the just exchange
"Of death for glory. This right hand, O King,
"Can scatter shafts not few, nor do I wield
"Untempered steel. Whene'er I make a wound
"Blood follows. For my foeman when we meet
"Will find no goddess-mother near, with hand
"To hide him in her woman's skirt of cloud,
"Herself in dim, deluding shade concealed."

But now the Queen, whose whole heart shrank in fear
From these new terms of duel, wept aloud,
And like one dying clasped her fiery son:
"O Turnus, by these tears—if in thy heart
"Thou honorest Amata still—O thou

"Who art of our distressful, dark old age
"The only hope and peace, the kingly name
"And glory of Latinus rests in thee;
"Thou art the mighty prop whereon is stayed
"Our falling house. One favor I implore:
"Give o'er this fight with Trojans. In such strife
"Thy destined doom is destined to be mine
"By the same fatal stroke. For in that hour
"This hated life shall cease, nor will I look
"With slave's eyes on Æneas as my son."
Lavinia heard her mother's voice, and tears
O'erflowed her scarlet cheek, where blushes spread
Like flame along her warm, young face and brow:
As when the Indian ivory must wear
Ensanguined crimson stain, or lilies pale
Mingled with roses seem to blush, such hues
Her virgin features bore; and love's desire
Disturbed his breast, as, gazing on the maid,
His martial passion fiercer flamed; whereon
In brief speech he addressed the Queen: "No tears!
"No evil omen, mother, I implore!
"Make me no sad farewells, as I depart
"To the grim war-god's game! Can Turnus' hand
"Delay death's necessary coming? Go,
"Idmon, my herald, to the Phrygian King,
"And tell him this — a word not framed to please:
"Soon as Aurora from her crimson car
"Flushes to-morrow's sky, let him no more
"Against the Rutule lead the Teucrian line;
"Let Teucrian swords and Rutule take repose,
"While with our own spilt blood we twain will make

"An end of war; on yonder mortal field
"Let each man woo Lavinia for his bride."

So saying, he hied him to his lordly halls,
Summoned his steeds, and with pleased eye surveyed
Their action proud: them Orithyia, bride
Of Boreas, to Sire Pilumnus gave,
Which in their whiteness did surpass the snow
In speed the wind. The nimble charioteers
Stood by and smote with hollowed hand and palm
The sounding chests, or combed the necks and manes.
But he upon his kingly shoulders clasped
His corselet, thick o'erlaid with blazoned gold
And silvery orichalch; he fitted him
With falchion, shield, and helm of purple plume,
That falchion which the Lord of Fire had made
For Daunus, tempering in the Stygian wave
When white it glowed; next grasped he the good spear
Which leaned its weight against a column tall
In the mid-court, Auruncan Actor's spoil,
And waved it wide in air with mighty cry:
"O spear, that ne'er did fail me when I called,
"The hour is come! Once mighty Actor's hand,
"But now the hand of Turnus is thy lord.
"Grant me to strike that carcase to the ground,
"And with strong hand the corselet rip and rend
"From off that Phrygian eunuch: let the dust
"Befoul those tresses, tricked to curl so fine
"With singeing steel and sleeked with odorous oil."
Such frenzy goads him: his impassioned brow

Is all on flame, the wild eyes flash with fire.
Thus, bellowing loud before the fearful fray,
Some huge bull proves the fury of his horns,
Pushing against a tree-trunk; his swift thrusts
Would tear the winds in pieces; while his hoofs
Toss up the turf and sand, rehearsing war.

That self-same day with aspect terrible
Æneas girt him in the wondrous arms
His mother gave; made sharp his martial steel,
And roused his heart to ire; though glad was he
To seal such truce and end the general war.
Then he spoke comfort to his friends; and soothed
Iulus' fear, unfolding Heaven's intent;
But on Latinus bade his heralds lay
Unyielding terms and laws of peace impose.

Soon as the breaking dawn its glory threw
Along the hills, and from the sea's profound
Leaped forth the horses of the sun-god's car,
From lifted nostrils breathing light and fire,
Then Teucrian and Rutulian measured out
A place for duel, underneath the walls
Of the proud city. In the midst were set
Altars of turf and hearth-stones burning bright
In honor of their common gods. Some brought
Pure waters and the hallowed flame, their thighs
In priestly skirt arrayed, and reverend brows
With vervain bound. Th' Ausonians, spear in hand,
Out from the city's crowded portals moved
In ordered column: next the Trojans all,

With Tuscan host in various martial guise,
Equipped with arms of steel, as if they heard
Stern summons to the fight. Their captains, too,
Emerging from the multitude, in pride
Of gold and purple, hurried to and fro:
Mnestheus of royal stem, Asilas brave;
And Neptune's offspring, tamer of the steed,
Messapus. Either host, at signal given,
To its own ground retiring, fixed in earth
The long shafts of the spears and stacked the shields.
Then eagerly to tower and rampart fly
The women, the infirm old men, the throng
Of the unarmed, and sit them there at gaze,
Or on the columned gates expectant stand.

But Juno, peering from that summit proud
Which is to-day the Alban (though that time
Nor name nor fame the hallowed mountain knew),
Surveyed the plain below and fair array
Of Trojan and Laurentine, by the walls
Of King Latinus. Whereupon straightway
With Turnus' sister she began converse,
Goddess with goddess; for that nymph divine
O'er Alba's calm lakes and loud rivers reigns;
Jove, the high monarch of th' ethereal sky,
Gave her such glory when he stole away
Her virgin zone. "O nymph," she said, "who art
"The pride of flowing streams, and much beloved
"Of our own heart! thou knowest thou alone
"Hast been my favorite of those Latin maids
"That to proud Jove's unthankful bed have climbed;

"And willingly I found thee place and share
"In our Olympian realm. So blame not me,
"But hear, Juturna, what sore grief is thine:
"While chance and destiny conceded aught
"Of strength to Latium's cause, I shielded well
"Both Turnus and thy city's wall; but now
"I see our youthful champion make his war
"With fates adverse. The Parcæ's day of doom
"Implacably impends. My eyes refuse
"To look upon such fight, such fatal league.
"If for thy brother's life thou couldst be bold
"To venture some swift blow, go, strike it now!
"'T is fit and fair! Some issue fortunate
"May tread on sorrow's heel." She scarce had said,
When rained the quick tears from Juturna's eyes.
Three times and yet again her desperate hand
Smote on her comely breast. But Juno cried,
"No tears to-day! But haste thee, haste and find
"What way, if way there be, from clutch of death
"To tear thy brother free; arouse the war;
"Their plighted peace destroy. I grant thee leave
"Such boldness to essay." With this command
She left the nymph dismayed and grieving sore.

Meanwhile the kings ride forth: Latinus first,
Looming tall-statured from his four-horse car;
Twelve rays of gold encircle his bright brow,
Sign of the sun-god, his progenitor;
Next Turnus, driving snow-white steeds, is seen,—
Two broad-tipped javelins in his hand he bears;
Æneas, of Rome's blood the source and sire,

With star-bright shield and panoply divine,
Far-shining comes; Ascanius by his side —
Of Roman greatness the next hope is he.
To camp they rode, where, garbed in blameless white
With youngling swine and two-year sheep unshorn,,
The priest before the flaming altars drove
His flock and offering: to the rising sun
All eyes are lifted, as with careful hand
The salted meal is scattered, while with knives
They mark each victim's brow, outpouring wine
From shallow bowls, the sacrifice to bless.

Then good Æneas, his sword drawn, put forth
This votive prayer: "O Sun in heaven; and thou,
"Italia, for whom such toils I bear,
"Be witness of my orison. On thee,
"Father omnipotent, I call; on thee,
"His Queen Saturnia, — now may she be
"More gracious to my prayer! O glorious Mars,
"Beneath whose godhead and paternity
"All wars begin and end, on thee I call;
"Hail, all ye river-gods and haunted springs;
"Hail, whatsoever gods have seat of awe
"In yonder distant sky, and ye whose power
"Is in the keeping of the deep, blue sea:
"If victory to Ausonian Turnus fall,
"Then let my vanquished people take its way
"Unto Evander's city! From these plains
"Iulus shall retire — so stands the bond;
"Nor shall the Trojans with rebellious sword
"Bring after-trouble on this land and King.

"But if on arms of ours success shall shine,
"As I doubt not it shall (may gods on high
"Their will confirm!), I purpose not to chain
"Italian captive unto Teucrian lord,
"Nor seek I kingly power. Let equal laws
"Unite in federation without end
"The two unconquered nations; both shall share
"My worshipped gods. Latinus, as my sire,
"Shall keep his sword, and as my sire receive
"Inviolable power. The Teucrians
"Shall build my stronghold, but our citadel
"Shall bear forevermore Lavinia's name."
Æneas thus: then with uplifted eyes
Latinus swore, his right hand raised to heaven:
"I too, Æneas, take the sacred vow.
"By earth and sea and stars in heaven I swear,
"By fair Latona's radiant children twain,
"And two-browed Janus; by the shadowy powers
"Of Hades and th' inexorable shrines
"Of the Infernal King; and may Jove hear,
"Who by his lightnings hallows what is sworn!
"I touch these altars, and my lips invoke
"The sacred altar-fires that 'twixt us burn:
"We men of Italy will make this peace
"Inviolate, and its bond forever keep,
"Let come what will; there is no power can change
"My purpose, not if ocean's waves o'erwhelm
"The world in billowy deluge and obscure
"The bounds of heaven and hell. We shall remain
"Immutable as my smooth sceptre is"
(By chance a sceptre in his hand he bore),

"Which wears no more light leaf or branching shade;
"For long since in the grove 't was plucked away
"From parent stem, and yielded to sharp steel
"Its leaves and limbs; erewhile 't was but a tree,
"Till the wise craftsman with fair sheath of bronze
"Encircled it and laid it in the hands
"Of Latium's royal sires."
With words like these
They swore the bond, in the beholding eyes
Of gathered princes. Then they slit the throats
Of hallowed victims o'er the altar's blaze,
Drew forth the quivering vitals, and with flesh
On loaded chargers heaped the sacrifice.

But to Rutulian eyes th' approaching joust
Seemed all ill-matched; and shifting hopes and fears
Disturbed their hearts the closer they surveyed
Th' unequal risks: still worse it was to see
How Turnus, silent and with downcast eyes,
Dejectedly drew near the place of prayer,
Worn, pale, and wasted in his youthful bloom.
The nymph Juturna, with a sister's fear,
Noted the growing murmur, and perceived
How all the people's will did shift and change;
She went from rank to rank, feigning the shape
Of Camers, scion of illustrious line,
With heritage of valor, and himself
Dauntless in war; unceasingly she ran
From rank to rank, spreading with skilful tongue
Opinions manifold, and thus she spoke:
"Will ye not blush, Rutulians, so to stake

"One life for many heroes? Are we not
"Their match in might and numbers? O, behold
"Those Trojan sons of Heaven making league
"With exiled Arcady; see Tuscan hordes
"Storming at Turnus. Yet we scarce could find
"One foe apiece, forsooth, if we should dare
"Fight them with half our warriors. Of a truth
"Your champion brave shall to those gods ascend
"Before whose altars his great heart he vows;
"And lips of men while yet on earth he stays
"Will spread his glory far. Ourselves, instead,
"Must crouch to haughty masters, and resign
"This fatherland upon whose fruitful fields
"We dwell at ease." So speaking, she inflamed
The warriors' minds, and through the legions ran
Increasing whisper; the Laurentine host
And even Latium wavered. Those who late
Prayed but for rest and safety, clamored loud
For arms, desired annulment of the league,
And pitied Turnus' miserable doom.

Whereon Juturna tried a mightier stroke,
A sign from heaven, which more than all beside
Confused the Latins and deceived their hearts
With prodigy. For through the flaming skies
Jove's golden eagle swooped, and scattered far
A clamorous tribe of river-haunting birds;
Then, swiftly to the waters falling, seized
One noble swan, which with keen, curving claws
He ruthless bore away: th' Italians all
Watched eagerly, while the loud-screaming flock

Wheeled upward (wondrous sight!), with host of wings
Shadowed the sky, and in a legion-cloud
Chased through the air the foe; till, overborne
By heavier odds, the eagle from his claws
Flung back his victim to the waves, and fled
To the dim, distant heaven. The Rutules then
Hailed the good omen with consenting cry,
And grasped the sword and shield. Tolumnius
The augur spoke first: "Lo, the sign I sought
"With many a prayer! I welcome and obey
"The powers divine. Take me for captain, me!
"And draw your swords, ye wretches, whom th' assault
"Of yonder foreign scoundrel puts in fear
"Like feeble birds, and with his violence
"Lays waste your shore. He too shall fly away,
"Spreading his ships' wings on the distant seas.
"Close up your ranks — one soul in all our breasts!
"Defend in open war your stolen King."

So saying, he hurled upon th' opposing foe
His javelin, running forward. The strong shaft
Of cornel whistled shrill, and clove the air
Unerring. Instantly vast clamor rose,
And all th' onlookers at the spectacle
Leaped up amazed, and every heart beat high.
The spear sped flying to the foeman's line,
Where stood nine goodly brethren, pledges all
Of one true Tuscan mother to her lord,
Gylippus of Arcadia; it struck full

On one of these at his gold-belted waist,
And where the clasp clung, pierced the rib clean
through.
And stretched the fair youth in his glittering arms
Full length and lifeless on the yellow sand.
His brothers then, bold band to wrath aroused
By sorrow, seize the sword or snatch the spear
And blindly charge. Opposing them, the host
Laurentine makes advance, and close-arrayed
The Trojans like a torrent pour, enforced
By Tuscans and the gay-accoutred clans
Of Arcady. One passion moved in all
To try the judgment of the sword. They tore
The altars down: a very storm of spears
Rose angrily to heaven, in iron rain
Down-pouring: while the priests bore far away
The sacrificial bowls and sacred fires.
Even Latinus fled; his stricken gods
Far from his violated oath he bore.

Some leaped to horse or chariot and rode
With naked swords in air. Messapus, wild
To break the truce, assailed the Tuscan King,
Aulestes, dight in kingly blazon fair,
With fearful shock of steeds; the Tuscan dropped
Helplessly backward, striking as he fell
His head and shoulders on the altar-stone
That lay behind him. But Messapus flew,
Infuriate, a javelin in his hand,
And, towering o'er the suppliant, smote him strong
With the great beam-like spear, and loudly cried:

"Down with him! Ah! no common victim he
"To give the mighty gods!" Italia's men
Despoiled the dead man ere his limbs were cold.
Then Corynæus snatched a burning brand
Out of the altar, and as Ebysus
Came toward him for to strike, he hurled the flame
Full in his face: the big beard quickly blazed
With smell of singeing; while the warrior bold
Strode over him, and seized with firm left hand
His quailing foe's long hair; then with one knee
He pushed and strained, compelled him to the ground —
And struck straight at his heart with naked steel.
The shepherd Alsus in the foremost line
Came leaping through the spears; when o'er him towered
Huge Podalirius with a flashing sword
In close pursuit; the mighty battle-axe
Clove him with swinging stroke from brow to chin,
And spilt along his mail the streaming gore:
So stern repose and iron slumber fell
Upon that shepherd's eyes, and sealed their gaze
In endless night.
But good Æneas now
Stretched forth his unarmed hand, and all unhelmed
Thus loudly to his people called: "What means
"This frantic stir, this quarrel rashly bold?
"Recall your martial rage! The pledge is given
"And all its terms agreed. 'T is only I
"Do lawful battle here. So let me forth,
"And tremble not. My own hand shall confirm

"The solemn treaty. For these rites consign
"Turnus to none but me." Yet while he spoke,
Behold, a wingèd arrow, hissing loud,
The hero pierced; but what bold hand impelled
Its whirling speed, none knew; nor if it were
Chance or some power divine that brought this fame
Upon Rutulia; for the glorious deed
Was covered o'er with silence: none would boast
An arrow guilty of Æneas' wound.

When Turnus saw Æneas from the line
Retreating, and the captains in dismay,
With sudden hope he burned: he called for steeds,
For arms, and, leaping to his chariot,
Rode insolently forth, the reins in hand.
Many strong heroes he dispatched to die,
As on he flew, and many stretched half-dead,
Or from his chariot striking, or from far
Raining his javelins on the recreant foe.
As Mars, forth-speeding by the wintry stream
Of Hebrus, smites his sanguinary shield
And whips the swift steeds to the front of war,
Who, flying past the winds of eve and morn,
Scour the wide champaign; the bounds of Thrace
Beneath their hoof-beats thunder; the dark shapes
Of Terror, Wrath, and Treachery move on
In escort of the god: in such grim guise
Bold Turnus lashed into the fiercest fray
His streaming steeds, that pitiful to see
Trod down the slaughtered foe; each flying hoof
Scattered a bloody dew; their path was laid

In mingled blood and sand.
                                        To death he flung
Pholus and Sthenelus and Thamyris:
Two smitten in close fight and one from far:
Also from far he smote with fatal spear
Glaucus and Lades, the Imbrasidæ,
Whom Imbrasus himself in Lycia bred,
And honored them with arms of equal skill
When grappling with a foe, or o'er the field
Speeding a war-horse faster than the wind.
Elsewhere Eumedes through a throng of foes
To battle rode, the high-born Dolon's child,
Famous in war, who bore his grandsire's name,
But seemed in might and courage like his sire:
That prince, who reconnoitring crept so near
The Argive camp, he dared to claim for spoil
The chariot of Achilles; but that day
Great Diomed for such audacious deed
Paid wages otherwise,— and he no more
Dreamed to possess the steeds of Peleus' son.
When Turnus recognized in open field
This warrior, though far, he aimed and flung
His javelin through the spacious air; then stayed
His coursers twain, and, leaping from his car,
Found the wretch helpless fallen; so planted he
His foot upon his neck, and from his hand
Wrested the sword and thrust it glittering
Deep in the throat, thus taunting as he slew:
"There's land for thee, thou Trojan! Measure there
"Th' Hesperian provinces thy sword would find.
"Such guerdon will I give to all who dare

"Draw steel on me; such cities they shall build."
To bear him company his spear laid low
Asbutes, Sybaris, Thersilochus,
Chloreus and Dares, and Thymœtes thrown
Sheer off the shoulders of his balking steed.
As when from Thrace the north wind thunders
down
The vast Ægean, flinging the swift flood
Against the shore, and where his blasts assail
The cloudy cohorts vanish out of heaven:
So before Turnus, where his path he clove,
The lines fell back, the wheeling legions fled.
The warrior's own wild impulse swept him on,
And every wind that o'er his chariot blew
Shook out his plume in air.
But such advance
So bold, so furious, Phegeus could not brook,
But, fronting the swift chariot's path, he seized
The foam-flecked bridles of its coursers wild,
While from the yoke his body trailed and swung;
The broad lance found his naked side, and tore
His double corselet, pricking lightly through
The outer flesh; but he with lifted targe
Still fought his foe and thrust with falchion bare;
But the fierce pace of whirling wheel and pole
Flung him down prone, and stretched him on the
plain.
Then Turnus, aiming with relentless sword
Between the corselet's edge and helmet's rim
Struck off his whole head, leaving on the sands
The mutilated corpse.

While thus afield
Victorious Turnus dealt out death and doom,
Mnestheus, Achates true, and by their side
Ascanius, have carried to the camp
Æneas, gashed and bleeding, whose long lance
Sustained his limping step. With fruitless rage
He struggled with the spear-head's splintered barb,
And bade them help him by the swiftest way
To carve the wound out with a sword, to rip
The clinging weapon forth, and send him back
To meet the battle. Quickly to his side
Came Iapyx, dear favorite and friend
Of Phœbus, upon whom the god bestowed
His own wise craft and power, love-impelled.
The gifts of augury were given, and song,
With arrows of swift wing: he when his sire
Was carried forth to die, deferred the doom
For many a day, by herbs of virtue known
To leechcraft; and without reward or praise
His silent art he plied. Æneas stood,
Bitterly grieving, propped upon his spear;
A throng of warriors were near him, and
Iulus, sorrowing. The aged man
Gathered his garments up as leeches do,
And with skilled hand and Phœbus' herbs of power
Bustled in vain; in vain his surgery
Pried at the shaft, and with a forceps strong
Seized on the buried barb. But Fortune gave
No remedy, nor did Apollo aid
His votary. So more and more grim fear
Stalks o'er the field of war, and nearer hies

The fatal hour; the very heavens are dust;
The horsemen charge, and in the midmost camp
A rain of javelins pours. The dismal cry
Of men in fierce fight, and of men who fall
Beneath relentless Mars, rends all the air.

Then Venus, by her offspring's guiltless woe
Sore moved, did cull from Cretan Ida's crest
Some dittany, with downy leaf and stem
And flowers of purple bloom — a simple known
To mountain goats, when to their haunches clings
An arrow gone astray. This Venus brought,
Mantling her shape in cloud; and this she steeped
In bowls of glass, infusing secretly
Ambrosia's healing essence and sweet drops
Of fragrant panacea. Such a balm
Aged Iapyx poured upon the wound,
Though unaware; and sudden from the flesh
All pain departed and the blood was staunched,
While from the gash the arrow uncompelled
Followed the hand and dropped: his wonted strength
Flowed freshly through the hero's frame. "Make haste!
"Bring forth his arms! Why tarry any more?"
Iapyx shouted, being first to fire
Their courage 'gainst the foe. "This thing is done
"Not of man's knowledge, nor by sovereign skill;
"Nor has my hand, Æneas, set thee free.
"Some mighty god thy vigor gives again
"For mighty deeds."

Æneas now put on,

All fever for the fight, his golden greaves,
And, brooking not delay, waved wide his spear.
Soon as the corselet and the shield were bound
On back and side, he clasped Ascanius
To his mailed breast, and through his helmet grim
Tenderly kissed his son. "My boy," he cried,
"What valor is and patient, genuine toil
"Learn thou of me; let others guide thy feet
"To prosperous fortune. Let this hand and sword
"Defend thee through the war and lead thee on
"To high rewards. Thou also play the man!
"And when thy riper vigor soon shall bloom,
"Forget not in thy heart to ponder well
"The story of our line. Heed honor's call,
"Like Sire Æneas and Hector thy close kin."

After such farewell word, he from the gates
In mighty stature strode, and swung on high
His giant spear. With him in serried line
Antheus and Mnestheus moved, and all the host
From the forsaken fortress poured. The plain
Was darkened with their dust; the startled earth
Shook where their footing fell. From distant hill
Turnus beheld them coming, and the eyes
Of all Ausonia saw: a chill of fear
Shot through each soldier's marrow; in their van
Juturna knew full well the dreadful sound,
And fled before it, shuddering. But he
Hurried his murky cohorts o'er the plain.
As when a tempest from the riven sky
Drives landward o'er mid-ocean, and from far

The hearts of husbandmen, foreboding woe,
Quake ruefully, — for this will come and rend
Their trees asunder, kill the harvests all,
And sow destruction broadcast; in its path
Fly roaring winds, swift heralds of the storm:
Such dire approach the Trojan chieftain showed
Before his gathered foes. In close array
They wedge their ranks about him. With a sword
Thymbræus cuts huge-limbed Osiris down;
Mnestheus, Arcetius; from Epulo
Achates shears the head; from Ufens, Gyas;
Tolumnius the augur falls, the same
Who flung the first spear to the foeman's line.
Uprose to heaven the cries. In panic now
The Rutules in retreating clouds of dust
Scattered across the plain. Æneas scorned
Either the recreant or resisting foe
To slaughter, or the men who shoot from far:
For through the war-cloud he but seeks the arms
Of Turnus, and to single combat calls.

The warrior-maid Juturna, seeing this,
Distraught with terror, strikes down from his place
Metiscus, Turnus' charioteer, who dropped
Forward among the reins and off the pole.
Him leaving on the field, her own hand grasped
The loosely waving reins, while she took on
Metiscus' shape, his voice, and blazoned arms.
As when through some rich master's spacious halls
Speeds the black swallow on her lightsome wing,
Exploring the high roof, or harvesting

Some scanty morsel for her twittering brood,
Round empty corridors or garden-pools
Noisily flitting: so Juturna roams
Among the hostile ranks, and wings her way
Behind the swift steeds of the whirling car.
At divers points she lets the people see
Her brother's glory, but not yet allows
The final tug of war; her pathless flight
Keeps far away.

Æneas too must take
A course circuitous, and follows close
His foeman's track; loud o'er the scattered lines
He shouts his challenge. But whene'er his eyes
Discern the foe, and fain he would confront
The flying-footed steeds, Juturna veers
The chariot round and flies. What can he do?
Æneas' wrath storms vainly to and fro,
And wavering purposes his heart divide.
Against him lightly leaped Messapus forth,
Bearing two pliant javelins tipped with steel;
And, whirling one in air, he aimed it well,
With stroke unfailing. Great Æneas paused
In cover of his shield and crouched low down
Upon his haunches. But the driven spear
Battered his helmet's peak and plucked away
The margin of his plume. Then burst his rage:
His cunning foes had forced him; so at last,
While steeds and chariot in the distance fly,
He plunged him in the fray, and called on Jove
The altars of that broken oath to see.
Now by the war-god's favor he began

Grim, never-pitying slaughter, and flung free
The bridle of his rage.
What voice divine
Such horror can make known? what song declare
The bloodshed manifold, the princes slain,
Or flying o'er the field from Turnus' blade,
Or from the Trojan King? Did Jove ordain
So vast a shock of arms should interpose
'Twixt nations destined to perpetual bond?

Æneas met the Rutule Sucro — thus
Staying the Trojan charge — and with swift blow
Struck at him sidewise, where the way of death
Is quickest, cleaving ribs and rounded side
With reeking sword. Turnus met Amycus,
Unhorsed him, though himself afoot, and slew
Diores, his fair brother (one was pierced
Fronting the spear, the other felled to earth
By stroke of sword), and both their severed heads
He hung all dripping to his chariot's rim.
But Talon, Tanais, and Cethegus brave,
Three in one onset, unto death went down
At great Æneas' hand; and he dispatched
Ill-starred Onites of Echion's line,
Fair Peridia's child. Then Turnus slew
Two Lycian brothers unto Phœbus dear,
And young Menœtes, an Arcadian,
Who hated war (though vainly) when he plied
His native fisher-craft in Lerna's streams,
Where from his mean abode he ne'er went forth
To wait at great men's doors, but with his sire

Reaped the scant harvest of a rented glebe.
As from two sides two conflagrations sweep
Dry woodlands or full copse of crackling bay,
Or as, swift-leaping from the mountain-vales,
Two flooded, foaming rivers seaward roar,
Each on its path of death, not less uproused,
Speed Turnus and Æneas o'er the field;
Now storms their martial rage; now fiercely swells
Either indomitable heart; and now
Each hero's full strength to the slaughter moves.

Behold Murranus, boasting his high birth
From far-descended sires of storied name,
The line of Latium's kings! Æneas now
With mountain-boulder lays him low in dust,
Smitten with whirlwind of the monster stone;
And o'er him fallen under yoke and rein
Roll his own chariot wheels, while with swift tread
The mad hoofs of his horses stamp him down,
Not knowing him their lord.
But Turnus found
Proud Hyllus fronting him with frantic rage,
And at his golden helmet launched the shaft
That pierced it; in his cloven brain it clung.
Nor could thy sword, O Cretheus, save thee then
From Turnus, though of bravest Greeks the peer;
Nor did Cupencus' gods their priest defend
Against Æneas, but his breast he gave
Unto the hostile blade; his brazen targe
Delayed no whit his miserable doom.
Thee also, Æolus, Laurentum saw

Spread thy huge body dying on the ground;
Yea, dying, thou whom Greeks in serried arms
Subdued not, nor Achilles' hand that hurled
The throne of Priam down: here didst thou touch
Thy goal of death; one stately house was thine
On Ida's mountain, at Lyrnessus, one;
Laurentum's hallowed earth was but thy grave.
Now the whole host contends; all Latium meets
All Ilium; Mnestheus and Serestus bold;
Messapus, the steed-breaker, and high-souled
Asilas; Tuscans in a phalanx proud;
Arcadian riders of Evander's train:
Each warrior lifts him to his height supreme
Of might and skill; no sloth nor lingering now,
But in one far-spread conflict all contend.

His goddess-mother in Æneas' mind
Now stirred the purpose to make sudden way
Against the city-wall, in swift advance
Of all his line, confounding Latium so
With slaughter and surprise. His roving glance,
Seeking for Turnus through the scattered lines
This way and that, beholds in distant view
The city yet unscathed and calmly free
From the wide-raging fight. Then on his soul
Rushed the swift vision of a mightier war.
Mnestheus, Sergestus, and Serestus brave,
His chosen chiefs, he summons to his side,
And stands upon a hillock, whither throng
The Teucrian legions, each man holding fast
His shield and spear. He, towering high,

Thus from the rampart to his people calls:
"Perform my bidding swiftly: Jove's own hand
"Sustains our power. Be ye not slack, because
"The thing I do is sudden. For this day
"I will pluck out th' offending root of war,—
"Yon city where Latinus reigns. Unless
"It bear our yoke and heed a conqueror's will,
"I will lay low in dust its blazing towers.
"Must I wait Turnus' pleasure, till he deign
"To meet my stroke, and have a mind once more,
"Though vanquished, to show fight? My countrymen,
"See yonder stronghold of their impious war!
"Bring flames; avenge the broken oath with fire!"

Scarce had he said, when with consenting souls,
They speed them to the walls in dense array,
Forming a wedge. Ladders now leap in air,
And sudden-blazing fires. In various war
Some troops run charging at the city-gates,
And slay the guards; some fling the whirling spear
And darken heaven with arrows. In their van,
His right hand lifted to the walls and towers,
Æneas, calling on the gods to hear,
Loudly upbraids Latinus that once more
Conflict is thrust upon him; that once more
Italians are his foes and violate
Their second pledge of peace. So blazes forth
Dissension 'twixt the frighted citizens:
Some would give o'er the city and fling wide
Its portals to the Trojan, or drag forth

The King himself to parley; others fly
To arms, and at the rampart make a stand.
'T is thus some shepherd from a caverned crag
Stirs up the nested bees with plenteous fume
Of bitter smoke; they, posting to and fro,
Fly desperate round the waxen citadel,
And whet their buzzing fury; through their halls
The stench and blackness rolls; within the caves
Noise and confusion ring; the fatal cloud
Pours forth incessant on the vacant air.

But now a new adversity befell
The weary Latins, which with common woe
Shook the whole city to its heart. The Queen,
When at her hearth she saw the close assault
Of enemies, the walls beset, and fire
Spreading from roof to roof, but no defence
From the Rutulian arms, nor front of war
With Turnus leading, — she, poor soul, believed
Her youthful champion in the conflict slain;
And, mad with sudden sorrow, shrieked aloud
Against herself, the guilty chief and cause
Of all this ill; and, babbling her wild woe
In endless words, she rent her purple pall,
And with her own hand from the rafter swung
A noose for her foul death. The tidings dire
Among the moaning wives of Latium spread,
And young Lavinia's frantic fingers tore
Her rose-red cheek and hyacinthine hair.
Then all her company of women shrieked
In anguish, and the wailing echoed far

Along the royal seat; from whence the tale
Of sorrow through the peopled city flew;
Hearts sank; Latinus rent his robes, appalled
To see his consort's doom, his falling throne;
And heaped foul dust upon his hoary hair.

Meanwhile the warrior Turnus far afield
Pursued a scattered few; but less his speed,
For less and less his worn steeds worked his will;
And now wind-wafted to his straining ear
A nameless horror came, a dull, wild roar,
The city's tumult and distressful cry.
"Alack," he cried, "what stirs in yonder walls
"Such anguish? Or why rings from side to side
"Such wailing through the city?" Asking so,
He tightened frantic grasp upon the rein.
To him his sister, counterfeiting still
The charioteer Metiscus, while she swayed
Rein, steeds, and chariot, this answer made:
"Hither, my Turnus, let our arms pursue
"The sons of Troy. Here lies the nearest way
"To speedy triumph. There be other swords
"To keep yon city safe. Æneas now
"Storms against Italy in active war;
"We also on this Trojan host may hurl
"Grim havoc. Nor shalt thou the strife give o'er
"In glory second, nor in tale of slain."
Turnus replied, "O sister, long ago
"I knew thee what thou wert, when guilefully
"Thou didst confound their treaty, and enlist
"Thy whole heart in this war. No longer now

"Thy craft divine deceives me. But what god
"Compelled thee, from Olympus fallen so far,
"To bear these cruel burdens? Wouldst thou see
"Thy wretched brother slaughtered? For what else
"Is in my power? What flattering hazard still
"Holds forth deliverance? My own eyes have seen
"Murranus (more than any now on earth
"My chosen friend) who, calling on my name,
"Died like a hero by a hero's sword.
"Ill-fated Ufens fell, enduring not
"To look upon my shame; the Teucrians
"Divide his arms for spoil and keep his bones.
"Shall I stand tamely, till my hearth and home
"Are levelled with the ground? For this would be
"The only blow not fallen. Shall my sword
"Not give the lie to Drances' insolence?
"Shall I take flight and let my country see
"Her Turnus renegade? Is death a thing
"So much to weep for? O propitious dead,
"O spirits of the dark, receive and bless
"Me whom yon gods of light have cast away!
"Sacred and guiltless shall my soul descend
"To join your company; I have not been
"Unworthy offspring of my kingly sires."

Scarce had he said, when through the foeman's line
Saces dashed forth upon a foaming steed,
His face gashed by an arrow. He cried loud
On Turnus' name: "O Turnus, but in thee
"Our last hope lies. Have pity on the woe
"Of all thy friends and kin! Æneas hurls

"His thunderbolt of war, and menaces
"To crush the strongholds of all Italy,
"And lay them low; already where we dwell
"His firebrands are raining. Unto thee
"The Latins look, and for thy valor call.
"The King sits dumb and helpless, even he,
"In doubt which son-in-law, which cause to choose.
"Yea, and the Queen, thy truest friend, is fallen
"By her own hand; gone mad with grief and fear,
"She fled the light of day. At yonder gates
"Messapus only and Atinas bear
"The brunt of battle; round us closely draw
"The serried ranks; their naked blades of steel
"Are thick as ripening corn; wilt thou the while
"Speed in thy chariot o'er this empty plain?"

Dazed and bewildered by such host of ills,
Turnus stood dumb; in his pent bosom stirred
Shame, frenzy, sorrow, a despairing love
Goaded to fury, and a warrior's pride
Of valor proven. But when first the light
Of reason to his blinded soul returned,
He strained his flaming eyeballs to behold
The distant wall, and from his chariot gazed
In wonder at the lordly citadel.
For, lo, a pointed peak of flame uprolled
From tier to tier, and surging skyward seized
A tower — the very tower his own proud hands
Had built of firm-set beams and wheeled in place,
And slung its lofty bridges high in air.
"Fate is too strong, my sister! Seek no more

"To stay the stroke. But let me hence pursue
"That path where Heaven and cruel Fortune call.
"Æneas I must meet; and I must bear
"The bitterness of death, whate'er it be.
"O sister, thou shalt look upon my shame
"No longer. But first grant a madman's will!"
He spoke; and leaping from his chariot, sped
Through foes and foemen's spears, not seeing now
His sister's sorrow, as in swift career
He burst from line to line. Thus headlong falls
A mountain-boulder by a whirlwind flung
From lofty peak, or loosened by much rain,
Or by insidious lapse of seasons gone;
The huge, resistless crag goes plunging down
By leaps and bounds, o'erwhelming as it flies
Tall forests, flocks and herds, and mortal men:
So through the scattered legions Turnus ran
Straight to the city walls, where all the ground
Was drenched with blood, and every passing air
Shrieked with the noise of spears. His lifted hand
Made sign of silence as he loudly called:
"Refrain, Rutulians! O ye Latins all,
"Your spears withhold! The issue of the fray
"Is all my own. I only can repair
"Our broken truce by judgment of the sword."
Back fell the hostile lines, and cleared the field.

But Sire Æneas, hearing Turnus' name,
Down the steep rampart from the citadel
Unlingering hied, all lesser task laid by,
With joy exultant and dread-thundering arms.

Like Athos' crest he loomed, or soaring top
Of Eryx, when the nodding oaks resound,
Or sovereign Apennine that lifts in air
His forehead of triumphant snow. All eyes
Of Troy, Rutulia, and Italy
Were fixed his way; and all who kept a guard
On lofty rampart, or in siege below
Were battering the foundations, now laid by
Their implements and arms. Latinus too
Stood awestruck to behold such champions, born
In lands far-sundered, met upon one field
For one decisive stroke of sword with sword.

Swift striding forth where spread the vacant plain,
They hurled their spears from far; then in close fight
The brazen targes rang. Beneath their tread
Earth groaned aloud, as with redoubling blows
Their falchions fell; nor could a mortal eye
'Twixt chance and courage the dread work divide.
As o'er Taburnus' top, or upland vale
Of Sila, in relentless shock of war,
Two bulls rush brow to brow, while terror-pale
The herdsmen fly; the herd is hushed with fear;
The heifers dumbly marvel which shall be
True monarch of the grove, whom all the kine
Obedient follow; but the rival twain,
Commingling mightily wound after wound,
Thrust with opposing horns, and bathe their necks
In streams of blood; the forest far and wide
Repeats their bellowing rage: not otherwise
Trojan Æneas and King Daunus' son

Clashed shield on shield, till all the vaulted sky
Felt the tremendous sound. The hand of Jove
Held scales in equipoise, and threw thereon
Th' unequal fortunes of the heroes twain:
One to vast labors doomed and one to die.

Soon Turnus, reckless of the risk, leaped forth,
Upreached his whole height to his lifted sword,
And struck: the Trojans and the Latins pale
Cried mightily, and all eyes turned one way
Expectant. But the weak, perfidious sword
Broke off, and as the blow descended, failed
Its furious master, whose sole succor now
Was flight; and swifter than the wind he flew.
But, lo! a hilt of form and fashion strange
Lay in his helpless hand. For in his haste,
When to the battle-field his team he drove,
His father's sword forgotten (such the tale),
He snatched Metiscus' weapon. This endured
To strike at Trojan backs, as he pursued,
But when on Vulcan's armory divine
Its earthly metal smote, the brittle blade
Broke off like ice, and o'er the yellow sands
In flashing fragments scattered. Turnus now
Takes mad flight o'er the distant plain, and winds
In wavering gyration round and round;
For Troy's close ring confines him, and one way
A wide swamp lies, one way a frowning wall.
But lo! Æneas — though the arrow's wound
Still slackens him and oft his knees refuse
Their wonted step — pursues infuriate

His quailing foe, and dogs him stride for stride.
As when a stag-hound drives the baffled roe
To torrent's edge (or where the flaunting snare
Of crimson feathers fearfully confines)
And with incessant barking swift pursues;
While through the snared copse or embankment high
The frightened creature by a thousand ways
Doubles and turns; but that keen Umbrian hound
With wide jaws, undesisting, grasps his prey,
Or, thinking that he grasps it, snaps his teeth
Cracking together, and deludes his rage,
Devouring empty air: then peal on peal
The cry of hunters bursts; the lake and shore
Reëcho, and confusion fills the sky:—
Such was the flight of Turnus, who reviled
The Rutules as he fled, and loudly sued
Of each by name to fetch his own lost sword.
Æneas vowed destruction and swift death
To all who dared come near, and terrified
Their trembling souls with menace that his power
Would raze their city to the ground. Straightway,
Though wounded, he gave chase, and five times
round
In circles ran; then winding left and right
Coursed the swift circles o'er. For, lo! the prize
Is no light laurel or a youthful game:
For Turnus' doom and death their race is run.

But haply in that place a sacred tree,
A bitter-leaved wild-olive, once had grown,
To Faunus dear, and venerated oft

By mariners safe-rescued from the waves,
Who nailed their gifts thereon, or hung in air
Their votive garments to Laurentum's god.
But, heeding not, the Teucrians had shorn
The stem away, to clear the field for war.
'T was here Æneas' lance stuck fast; its speed
Had driven it firmly inward, and it clave
To the hard, clinging root. Anchises' son
Bent o'er it, and would wrench his weapon free,
And follow with a far-flung javelin
The swift out-speeding foe. But Turnus then,
Bewildered and in terror, cried aloud:
"O Faunus, pity me and heed my prayer!
"Hold fast his weapon, O benignant Earth!
"If ere these hands have rendered offering due,
"Where yon polluting Teucrians fight and slay."
He spoke; invoking succor of the god,
With no lost prayer. For tugging valiantly
And laboring long against the stubborn stem,
Æneas with his whole strength could but fail
To loose the clasping tree. While fiercely thus
He strove and strained, Juturna once again,
Wearing the charioteer Metiscus' shape,
Ran to her brother's aid, restoring him
His own true sword. But Venus, wroth to see
What license to the dauntless nymph was given,
Herself came near, and plucked from that deep root
The javelin forth. So both with lofty mien
Strode forth new-armed, new-hearted: one made bold
By his good sword, the other, spear in hand,
Uptowered in wrath, and with confronting brows

They set them to the war-god's breathless game.

Meanwhile th' Olympian sovereign supreme
To Juno speaks, as from an amber cloud
The strife she views: "My Queen, what end shall be?
"What yet remains? Thou seest Æneas' name
"Numbered with tutelary gods of power;
"And well thou know'st what station in the sky
"His starward destiny intends. What scheme
"Vexes thy bosom still? What stubborn hope,
"Fostered in cloud and cold? O, was it well
"To desecrate a god with mortal wound;
"Or well (what were a nymph unhelped by thee?)
"To give back Turnus his lost sword, and lend
"Strength unavailing to the fallen brave?
"Give o'er, and to our supplication yield;
"Let not such grief thy voiceless heart devour;
"Nor from thy sweet lips let thy mournful care
"So oft assail my mind. For now is come
"The last decisive day. Thy power availed
"To vex the Trojans upon land and sea,
"To wake abominable war, bring shame
"Upon a royal house, and mix the songs
"Of marriage and the grave: but further act
"I thee refuse."
Such was the word of Jove.
Thus Saturn's daughter answered, drooping low
Her brows divine: "Because, great Jove, I knew
"Thy pleasure, I from yonder earth retired
"And Turnus' cause, tho' with unwilling mind.
"Else shouldst thou not behold me at this hour

"Upon my solitary throne of air
"Enduring fair and foul; I should be found
"Flame-girded on the battle's deadly verge,
"Tempting the Teucrians to a hated war.
"Yea, 't was my motion thrust Juturna forth
"To help her hapless brother. I approved —
"To save his life — that she should be too bold;
"But bade no whirl of spear nor bending bow:
"I swear it by th' inexorable fount
"Whence flow the Stygian rivers, the sole seat
"Where gods of light bow down in awful prayer.
"I yield me now; heart-sick I quit the war.
"But ask one boon, which in the book of fate
"Is not denied; for Latium's good I sue,
"And high prerogatives of men that be
"Thy kith and kin: when happy wedlock vows
"(Aye, be it so!) shall join them by strong laws
"Of chartered peace, let not the Latins lose
"Their ancient, native name. Bid them not pass
"For Trojans, nor be hailed as Teucer's sons;
"No alien speech, no alien garb impose.
"Let it be Latium ever; let the lords
"Of Alba unto distant ages reign;
"Let the strong, master blood of Rome receive
"The manhood and the might of Italy.
"Troy perished: let its name and glory die!

The Author of mankind and all that is,
Smiling benignant, answered thus her plea:
"Jove's sister true, and Saturn's second child,
"What seas of anger vex thy heart divine!

"But come, relinquish thy rash, fruitless rage:
"I give thee this desire, and yield to thee
"A free submission. The Ausonian tribes
"Shall keep the speech and customs of their sires;
"The name remains as now; the Teucrian race,
"Abiding in the land, shall but infuse
"The mixture of its blood. I will bestow
"A league of worship, and to Latins give
"One language only. From the mingled breed
"A people shall come forth whom thou shalt see
"Surpass all mortal men and even outvie
"The faithfulness of gods; for none that live
"Shall render to thy name an equal praise."
So Juno bowed consent, and let her will
Be changed, as with much comfort in her breast
She left Olympus and her haunt of cloud.

After these things Jove gave his kingly mind
To further action, that he might forthwith
Cut off Juturna from her brother's cause.
Two plagues there be, called Furies, which were spawned
At one birth from the womb of wrathful Night
With dread Megæra, phantom out of hell;
And of their mother's gift, each Fury wears
Grim-coiling serpents and tempestuous wings.
These at Jove's throne attend, and watch the doors
Of that stern King — to whet the edge of fear
For wretched mortals, when the King of gods
Hurls pestilence and death, or terrifies
Offending nations with the scourge of war.

'T was one of these which Jove sent speeding down
From his ethereal seat, and bade her cross
The pathway of Juturna for a sign.
Her wings she spread, and earthward seemed to ride
Upon a whirling storm. As when some shaft,
With Parthian poison tipped or Cretan gall,
A barb of death, shoots cloudward from the bow,
And hissing through the dark hastes forth unseen:
So earthward flew that daughter of the night.

Soon as she spied the Teucrians in array
And Turnus' lines, she shrivelled to the shape
Of that small bird which on lone tombs and towers
Sits perching through the midnight, and prolongs
In shadow and deep gloom her troubling cry.
In such disguise the Fury, screaming shrill,
Flitted in Turnus' face, and with her wings
Smote on his hollow shield. A strange affright
Palsied his every limb; each several hair
Lifted with horror, and his gasping voice
Died on his lips. But when Juturna knew
From far the shrieking fiend's infernal wing,
She loosed her tresses, and their beauty tore,
To tell a sister's woe; with clenching hands
She marred her cheeks and beat her naked breast.
"What remedy or help, my Turnus, now
"Is in a sister's power? What way remains
"For stubborn me? Or with what further guile
"Thy life prolong? What can my strength oppose
"To this foul thing? I quit the strife at last.
"Withdraw thy terror from my fearful eyes,

"Thou bird accurst! The tumult of thy wings
"I know full well, and thy death-boding call.
"The harsh decrees of that large-minded Jove
"I plainly see. Is this the price he pays
"For my lost maidenhood? Why flatter me
"With immortality, and snatch away
"My property of death? What boon it were
"To end this grief this hour, and hie away
"To be my brother's helpmeet in his grave!
"I, an immortal? O, what dear delight
"Is mine, sweet brother, living without thee?
"O, where will earth yawn deep enough and wide
"To hide a goddess with the ghosts below?"
She spoke; and veiled in glistening mantle gray
Her mournful brow; then in her stream divine
The nymph sank sighing to its utmost cave.

Æneas now is near; and waving wide
A spear like some tall tree, he called aloud
With unrelenting heart: "What stays thee now?
"Or wherefore, Turnus, backward fly? Our work
"Is not a foot-race, but the wrathful strife
"Of man with man. Aye, hasten to put on
"Tricks and disguises; gather all thou hast
"Of skill or courage; wish thou wert a bird
"To fly to starry heaven, or hide thy head
"Safe in the hollow ground!"
The other then
Shook his head, saying: "It is not thy words,
"Not thy hot words, affright me, savage man!
"Only the gods I fear, and hostile Jove."

Silent he stood, and glancing round him saw
A huge rock lying by, huge rock and old,
A landmark justly sundering field from field,
Which scarce six strong men's shoulders might up-
raise,
Such men as mother-Earth brings forth to-day:
This grasped he with impetuous hand and hurled,
Stretched at full height and roused to all his speed,
Against his foe. Yet scarcely could he feel
It was himself that ran, himself that moved
With lifted hand to fling the monster stone;
For his knees trembled, and his languid blood
Ran shuddering cold; nor could the stone he threw,
Tumbling in empty air, attain its goal
Nor strike the destined blow. But as in dreams,
When helpless slumber binds the darkened eyes,
We seem with fond desire to tread in vain
Along a lengthening road, yet faint and fall
When straining to the utmost, and the tongue
Is palsied, and the body's wonted power
Obeys not, and we have no speech or cry:
So unto Turnus, whatsoever way
His valiant spirit moved, the direful Fiend
Stopped in the act his will. Swift-changing thoughts
Rush o'er his soul; on the Rutulian host,
Then at the town he glares, shrinks back in fear,
And trembles at th' impending lance; nor sees
What path to fly, what way confront the foe:—
No chariot now, nor sister-charioteer!

Above his faltering terror gleams in air

Æneas' fatal spear; whose eye perceived
The moment of success, and all whose strength
Struck forth: the vast and ponderous rock outflung
From engines which make breach in siegèd walls
Not louder roars nor breaks in thunder-sound
More terrible; like some black whirlwind flew
The death-delivering spear, and, rending wide
The corselet's edges and the heavy rim
Of the last circles of the seven-fold shield,
Pierced, hissing, through the thigh. Huge Turnus sinks
O'erwhelmed upon the ground with doubling knee.
Upspring the Rutules, groaning; the whole hill
Roars answering round them, from far and wide
The lofty groves give back an echoing cry.

Lowly, with suppliant eyes, and holding forth
His hand in prayer: "I have my meed," he cried,
"Nor ask for mercy. Use what Fate has given!
"But if a father's grief upon thy heart
"Have power at all,—for Sire Anchises once
"To thee was dear,—I pray thee to show grace
"To Daunus in his desolate old age;
"And me, or, if thou wilt, my lifeless clay,
"To him and his restore. For, lo, thou art
"My conqueror! Ausonia's eyes have seen
"Me suppliant, me fallen. Thou hast made
"Lavinia thy bride. Why further urge
"Our enmity?"
With swift and dreadful arms
Æneas o'er him stood, with rolling eyes,

But his bare sword restraining; for such words
Moved on him more and more: when suddenly,
Over the mighty shoulder slung, he saw
That fatal baldric studded with bright gold
Which youthful Pallas wore, what time he fell
Vanquished by Turnus' stroke, whose shoulders now
Carried such trophy of a foeman slain.
Æneas' eyes took sure and slow survey
Of spoils that were the proof and memory
Of cruel sorrow; then with kindling rage
And terrifying look, he cried, "Wouldst thou,
"Clad in a prize stripped off my chosen friend,
"Escape this hand? In this thy mortal wound
"'T is Pallas has a victim; Pallas takes
"The lawful forfeit of thy guilty blood!"
He said, and buried deep his furious blade
In the opposer's heart. The failing limbs
Sank cold and helpless; and the vital breath
With moan of wrath to darkness fled away.

THE END